the food of the mediterranean

SANLUCAR DE BARRAMEDA
7 €
100 grs.

the food of the mediterranean

a journey for food lovers through France, Italy, Morocco & Spain

bay books

CONTENTS

the food of the MEDITERRANEAN

FRANCE

FROM RIPE CAMEMBERT TO WARM CROISSANTS, EXQUISITE PÂTISSERIE TO VINTAGE CHAMPAGNE, NOWHERE IS FRENCH FARE BETTER, OR ENJOYED MORE, THAN IN FRANCE ITSELF.

Eating and drinking are at the heart of French culture. The morning ritual of a petit déjeuner of a fresh croissant and café au lait is a daily treat, but for many, lunch is still the main meal of the day, extending to three or four courses with wine – and dinner may be equally substantial.

Growers and food producers are held in the highest respect, as are the ingredients they supply to the table, many of which are eaten only at the height of their season. Recipes change to reflect the best that each month has to offer, and seasonal fruits and vegetables are eagerly awaited, from the summer melons of Provence to autumn walnuts and winter truffles in the Dordogne. Each area of France grows or produces food uniquely suited to its terrain and climate, and these produits du terroir are a source of great regional pride.

A strict system of controls and naming rights, called the appellation d'origine contrôlée (AOC), ensures the authenticity of regional specialties, ranging from poultry from Bresse to honey from Corsica. As an example, the AOC designates more than 300 appellations to identify the origins of French wine and spirits, and thus French wine the world over is identified by the place it was produced, from the underground caves of the Champagne district to the vast wine-growing regions of Bordeaux.

Cheese making is a grand tradition with numerous regional specialties. Normandy's rich pasture produces fine Camembert, Pont l'Evêque and Livarot; while the Champagne region produces Brie and Chaource. Magnificent blue cheeses include Bleu d'Auvergne and Fourme d'Ambert from Auvergne, and of course Roquefort, ripened in caves in the Pyrenees, and hailed as the king of cheeses. In the Alps, cheeses such as Reblochon are still made from animals taken up to the high meadows in the summer time, and Swiss-style cheeses such as raclette and gruyère are popular.

Neighbourly influences can also be detected in other border regions. The cuisine of Alsace-Lorraine reflects the proximity of Germany. Bakery items include pretzels, rye bread and kugelhopf, while meat dishes à la

lorraine are served with red cabbage cooked in wine. Corsica is closer to Italy and Sardinia than France, and has a tradition of Italian charcuterie, pasta and polenta – a classic example is stufato, a rich beef stew served over pasta. Similarly, favourite ingredients in Provence are those of the Mediterranean: olives, olive oil, garlic, eggplants (aubergines), zucchini (courgettes), tomatoes and herbes de Provence, with strong flavours of aïoli, anchoïade, tapenade, pissaladière and pistou from the Italian-bordering Côte d' Azur. The southwest Basque country close to Spain flavours its food with spicy piment d'Espelette (dried chillies), which are also often used in the salting mixture for the local Bayonne ham.

Elsewhere, the rich flavours that are quintessentially French dominate regional cooking, and recipes often incorporate the local wines. Entrecote à la bordelaise is a classic example using the red wine of Bordeaux, just as boeuf à la bourguignonne is characteristic of Burgundy, along with coq au vin (Bresse chicken cooked with cream and wild morels), snails filled with garlic herb butter and slices of jambon persillé (ham and parsley set in aspic).

Hearty dishes such as aligot and potée auvergnate (one-pot pork and cabbage stew) are perfect for the cold winters of central France, and in the south and south-west, Gascony and the Dordogne are famous for their foie gras, duck and goose confit, pâtés and terrines and for the use of goose fat in their cooking.

But the epitome of all French culinary experiences is to be found in the country's restaurants. Haute cuisine employs extravagant ingredients and time-consuming processes that elevate cooking to a fine art, and is found mostly in expensive restaurants, celebrated in stars by the famous Michelin guide. Parisians are legendarily discerning about their food, and although Paris is home to many world-class haute cuisine restaurants, even neighbourhood brasseries offer high quality fare. Lyon is another culinary capital, dotted with simple bouchons (traditional working-class cafés) and brasseries serving Lyonnaise favourites including poulet au vinaigre (chicken stewed in vinegar), pike quenelles, and potato gratins. In rural areas, homemade and local specialities can be tasted at fermes auberges (farmhouse restaurants).

ITALY

EATING AND DRINKING WELL IS A NATIONAL PASTIME. FROM SELECTING VEGETABLES IN THE MARKET TO ENJOYING A MID-MORNING ESPRESSO, LUNCHING IN A TRATTORIA, OR BUYING ANTIPASTO ON THE WAY HOME, THE DAY REVOLVES AROUND FOOD.

The market is the preferred option for buying fresh produce, but even the smallest village may be home to a host of specialty food purveyors.

Fresh meat and poultry come from the macellaria (butcher), but salumi (cured pork products) are purchased at either the norcineria or salumeria. The pescheria is the fishmonger, but as Italians love to buy at source, in coastal areas many prefer to get seafood straight from the fishermen on their trawlers. The caseificio and latteria sell dairy products and eggs. The panificio, panetteria and forno sell breads and baked goods, while the pasticceria is a specialist bakery for pastries. The gelateria is the ice cream shop, and wine is available at the enoteca by the bottle and often also in larger volumes, decanted from huge containers. And of course, in every town you will also find the cafes and bars that are a mainstay of Italian life.

Cucina regionale (regional food) is alive and flourishing throughout the 20 regions of Italy.

Some of the northern specialties show an affinity with those of the neighbouring countries. The northernmost part of Trentino-Alto Adige is Austrian Italy, with a cuisine that features speck (cured ham), canederli (dumplings) and gulasch. Further west, mountainous Valle d'Aosta is famous for dairy products – just like adjacent Switzerland.

The tradition of cheese making is also strong in the northern region of Lombardia, where Gorgonzola, Taleggio and grana padano are made. Other specialties of the area include bresaola (air-dried beef) and pizzoccheri (buckwheat pasta), both from Valtellini. The saffron-infused risotto alla milanese, is the signature dish of Milan, the region's capital.

An equally simple risotto, risi e bisi (rice with peas), is characteristic of the Veneto region outside Venice. Most local food is similarly rustic and unfussy, including bean soups such as pasta e fagioli. Veneto produces some of Italy's great wines, including Bardolino, Valpolicella and Soave.

Central Italy is an area of fresh pasta, great cheeses and salumi, and gutsy wines. It encompasses some of the best-known gastronomic regions of Italy: Le Marche, Tuscany, Umbria, and, most highly regarded of all, Emilia-Romagna.

The list of specialties from Emilia-Romagna includes Aceto balsamico tradizionale di Modena (traditionally produced aged balsamic vinegar from Modena) and prosciutto di Parma. Parmiggiano Reggiano is eaten in chunks or grated over fresh egg pasta, especially tortellini, the region's favourite. Ragù has been reinterpreted worldwide as spaghetti Bolognese.

Le Marche is renowned for its Adriatic seafood, used to produce local versions of the rich fish stew, brodetto. Other famed regional dishes include porchetta (roast suckling pig) and vincisgrassi (lasagne with chicken livers and prosciutto).

Tuscany produces the world's finest extra virgin olive oils, and Italy's most famous red wine, Chianti. Meals are centred on meat, especially beef, and the capital Florence is famous for its huge servings of bistecca alla fiorentina. The popularity of bean dishes – including soups such as ribollita and papa al pomodoro – has earned the Tuscans the nickname 'i mangiafagioli' (the bean-eaters). Siena's spicy cakes pan pepato and panforte date back to medieval times.

Italy's south is home to robust cucina povera (peasant cooking) – created from whatever was available. The Romans make use of pasta, beans, artichokes, meat and offal. Bucatini all'amatriciana includes the local guanciale (cured pig's cheek), while in the surrounding rural area, lamb is used in dishes such as abbacchio (milk-fed baby lamb).

The cuisine of Campania and Naples has been duplicated around the world: eggplant (aubergine) Parmigiana, spaghetti alle vongole, and pizza topped with fresh mozzarella. Cheeses include fresh buffalo and cows' milk mozzarella, goats' cheese and caciocavallo.

With extensive coastlines, the Calabrians and Sicilians incorporate seafood into their cooking. Citrus trees thrive in these regions, providing just some of the flavours for Sicily's granita and gelati – regarded as the finest in Italy.

MOROCCO

MOROCCAN FOOD IS A RICH BLEND OF ARABIC, FRENCH, OTTOMAN, SPANISH AND AFRICAN TRADITIONS AND FLAVOURS – ALL LEGACIES OF MOROCCO'S EXOTIC BACKGROUND AS A TRADING CENTRE AT THE STRATEGIC GATEWAY BETWEEN AFRICA AND EUROPE.

The international influences on Moroccan cooking are legion, reading like a roll call from the history books. Arabic influences dominate, although the majority of the population are Berbers, a race that is believed to have originated in modern-day Libya. African elements are contributed by a significant population from Senegal, Mauritania and Mali – a result of early trading caravans that entered Morocco from across the Sahara. Ties with Spain and Portugal have been close ever since the Arabs invaded the Iberian Peninsula in the early 8th century, and the cuisines of the three countries still have many common features. Sweet and hot peppers, potatoes, chilli, cayenne pepper and paprika were eagerly adopted into Moroccan dishes when they were introduced from the New World. Traces of Ottoman cooking filtered into Morocco's northeast from Algeria, and the prevalence of stuffed vegetables and kebabs can be attributed to this influence. Even the Chinese have had an impact on Moroccan cooking; warkha (the tissue-thin pastry used to make the famed pigeon pie bestilla) was brought to Morocco by the Persians, who had learnt the skills of pastry making from the Chinese via the Silk Road. The more recent French presence in the country from 1912 to 1962 can still be felt, too, not just because French is still one of the two official languages (the other being Arabic), but also in a cuisine that includes wine, coffee, baguettes and croissants.

Throughout Morocco, salads are finely grated or chopped, grains are ground into couscous before steaming, and tagines are cooked over charcoal (or, in more modern kitchens, in pressure cookers called majottes before being transferred into a traditional earthenware tagine for serving). These three elements are at the heart of Moroccan cuisine, with historical influences and the local availability of grains, nuts and fresh produce determining the regional variations on these core dishes as well as other local specialties.

Spanish influences are prevalent around the northern cities of Tetuan and Tangier, where capsicums (peppers), tomatoes, olive oil, saffron and artichokes are widely used. Spanish-style rice dishes, tortilla-like omelettes and even nougat feature in the cuisine, and the blossoms of Seville oranges are distilled to make orange flower water.

Lying to the west of the Middle Atlas Mountains, the walls of Marrakesh are surrounded by date palms and orange groves. Almonds feature in two specialties of the city – kneffa, a festive dish of fried warkha pastry layered with custard, and tkout (or sellou), a mixture of browned flour, almonds, sesame and anise seeds, honey, cinnamon and butter that is served in a peaked mound to be eaten communally. A slow-cooked meat stew called tangia that is traditionally prepared by men is another classic dish of Marrakesh.

The Middle Atlas mountains are also home to the famous rose gardens of Kelaa el M'gouna (a renowned source of rosewater), and to the Erfoud Oases that border Algeria – Tafilalt, Rissania, Seffalat, Aoufous and Jorf – where a million palms produce some 30 varieties of dates.

The city of Fes is famous for its bestilla, and the sweet, almond-flavoured version prepared here is the one preferred throughout most of the country (although the recipe used in Tetuan features more lemon). Another favourite from Fes is the dish aloes bil tamra, in which shad from the Sebou River are stuffed with dates that have themselves been stuffed with almonds.

The fertile land on the western and southern coasts produces a myriad of fruits, vegetables and grains. Almond, orange and olive groves grow in the region, as well as argan trees in the inland area between Essaouira and Agadir. This nut is unique to Morocco and neighbouring Algeria, and among other uses, its oil is combined with almond meal and honey to create a dip called amalou that is eaten with bread.

Fish and other seafood proliferate along the coastline, where popular dishes including sardin mraqad (fried sardines stuffed with chermoula), tagine bil hout (fish tagine), kseksou bil hout (fish couscous) and bestilla bil hout (fish pie).

In the Anti-Atlas and pre-Sahara region in the south of the country, availability dictates the menu. Couscous is likely to be made from cracked barley, maize or millet, or otherwise from semolina, while meat sources may include camel, hedgehog or wild fox. Staples include milk and buttermilk, dates, pulses, bread (made from barley, millet or wheat), and a white maize porridge called asida.

The forests of the Rif and Atlas Mountains and the Souss are an important food source, providing acorns, pine nuts, mushrooms, carob, capers, wild pears, blackberries and mulberries, jujubes, various edible greens and herbs, and a superb wild honey.

Regardless of what's on the menu, at a Moroccan meal there are customs to follow and etiquette to be observed.

Firstly, diners must wash their hands. This is usually done in the bathroom, but sometimes the custom is more ceremonial, with a young family member or servant offering the seated diners a jug of warm water and basin with which to rinse the fingers of the right hand, and proffering a linen towel to dry them with.

A daughter of the household places a wedge of bread before each diner, and this, along with more bread that will be passed around during the meal, will be used to pick up food, soak up sauces, and wipe fingers (for fingers are never licked during the meal).

Vegetable dishes and salads are served in shallow bowls at the beginning of the meal, and are either removed before the main dish (or dishes) is served, or left on the table for people to pick at as the meal progresses.

The main course is served in a tagine or on a large platter, and diners help themselves, using the thumb and first two fingers of the right hand to select morsels of food from the closest section of the serving plate. If the dish is couscous, morsels of meat and vegetable are deftly combined with couscous and rolled into a ball before being popped into the mouth.

Hands are washed again when the meal is complete, this time more thoroughly. At formal gatherings, the water may be perfumed with rosewater and lightly sprinkled over the hands using a special flask called a rashasha.

To finish the meal, guests move from the dining table to the living room for relaxed conversation over mint tea and pastries.

SPAIN

THE THREE MAJOR INFLUENCES ON THE CUISINE OF A COUNTRY ARE ITS GEOGRAPHY, ITS HISTORY AND THE PERSONALITY AND HABITS OF ITS PEOPLE, AND NOWHERE IS THIS MORE EVIDENT THAN IN THE FOOD OF SPAIN.

The Iberian Peninsula, comprising both Spain and Portugal, stretches from southern France to the Mediterranean, just a sliver of which separates it from northern Africa. Along the way it encompasses the most varied range of landscapes in all of Europe, from the permanently snow-capped Sierra Nevada to an almost tropical coast and a windswept treeless meseta (high central plain).

To the north and northwest, bordering the Atlantic, is green Spain: mists and mountains; high rainfall; and lush forests. The Cantabrian coast (Costa Verde) has dramatic peaks and valleys, and rivers teem with salmon and trout. To the south, the chalky soil of Jerez de la Frontera is inland, with the coastline stretching to the Donaña National Park, sandy woodlands sheltering red deer, and a wilderness of wetlands. The province of Almeria, in the far south-eastern corner of the country includes Europe's only desert. Then there are the islands, including mountainous Mallorca, gently rolling Menorca, pine-clad Ibiza, almost barren Formentera, plus the seven islands of the Canaries, each with its own unique natural features. This immensely varied landscape is home to an equally wide variety of produce and livestock, and a multitude of seafood is sourced from the waters that lap Spain's shores.

Over the centuries, Spain has been subject to many invasions, each leaving its culinary imprint on the land and its cuisine. The Phoenicians brought the first olive trees, which were later cultivated by the Romans and Moors. The Romans introduced new methods of cooking (roasting and grilling), as well as the first cereals and the techniques for creating bread. Next came the Visigoths, who helped develop the livestock farming and cheese making that still flourish today. They also introduced legumes and vegetables from northern Europe, including spinach and radishes, which were well suited to the Spanish soil.

But the people who left the greatest mark on Spanish food and culture were the Moors – the Berbers and Arabs from northern Africa (and as far afield as Syria), who ruled the Iberian Peninsula for almost 800 years.

The Moors referred to the region as Al-Andalus, and regarded it as an earthly paradise, especially after they had transformed large areas of this once arid land into green and well-watered oases using gravity-flow canals and waterwheels.

These changes saw new crops being introduced to the region – citrus, including sour (later Sevilla) oranges, lemons and limes; apricots, bananas and almonds; rice, taro and sugarcane from Asia; and vegetables such as artichokes, eggplant (aubergine) and celery. Perhaps most important of all, the Moors contributed the hard wheat from which pasta was made, as well as the spices that now form the essence of Spanish cuisine, saffron and cinnamon.

Later, the importation from the New World of those strange, new and, at first, suspicious foods – the tomato, the potato, the capsicum (pepper), the chilli and chocolate – contributed to the unique, hybrid nature of Spanish cuisine.

To this day, Spain remains a political construct, made up of several distinct culture groups, many with their own languages as well as their own cuisines. There are the Basques, whose lands are in the north-east, along a porous border with France; to their west, the Galicians; south and east the Catalans and the Valencians; off the shores of these two provinces the Balearic Islands, holding Mallorquins, Menorcans and Ibicencans (natives of Ibiza), all of whom speak a variation of the Catalan language. Then there are the Asturians, Andalucians, Extremadurans and the Navarrans.

It's no surprise then that the Spaniards are unified more by their customs and traditions than they are by any political directives handed down from Madrid. One practice that has become a defining characteristic of modern Spanish life is taking tapas, a tradition that suits – and unites – the gregarious Spaniards.

On the whole, the Spanish don't start their evening meal until late – often as late as 10 pm – so they eat tapas to stave off the pangs of hunger. If you are visiting Spain for the first time, you may find you need to adjust to this Spanish eating schedule, winding your gastric clock back by at least a few hours. Late for everything else, the Spanish are habitually late for the evening meal – hence the success of tapas.

From Malaga to Palma de Mallorca, from Barcelona to Badajoz, almost everyone participates in this tradition of bar hopping and feasting on tiny plates with friends after work and before the evening meal.

Tapas is almost always washed down with an accompanying glass (or two) of wine – perhaps a rioja tinto, blanco or rosado (red, white or rosé) or a carafe of sangria shared among friends.

Whether served as tapas or incorporated into more substantial meals, the produce of Spain offers a myriad of flavours.

Olives and their oil range from lightly coloured and flavoured to darker, richer varieties, and many tapas dishes – such as champiñones al ajillo (garlic mushrooms) – are served in oil.

Seafood is enjoyed fresh, plucked directly from the ocean, cured as in the Portuguese-style salted cod called bacalao, popular in the Basque country, or deep fried, as pescadito frito (sometimes referred to as pescaito frito).

Jamón – from jamón serrano (dry cured mountain ham) to the more expensive jamón iberico (produced from acorn-fed black Iberian pigs) – is at its best when served simply, with no garnish to detract from the subtle combination of its flesh and fat.

Other dishes are heartier – from the slow-roasted suckling lamb of Segovia to the humble tortilla de patatas found in every tapas bar in the land.

Paella is ubiquitous, served with meat, seafood or a combination of the two, and rice is also used in desserts – arroz con leche is a popular rice pudding made with milk, cinnamon, sugar and lemon. The other sweet that is a traditional favourite is churros, the fried Spanish doughnut that is typically dipped in chocolate and eaten for breakfast.

Spanish cooking is still evolving, and today la nueva cocina ('the new cooking of Spain'), attracts great interest and enthusiasm from gourmands around the world. Its most famous exponent is a Catalan, Ferran Adrià, who has popularised audacious combinations of ingredients and new culinary methods such as espuma (foams created by aerating the main ingredient) at his restaurant El Bulli on the Costa Brava.

SNACKS

FROM FRANCE

AÏOLI

A mortar and pestle is ideal for making tapenade, which should be a worked to a fairly rough paste. The name comes from *tapenado*, the Provençal word for caper.

OFTEN REFERRED TO AS 'PROVENCE BUTTER', AÏOLI IS A SIMPLE BUT SUPERB GARLIC-FLAVOURED MAYONNAISE. IT IS SERVED WITH A SELECTION OF CRUDITÉS OR HOT VEGETABLES, POACHED CHICKEN, SNAILS OR FISH, AND IT CAN ALSO BE ADDED TO FISH SOUPS.

4 egg yolks
8 garlic cloves, crushed
½ teaspoon salt
2 tablespoons lemon juice
500 ml (17 fl oz/2 cups) olive oil

CRUDITÉS
6 baby carrots, trimmed with stalks left on
6 asparagus spears, trimmed and blanched
6 French beans, trimmed and blanched
6 button mushrooms, halved
1 yellow capsicum (pepper), seeded and cut into batons
1 red capsicum (pepper), seeded and cut into batons
6 cauliflower florets
1 fennel bulb, cut into batons

SERVES 6

PUT the egg yolks, garlic, salt and half the lemon juice in a mortar and pestle or food processor and pound or mix until light and creamy. Add the oil, drop by drop from the tip of a teaspoon, whisking constantly until it begins to thicken, then add the oil in a very thin stream. (If you're using a processor, pour in the oil in a thin stream with the motor running.) Season, add the remaining lemon juice and, if necessary, thin with a little warm water.

ARRANGE crudités around a large platter and serve the aïoli in a bowl in the centre. You can keep aïoli sealed in a sterilised jar in the fridge. It will last for up to 3 weeks.

TAPENADE

TAPENADE

350 g (12 oz) black olives, pitted
3 tablespoons capers, rinsed
8 anchovies
1 garlic clove, crushed
180 ml (6 fl oz) olive oil
1 tablespoon lemon juice
2 teaspoons dijon mustard
1 teaspoon chopped thyme
1 tablespoon chopped parsley

SERVES 6

POUND together the olives, capers, anchovies and garlic, either using a mortar and pestle or a food processor. Add the olive oil, lemon juice, mustard and herbs and pound or process again until you have a fairly rough paste.

SERVE with a selection of breads or crudités for dipping. Tapenade can be kept, covered, in the fridge for several days.

FROM SPAIN

SALTED ALMONDS

- 1 egg white
- ¼ teaspoon sweet paprika (pimentón)
- 500 g (1 lb 2 oz) whole blanched almonds
- 1½ tablespoons coarse sea salt grains (not flakes)

SERVES 6–8

PREHEAT the oven to 120°C (235°F/Gas ½). In a large bowl, lightly whip the egg white and paprika with a fork until the mixture starts to froth. Add the blanched almonds and toss to coat evenly.

DIVIDE the nuts between two non-stick baking trays. Sprinkle with sea salt, turning the nuts several times so that the salt adheres to them. Spread over the trays. Bake for 30 minutes, turning the nuts over occasionally to prevent them from sticking. Turn off the heat and leave the almonds in the oven for 30 minutes. When completely cooled, store in airtight jars.

Spanish sweet paprika is also known as pimentón. It is a popular ingredient in many Mediterranean recipes. Anyone from Spain swears by this paprika, and its flavour is essential for authentic Spanish cooking. The peppers are dried, slowly over an oak burning fire for several weeks. The result is a sweet, cool, smokey flavour.

Using a mixture of green and black olives adds more appeal to these warm olives. Shred the lemon zest finely; however, if you have preserved lemon on hand, use strips of rind instead.

FROM MOROCCO

WARM OLIVES WITH LEMON AND HERBS

WHILE A CHOICE OF OLIVES IS GIVEN, A COMBINATION OF BOTH ADDS VARIETY IN COLOUR AND FLAVOUR. BOILING REDUCES SALT CONTENT AND 'SWEETENS' THE OLIVES. CRACKED GREEN OLIVES CAN BE DIFFICULT TO OBTAIN; IF GREEN OLIVES ARE USED, SICILIAN GREEN OLIVES ARE IDEAL.

350 g (12 oz/2 cups) cured cracked green or black Kalamata olives
80 ml (2½ fl oz/⅓ cup) olive oil
1 teaspoon fennel seeds
2 garlic cloves, finely chopped
pinch of cayenne pepper
finely shredded zest and juice of 1 lemon
1 tablespoon finely chopped coriander (cilantro) leaves
1 tablespoon finely chopped flat-leaf (Italian) parsley

SERVES 4

RINSE the olives, drain and place in a saucepan with enough water to cover.

BRING to the boil and cook for 5 minutes, then drain in a sieve. Set aside. Add the olive oil and fennel seeds to the saucepan and heat gently until fragrant.

ADD the garlic, olives, cayenne pepper and the lemon zest and juice. Toss for 2 minutes, or until the olives are hot.

TRANSFER to a bowl and toss with the coriander and parsley. Serve hot with crusty bread to soak up the juices.

Shops specialising in selling pickles are common to Morocco. Preserved lemons and cured olives dominate such outlets.

FROM FRANCE

CHICKEN LIVER PÂTÉ

500 g (1 lb 2 oz) chicken livers
80 ml (2½ fl oz/⅓ cup) brandy
90 g (3¼ oz) unsalted butter
1 onion, finely chopped
1 garlic clove, crushed
1 teaspoon chopped thyme
60 ml (2 fl oz/¼ cup) cream
4 slices white bread

SERVES 6

TRIM chicken livers, cutting away any discoloured bits and veins. Rinse them, pat dry with paper towels and cut in half. Place in a small bowl with the brandy, cover and leave for a couple of hours. Drain the livers, reserving the brandy.

MELT half of the butter in a frying pan, add the onion and garlic and cook over low heat until the onion is soft and transparent. Add the livers and thyme and stir over moderate heat until the livers change colour. Add the reserved brandy and simmer for 2 minutes. Cool for 5 minutes.

PLACE livers and liquid in a food processor and whiz until smooth. Add remaining butter, chopped, and process again until smooth. (Or, roughly mash the livers with a fork, then push them through a sieve and mix with the melted butter.) Pour in the cream and process until just incorporated.

SEASON pâté and spoon into an earthenware dish or terrine, smoothing the surface. Cover and refrigerate until firm. If the pâté is to be kept for more than a day, chill it and then pour clarified butter over the surface to seal.

TO MAKE Melba toasts, preheat the grill and cut the crusts off the bread. Toast the bread on both sides and then slice horizontally with a sharp serrated knife, to give you eight pieces. Carefully toast the uncooked side of each slice and then cut it into two triangles. Serve with the pâté.

Gently fry the onion and garlic before adding the chicken livers and thyme. Once the livers have changed colour, add the brandy.

FROM ITALY

Bruschetta is a traditional Italian antipasto. Use slightly stale bread (this is an excellent dish for using up leftovers) that is dense enough to stop the olive oil seeping through. Technically speaking, bruschetta is just plain grilled (broiled) bread, rubbed with garlic while it is hot and then drizzled with good-quality olive oil.

BRUSCHETTA

4 large slices of 'country-style' bread, such as ciabatta
1 garlic clove
drizzle of extra virgin olive oil

MAKES 4

GRILL (broil), chargrill or toast the bread until it is crisp. Cut the garlic clove in half and rub the cut edge over both sides of each bread slice. Drizzle a little olive oil over each bread slice.

TOMATO AND BASIL BRUSCHETTA

4 ripe tomatoes
1 tablespoon shredded basil
4 pieces basic bruschetta

SERVES 4

ROUGHLY chop the tomatoes and mix with the basil. Season well and pile onto the bruschetta.

WILD MUSHROOM BRUSCHETTA

2 tablespoons olive oil
400 g (14 oz) selection of wild mushrooms, particularly fresh porcini, sliced if large, or chestnut mushrooms
2 garlic cloves, crushed
1 heaped tablespoon chopped thyme
4 pieces basic bruschetta

SERVES 4

HEAT olive oil in a large saucepan or frying pan. When oil is hot, add just enough mushrooms to cover the base of the pan and cook over high heat, stirring frequently. Season with salt and pepper. (Mushrooms can become watery when cooked. Continue cooking until no liquid remains.)

ADD a little crushed garlic and thyme. Cook for a further minute. Remove from the pan and repeat with remaining mushrooms. Spoon over the bruschetta and serve immediately.

EGGPLANT BRUSCHETTA

EGGPLANT BRUSCHETTA

2 large eggplants (aubergines), sliced
2 garlic cloves, crushed
170 ml (5½ fl oz/⅔ cup) extra virgin olive oil
juice of 1 small lemon
3 tablespoons roughly chopped mint
4 pieces basic bruschetta

SERVES 4

HEAT a chargrill pan (griddle) on the stove. Place a few eggplant slices in the pan and cook over moderately high heat, turning once, until the eggplant is soft and cooked.

MIX together the garlic, oil, lemon juice and mint and season well. Put the eggplant in a dish with the marinade and leave for 30 minutes. Place a couple of eggplant pieces on each bruschetta and spoon the marinade over the top.

FROM FRANCE

HAM, MUSHROOM AND CHEESE CRÊPES

1 quantity crêpe batter (see recipe on page 478)
20 g (3/4 oz) butter
150 g (5½ oz) mushrooms, sliced
2 tablespoons single cream
150 g (5½ oz) Gruyère, grated
100 g (3½ oz) ham, chopped

SERVES 6

HEAT a large crêpe or frying pan and grease with a little butter or oil. Pour in enough batter to coat the base of the pan in a thin even layer and tip out any excess. Cook over moderate heat for about a minute, or until the crêpe starts to come away from the side of the pan. Turn crêpe and cook on the other side for 1 minute or until lightly golden. Stack crêpes on a plate, with pieces of baking paper between them, and cover with plastic wrap while you cook the rest of the batter to make six large crêpes.

PREHEAT the oven to 180°C (350°F/Gas 4). Heat the butter in a frying pan, add mushrooms, season well and cook, stirring, for 5 minutes, or until all the liquid from the mushrooms has evaporated. Stir in the cream, cheese and ham.

LAY one crêpe on a board or work surface. Top with about a sixth of the filling and fold the crêpe into quarters. Place it on a baking tray and then fill and fold the remaining crêpes. Bake for 5 minutes and then serve immediately.

Once the crêpe starts to come away from the side of the pan, turn it over.

CERVELLE DE CANUT

CERVELLE DE CANUT IS A LYONNAIS DISH. THE NAME MEANS 'SILK WEAVERS' BRAINS' (APPARENTLY SILK WEAVERS WERE CONSIDERED TO BE QUITE STUPID). DEPENDING ON THE TYPE OF CHEESE THAT YOU USE, THE DISH CAN BE SMOOTH AND CREAMY OR RATHER MORE COARSE.

500 g (1 lb 2 oz) fromage blanc or curd cheese
2 tablespoons olive oil
1 garlic clove, finely chopped
2 tablespoons chopped chervil
4 tablespoons chopped parsley
2 tablespoons chopped chives
1 tablespoon chopped tarragon
4 shallots, finely chopped

SERVES 8

BEAT the fromage blanc or curd cheese with a wooden spoon, then add the olive oil and garlic and beat it into the cheese. Add the herbs and shallots and mix together well. Season and serve with pieces of toast or bread, perhaps after a dessert, as you would cheese and biscuits.

CERVELLE DE CANUT

HAM, MUSHROOM AND CHEESE CRÊPES

FROM SPAIN

FRIED BREADCRUMBS WITH EGGS

BREADCRUMBS ARE AN INGREDIENT OF 'LA COCINA POBRE' – THE CUISINE OF THE POOR – AS WAS BACALAO. AND BREADCRUMBS, LIKE BACALAO, HAVE BECOME, IN THE NEWLY PROSPEROUS SPAIN, CHIC – OR, AS THE SPANISH WOULD SAY, 'LA MODA'. HERE, THEY TEAM PERFECTLY WITH EGGS.

- 4 thick slices white bread, crusts removed
- 2 tablespoons extra virgin olive oil
- 125 ml (4 fl oz/½ cup), mild olive oil
- 1 red onion, cut into 2 cm cubes
- 2 garlic cloves, crushed
- 2 red capsicums (peppers) cut into 2 cm (¾ inch) squares
- 100 g (3½ oz) thinly sliced jamón, cut into fine strips
- 2 chorizo, cut into 2 cm (¾ inch) cubes
- ½ teaspoon smoked Spanish paprika
- 4 eggs
- 2 tablespoons chopped flat-leaf (Italian) parsley

SERVES 4

CUT or tear the bread into small pieces or large crumbs. Heat the extra virgin olive oil in a large heavy-based frying pan over medium heat. Add the bread pieces and toss to coat in the oil then stir continuously for 3–4 minutes or until lightly golden. Remove and drain on paper towel. Season with salt and pepper. Allow to cool.

HEAT 2 tablespoons of the mild olive oil in the same pan used for the bread over medium heat. Add the onion, garlic and red capsicum and stir until softened, about 10 minutes. Add the jamón, chorizo and paprika and continue to cook on medium heat until lightly browned, another 10 minutes. Sprinkle with half the bread pieces and stir through. Remove from heat and keep warm in a low oven while cooking eggs.

PUT the remaining oil in a clean frypan over medium heat. When hot, quickly crack 4 eggs into the oil. Using a metal spoon, scoop hot oil from the base of the pan over the eggs so that they become crisp around the edges while yolk remains soft. Remove from oil and drain eggs.

TO SERVE, divide the breadcrumb mixture between 4 serving dishes; top each with a fried egg and sprinkle with parsley.

FROM ITALY

CALZONE

CALZONE DIFFERS FROM A PIZZA IN THAT THE BASE IS FOLDED OVER THE TOPPING. THIS NEAPOLITAN SPECIALITY MEANS 'TROUSER LEG', PRESUMABLY BECAUSE THERE IS A RESEMBLANCE. EACH OF THE FOLLOWING FILLINGS MAKES ONE 25 CM (10 INCH) CALZONE – ENOUGH FOR ONE TO TWO PEOPLE.

cornmeal
½ quantity pizza dough (see recipe on page 469) for each calzone
1½ tablespoons olive oil

MOZZARELLA AND PROSCIUTTO
170 g (6 oz) mozzarella cheese, cut into 2 cm (¾ inch) cubes
2 thin slices prosciutto, cut in half
1 artichoke heart, marinated in oil, drained and cut into 3 slices from top to bottom

POTATO, ONION AND SALAMI
2 tablespoons vegetable oil
1 small onion, very thinly sliced
75 g (2½ oz) small red potatoes, unpeeled, very thinly sliced
75 g (2½ oz) mozzarella cheese, chopped
60 g (2¼ oz) sliced salami
2 tablespoons grated parmesan cheese

EACH RECIPE MAKES ONE 25 CM (10 INCH) CALZONE

PREHEAT the oven to 230°C (450°F/Gas 8). Lightly oil a baking tray and dust with cornmeal.

ON a lightly floured surface roll out the dough into an 18 cm (7 inch) circle. Now, using the heels of your hands and working from the centre outwards, press the circle out to a diameter of about 30 cm (12 inches). Transfer to the baking tray. Brush the entire surface lightly with the oil.

TO MAKE the mozzarella and prosciutto calzone, spread the mozzarella cheese over one half of the pizza base, leaving a narrow border around the edge. Roll the half slices of prosciutto into little tubes and place on top of the cheese. Top with the artichoke slices, then season well.

TO MAKE the potato, onion and salami calzone, heat the oil in a frying pan and add the onion slices. Cook for 1 minute, then scatter potato on top. Cook, stirring, for 3–4 minutes, until beginning to brown. Season with salt and pepper. Spread over one half of the pizza base, leaving a narrow border around the edge. Scatter the mozzarella on top, followed by the salami slices and parmesan.

WHICHEVER calzone you are making, now fold the plain side of the base over the filling to make a half-moon shape. Match the cut edges and press them firmly together to seal. Fold them over and press into a scrolled pattern to thoroughly seal in the filling. Brush the surface with a little extra olive oil, then transfer to the oven. Bake for about 20 minutes, until the crust is golden.

Calzones are an Italian delicacy that means *baggy pants*. Calzones are made with floppy soft doughs but are strong enough to be carried.

POTATO, ONION AND SALAMI CALZONE

FROM MOROCCO

FRIED POTATO CAKES

POTATO CAKES ARE OFTEN FOUND IN THE WEEKLY SOUKS IN REMOTE REGIONS AND ARE EASY TO ASSEMBLE. THE POTATOES ARE USUALLY BOILED IN THEIR SKINS, BUT PEELING AND SLICING, THEN DRYING OUT THE POTATOES OVER HEAT, WORKS JUST AS WELL.

600 g (1 lb 5 oz) boiling potatoes
2 garlic cloves, unpeeled
1½ teaspoons ground cumin
½ teaspoon ground coriander
1 teaspoon paprika
⅛ teaspoon cayenne pepper
2 tablespoons finely chopped flat-leaf (Italian) parsley
2 tablespoons finely chopped coriander (cilantro) leaves
2 small eggs
oil for frying

MAKES 8

PEEL potatoes, cut in thick slices and place in a saucepan with water to cover. Add garlic and bring to the boil. Boil for 15–20 minutes until tender, drain and return to medium heat to dry the potatoes, shaking pan occasionally until excess moisture evaporates. Squeeze the pulp from the garlic cloves into the potatoes, then mash. Add cumin, ground coriander, paprika and cayenne pepper. Mix in lightly and leave until cool.

ADD parsley, coriander leaves and one egg to the mash. Season to taste. Mix well but do not overwork. Divide into 8 even portions. Lightly moisten hands and shape each portion into a smooth cake 1.5 cm (½ inch) thick and about 8 cm (3¼ inch) in diameter. Place on a baking paper-lined baking tray. Beat remaining egg in a shallow dish.

IN A frying pan, add oil to a depth of 5 mm (¼ inch), and place over medium–high heat. When hot, dip potato cakes one at a time into beaten egg to coat completely and fry for about 3 minutes each side, or until golden and heated through. Drain on paper towel and serve hot.

Traditionally the potatoes are cooked whole and peeled. It is quicker, and easier on the fingers, however, if they are peeled and sliced before they are boiled with the garlic. Dry them by shaking the pan over heat, then mash.

FROM FRANCE

TERRINE DE CAMPAGNE

THIS IS THE DISH THAT YOU WILL FIND IN RESTAURANTS IF YOU ORDER *PÂTÉ MAISON*. IT IS OFTEN SERVED WITH PICKLED VEGETABLES AND COARSE COUNTRY BREAD. TERRINE DE CAMPAGNE FREEZES VERY WELL IF YOU HAVE SOME LEFT OVER OR WANT TO MAKE IT IN ADVANCE.

700 g (1 lb 9 oz) lean pork, cut into cubes
200 g (7 oz) pork belly, cut into strips
200 g (7 oz) chicken livers, trimmed
125 g (4 oz) streaky bacon, chopped
1½ teaspoons sea salt
½ teaspoon black pepper
pinch of grated nutmeg
8 juniper berries, lightly crushed
3 tablespoons brandy
2 shallots, finely chopped
1 large egg, lightly beaten
sprig of bay leaves
8 thinly sliced rashers bacon

SERVES 8

PUT the lean pork, pork belly, chicken livers and chopped bacon in a food processor and roughly chop into small dice (you will need to do this in two or three batches). Alternatively, finely dice the meat with a sharp knife.

PUT the diced meat in a large bowl and add sea salt, pepper, nutmeg, juniper berries and brandy. Mix carefully and leave to marinate in the fridge for at least 6 hours or overnight.

PREHEAT the oven to 180°C (350°F/Gas 4). Lightly butter a 20 x 7 x 9 cm (8 x 2¾ x 3½ inch) terrine or loaf tin. Add the shallots and egg to the marinated meat and carefully combine.

PUT a sprig of bay leaves in the base of the terrine. Line with the bacon slices, leaving enough hanging over the sides to cover the top. Spoon the filling into the terrine and fold the ends of the bacon over the top. Cover the top with a layer of well-buttered baking paper and then wrap the whole terrine in a layer of foil.

PLACE the terrine in a large baking dish and pour water into the dish to come halfway up the sides of the terrine. Bake in this bain-marie (water bath) for 1½ hours, or until the pâté is shrinking away from the sides of the terrine.

LIFT the terrine out of the bain-marie and leave pâté to cool, still wrapped in the paper and foil. Once cold, drain off excess juices and refrigerate for up to a week. You may find that a little moisture has escaped from the pâté. This is normal and prevents it from drying out. Run a knife around the inside of the terrine to loosen the pâté and then turn out onto a board and serve in slices.

The free-range chicken and egg stall at a Lyon market.

FROM SPAIN

CÓRDOBAN PORK ROLLS

THESE PORK ROLLS ARE A SPECIALTY OF THE CITY OF CÓRDOBA, IN ANDALUCÍA. THEY ARE CALLED FLAMENQUINES AFTER THE FLEMISH SOLDIERS WHO ACCOMPANIED EMPEROR CARLOS V. MUCH LIKE THE COATING OF BEATEN EGG IN THE DISH, THE SOLDIERS WERE BLOND.

100 g (3½ oz) butter
60 g (2¼ oz/½ cup) plain (all-purpose) flour
185 ml (6 fl oz/¾ cup) milk
185 ml (6 fl oz/¾ cup) chicken stock
4 pork schnitzel pieces, 100 g (3½ oz) each
4 thin slices jamón, 100 g (3½ oz) each
2 tablespoons finely chopped flat-leaf (Italian) parsley
2 garlic cloves, finely chopped
2 large eggs
dash of milk
plain flour, for coating
dried breadcrumbs, for coating
olive oil, for deep-frying

SERVES 4–6

MELT the butter in a saucepan over low–medium heat. Add the flour and cook for 1–2 minutes, stirring. Slowly whisk in the combined milk and stock mixture. Season and stir for 8–10 minutes, or until quite thick. Cool to room temperature, then cover and refrigerate until well chilled.

USING a mallet, pound the pork until about 5 mm thick and slightly longer and wider than the jamón slices. Trim the edges to form neat rectangles.

LAY a piece of jamón over the top of each rectangle. Combine the parsley and garlic and sprinkle on top. Roll up and hold in place with a toothpick. Refrigerate until ready to use.

WHEN the white sauce is cold and firm remove from refrigerator. You will need to mould the sauce around the pork. Add a little milk if mix is too thick and won't stick to the pork. Note that the mixture just needs to coat the pork – work quickly, it doesn't need to look too neat as the pork will be coated in crumbs. Place on a tray in a single layer, cover and refrigerate for 1 hour to firm up again.

PLACE the eggs and a dash of milk in a bowl and combine. Place the flour and breadcrumbs on separate plates. Lightly coat the pork rolls in the flour then dip into the egg wash, then lift out allowing any excess to drip off then roll in the breadcrumbs. Continue until all are coated. Refrigerate until ready to cook to firm crumbs. Preheat the oven to 180°C (350°F/Gas 4).

MEANWHILE fill a deep-fryer or a heavy-based casserole dish one-third full of oil and heat the oil to 180°C (350°F). Fry the pork until golden, about 1 minute on each side. Place in the oven for 15–20 minutes, or until firm to touch. Remove toothpicks and serve.

Roll up the pork and secure with toothpick before coating it with the thick white sauce.

FROM FRANCE

OMELETTE AUX FINES HERBES

THE OMELETTE IS WONDERFULLY ACCOMMODATING TO PERSONAL TASTE – IT CAN BE FOLDED, ROLLED OR LEFT FLAT, COOKED ON ONE SIDE OR BOTH. THIS FOLDED OMELETTE IS TRADITIONALLY *BAVEUSE* (CREAMY) IN THE MIDDLE AND COOKED ON ONE SIDE ONLY BEFORE BEING FOLDED.

15 g (½ oz) butter
2 shallots, finely chopped
1 garlic clove, crushed
2 tablespoons chopped parsley
2 tablespoons chopped basil
½ tablespoon chopped tarragon
2 tablespoons thick (double/heavy) cream
8 eggs, lightly beaten
oil

SERVES 4

MELT the butter in a frying pan and cook the shallots and garlic over low heat until tender. Stir in the herbs and then tip into a bowl. Mix in the cream and eggs and season well.

HEAT a little oil in a non-stick frying pan. Pour a quarter of the batter into the pan and cook gently, constantly pulling the set egg around the edge of the pan into the centre, until the omelette is set and browned underneath and the top is just cooked. Fold the omelette into three and slide it out of the pan onto a plate with the seam underneath. Serve hot, for someone else to eat while you cook up the remaining three omelettes.

When the omelette is set and browned underneath, fold it in three so the inside stays creamy.

CROQUE MONSIEUR

80 g (2¾ oz) unsalted butter
20 g (¾ oz) plain (all-purpose) flour
185 ml (6 fl oz/¾ cup) milk
½ teaspoon dijon mustard
1 egg yolk
grated nutmeg
12 slices white bread
6 slices ham
125 g (4½ oz) gruyère, grated

SERVES 6

MELT 20 g (¾ oz) of the butter in a saucepan, add flour and stir over low heat for 3 minutes. Slowly add the milk and mustard, whisking constantly. Leave to simmer until the mixture has thickened and reduced by about a third. Remove from heat, stir in the egg yolk and season with salt, pepper and nutmeg. Leave to cool completely.

PLACE HALF the bread slices on a baking tray. Top each piece of bread with a slice of ham, then with some sauce, then gruyère and finally with another piece of bread. Melt half the remaining butter in a large frying pan and fry the sandwiches on both sides until they are golden brown, adding the remaining butter when you need it. Cut each sandwich in half to serve.

CROQUE MONSIEUR

An old olive oil press at the Ravida estate in Menfi in Sicily. This stone was turned by a donkey who walked around it in a circle. Olives were ground between the two stones before being pressed to extract the oil.

FROM ITALY

PIZZETTE

½ quantity pizza dough (see recipe on page 469)
cornmeal, to dust
250 g (9 oz) mozzarella cheese
1 tablespoon olive oil

GARLIC AND ROSEMARY PIZZETTE
50 g (1¾ oz) parmesan cheese
4 garlic cloves, crushed
2 teaspoons chopped rosemary
1½ tablespoons olive oil
3 garlic cloves, thinly sliced

TOMATO AND OLIVE PIZZETTE
200 g (7 oz) pitted black olives
400 g (14 oz) roma (plum) tomatoes
3 garlic cloves, crushed
2 tablespoons finely shredded basil
3 tablespoons olive oil
5 small sprigs of basil

MAKES 10 PIZZETTE

PREHEAT the oven to 240°C (475°C/Gas 9). Form the pizza dough into ten bases. Place the pizza bases on two baking trays dusted with cornmeal. Grate the mozzarella cheese. Brush the pizza bases with the oil, then sprinkle with mozzarella. Make five garlic and rosemary pizzette and five tomato and olive pizzette.

TO MAKE the garlic and rosemary pizzette, grate the parmesan. Scatter five bases with the garlic and rosemary and drizzle with the oil. Sprinkle with parmesan and garnish with some slices of garlic.

TO MAKE the tomato and olive pizzette, dice the olives and tomatoes. Mix together the olives, tomato, garlic and shredded basil and spoon over the remaining bases. Drizzle with oil and garnish with the basil sprigs.

BAKE the pizzette for 10 minutes, or until the bases are crisp and golden.

GRISSINI

1 tablespoon malt syrup
2 teaspoons dried yeast or 15 g (½ oz) fresh yeast
500 g (4 cups) plain (all-purpose) flour
1½ teaspoons salt
2 tablespoons olive oil
fine semolina

MAKES 20

PUT 310 ml (11 fl oz/1¼ cups) warm water in a bowl and stir in the malt and yeast. Leave until the yeast foams. Sift the flour and salt into a bowl, add the yeast and oil and mix until it clumps together.

FORM into a ball and knead on a lightly floured surface for 5–6 minutes, or until smooth and elastic. Put the dough on a lightly oiled tray and squash out to fill the shape of the tray. Brush with oil. Slide into a plastic bag and leave for 1 hour, or until doubled in size.

PREHEAT the oven to 230°C (450°F/Gas 8) and lightly oil two baking trays. Sprinkle the dough with semolina. Cut into four portions along its length, then slice each one into five strips. Pick up each strip by both ends and stretch out to 20 cm (8 inches) long. Place on the trays, 5 cm (2 inches) apart. Bake for 20 minutes, or until crisp and golden. Cool slightly on the trays and then on wire racks.

GRISSINI

FROM ITALY

ARTICHOKE FRITTATA

ALMOST AN OMELETTE, BUT FLASHED UNDER THE GRILL (BROILER) TO FINISH COOKING, THE FRITTATA VARIES FROM THIN AND PANCAKE-LIKE, TO THICKER, WITH A GOLDEN CRUST AND CREAMY CENTRE. IT IS A FAVOURITE THROUGHOUT ITALY, BUT THE ARTICHOKE FRITTATA IS A SPECIALITY OF TRENTINO.

175 g (6 oz) broad beans, fresh or frozen
1 onion
400 g (14 oz) tin artichoke hearts, drained
3 tablespoons olive oil
6 eggs
2 tablespoons chopped parsley
45 g (1½ oz/½ cup) grated pecorino cheese
pinch of nutmeg

SERVES 4

BRING a small saucepan of water to the boil. Add a large pinch of salt and the broad beans. Boil for 2 minutes, then drain and rinse under cold water. Peel off the skins from the beans.

HALVE the onion and slice thinly. Cut the artichoke hearts from bottom to top into slices about 5 mm (¼ inch) wide. Discard any slices that contain the tough central choke.

HEAT the oil in a 30 cm (12 inch) frying pan and fry the onion over low heat for 6–8 minutes, without allowing it to brown. Add the artichoke slices and cook for 1–2 minutes. Stir in the broad beans.

PREHEAT the grill (broiler). Lightly beat together the eggs, parsley, pecorino and nutmeg and season well with salt and pepper. Pour into the frying pan and cook over low heat until three-quarters set, shaking the pan often to stop the frittata sticking.

FINISH the top off under the grill and leave to cool before serving in wedges.

Preparing artichokes by hand at the Rialto market in Venice.

RED CAPSICUM AND ZUCCHINI FRITTATA

1 tablespoon olive oil
1 onion, sliced
1 red capsicum (pepper), sliced
2 zucchini (courgettes), sliced
6 eggs
1 tablespoon chopped basil
60 g (2 oz/½ cup) grated Parmesan cheese

SERVES 4

HEAT the olive oil in a 30 cm (12 inch) frying pan and cook the onion until soft. Add the red capsicum and zucchini and fry until soft. Preheat the grill (broiler).

LIGHTLY beat the eggs, basil and Parmesan and season well. Pour into the frying pan and cook over low heat until three-quarters set, shaking the pan to stop the frittata sticking. Finish the top off under the grill and leave to cool before serving in wedges.

The zucchini (courgette) is one of Italy's favourite vegetables. In the north it's baked in béchamel, in the south fried with tomatoes and basil. These are from Sicily.

ARTICHOKE FRITTATA WITH RED CAPSICUM AND ZUCCHINI FRITTATA

FROM MOROCCO

LAMB KEBABS

OF ALL THE STREET-FOOD OFFERINGS, THESE WOULD HAVE TO BE THE MOST POPULAR. LITTLE CUBES OF LAMB FAT ARE PLACED BETWEEN THE MEAT TO KEEP THE LAMB MOIST AS THE KEBABS COOK OVER A CHARCOAL FIRE. THE OIL IN THE FOLLOWING MARINADE SERVES THE SAME PURPOSE.

750 g (1 lb 10 oz) boneless lamb from leg
1 brown onion, grated
1 teaspoon paprika
1 teaspoon ground cumin
2 tablespoons finely chopped flat-leaf (Italian) parsley
3 tablespoons olive oil
1 round of Moroccan bread or pitta breads, to serve

HARISSA AND TOMATO SAUCE
2 tomatoes
½ brown onion, grated
1 tablespoon olive oil
1 teaspoon harissa, or to taste, or ¼ teaspoon cayenne pepper
½ teaspoon caster (superfine) sugar

SERVES 4

SOAK eight bamboo skewers in water for 2 hours, or use metal skewers.

DO NOT trim the fat from the lamb. Cut the meat into 3 cm (1¼ inch) cubes and put in a bowl. Add the onion, paprika, cumin, parsley, olive oil and a generous grind of black pepper. Toss well to coat the lamb with the marinade, then cover and leave in the refrigerator to marinate for at least 2 hours.

TO MAKE the harissa and tomato sauce, halve the tomatoes crossways and squeeze out the seeds. Coarsely grate the tomatoes into a bowl down to the skin, discarding the skin. In a saucepan, cook the onion in the olive oil for 2 minutes, stir in the harissa or cayenne pepper, and add the grated tomatoes, sugar and ½ teaspoon salt. Cover and simmer for 10 minutes, then remove the lid and simmer for a further 4 minutes, or until the sauce becomes thick and pulpy. Transfer to a bowl.

THREAD the lamb cubes onto the skewers, leaving a little space between the meat cubes. Heat the barbecue grill to high and cook for 5–6 minutes, turning and brushing with the marinade. Alternatively, cook in a chargrill pan or under the grill (broiler).

IF SERVING kebabs with Moroccan bread, cut the bread into quarters and slit each piece in half almost to the crust. Slide meat from the skewers into the bread pocket and drizzle with a little tomato and harissa sauce. If using pitta bread, don't split it; just slide the lamb from the skewers onto the centre, add sauce and fold up the sides.

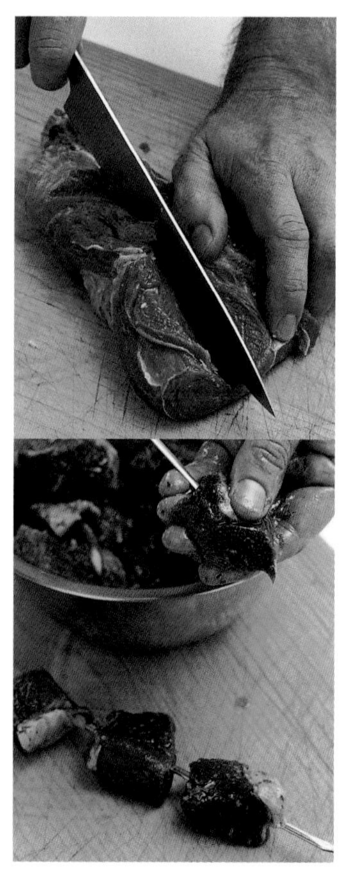

For moist, tender kebabs, thread the marinated meat onto skewers and cook on a heated barbecue grill.

FROM SPAIN

CROQUETTES

THESE LITTLE DEEP-FRIED SNACKS ARE UNIVERSALLY LOVED FOR THEIR SUBLIME SYMPHONY OF CRUNCHY OUTSIDE AND CREAMY INSIDE. THE INSIDE, IF PERFECT, WILL EXPLODE IN THE MOUTH WITH RICH FLAVOUR – IN THE CASE OF THIS PARTICULAR RECIPE, OF JAMÓN.

90 g (3 oz) butter
1 small brown onion, finely chopped
115 g (4 oz) open cap mushrooms, finely chopped
125 g (4½ oz/1 cup) plain (all-purpose) flour
250 ml (9 fl oz/1 cup) milk
185 ml (6 fl oz/¾ cup) chicken stock
115 g (4 oz) jamón or prosciutto, finely chopped
60 g (2¼ oz/½ cup) plain (all-purpose) flour, extra
2 eggs, lightly beaten
50 g (1¾ oz/½ cup) dry breadcrumbs
olive oil, for deep-frying

MAKES 24

MELT the butter in a saucepan over low heat, add the onion and cook for 5 minutes, or until translucent. Add the mushrooms and cook over low heat, stirring occasionally, for 5 minutes. Add the flour and stir over low–medium heat for 1 minute, or until the mixture is dry and crumbly and begins to change colour. Remove from the heat and gradually add the milk, stirring until smooth. Stir in the stock and return to the heat, stirring until the mixture boils and thickens. Stir in the jamón and some black pepper, then transfer the mixture to a bowl to cool for about 2 hours.

ROLL heaped tablespoons of the mixture into croquette shapes about 6 cm (2½ inches) long. Put the extra flour, beaten egg and breadcrumbs in three separate shallow bowls. Toss croquettes in the flour, dip in the egg, allowing the excess to drain away, then roll in the breadcrumbs. Put on a baking tray and refrigerate for about 30 minutes.

FILL a deep, heavy-based saucepan one-third full of oil and heat to 170°C (325°F), or until a cube of bread dropped into the oil browns in 20 seconds. Add the croquettes in batches and deep-fry for 3 minutes, turning, until brown. Drain well on paper towel. Sprinkle with salt before serving hot.

Before frying, refrigerate the croquettes to help set the flour, egg and breadcrumb coating.

Ensure the basil and mozzarella filling is fully enclosed so it doesn't spill out when the suppli are fried.

FROM ITALY

SUPPLI

WHEN THESE CROQUETTES ARE BITTEN INTO, THE MOZZARELLA PULLS OUT TO RESEMBLE STRANDS OF TELEPHONE WIRES, HENCE THE ITALIAN NAME FOR THIS DISH, *SUPPLI AL TELEFONO*. SUPPLI ARE EXCELLENT FOR USING UP LEFT-OVER RISOTTO.

3 tablespoons butter
1 small onion, finely chopped
1.5 litres (52 fl oz/6 cups) chicken stock
440 g (15½ oz/2 cups) risotto rice (arborio, vialone nano or carnaroli)
75 g (2½ oz/¾ cup) grated parmesan cheese
2 eggs, beaten
9 basil leaves, torn in half
150 g (5½ oz) mozzarella cheese, cut into 18 cubes (about 1.5 cm/⅝ inch square)
150 g (5½ oz/1½ cups) dried breadcrumbs
oil for deep-frying

MAKES 18

MELT the butter in a large saucepan. Add the onion and cook over low heat for 3–4 minutes until softened but not browned. Heat the stock to simmering point in another saucepan.

ADD the rice to the onion and cook, stirring, for 1 minute to seal the rice. Add several ladles of the hot stock, stirring continuously so that the rice cooks evenly. Keep adding enough stock to just cover the rice, stirring frequently. Continue in this way for about 20 minutes, or until the rice is creamy on the outside but still al dente.

REMOVE from the heat and stir in the parmesan and eggs. Season with salt and pepper. Spread out on a large baking tray to cool completely.

DIVIDE the rice into 18 portions. Take one portion in the palm of your hand and place a piece of basil and a cube of mozzarella in the centre. Fold rice over to encase the cheese and at the same time mould the croquette into an egg shape. Roll the croquette in breadcrumbs and place on a baking tray while you make the rest.

HEAT enough oil in a deep-fat fryer or deep frying pan to fully cover the croquettes. Heat the oil to 180°C (350°F), or until a piece of bread fries golden brown in 15 seconds when dropped in the oil. Deep-fry the suppli in batches, without crowding, for about 4 minutes, or until evenly golden brown. Drain on paper towels and serve at once, as they are or with a fresh tomato sauce.

FROM FRANCE

DUCK RILLETTES

OFTEN KNOWN AS *RILLETTES DE TOURS*, THIS SPECIALITY OF THE LOIRE VALLEY IS THE FRENCH VERSION OF POTTED MEAT. SPREAD ON TOAST OR BREAD AND SERVE WITH A GLASS OF WINE, OR STIR A SPOONFUL INTO SOUPS AND STEWS TO ADD FLAVOUR.

600 g (1 lb 5 oz) pork belly, rind and bones removed
800 g (1 lb 12 oz) duck legs
100 ml (3½ fl oz) dry white wine
1 teaspoon sea salt
¼ teaspoon black pepper
½ teaspoon ground nutmeg
¼ teaspoon ground allspice
1 large garlic clove, crushed

SERVES 8

PREHEAT oven to 140°C (275°F/Gas 1). Cut pork belly into small pieces and put in a casserole dish with the rest of the ingredients and 200 ml (7 fl oz) water. Mix well. Bake, covered, for 4 hours. The meat should be soft and surrounded by liquid fat.

TIP the meat and fat into a sieve placed over a bowl to collect the fat. Remove the meat from the duck legs and shred all the warm meat with two forks. Season to taste. Pack meat into a 750 ml (26 fl oz/3 cups) terrine. Leave until cold. Strain hot fat through a sieve lined with damp muslin.

ONCE the meat is cold, pour the fat over it (you may need to melt the fat first, if it has solidified as it cooled). Cover and refrigerate for up to a week. Serve at room temperature.

Use two forks to shred the meat.

PORK RILLETTES

750 g (1 lb 10 oz) pork neck or belly, rind and bones removed
150 g (5 oz) pork back fat
100 ml (3½ fl oz) dry white wine
3 juniper berries, lightly crushed
1 teaspoon sea salt
2 teaspoons dried thyme
½ teaspoon ground nutmeg
¼ teaspoon ground allspice
pinch of ground cloves
1 large garlic clove, crushed

SERVES 8

PREHEAT oven to 140°C (275°F/Gas 1). Cut the meat and fat into short strips. Place in a casserole dish with the rest of the ingredients. Combine thoroughly. Bake, covered, for 4 hours; the pork should be soft and surrounded by liquid fat.

TIP the meat and fat into a sieve placed over a bowl to collect the fat. Shred the warm meat with two forks. Season if necessary. Pack meat into a 750 ml (26 fl oz/3 cups) dish or terrine and leave until cold. Strain the hot fat through a sieve lined with damp muslin.

ONCE the pork is cold, pour the fat over it (you may need to melt the fat first, if it has solidified as it cooled). Cover and refrigerate for up to a week. Serve at room temperature.

PORK RILLETTES

DUCK RILLETTES

FROM SPAIN

TUNA EMPANADAS

ORIGINALLY FROM GALICIA, THE EMPANADA IS SPAIN'S VERSION OF THE PIE. IT WOULD HAVE BEEN A SATISFYING SNACK FOR THE HARDY GALICIANS, WHO FOR CENTURIES HAVE BEEN FARMERS AND FISHERMEN. TODAY, IT COMES WITH A VARIETY OF FILLINGS, BUT THE TUNA VERSION IS A FAVOURITE.

Carefully 'cut' the liquid into the breadcrumb-like mixture. Fold the dough over the filling and pinch around the edges to seal.

400 g (14 oz/3¼ cups) plain (all-purpose) flour, plus extra for rolling
75 g (2¾ oz) butter, softened
2 eggs
60 ml (2 fl oz/¼ cup) fine sherry
1 egg, extra, lightly beaten

FILLING
1 tablespoon olive oil
1 small brown onion, finely diced
2 teaspoons tomato paste (concentrated purée)
125 g (4½ oz/½ cup) tinned chopped tomatoes
85 g (3 oz) tinned tuna, drained
1½ tablespoons chopped roasted red capsicum (pepper)
2 tablespoons chopped flat-leaf (Italian) parsley

MAKES 24

SIFT the flour and 1 teaspoon of salt into a large bowl. Rub the butter into the flour until mixture resembles fine breadcrumbs. Combine the eggs and sherry and add to the bowl, cutting the liquid in with a flat-bladed knife until the mixture clumps and forms a dough. Turn onto a lightly floured surface and gather into a smooth ball (do not knead or you will have tough pastry). Cover with plastic wrap and refrigerate for 30 minutes.

TO MAKE the filling, heat the olive oil in a frying pan over medium heat and cook the onion for about 5 minutes, or until softened and translucent. Add the tomato paste and chopped tomato and cook for 10 minutes, or until pulpy. Add the tuna, roasted capsicum and parsley and season well.

PREHEAT the oven to 190°C (375°F/Gas 5). Dust a work surface with the extra flour. Roll out half the pastry to a thickness of 2 mm (1/16 inch). Using a 10 cm (4 inch) cutter, cut into 12 rounds. Put a heaped tablespoon of filling on each round, fold over and brush the edges with water, then pinch to seal. Continue with the remaining rounds, then repeat with the remaining dough and filling to make 24 empanadas.

TRANSFER to a lightly oiled baking tray and brush each empanada with extra beaten egg. Bake for 30 minutes, or until golden. Serve warm or cold.

STARTERS, TAPAS & ANTIPASTO

Add the leeks to the simmering liquid and cook in a single layer.

FROM FRANCE

LEEKS A LA GRECQUE

A LA GRECQUE REFERS TO THE GREEK STYLE OF COOKING, USING OLIVE OIL, LEMON, HERBS AND SPICES. THESE INGREDIENTS THAT ARE SO READILY FOUND IN THE DUSTY GREEK HILLSIDES ARE EQUALLY AT HOME IN THE MORE VERDANT LANDSCAPE OF FRANCE.

60 ml (2 fl oz/¼ cup) extra virgin olive oil
30 ml (1 fl oz) white wine
1 tablespoon tomato purée
¼ teaspoon sugar
1 bay leaf
1 thyme sprig
1 garlic clove, crushed
4 coriander seeds, crushed
4 peppercorns
8 small leeks, trimmed
1 teaspoon lemon juice
1 tablespoon chopped parsley

SERVES 4

PUT the oil, wine, tomato purée, sugar, bay leaf, thyme, garlic, coriander seeds, peppercorns and 250 ml (9 fl oz/1 cup) water in a large non-aluminium frying pan. Bring to the boil, cover and simmer for 5 minutes.

ADD leeks in a single layer and bring to simmering point. Reduce heat, cover pan again and cook for 20–30 minutes, or until the leeks are tender (pierce with a fine skewer). Lift out the leeks and put them in a serving dish.

ADD the lemon juice to the cooking liquid and boil rapidly until the liquid is slightly syrupy. Remove the bay leaf, thyme and peppercorns. Season with salt and pour over the leeks. Serve the leeks cold, sprinkled with chopped parsley.

MUSHROOMS Á LA GRECQUE

MUSHROOMS A LA GRECQUE

2 tomatoes
80 ml (2½ fl oz/⅓ cup) extra virgin olive oil
60 ml (2 fl oz/¼ cup) white wine
2 shallots, finely chopped
1 garlic clove, crushed
6 coriander seeds, lightly crushed
1 bay leaf
1 thyme sprig
500 g (1 lb 2 oz) button mushrooms
2 teaspoons lemon juice
pinch of sugar
1 tablespoon chopped parsley

SERVES 4

SCORE a cross in the top of each tomato. Plunge tomatoes into boiling water for 20 seconds, then drain and peel the skin away from the cross. Chop the tomatoes, discarding the cores.

PUT the oil, wine, tomato, shallots, garlic, coriander seeds, bay leaf, thyme and 250 ml (9 fl oz/1 cup) water in a non-aluminium saucepan. Bring to the boil, cover and simmer for 10 minutes. Uncover the pan, add mushrooms and simmer for a further 10 minutes, stirring occasionally. Lift out the mushrooms with a slotted spoon and put them in a serving dish.

BOIL the cooking liquid rapidly until you have only about 250 ml (9 fl oz/1 cup) left. Remove the bay leaf and thyme. Add lemon juice and season with salt, pepper and the sugar. Pour the liquid over the mushrooms and leave to cool. Serve the mushrooms cold, sprinkled with chopped parsley.

LEEKS Á LA GRECQUE

FROM SPAIN

GARLIC PRAWNS

AS AN APPETISER FOR A DINNER PARTY, OR ONE OF THE MANY TAPAS YOU TUCK IN TO OVER A GLASS OF WINE AND SOME GOOD CONVERSATION, THIS DISH IS SURE TO BE A HIT. SERVE IN CAZUELAS DE BARRO (EARTHENWARE RAMEKINS) FOR A PARTICULARLY AUTHENTIC APPROACH.

1¼ kg (2 lb 12 oz) raw prawns (shrimp)
80 g (2¾ oz) butter, melted
185 ml (6 fl oz/¾ cups) olive oil
8 garlic cloves, crushed
2 spring onions (scallions), thinly sliced
crusty bread, to serve

SERVES 4

PREHEAT the oven to 250°C (500°F/Gas 9). Peel the prawns, leaving the tails intact. Pull out the vein from the back, starting at the head end. Cut a slit down the back of each prawn.

COMBINE the butter and oil and divide among four 500 ml (17 fl oz/2 cup) cast-iron pots. Divide half the crushed garlic among the pots.

PLACE the pots on a baking tray and heat in the oven for 10 minutes, or until the mixture is bubbling. Remove from the oven and divide the prawns and remaining garlic among the pots. Return to the oven for 5 minutes, or until prawns are cooked. Stir in the spring onion. Season to taste. Serve with bread to mop up the juices.

TOAST WITH TOMATO

ALSO KNOWN AS PAN A LA CATALANA, THIS HUMBLE, STRAIGHTFORWARD DISH IS A FAVOURITE IN TAPAS BARS THROUGHOUT SPAIN. IF YOU CAN, SERVE WITH THE FRESHEST, RIPEST TOMATOES YOU CAN FIND FOR A TRULY LUSCIOUS EXPERIENCE.

1 crusty bread stick
6 garlic cloves, halved
3 tomatoes, halved
extra virgin olive oil, for drizzling

SERVES 6

SLICE the bread stick diagonally and toast the slices very lightly. Rub them on one side with a cut garlic clove, then with half a tomato, squeezing the juice onto the bread. Season with a little salt and drizzle with extra virgin olive oil.

TOAST WITH TOMATO

GARLIC PRAWNS

FROM MOROCCO

BEETROOT AND CUMIN SALAD

THIS WARM BEETROOT (BEET) SALAD, WITH FLAVOURS HEIGHTENED BY GROUND CUMIN, IS ONE YOU WILL MAKE AGAIN AND AGAIN. IF SERVING AS PART OF A MOROCCAN DINNER, DICE THE BEETROOT RATHER THAN CUTTING INTO WEDGES, SO THAT IT CAN BE EASILY PICKED UP WITH THE FINGERS.

6 beetroot (beets)
80 ml (2½ fl oz/⅓ cup) olive oil
1 tablespoon red wine vinegar
½ teaspoon ground cumin
1 red onion
2 tablespoons chopped flat-leaf (Italian) parsley

SERVES 4–6

CUT the stems from the beetroot bulbs, leaving 2 cm (¾ inch) attached. Do not trim the roots. Wash well to remove all traces of soil, and boil in salted water for 1 hour, or until tender. Leave until cool enough to handle.

IN A deep bowl, beat the olive oil with the red wine vinegar, cumin and a good grinding of black pepper to make a dressing.

WEARING rubber gloves so the beetroot juice doesn't stain your hands, peel the warm beetroot bulbs and trim the roots. Halve them and cut into slender wedges. Place in the dressing. Halve the onion, slice into slender wedges and add to the beetroot. Add parsley and toss well. Serve this salad warm or at room temperature.

Gloved hands are a must when handling hot beetroot. Rub gently and the skins and stem remains slip off easily.

OKRA WITH TOMATO SAUCE

WHEN PREPARING FRESH OKRA, CAREFULLY TRIM THE TIP OF EACH STEM ONLY, LEAVING MOST OF THE STEM IN PLACE. IF YOU CUT INTO THE OKRA ITSELF, THE VISCOUS SUBSTANCE IT CONTAINS BECOMES MORE NOTICEABLE. ALWAYS STIR GENTLY, OR SHAKE THE PAN, DURING COOKING.

3 tablespoons olive oil
1 brown onion, chopped
2 garlic cloves, crushed
500 g (1 lb 2 oz) fresh okra
400 g (14 oz) tin chopped tomatoes
2 teaspoons caster (superfine) sugar
3 tablespoons lemon juice
3 large handfuls coriander (cilantro) leaves, finely chopped

SERVES 4–6

HEAT the oil in a large frying pan over medium heat, add the onion and cook for 5 minutes, or until the onion is softened. Add garlic and cook for a further 1 minute.

ADD okra to pan and cook, stirring occasionally, for 4–5 minutes. Add the tomatoes, sugar and lemon juice and simmer, covered, for 3–4 minutes. Stir in coriander, cover and simmer for 5 minutes, then serve.

OKRA WITH TOMATO SAUCE

FROM FRANCE

PROVENÇAL TART

PASTRY
250 g (9 oz/2 cups) plain (all-purpose) flour
150 g (5½ oz) butter, diced
1 egg yolk, beaten

2 tablespoons olive oil
1 large white onion, finely chopped
10 tomatoes (or 2 x 400 g/14 oz tins chopped tomatoes)
1 teaspoon tomato purée
2 garlic cloves, finely chopped
1 tablespoon roughly chopped oregano, plus a few whole leaves to garnish
1 red capsicum (pepper)
1 yellow capsicum (pepper)
6 anchovies, halved
12 pitted olives
drizzle of olive oil

SERVES 6

TO MAKE the pastry, sift the flour into a bowl, add the butter and rub in with your fingertips until the mixture resembles breadcrumbs. Add the egg yolk and a little cold water (about 2–3 teaspoons) and mix with the blade of a palette knife until the dough just starts to come together. Bring dough together with your hands and shape into a ball. Wrap in plastic wrap and refrigerate for at least 30 minutes.

HEAT oil in a frying pan, add the onion, cover and cook over very low heat for 20 minutes, stirring often, until softened but not browned.

SCORE a cross in the top of each tomato. Plunge tomatoes into boiling water for 20 seconds, drain and peel. Chop the tomatoes, discarding cores. Add tomato, tomato purée, garlic and oregano to the pan. Simmer, uncovered, for 20 minutes, stirring occasionally. Once tomato is soft and the mixture has become a paste, leave to cool.

ROLL OUT the pastry to fit a 34 x 26 cm (13½ x 10½ inch) shallow baking tray. Prick pastry gently all over, without piercing right through, then cover with plastic wrap and chill for 30 minutes. Preheat oven to 200°C (400°F/Gas 6) and preheat the grill (broiler).

CUT capsicum in half, remove the seeds and membrane and place, skin side up, under hot grill until skin blackens and blisters. Leave to cool. Peel away skin. Cut capsicum into thin strips.

LINE the pastry shell with a crumpled piece of baking paper and fill with baking beads (use dried beans or rice if you don't have beads). Blind bake the pastry for 10 minutes, remove the paper and beads and bake for a further 3–5 minutes, or until pastry is just cooked but still very pale. Reduce the oven to 180°C (350°F/Gas 4).

SPREAD tomato over the pastry and scatter with capsicum. Arrange anchovies and olives over the top. Brush with olive oil and bake for 25 minutes. Scatter with oregano leaves to serve.

Simmer the filling until the tomato is so soft that it forms a paste.

FROM ITALY

CARPACCIO

Fresh tuna has a dark meaty flesh that is delicious both raw and cooked. Tuna is fished off the coasts of Sicily and Calabria where the fish come to spawn. The better-tasting red flesh indicates that the tuna was caught by hand, killed and bled quickly, while muddy-brown flesh means the fish drowned and so probably was caught by net.

CARPACCIO IS NAMED AFTER THE RENAISSANCE PAINTER WHOSE USE OF REDS IS REFLECTED IN THE DISH. IT WAS CREATED IN HARRY'S BAR IN VENICE FOR A FAVOURITE CUSTOMER WHOSE DOCTOR HAD PLACED HER ON A DIET FORBIDDING COOKED MEAT.

700 g (1 lb 9 oz) good-quality beef fillet
1 egg yolk
3 teaspoons dijon mustard
3 tablespoons lemon juice
2 drops Tabasco sauce
80 ml (2½ fl oz/⅓ cup) olive oil
1 tablespoon cream
2–3 tablespoons capers, rinsed

SERVES 6

PLACE the beef in the freezer for about half an hour, or until it is firm. Using a sharp knife or mandolin, cut the beef into paper-thin slices. Cover six serving plates with the beef in an even layer.

BLEND the egg yolk, mustard, lemon juice and Tabasco in a bowl or food processor. Add olive oil in a thin, steady stream, whisking or processing continuously until the mayonnaise thickens. Whisk in the cream. Season to taste. Drizzle over beef slices and sprinkle with capers.

TUNA CARPACCIO

TUNA CARPACCIO

400 g (14 oz) sashimi-quality tuna
2 very large handfuls basil leaves
1 garlic clove
80 ml (2½ fl oz/⅓ cup) extra virgin olive oil
1 teaspoon lemon juice

SERVES 4

PLACE the tuna in the freezer for about half an hour, or until it is firm. Using a sharp knife or a mandolin, cut the tuna into paper-thin slices. Cover four serving plates with the slices in a thin even layer.

BLANCH basil leaves in salted boiling water for 10 seconds, then drain well. Place leaves in a food processor or blender with the garlic, olive oil and lemon juice and mix well. Season with salt and pepper. Drizzle over tuna. Serve with bread.

Crisp and sweet, fresh broad beans are well complemented by the rich and salty jamón.

FROM SPAIN

BROAD BEANS WITH JAMÓN

THE SPANISH LOVE THEIR VEGETABLES – ESPECIALLY PULSES. THEY PARTICULARLY LOVE TO COMBINE VEGETABLES WITH THE SALTINESS OF JAMÓN. THIS DISH CAN BE SEEN IN A TAPAS BAR, OR ON A MENU AS A STARTER, AND IS TRADITIONALLY SERVED IN SPANISH HOMES AS A SIDE DISH.

20 g (¾ oz) butter
1 brown onion, chopped
175 g (6 oz) jamón or prosciutto, roughly chopped
2 garlic cloves, crushed
500 g (1 lb 2 oz) broad (fava) beans, fresh or frozen
125 ml (4 fl oz/½ cup) dry white wine
185 ml (6 fl oz/¾ cup) chicken stock

SERVES 4

MELT the butter in a large saucepan and add the onion, jamón and garlic. Cook over medium heat for 5 minutes, stirring often, until the onion softens.

ADD the broad beans and wine and cook over high heat until the liquid is reduced by half. Add the stock, reduce the heat to low–medium, cover and cook for 10 minutes. Uncover and simmer for another 10 minutes or until the broad beans are tender and most of the liquid has evaporated. Serve hot as a tapas dish with crusty bread, or as a side dish.

Jamón – the pig from which this delicacy is made is a decendant of the original wild animal that roamed the shores of the Mediterranean millennia before the birth of Christ. Accounting for only 10% of Jamón produced, the four denominations of origin are: Extremadura, Guijelo, Huelva and Los Pedrones. High-quality jamón comes from Iberian pigs and under strict controls, is graded and quality checked.

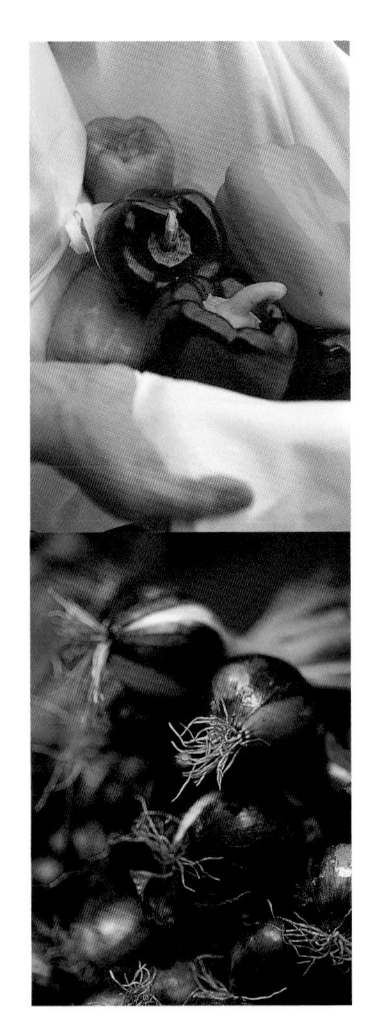

FROM ITALY

STUFFED CAPSICUMS

- 3 red or yellow capsicums (peppers)
- 1 tablespoon olive oil
- 1 small onion, finely chopped
- 2 garlic cloves, crushed
- 50 g (1¾ oz) butter
- 180 g (6 oz/2¼ cups) fresh breadcrumbs
- 1 egg
- 35 g (1¼ oz/⅓ cup) grated parmesan cheese
- 2 tomatoes, peeled, seeded and chopped
- 150 g (5½ oz/1 cup) grated mozzarella cheese
- 2 tablespoons chopped basil
- 3 tablespoons extra virgin olive oil

SERVES 6

PREHEAT the oven to 170°C (325°F/Gas 3). Cut capsicums in half and remove the seeds. Place on a lightly oiled baking tray.

HEAT the olive oil in a frying pan, add the onion and garlic and cook, stirring, for 5 minutes. Remove from the heat and stir in the butter and breadcrumbs. Transfer to a bowl and add the egg, parmesan, tomato, mozzarella, basil and 3 tablespoons water. Stir well and season.

FILL capsicum halves with stuffing, drizzle with the extra virgin olive oil and bake for 40–45 minutes, or until capsicums are cooked through and the tops are golden brown.

STUFFED ONIONS

- 8 medium white or red onions, peeled but left whole
- 3 tomatoes
- 1 tablespoon olive oil
- 15 g (½ oz) butter
- 1 onion, finely chopped
- 1 garlic clove, crushed
- 250 g (9 oz) minced (ground) beef
- 2 tablespoons chopped parsley
- 1 egg
- 30 g (1 oz/⅓ cup) grated parmesan cheese

SERVES 4

PLACE onions in a large saucepan, cover with water and simmer for 10 minutes. Drain and cool. Preheat the oven to 180°C (350°F/Gas 4). Score a cross in the top of each tomato. Plunge into boiling water for 20 seconds, then drain and peel. Chop the tomatoes, discarding the cores.

HEAT the olive oil and butter in a frying pan until the butter has melted. Add the onion and garlic and cook, stirring, for 5 minutes or until tender. Add the tomato and cook for a further 6 minutes over low heat. Add the beef and cook until lightly browned. Remove from the heat and cool. Add the parsley, egg and parmesan and stir well.

Cut off the top of each onion and, using a melon baller or a spoon, remove some of the inside (being careful not to lose the shape). Place them on a baking tray and stuff with the filling. Bake for 20 minutes and serve hot or at room temperature.

FROM FRANCE

ZUCCHINI SOUFFLÉ

SOUFFLÉS HAVE DEVELOPED A REPUTATION AS UNPREDICTABLE CREATIONS, BUT THEY ARE NOT HARD TO MAKE. THE SECRET LIES IN BEATING THE EGG WHITES TO THE RIGHT STIFFNESS AND SERVING THE SOUFFLÉ STRAIGHT FROM OVEN TO TABLE. YOU COULD USE BROCCOLI INSTEAD OF ZUCCHINI.

15 g (½ oz)butter, melted
1½ tablespoons dried breadcrumbs
350 g (12 oz) zucchini (courgettes), chopped
125 ml (4 fl oz/½ cup) milk
30 g (1 oz) butter
30 g (1 oz) plain flour
75 g (2½ oz) gruyère or parmesan, finely grated
3 spring onions (scallions), finely chopped
4 eggs, separated

SERVES 4

BRUSH a 1.5 litre (52 fl oz/6 cups) soufflé dish with the melted butter and tip the breadcrumbs into it. Rotate the dish to coat the side completely with breadcrumbs. Tip out excess breadcrumbs.

COOK the zucchini in boiling water for 8 minutes until tender, then drain. Place zucchini in a food processor with the milk and mix until smooth. Or, mash zucchini with milk and press through a sieve with a wooden spoon. Preheat the oven to 180°C (350°F/Gas 4).

MELT butter in a heavy-based saucepan. Stir in the flour to make a roux. Cook, stirring, 2 minutes over low heat without allowing the roux to brown. Remove from the heat and add zucchini purée, stirring until smooth. Return to the heat and bring to the boil. Simmer, stirring, for 3 minutes, then remove from the heat. Pour into a bowl, add the cheese and spring onion. Season well. Mix until smooth. Add egg yolks and beat until smooth.

WHISK the egg whites in a clean dry bowl until they form soft peaks. Spoon a quarter of the egg white onto the soufflé mixture and quickly but lightly fold it in, to loosen the mixture. Lightly fold in the remaining egg white. Pour into the soufflé dish and run your thumb around the inside rim of the dish, about 2 cm into the soufflé mixture (try not to wipe off the butter and breadcrumbs). This ridge helps the soufflé to rise without sticking.

BAKE for 45 minutes, or until the soufflé is well risen and wobbles slightly when tapped. Test with a skewer through a crack in the side of the soufflé. The skewer should come out clean or slightly moist. If the skewer is slightly moist, by the time the soufflé makes it to the table it will be cooked in the centre. Serve immediately.

Finely grate the cheese for soufflés so that it melts quickly without forming bubbles of oil.

Round zucchini are used in the same way as the more common long variety.

FROM MOROCCO

FRIED TUNA PASTRIES

TO EAT THIS TUNISIAN PASTRY (ADOPTED BY MOROCCANS), HOLD IT BY THE CORNERS, FILLING-SIDE UP, AND BITE INTO THE EGG, ALLOWING THE YOLK TO RUN INTO THE TUNA MIXTURE. WHILE SPRING-ROLL WRAPPERS ARE USED, WARKHA PASTRY IS NOW AVAILABLE IN SOME WESTERN MARKETS.

Take care when assembling and cooking to keep the egg yolk intact. Break egg into a small bowl and slide it into the filling. With spring-roll wrappers, the normally semicircular pastries become triangles.

2 tablespoons finely chopped brown onion
2 teaspoons olive oil
3 anchovy fillets, finely chopped
95 g (3¼ oz) tin tuna, in brine
2 teaspoons capers, rinsed, drained and chopped
2 tablespoons finely chopped flat-leaf (Italian) parsley
olive oil, for frying
4 x 21 cm (8¼ inch) square spring-roll wrappers (egg roll skins) or warkha pastry rounds
1 egg white, lightly beaten
4 small eggs

MAKES 4

IN A small frying pan, gently cook onion in the olive oil until softened. Add anchovies. Cook, stirring, until they have melted. Tip into a bowl. Drain the tuna well and add to the bowl with capers and parsley. Mix well, breaking up the chunks of tuna. Divide the mixture in the bowl into four portions.

POUR the oil into a large frying pan to a depth of 1 cm (½ inch) and place over medium heat.

PUT a spring-roll wrapper on the work surface and brush the edge with beaten egg white. Place a quarter of the filling on one corner of the wrapper, with the edge of the filling just touching the centre of the wrapper. Make an indent in the filling with the back of a spoon and break an egg into the centre of the filling. Fold the pastry over to form a triangle. Firmly press the edges together to seal.

AS SOON as you have finished the first pastry triangle, carefully lift it up using a wide spatula to help support the filling, and slide it into the hot oil. Fry for about 30 seconds on each side, spooning hot oil on top at the beginning of frying. If a firmly cooked egg is preferred, cook for 50 seconds on each side. When golden brown and crisp, remove with the spatula and drain on paper towel. Repeat with the remaining wrappers and filling. Do not prepare all the pastry triangles before frying them, as the moist filling soaks through the wrapper.

EITHER eat the traditional way by holding the brek by the corners, or use a knife and fork.

FROM ITALY

FRITTO MISTO DI MARE

FRITTO MISTO IS TRADITIONALLY A MIXED PLATTER. WE USUALLY THINK OF THIS AS SEAFOOD, AS IN THIS RECIPE, BUT FRITTO MISTO IS ANOTHER OF THOSE ITALIAN DISHES THAT VARIES FROM REGION TO REGION. SOME FAVOUR MEAT OR VEGETABLES, OTHERS USE FRUIT AND EVEN CHOCOLATE.

250 g (9 oz) baby squid
12 large prawns (shrimp)
8 small octopus
16 scallops, cleaned
12 fresh sardines, gutted and heads removed
250 g (9 oz) firm white fish fillets (such as ling, cod or snapper), skinned and cut into large cubes

GARLIC AND ANCHOVY SAUCE
125 ml (4 fl oz/½ cup) extra virgin olive oil
2 garlic cloves, crushed
3 anchovy fillets, finely minced
2 tablespoons finely chopped parsley
pinch of chilli flakes

BATTER
200 g (7 oz/1⅔ cups) plain (all-purpose) flour
80 ml (2½ oz/⅓ cup) olive oil
1 large egg white

oil for deep-frying
lemon wedges, to serve

SERVES 4

PREHEAT the oven to 140°C (275°F/Gas 1). Clean the squid by pulling the heads and tentacles out of the bodies along with any innards. Cut heads off below the eyes, just leaving the tentacles. Discard the heads and set the tentacles aside. Rinse the bodies, pulling out the clear quills, and cut the bodies into rings. Peel and devein the prawns, leaving the tails intact.

CLEAN the octopus by slitting the head and pulling out the innards. Cut out the eyes and hard beak and rinse. If the octopus seem a bit big, cut them into halves or quarters.

TO MAKE the sauce, warm the oil in a frying pan. Add the garlic, anchovy, parsley and chilli flakes. Cook over low heat for 1 minute, or until the garlic is soft but not brown. Serve warm or chilled.

TO MAKE the batter, sift the flour into a bowl and stir in ¼ teaspoon salt. Mix in the oil with a wooden spoon, then add 315 ml (10¾ fl oz/1¼ cups) tepid water gradually, changing to a whisk when the mixture becomes liquid. Continue whisking until the batter is smooth and thick. Stiffly whisk the egg white and fold into the batter. Heat oil in a deep-fat fryer or deep frying pan to 190°C (375°F), or until a piece of bread fries golden brown in 10 seconds when dropped in the oil.

DRY the seafood on paper towels so the batter will stick. Working with one type of seafood at a time, dip the pieces in batter. Shake off the excess batter, then carefully lower into the oil. Deep-fry for 2–3 minutes, depending on the size of the pieces. Drain on paper towels, then transfer to the oven. Do not crowd the seafood. Keep warm while you fry the remaining seafood. Serve with lemon wedges and the sauce.

Palermo's wholesale fish market (*Mercato Ittico*) sells fish caught all around Sicily's long coastline.

FROM SPAIN

SCRAMBLED EGGS WITH ASPARAGUS

CREAMY SCRAMBLED EGGS AS A STARTER? WHY NOT? THAT'S WHAT THE SPANISH CALL A REVUELTO: SCRAMBLED EGGS WITH FRESH SEASONAL INGREDIENTS SUCH AS PRAWNS, MUSHROOMS, GARLIC SHOOTS, BABY ARTICHOKES – AND, IN THE CASE OF THIS DELICIOUS RECIPE – ASPARAGUS.

2 garlic cloves, chopped
1 thick slice bread, crusts removed
60 ml (2 fl oz/¼ cup) olive oil
175 g (6 oz/1 bunch) asparagus, cut into 2 cm (¾ inch) lengths
1 teaspoon sweet paprika (pimentón)
2 tablespoons white wine vinegar
6 eggs, beaten

SERVES 4

PUT the garlic and bread in a food processor or mortar and pestle and grind to a loose paste, adding a small amount of water (1–2 tablespoons).

HEAT oil in a frying pan and sauté asparagus over medium heat for 2 minutes, or until just starting to become tender. Add the garlic and bread paste, paprika, vinegar and a pinch of salt, and stir to combine. Cover and cook over medium heat for 2–3 minutes, or until asparagus is tender.

POUR in the eggs and stir for a few minutes. Remove the mixture from the heat just before it is fully cooked (the perfect revuelto is creamy in consistency), then season to taste and serve.

Combine the asparagus and garlic paste and cook until tender before stirring in the eggs.

FROM FRANCE

POACHED SEAFOOD WITH HERB AÏOLI

THE BEST WAY TO APPROACH THIS RECIPE IS TO USE IT AS A GUIDE. AS WITH ALL SEAFOOD COOKING, YOU SHOULD ALWAYS ASK YOUR FISHMONGER'S ADVICE AS TO WHAT'S THE BEST CATCH THAT DAY. DON'T FORGET TO PROVIDE FINGERBOWLS.

2 raw lobster tails
12 mussels
250 g (9 oz) scallops on their shells
500 g (1 lb 2 oz) prawns (shrimp)
250 ml (9 fl oz/1 cup) dry white wine
250 ml (9 fl oz/1 cup) fish stock
pinch of saffron threads
1 bay leaf
4 black peppercorns
4 x 50 g (1¾ oz) salmon fillets

HERB AÏOLI
4 egg yolks
4 garlic cloves, crushed
1 tablespoon chopped basil
4 tablespoons chopped flat-leaf parsley
1 tablespoon lemon juice
200 ml (7 fl oz) olive oil

lemon wedges, to serve

SERVES 4

REMOVE the lobster meat from the tail by cutting down each side of the underside with scissors and peeling back the middle piece of shell. Scrub the mussels and remove their beards, discarding any that are open and don't close when tapped on the work surface. Remove scallops from their shells and pull away the white muscle and digestive tract around each one, leaving the roes intact. Clean scallop shells and keep them for serving. Peel and devein prawns, leaving the tails intact. Butterfly them by cutting them open down the backs.

TO MAKE the herb aïoli, put the egg yolks, garlic, basil, parsley and lemon juice in a mortar and pestle or food processor and pound or mix until light and creamy. Add oil, drop by drop from the tip of a teaspoon, pounding constantly until the mixture begins to thicken, then add the oil in a very thin stream. (If you're using a processor, pour in the oil in a thin stream with the motor running.)

PUT the wine, stock, saffron, bay leaf and peppercorns in a frying pan and bring to a very slow simmer. Add lobster and poach 5 minutes, then remove, cover and keep warm.

POACH the remaining seafood in batches: the mussels and scallops will take about 2 minutes to cook and open (discard any mussels that have not opened after this time). The prawns will take 3 minutes and the salmon a little longer, depending on the thickness. (Keep poaching liquid to use as soup stock.) Cut the lobster into thick medallions, put the scallops back on their shells and arrange the seafood on a large platter with the aïoli in a bowl in the centre. Serve with lemon wedges.

Cut down each side of the underside of the lobster tail and peel back the shell.

A busy port in Provence.

FROM SPAIN

CHICKPEAS WITH CHORIZO

THIS COMBINATION OF TWO EMBLEMATIC INGREDIENTS OF SPANISH COOKING PROVIDES A SIMPLE BUT SATISFYING TAPAS DISH. CHORIZO, A SOMETIMES FIERY SAUSAGE OF PORK AND PIMENTÓN, IS EATEN RIGHT ACROSS SPAIN, FROM SAN SEBASTIÁN TO SEVILLA, BARCELONA TO BADAJOZ.

165 g (5¾ oz/¾ cup) dried chickpeas
1 bay leaf
4 cloves
1 cinnamon stick
750 ml (26 fl oz/3 cups) chicken stock
2 tablespoons olive oil
1 brown onion, finely chopped
1 garlic clove, crushed
pinch of dried thyme
375 g (13 oz) chorizo, chopped (slightly larger than the chickpeas)
1 tablespoon chopped flat-leaf (Italian) parsley

SERVES 6

PUT chickpeas in a large bowl, cover with water and soak overnight. Drain well. Place in a large saucepan with the bay leaf, cloves, cinnamon stick and stock. Cover completely with water, bring to the boil, then reduce heat and simmer for 1 hour, or until the chickpeas are tender. If they need more time, add a little more water. There should be just a little liquid left in the saucepan. Drain and remove the bay leaf, cloves and cinnamon stick.

HEAT the oil in a large frying pan, add the onion and cook over medium heat for 3 minutes, or until translucent. Add the garlic and thyme and cook, stirring, 1 minute. Increase heat to medium–high, add the chorizo and cook for 3 minutes.

ADD the chickpeas to the frying pan, mix well, then stir over medium heat for about 4 minutes or until they are heated through. Remove from the heat and mix in the parsley. Taste before seasoning with salt and freshly ground black pepper. This dish is equally delicious served hot or at room temperature.

Chorizo is the best known of all Spanish sausages. Sometimes sold soft for cooking in wet dishes (such as soups or stews), it is more commonly found as a hard, cured sausage that can be eaten as is, but is often sliced and fried.

FROM ITALY

INSALATA CAPRESE

INSALATA CAPRESE IS TRADITIONALLY SERVED WITH NO OTHER DRESSING THAN A DRIZZLE OF EXTRA VIRGIN OLIVE OIL. HOWEVER, IF YOU'RE NOT ABSOLUTELY CONFIDENT THAT YOUR TOMATOES HAVE THE BEST FLAVOUR, A LITTLE BALSAMIC VINEGAR WILL HELP THEM ALONG.

6 ripe roma (plum) tomatoes
3–4 balls fresh baby mozzarella (bocconcini)
2 tablespoons extra virgin olive oil
15 young basil leaves
½ teaspoon balsamic vinegar (optional)

SERVES 4

SLICE the tomatoes, pouring off any excess juice, and cut the mozzarella into slices of a similar thickness.

ARRANGE alternating rows of tomato and mozzarella on a serving plate. Sprinkle with salt and pepper and drizzle the olive oil over the top. Tear the basil leaves into pieces and scatter over the oil. To serve, take to the table and sprinkle with the balsamic vinegar.

Caprese is also known as *insalata tricolore* – the mozzarella, ripe tomatoes and basil reflect the colours of the Italian flag.

INSALATA DI RINFORZO

250 g (9 oz) carrots
150 g (5½ oz) green beans
¼ red onion
625 ml (21½ fl oz/2½ cups) white wine vinegar
1 tablespoon sea salt
1 tablespoon sugar
1 bay leaf
300 g (10½ oz) cauliflower florets

DRESSING
80 ml (2½ fl oz/⅓ cup) extra virgin olive oil
2 tablespoons lemon juice
1 tablespoon finely chopped parsley
1 tablespoon chopped capers
1 garlic clove, halved

4 anchovy fillets, halved lengthways
85 g (3 oz) small black olives, such as Ligurian
1 tablespoon roughly chopped parsley
1–2 tablespoons extra virgin olive oil

SERVES 4

CUT the carrots into lengths the size of your little finger, slice the beans into similar lengths and slice the onion into rings.

COMBINE the vinegar, salt, sugar and bay leaf in a saucepan with 500 ml (17 fl oz/2 cups) water. Bring to the boil. Cook carrots for 3 minutes, or until just tender. Transfer to a bowl with a slotted spoon. Add the beans to the pan and cook for 2 minutes, or until just tender. Add to the carrots in the bowl. Add the onion and cauliflower to the pan and cook for 3 minutes, or until the cauliflower just starts to soften. Drain, add to the bowl and cool.

TO MAKE the dressing, combine the olive oil, lemon juice, parsley, capers and garlic and season well. Pour over cooled vegetables and toss gently. This salad can be stored in an airtight container for up to 2 weeks at this stage.

TO SERVE toss through the anchovy fillets, olives, parsley and oil.

INSALATA DI RINFORZO

INSALATA CAPRESE

FROM ITALY

PINZIMONIO

8 spring onions (scallions)
4 young Romanesco or Violetto Toscano artichokes
2 tablespoons lemon juice
2 baby fennel bulbs
8 celery stalks
8 red or white radishes
8 baby carrots
1 red capsicum (pepper)
185 ml (6 fl oz/¾ cup) extra virgin olive oil

SERVES 4

TRIM the spring onions at both ends. Cut off and discard the top third of each artichoke and the tough outer leaves, and snip off any spikes from the remaining leaves. Trim the stem and peel with a potato peeler.

SLICE EACH artichoke in half and scrape out the furry choke and discard. Place the artichokes in a bowl of lemon water to avoid discolouring. Trim the tops of the fennel. Cut the bulbs into quarters. Trim the celery and radishes. Peel carrots, leaving any greenery attached. Cut the red capsicum into strips. Arrange the vegetables on a platter.

DIVIDE the oil among four small dishes and season with salt and pepper. Give each person a dish of oil into which to dip the vegetables.

BAGNA CAÔDA

A FONDUE BOWL AND BURNER WORKS VERY WELL TO HEAT THE BAGNA CAÔDA (THE NAME MEANS LITERALLY 'HOT BATH'). THIS PIEMONTESE SPECIALITY IS A POPULAR GROUP MEAL ALL YEAR ROUND, BUT IS ESPECIALLY ASSOCIATED WITH THE VIBRANT ATMOSPHERE OF THE GRAPE HARVEST.

40 pieces assorted raw vegetables (carrot, celery, fennel or cauliflower florets)
185 ml (6 fl oz/¾ cup) olive oil
6 garlic cloves, crushed
120 g (4 oz) anchovy fillets, finely minced
90 g (3½ oz) butter
'country-style' bread, such as ciabatta

SERVES 4

TRIM, wash and dry the vegetables and cut them into strips for dipping.

PUT the oil, garlic and anchovies in a saucepan and place over moderately low heat. Cook gently, stirring once or twice, until the anchovies dissolve. Do not let the garlic brown. Add the butter and leave over low heat until it has melted. Season with pepper.

TRANSFER the sauce to a bowl and keep warm at the table by placing on a food warmer or over a burner or spirit stove. Serve the vegetables and bread arranged on a platter. Guests dip their choice of vegetable into the bagna caôda, using a piece of bread to catch any stray drips.

BAGNA CAÔDA

FROM FRANCE

PÂTÉ EN CROÛTE

THE WORD 'PÂTÉ' WAS TRADITIONALLY ONLY USED WHEN REFERRING TO THIS DISH. THESE DAYS THE NAME IS SYNONYMOUS WITH ALL KINDS OF PÂTÉS (MEANING MEATS SMOOTHED TO MAKE A PASTE) AND NOT JUST THOSE WITH A PASTRY CRUST.

- 600 g (1 lb 5 oz) veal fillet, finely diced
- 250 g (9 oz) lean pork, finely diced
- 200 g (7 oz) streaky bacon, finely diced
- large pinch of ground cloves
- large pinch of allspice
- finely grated zest of 1 lemon
- 2 tablespoons brandy
- 2 bay leaves
- 1 tablespoon butter
- 1 large garlic clove, crushed
- 1 onion, finely chopped
- 200 g (7 oz) wild or chestnut mushrooms, finely chopped
- 3 tablespoons finely chopped parsley
- 1 quantity puff pastry (see recipe on page 474)
- 1 egg, lightly beaten

SERVES 8

COMBINE the veal, pork, streaky bacon, cloves, allspice, lemon zest and brandy. Stir well, tuck the bay leaves into the mixture, then cover and leave to marinate in the fridge for at least 6 hours or preferably overnight.

MELT the butter in a frying pan and add the garlic and onion. Cook over a low heat for 10 minutes, add mushrooms and cook for about 10 minutes, or until softened and liquid from the mushrooms has evaporated. Stir in the parsley. Leave to cool.

REMOVE the bay leaves from the marinated meat. Add the cold mushroom mixture to the raw meat, season well and combine thoroughly.

PREHEAT the oven to 200°C (400°F/Gas 6). Roll out the pastry on a lightly floured surface into a 38 cm (15 inch) square, trim the edges and keep for decoration. Pile meat mixture onto the middle of the pastry, shaping it into a rectangle about 30 cm (12 inches) long. Brush the edges of the pastry with a little beaten egg. Fold pastry over the meat as if wrapping a parcel, then place on a baking tray, seam side down.

DECORATE parcel with shapes cut from pastry scraps and brush all over with beaten egg. Cook on the middle shelf of the oven for 15 minutes. Reduce the temperature to 180°C (350°F/Gas 4) and cook for 1–1¼ hours, or until the filling is cooked and the pastry is golden brown. Cool completely before serving in slices with pickles.

Pâté for sale at a Provence market.

Pound the garlic pulp and the parsley together to form a paste.

FROM SPAIN

CHICKEN IN GARLIC SAUCE

A FINE EXAMPLE OF A MODERN SPANISH RECIPE THAT TAKES TYPICAL AND TRADITIONAL INGREDIENTS – IN THIS PARTICULAR CASE, LOTS OF GARLIC AND SHERRY – AND COMBINES THEM IN A WAY THAT IS SO IMPRESSIVE THE DISH WILL SOON ENTER YOUR REPERTOIRE OF EVERYDAY MEALS.

1 kg (2 lb 4 oz) boneless, skinless chicken thighs
1 tablespoon sweet paprika (pimentón)
2 tablespoons olive oil
8 garlic cloves, unpeeled
60 ml (2 fl oz/¼ cup) fino sherry
125 ml (4 fl oz/½ cup) chicken stock
1 bay leaf
2 tablespoons chopped flat-leaf (Italian) parsley

SERVES 6

TRIM any excess fat from the chicken and cut the thighs into thirds. Combine the paprika with some salt and pepper in a bowl, add the chicken and toss to coat.

HEAT half the oil in a large frying pan over high heat and cook the garlic cloves for 1–2 minutes, or until brown. Remove from the pan. Cook the chicken in batches for 5 minutes, or until brown all over. Return all the chicken to the pan, add sherry, boil for 30 seconds, then add the stock and bay leaf. Reduce the heat and simmer, covered, over low heat for 10 minutes.

MEANWHILE, squeeze the garlic pulp from the skins and pound with the parsley into a paste using a mortar and pestle or a small bowl and the back of a spoon. Stir into the chicken, then cover and cook for 10 minutes, or until tender. Serve hot.

FROM ITALY

SEAFOOD ANTIPASTI

THE GOLDEN RULE FOR COOKING SEAFOOD IS THAT ALL YOUR INGREDIENTS MUST BE ABSOLUTELY STRAIGHT-FROM-THE-SEA FRESH. BUY LIVING SHELLFISH FROM THE FISHMONGER AND BE ADVISED AS TO WHAT IS IN SEASON, A REGIONAL SPECIALITY, OR A GOOD CATCH OF THE DAY.

500 g (1 lb 2 oz) mussels
500 g (1 lb 2 oz) clams (vongole)
250 g (9 oz) octopus
250 g (9 oz) small squid
250 g (9 oz) prawns (shrimp)
80 ml (2½ fl oz/⅓ cup) olive oil
juice of 2 lemons
2 tablespoons finely chopped parsley
lemon wedges, to serve

SERVES 6

CLEAN the mussels and clams by scrubbing them thoroughly and scraping off any barnacles. Pull off the beards from the mussels and rinse well under running water. Discard any mussels or clams that are broken or open and do not close when tapped on the work surface.

CLEAN the octopus by slitting the head and pulling out the innards. Cut out the eyes and hard beak and rinse. If the flesh is still springy and has not been tenderised, beat with a mallet until soft.

PREPARE the squid by pulling the heads and tentacles out of the bodies along with any innards. Cut the heads off below the eyes, just leaving the tentacles. Discard heads and set tentacles aside. Rinse the bodies, pulling out the clear quills, then cut the bodies into rings. Peel and devein the prawns, leaving the tails intact.

BRING a large pan of water to the boil and add the octopus. Reduce the heat and simmer for about 20 minutes or until tender. Add the squid and prawns. Cook for about 2 minutes, or until the prawns turn pink. Drain well.

PUT the mussels and clams in an even layer in a steamer. Steam over boiling water for 2 minutes or until the shells have just opened (discard any that stay closed). Pull the top shell off each mussel and clam. Arrange on a platter.

IF YOU have one octopus, cut it into pieces; if you have baby ones, leave whole. Arrange octopus, squid and prawns on the platter and sprinkle with sea salt and black pepper. Combine olive oil and lemon juice and drizzle over seafood. Cover with plastic wrap and marinate in the fridge for at least 2 hours. Sprinkle with the parsley and serve with lemon wedges and bread to mop up the juices.

FROM SPAIN

POTATOES IN SPICY TOMATO SAUCE

A DISH RARELY SEEN OUTSIDE THE TAPAS BAR, IT CAN, LIKE THE SIMPLE SPANISH TORTILLA, REVEAL THE QUALITY OF THE REST OF THE OFFERINGS AT A BAR. THE SIGNS OF A GOOD PATATAS BRAVAS ARE POTATOES THAT ARE FIRM TO THE MOUTH BUT NOT STARCHY, AND A SAUCE THAT IS DEEPLY SPICY.

1 kg (2 lb 4 oz) all-purpose potatoes, such as desiree
oil, for deep-frying
2 tablespoons olive oil
¼ red onion, finely chopped
2 garlic cloves, crushed
3 teaspoons sweet paprika (pimentón)
¼ teaspoon cayenne pepper
500 g (1 lb 2 oz) ripe roma (plum) tomatoes, peeled, seeded and chopped (see recipe on page 490)
1 bay leaf
1 teaspoon white sugar

SERVES 6

PEEL, then cut potatoes into 2 cm (¾ inch) cubes. Rinse, drain well and pat completely dry. Fill a deep-fryer or large heavy-based saucepan one-third full of oil and heat to 180°C (350°F), or until a cube of bread browns in it in 15 seconds. Cook potato in batches for 5 minutes, or until golden. Drain well on paper towel. Do not discard the oil.

HEAT olive oil in a saucepan over medium heat and cook onion for 5 minutes, or until softened. Add the garlic, paprika and cayenne pepper and cook for 1–2 minutes, or until fragrant.

ADD tomato, bay leaf, sugar and 80 ml (2½ fl oz/⅓ cup) water and cook, stirring occasionally, for 20 minutes, or until thick and pulpy. Cool slightly and remove bay leaf. Blend in a food processor until smooth, adding a little water if necessary. Before serving, return the sauce to the saucepan and simmer over low heat for 2 minutes, or until heated through. Season well.

REHEAT the oil to 180°C (350°F) and cook the potato again, in batches, for 2 minutes, or until very crisp and golden. Drain on paper towel. This second frying makes the potato extra crisp and stops the sauce soaking in immediately. Put on a platter and cover with sauce. Serve immediately.

A double-frying of the cubes of potato gives them an especially crunchy result.

To an outsider, it is remarkable the extent to which Spanish life and cuisine are lubricated by the fruit of the olive tree. Of the 262 varieties of olive grown in Spain, only about 24 are used in the production of olive oil.

FROM FRANCE

ARTICHOKES VINAIGRETTE

THIS IS THE CLASSIC WAY TO SERVE ARTICHOKES: YOU JUST NEED TO MAKE SURE YOU BUY THE BEST ONES AVAILABLE. SMALLER ARTICHOKES CAN ALSO BE PREPARED IN THIS FASHION, BUT CUT THEM INTO QUARTERS AND SERVE WITH THE DRESSING RATHER THAN REMOVING THE LEAVES ONE BY ONE.

juice of 1 lemon
4 globe artichokes

VINAIGRETTE
5 tablespoons olive oil
2 spring onions (scallions), finely chopped
2 tablespoons white wine
2 tablespoons white wine vinegar
¼ teaspoon dijon mustard
pinch of sugar
1 tablespoon finely chopped parsley

SERVES 4

TO PREPARE artichokes, bring a large saucepan of salted water to the boil and add the lemon juice. Break the stalks from the artichokes, pulling out any strings at the same time, and then trim the bases flat. Add the artichokes to the water and put a small plate on top of them to keep them submerged. Cook at a simmer for 25–30 minutes, or until a leaf from the base comes away easily. (The base will be tender when pierced with a skewer.) Cool quickly under cold running water, then drain upside down on a tray.

TO MAKE vinaigrette, heat 1 tablespoon of oil in a small saucepan, add the spring onion and cook over low heat for 2 minutes. Leave to cool a little, then add the white wine, vinegar, mustard and sugar and gradually whisk in the remaining oil. Season well and stir in half the parsley.

PLACE an artichoke on each plate and gently prise it open a little. Spoon the dressing over the top, allowing it to drizzle into the artichoke and around the plate. Pour the remaining dressing into a small bowl for people to dip the leaves. Sprinkle each artichoke with a little parsley.

EAT the leaves one by one, dipping them in the vinaigrette and scraping the flesh off the leaves between your teeth. When you reach the middle, pull off any really small leaves and then use a teaspoon to remove the furry choke. Once you've got rid of the choke, you can eat the tender base or 'heart' of the artichoke.

Whisking the remaining oil into the vinaigrette.

FROM MOROCCO

HOT CHICKPEAS

CHICKPEAS ARE A STAPLE IN ALL MOROCCAN KITCHENS, A MEANS OF EXTENDING THE PROTEIN CONTENT OF MEAT TAGINES AND SOUPS. AS STREET FOOD, THEY ARE SERVED IN PAPER CONES WITH A LIGHT SPRINKLING OF CUMIN AND EATEN WITH YOUR FINGERS, OR IN SMALL BOWLS WITH A SPOON.

- 220 g (7¾ oz/1 cup) dried chickpeas, or 2 x 420 g (15 oz) tins chickpeas
- 2 tablespoons olive oil
- 1 brown onion, finely chopped
- 1 small green capsicum (pepper), chopped
- 1 teaspoon ground cumin
- 2 tablespoons finely chopped coriander (cilantro) leaves

SERVES 4–6

TO COOK dried chickpeas, soak them overnight in three times their volume of cold water. Drain and place in a saucepan with fresh water to cover well. Simmer gently for 1 hour, or until tender, adding salt to taste towards the end of cooking. Drain, reserving 250 ml (9 fl oz/1 cup) of cooking liquid.

IF USING tinned chickpeas, drain them, reserving 250 ml (9 fl oz/1 cup) of the liquid.

WARM the olive oil in a saucepan over medium heat. Add the onion and cook until lightly golden, then add the capsicum, cumin and coriander and cook for a few seconds. Add the chickpeas and their liquid, and freshly ground black pepper, to taste. Bring to a simmer, cover and simmer until heated through.

ADJUST the seasoning and serve hot in small bowls with bread.

Tinned chickpeas may be used. If preferred, leave the skins on for all recipes as modern Moroccan cooks do.

HOT CHICKPEAS

FROM ITALY

OCTOPUS SALAD

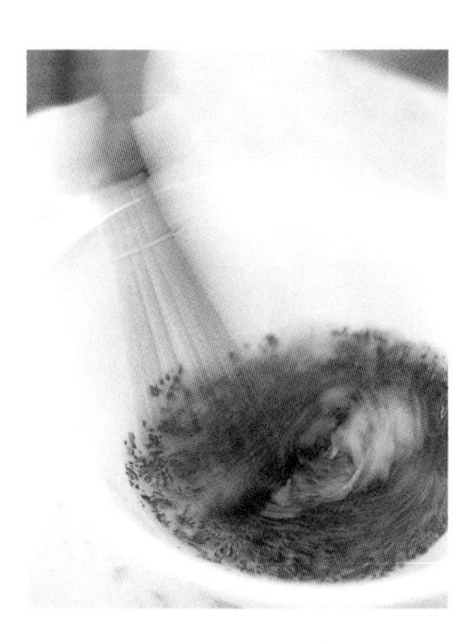

Whisking the dressing for the octopus salad.

650 g (1 lb 7 oz) baby octopus
2 tablespoons lemon juice
80 ml (2½ fl oz/⅓ cup) olive oil
1 garlic clove, thinly sliced
1 tablespoon chopped mint
1 tablespoon chopped parsley
1 teaspoon dijon mustard
pinch of cayenne pepper
115 g (4 oz) misticanza (mixed salad leaves)
lemon wedges, to serve

SERVES 4

CLEAN the octopus by slitting the head and pulling out the innards. Cut out the eyes and hard beak and rinse. If the octopus seem a bit big, cut them into halves or quarters.

BRING a large pan of water to the boil and add the octopus. Simmer for about 8–10 minutes, or until they are tender.

MEANWHILE, make a dressing by mixing together the lemon juice, olive oil, garlic, mint, parsley, mustard and cayenne with some salt and pepper.

DRAIN octopus well and put in a bowl. Pour the dressing over the top and cool for a few minutes before transferring to the fridge. Chill for at least 3 hours before serving on a bed of misticanza. Drizzle a little of the dressing over the top and serve with lemon wedges.

MARINATED FRESH ANCHOVIES

FRESH ANCHOVIES ARE FISHED ALL OVER THE MEDITERRANEAN, AS WELL AS THE ATLANTIC COASTS OF FRANCE AND SPAIN. YOU WILL NEED VERY FRESH FISH FOR THIS SIMPLE DISH, WITH PERHAPS JUST SOME BREAD TO MOP UP JUICES. THE DISH CAN BE KEPT REFRIGERATED FOR UP TO THREE DAYS.

400 g (14 oz) fresh anchovies
60 ml (2 fl oz/¼ cup) olive oil
1 tablespoon extra virgin olive oil
3 tablespoons lemon juice
2 garlic cloves, crushed
2 tablespoons finely chopped parsley
2 tablespoons finely chopped basil
1 small red chilli, seeded and chopped

SERVES 4

FILLET the anchovies by running your thumbnail or a sharp knife along the backbone, then pulling the head upwards. The head, bones and guts should all come away together, leaving you with the fillets. Carefully wash under cold water and pat dry with paper towels. Place fillets in a shallow serving dish.

COMBINE all the remaining ingredients together with some salt and pepper and pour over the anchovies. Cover with plastic wrap and marinate in the fridge for at least 3 hours before serving.

MARINATED FRESH ANCHOVIES

OCTOPUS SALAD

FROM FRANCE

PETITS FARCIS

THIS WONDERFUL DISH FROM PROVENCE MAKES GOOD USE OF THE REGION'S ABUNDANCE OF GARDEN PRODUCE AND THE STUFFING CAN INCLUDE ANY HERBS, MEAT OR CHEESES AT HAND. SERVE HOT OR COLD WITH BREAD FOR A SIMPLE SUMMER LUNCH.

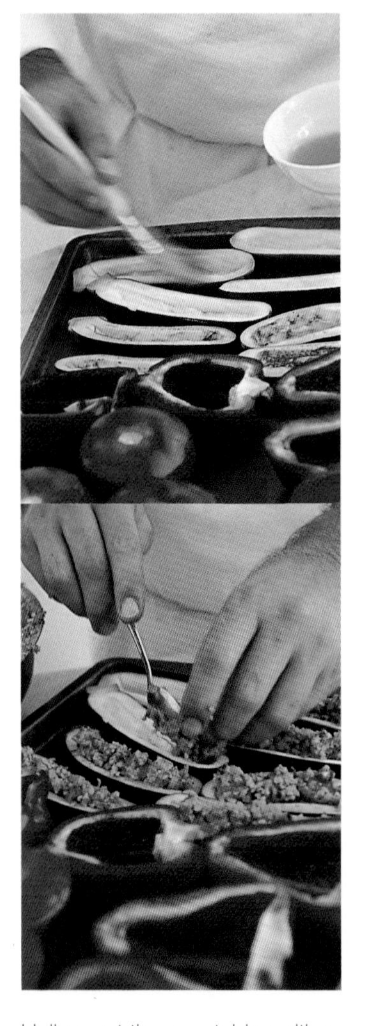

Hollow out the vegetables with a spoon and brush the edges with a little oil before filling with the mince stuffing.

2 small eggplant (aubergines), halved lengthways
2 small zucchini (courgettes), halved lengthways
4 tomatoes
2 small red capsicum (peppers), halved lengthways and seeded
4 tablespoons olive oil
2 red onions, chopped
2 garlic cloves, crushed
250 g (9 oz) minced (ground) pork
250 g (9 oz) minced (ground) veal
50 g (1¾ oz) tomato purée
80 ml (2½ fl oz/⅓ cup) white wine
2 tablespoons chopped parsley
50 g parmesan cheese, grated
80 g (2¾ oz/1 cup) fresh breadcrumbs

SERVES 4

PREHEAT oven to 180°C (350°F/Gas 4). Grease a large roasting tin with oil. Hollow out the centres of the eggplant and zucchini, using a teaspoon, leaving a border around the edge. Chop flesh finely.

CUT the tops from the tomatoes (don't throw away the tops). Use a teaspoon to hollow out the centres, catching the juice in a bowl, and chop the flesh roughly. Arrange the vegetables, including the red capsicum, in the roasting tin. Brush edges of eggplant and zucchini with a little of the oil. Pour 125 ml (4 fl oz/½ cup) water into the roasting tin.

HEAT half the oil in a large frying pan. Cook the onion and garlic for 3 minutes, or until they have softened. Add the minced pork and veal and stir for 5 minutes until the meat browns, breaking up any lumps with the back of a fork. Add the chopped eggplant and zucchini and cook for a further 3 minutes. Add the tomato pulp and juice, tomato purée and wine. Cook for 10 minutes, stirring occasionally.

REMOVE the frying pan from the heat and stir in parsley, parmesan and breadcrumbs. Season well with salt and pepper. Spoon the mixture into the vegetables. Place the tops back on the tomatoes. Sprinkle vegetables with remaining oil and bake for 45 minutes, or until they are tender.

FROM SPAIN

STUFFED MUSSELS

MUSSELS ARE CHEAPER AND MORE VERSATILE THAN THEIR MOLLUSC RELATION, THE OYSTER, AND AS SUCH, ARE MORE COMMON. THEY LEND THEMSELVES TO A GREAT NUMBER OF PREPARATIONS, INCLUDING THIS TEXTURALLY APPEALING DISH, INFUSED WITH THE DELICIOUS FLAVOUR OF GARLIC.

18 black mussels
2 teaspoons olive oil
2 spring onions (scallions), finely chopped
1 garlic clove, crushed
1 tablespoon tomato paste (concentrated purée)
2 teaspoons lemon juice
1 large handful flat-leaf (Italian) parsley, chopped
75 g (2¾ oz/¾ cup) dry breadcrumbs
2 eggs, beaten
olive oil, for deep-frying

WHITE SAUCE
20 g (¾ oz) butter
1½ tablespoons plain (all-purpose) flour
2 tablespoons milk

MAKES 18

SCRUB the mussels and remove the hairy beards. Discard any open mussels or those that don't close when tapped on the bench. Bring 250 ml (9 fl oz/1 cup) water to the boil in a saucepan, add the mussels, then cover and cook for 3–4 minutes, shaking the pan occasionally, until the mussels have just opened. Remove them as soon as they open or they will be tough. Strain the cooking liquid into a pitcher until you have 80 ml (2½ fl oz/⅓ cup). Discard any unopened mussels. Remove the other mussels from their shells and discard one half shell from each. Finely chop the mussel meat.

HEAT the oil in a frying pan, add the spring onion and cook for 1 minute. Add the garlic and cook for 1 minute. Stir in the mussel meat, tomato paste, lemon juice, 2 tablespoons of the parsley and season with salt and pepper. Set aside to cool.

TO MAKE the white sauce, melt the butter in a saucepan over low heat. Stir in the flour and cook for 1 minute, or until pale and foaming. Remove from the heat and gradually whisk in the reserved mussel liquid, the milk and some pepper. Return to the heat and cook, stirring, for 1 minute, or until sauce boils and thickens. Reduce the heat and simmer for 2 minutes until quite thick. Cool.

SPOON the mussel mixture into the shells. Top each generously with the thick white sauce and smooth the surface, to form a mound.

COMBINE breadcrumbs and remaining parsley. Dip mussels in the egg, then press in crumbs to cover the top. Fill a deep, heavy-based saucepan one-third full of oil and heat to 180°C (350°F), or until a cube of bread browns in 15 seconds. Cook mussels in batches for 10–15 seconds, or until lightly browned. Remove with a slotted spoon and drain well. Serve hot.

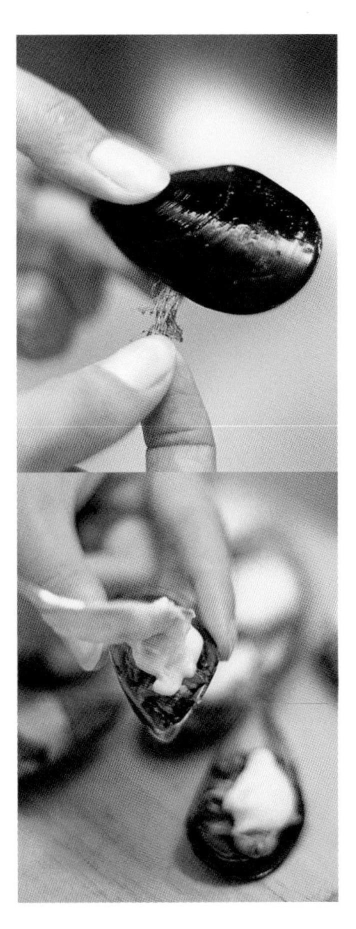

Discard the hairy beards. Spoon mussel mixture into the shells and top with white sauce.

FROM SPAIN

TUNA SKEWERS

TAPAS ON SKEWERS – BANDERILLAS IN THE SOUTH, PINCHOS IN THE NORTH – ARE YOUR CHANCE TO ASSEMBLE, ON THE LITTLE STICK, A CLEVER COLLECTION OF COMPLEMENTARY FLAVOURS, AS EXEMPLIFIED HERE WITH TUNA, CAPER BERRIES AND GREEN OLIVES.

250 g (9 oz) raw tuna
1 lemon
1 tablespoon lemon juice
1 tablespoon extra virgin olive oil
16 caperberries
8 green olives, stuffed with anchovies

MAKES 8

SOAK eight wooden skewers in cold water for 1 hour to prevent them burning during cooking. Cut the raw tuna into 24 even-sized cubes. Remove the zest from the lemon, avoiding the bitter white pith, and cut the zest into thin strips.

COMBINE the tuna, lemon zest, lemon juice and olive oil in a bowl.

THREAD three pieces of tuna, two caperberries and one green olive onto each skewer, alternating each ingredient. Put in a non-metallic dish and pour the marinade over them. Cook under a hot grill (broiler), turning to cook each side, for 4 minutes, or until done to your liking.

FRIED CALAMARI

FRIED CALAMARI

NO OTHER TAPA, WITH THE EXCEPTIONS OF THE TORTILLA AND RUSSIAN SALAD, CAN BE SEEN IN TAPAS BARS FROM JEREZ DE LA FRONTERA TO SANTIAGO DE COMPOSTELA. FRIED CALAMARI ON THE MENU IS ANOTHER PERFECT BAROMETER OF A GOOD TASCA, SPANISH BAR OR GATHERING PLACE.

500 g (1 lb 2 oz) cleaned squid tubes
185 g (6½ oz/1½ cups) plain (all-purpose) flour
2 teaspoons sweet paprika (pimentón)
olive oil, for deep-frying
lemon wedges, to serve
allioli (see recipe on page 490), to serve (optional)

SERVES 4–6

WASH the calamari and cut into rings about 1 cm (½ inch) wide. Combine flour and paprika. Season calamari rings well with salt and pepper and toss in the flour to lightly coat.

FILL a deep, heavy-based saucepan one-third full of oil and heat to 180°C (350°F), or until a cube of bread dropped into the oil browns in 15 seconds. Add calamari in batches and cook for 2 minutes, or until golden. Drain and serve hot with the lemon wedges and allioli if desired.

TUNA SKEWERS

FROM FRANCE

PIPERADE

THIS TRADITIONAL BASQUE DISH IS A DELICIOUS MELDING OF RATATOUILLE AND EGGS. THE NAME IS DERIVED FROM *'PIPER'*, MEANING RED CAPSICUM IN THE LOCAL DIALECT. THE EGGS CAN EITHER BE COOKED MORE LIKE AN OMELETTE OR SCRAMBLED AS DONE HERE.

2 tablespoons olive oil
1 large onion, thinly sliced
2 red capsicum (peppers), seeded and cut into batons
2 garlic cloves, crushed
750 g (1 lb 10 oz) tomatoes
pinch of cayenne pepper
8 eggs, lightly beaten
1 tablespoon butter
4 thin slices of ham, such as Bayonne

SERVES 4

HEAT oil in a large heavy-based frying pan and cook onion for 3 minutes, or until it has softened. Add the capsicum and garlic, cover and cook for 8 minutes to soften. Stir frequently and don't allow mixture to brown.

SCORE a cross in the top of each tomato. Plunge into boiling water for 20 seconds, then drain and peel skin away from the cross. Chop tomatoes, discarding the cores. Spoon the chopped tomato and cayenne over the capsicum, cover the pan and cook for a further 5 minutes.

UNCOVER the pan and increase the heat. Cook for 3 minutes or until the juices have evaporated, shaking the pan often. Season well with salt and pepper. Add the eggs and scramble into the mixture until they are cooked.

HEAT the butter in a small frying pan and fry the ham. Arrange on the piperade and serve at once.

Add the egg and scramble lightly into the piperade, remembering that it will continue to cook after it is removed from the heat.

OEUFS EN COCOTTE

15 g (½ oz) butter, melted
125 ml (4 fl oz/½ cup) thick (double/heavy) cream
4 button mushrooms, finely chopped
40 g (1½ oz) ham, finely chopped
40 g gruyère cheese, finely chopped
4 eggs
1 tablespoon finely chopped herbs such as chervil, parsley, chives

SERVES 4

PREHEAT the oven to 200°C (400°F/Gas 6) and put a baking tray on the top shelf. Grease four ramekins with melted butter. Pour half the cream into the ramekins and then put a quarter of the mushrooms, ham and cheese into each. Break an egg into each ramekin. Mix the remaining cream with the herbs and pour over the top.

BAKE for 15–20 minutes on the hot baking tray, depending on how runny you like your eggs. Remove from the oven while still a little runny as the eggs will continue to cook. Season well and serve immediately with crusty toasted bread.

OEUFS EN COCOTTE

PIPERADE

FROM SPAIN

POTATO OMELETTE

SUCH A SIMPLE DISH, SO DIFFICULT TO PERFECT. A TORTILLA MUST BE LIGHT, THE POTATO FIRM, THE ONIONS EVER SO SLIGHTLY CARAMELISED, AND THE EGGS COOKED ENOUGH TO HOLD THE WHOLE DISH TOGETHER BUT NO MORE. THE TORTILLA IS THE DISH BY WHICH TO JUDGE A TAPAS BAR.

500 g (1 lb 2 oz) all-purpose potatoes, peeled and cut into 1 cm (½ inch) slices
60 ml (2 fl oz/¼ cup) olive oil
1 brown onion, thinly sliced
4 garlic cloves, thinly sliced
2 tablespoons finely chopped flat-leaf (Italian) parsley
6 eggs

SERVES 6–8

PUT the potato slices in a large saucepan, cover with cold water and bring to the boil over high heat. Boil for 5 minutes, then drain and set aside.

HEAT the oil in a deep-sided non-stick frying pan over medium heat. Add the onion and garlic and cook for 5 minutes, or until the onion softens.

ADD the potato and parsley to the pan and stir to combine. Cook over medium heat for 5 minutes, gently pressing down into the pan.

WHISK the eggs with 1 teaspoon each of salt and freshly ground black pepper and pour evenly over the potato. Cover and cook over low–medium heat for 20 minutes, or until the eggs are just set. Slide onto a serving plate or serve directly from the pan.

Gently press down on the potato, onion, garlic and parsley combination as it cooks to help compact it.

FROM FRANCE

SMOKED TROUT GOUGÈRE

FOR A GOUGÈRE, CHOUX PASTRY IS TRADITIONALLY PIPED INTO A CIRCULAR OR OVAL SHAPE AND FILLED WITH A SAVOURY MIXTURE. IF YOU PREFER, THE PASTRY CAN ALSO BE MADE INTO SMALL CHOUX BUNS, SPLIT OPEN AND THE FILLING SPOONED INTO THE CENTRES.

75 g (2½ oz) butter
125 g (4 oz) plain (all-purpose) flour, sifted twice
¼ teaspoon paprika
3 large eggs, beaten
90 g (3 oz) gruyère cheese, grated

FILLING
400 g (14 oz) smoked trout
100 g (3 oz) watercress, trimmed
30 g (1 oz) butter
20 g (¾ oz) plain flour
300 (10 fl oz) ml milk

SERVES 4

PREHEAT the oven to 200°C (400°F/Gas 6) and put a baking tray on the top shelf to heat up.

MELT the butter with 185 ml (6 fl oz/¾ cup)water in a saucepan. Bring it to a rolling boil. Remove from heat and sift in all the flour and the paprika. Return to the heat and beat continuously with a wooden spoon to make a smooth shiny paste that comes away from the side of the pan. Cool for a few minutes. Beat in the eggs one at a time, until shiny and smooth. The mixture should drop off the spoon but not be too runny. Stir in two-thirds of the cheese.

SPOON the dough round the edge of a shallow, lightly greased baking dish. Put this in the oven on the hot tray and cook for about 45 minutes, or until the choux is well risen and browned.

MEANWHILE, to make the filling, peel the skin off the trout and lift off the top fillet. Pull out the bone. Break the trout into large flakes. Wash watercress and put in a large saucepan with just the water clinging to the leaves. Cover the pan and steam the watercress for 2 minutes, or until just wilted. Drain, cool and squeeze with your hands to get rid of the excess liquid. Roughly chop the watercress.

MELT the butter in a saucepan, stir in the flour to make a roux and cook, stirring, for 3 minutes over very low heat without allowing the roux to brown. Remove from the heat and add the milk gradually, stirring after each addition until smooth. Return to the heat and simmer for 3 minutes. Stir in the smoked trout and watercress and season well.

SPOON the trout filling into the centre of the cooked choux pastry and return to the oven for 10 minutes, then serve immediately.

Spoon the choux pastry around the edge of the baking dish and bake until well risen. To remove the bone from the trout, simply lift off the top fillet and then lift the bone away cleanly.

FROM SPAIN

RUSSIAN SALAD

THE MYSTERY OF THE RUSSIAN SALAD IS ONE PEOPLE LIKE TO SPECULATE ABOUT, AS THEY ENJOY IT WITH A COLD BEER. WHY IS A POTATO AND ARTICHOKE SALAD HAILING FROM RUSSIA TO BE FOUND IN EVERY TAPAS BAR IN SPAIN? NO MATTER — ONE BITE AND YOU WON'T CARE WHERE IT CAME FROM!

MAYONNAISE
2 egg yolks
1 teaspoon dijon mustard
125 ml (4 fl oz/½ cup) extra virgin olive oil (see Note)
2 tablespoons lemon juice
2 small garlic cloves, crushed

3 bottled artichoke hearts
3 all-purpose potatoes, such as desiree, unpeeled
100 g (3½ oz) baby green beans, trimmed and cut into 1 cm (½ inch) lengths
1 large carrot, cut into 1 cm (½ inch) dice
125 g (4 oz) fresh peas
30 g (1 oz) cornichons, chopped
2 tablespoons baby capers, rinsed and drained
4 anchovy fillets, finely chopped
10 black olives, each cut into 3 slices
whole black olives, extra, to garnish

SERVES 4–6

TO MAKE the mayonnaise, use electric beaters to beat the egg yolks with the mustard and ¼ teaspoon salt until creamy. Gradually add oil in a fine stream, beating constantly until all the oil has been added. Add the lemon juice, garlic and 1 teaspoon boiling water and beat for 1 minute, or until well combined. Season to taste.

CUT each artichoke into quarters. Rinse potatoes, cover with salted cold water and bring to a gentle simmer. Cook for about 15 minutes, or until tender when pierced with a knife. Drain and allow to cool slightly. Peel and set aside. When the potatoes are completely cool, cut into 1 cm (½ inch) dice.

BLANCH beans in salted boiling water until tender but still firm to the bite. Refresh in cold water, then drain thoroughly. Repeat with the carrot and peas.

SET aside a small quantity of each vegetable, including the cornichons, for the garnish and season to taste. Put the remainder in a bowl with the capers, anchovies and sliced olives. Add the mayonnaise, toss to combine and season to taste. Arrange on a serving dish and garnish with the reserved vegetables and the whole olives.

Note: Use a low-acid or mild flavoured olive oil to prevent any bitterness.

Beating constantly as the oil is slowly added ensures a smooth and creamy mayonnaise.

SOUPS

FROM MOROCCO

SPICED LENTILS

MOST BROAD-BEAN SOUP SELLERS ALSO OFFER THESE SPICY LENTILS, LADLED INTO BOWLS. WHEN COOKING GREEN (ALSO CALLED BROWN) LENTILS, IT IS TEMPTING TO DRAIN THEM AFTER THE FIRST STAGE OF COOKING AS THE LIQUID IS MUDDY, BUT IN DOING SO, PRECIOUS B VITAMINS ARE LOST.

375 g (13 oz/2 cups) green lentils
2 large ripe tomatoes
3 tablespoons olive oil
1 brown onion, finely chopped
2 garlic cloves, finely chopped
1 teaspoon ground cumin
½ teaspoon ground coriander seeds
½ teaspoon turmeric
½ teaspoon paprika
⅛ teaspoon cayenne pepper
1 red capsicum (pepper), cleaned and chopped
2 teaspoons tomato paste (concentrated purée)
3 tablespoons chopped flat-leaf (Italian) parsley
3 tablespoons chopped fresh coriander (cilantro) leaves

SERVES 4–6

PICK over the lentils and place in a bowl. Wash with 2–3 changes of cold water, then drain in a strainer. Tip into a large saucepan and add 1 litre (35 fl oz/4 cups) water. Bring to the boil, reduce to a simmer and cook for 30 minutes, skimming the surface as required.

WHILE lentils are cooking, halve the tomatoes crossways and squeeze out seeds. Using the shredder side of a grater, grate tomato halves down to the skin, discarding the skin. Set aside.

WARM oil in a frying pan over medium heat, add onion and cook for 5 minutes, or until soft. Stir in garlic and spices and cook, stirring occasionally for 2 minutes or until fragrant. Add capsicum, grated tomatoes, tomato paste, parsley and coriander and 250 ml (9 fl oz/1 cup) water. Combine well, then add to the well-skimmed lentils. Season, partly cover with lid and cook on low–medium heat for a further 30 minutes, or until lentils are tender. Serve hot in bowls.

Traditional lentils come in all hues, from green to beige to brown. Skim the surface early in the cooking.

FROM SPAIN

GALICIAN-STYLE SOUP

SIMPLY MEANING GALICIAN BROTH, THIS DISH IS SERVED AND COOKED IN ALL GALICIAN RESTAURANTS, AND IN MOST GALICIAN HOMES IN THE WINTER MONTHS. IT CAN ACCOMMODATE AS MANY DIFFERENT INGREDIENTS AS THERE ARE COOKS MAKING IT.

- 250 g (9 oz/1¼ cups) dried white haricot beans (such as navy beans)
- 500 g (1 lb 2 oz) smoked ham hock
- 2 tablespoons olive oil
- 1 leek, chopped
- 1 garlic clove, chopped
- 500 g (1 lb 2 oz) pork baby back or American-style ribs, separated into 5 cm (2 inch) widths
- 2 all-purpose potatoes, peeled and cubed
- 1 bay leaf
- 1 kg (2 lb 4 oz/1 bunch) silverbeet (Swiss chard), washed well and chopped

SERVES 4

RINSE beans, then soak them in cold water for at least 5 hours. Put the ham hock in a large heavy-based saucepan and cover with cold water. Bring to the boil, then reduce the heat and simmer for about 1 hour, or until meat starts to come away from the bone and is tender. Remove from heat. When hock is cool enough to handle, remove the meat from the bone. Cut into 2 cm (¾ inch) cubes. Reserve 625 ml (21½ fl oz/2½ cups) of the cooking liquid.

MEANWHILE, put the beans in a large saucepan and cover with cold water. Bring to the boil, then reduce heat and simmer for 30 minutes, or until tender. Drain, reserving 250 ml (9 fl oz/1 cup) of the cooking liquid.

HEAT olive oil in a large heavy-based saucepan over medium heat and cook the leek and garlic for about 5 minutes, or until translucent. Add the ham, beans, pork or ribs, potato, bay leaf and reserved cooking liquid (make sure the food is covered with liquid).

BRING to the boil, then reduce the heat, cover and simmer for 45 minutes. Stir in the silverbeet and cook for 5 minutes. Season before serving.

If short on time, pre-cooked white beans can be used. Simply skip the first step in the method.

The pig still roams free in the dehesa, the pastureland, of south-western Spain. Its meat is salted, cured and aged for up to 3 years. The result is called Jamón and it is a delicacy in Spain.

While picada is made in a food processor for convenience these days, it was originally prepared using a mortar and pestle.

FROM SPAIN

SPICY SEAFOOD SOUP

THIS CATALAN FISH SOUP IS NAMED AFTER A STYLE OF LIGHT OPERA. IT INCORPORATES A VARIETY OF SEAFOOD, AND IS BUILT AROUND A PICADA, DESCRIBED AS THE 'CATALAN ROUX'. A BLEND OF GARLIC, NUTS AND BREAD, A PICADA IS USED TO GIVE FORM TO, OR HOLD TOGETHER, DISHES.

300 g (10 oz) red mullet fillets
400 g (14 oz) firm white fish fillets
300 g (10 oz) cleaned squid tubes
1½ litres (52 fl oz/6 cups) fish stock
80 ml (2½ fl oz/⅓ cup) olive oil
1 white onion, chopped
6 garlic cloves, chopped
1 small red chilli, chopped
1 teaspoon sweet paprika (pimentón)
pinch of saffron threads
150 ml (5 fl oz) white wine
400 g (14 oz) tinned chopped tomatoes
16 raw prawns (shrimp), peeled and deveined, tails intact
2 tablespoons brandy
24 black mussels, cleaned
1 tablespoon chopped flat-leaf (Italian) parsley, to garnish

PICADA
2 tablespoons olive oil
2 slices day-old bread, cubed
2 garlic cloves
5 whole blanched almonds, toasted
2 tablespoons flat-leaf (Italian) parsley

SERVES 6–8

CUT the fish and squid into 4 cm (1½ inch) pieces and refrigerate (until ready to use). Pour the stock into a large saucepan, bring to the boil and boil for 15–20 minutes, or until reduced by half.

TO MAKE the picada, heat the olive oil in a frying pan, add the bread and stir for 2–3 minutes, or until golden, adding the garlic for the last minute. Process the bread, garlic, almonds and parsley in a food processor and add enough of the stock to make a smooth paste.

HEAT 2 tablespoons of the oil in a large saucepan, add the onion, garlic, chilli and paprika, and cook, stirring, for 1 minute. Add the saffron, white wine, tomato and remaining stock. Bring to the boil, then reduce the heat and leave to simmer.

HEAT the remaining oil in another frying pan over medium heat and cook the fish and squid for 3–5 minutes or until just opaque. Remove and set aside. Add the prawns, cook for 1 minute, then pour in the brandy. Add the prawn mixture to the fish.

ADD the mussels to the hot stock and simmer, covered, for 3–5 minutes, or until opened. Discard any that do not open. Return all the seafood to the pan, add the picada, and stir until the sauce has thickened slightly and seafood is cooked through. Season to taste. Serve garnished with parsley.

The soup base is called a *soffritto*, meaning 'underfried'. The slow-cooked mixture of onion, garlic, pancetta and herbs gives the soup its base flavour. Other types of minestrone simmer the vegetables in stock without frying them first, then add olive oil towards the end for flavour.

FROM ITALY

MINESTRONE ALLA GENOVESE

JUST ABOUT EVERY REGION OF ITALY HAS ITS OWN MINESTRONE. THIS VERSION HAS A SPOONFUL OF PESTO STIRRED THROUGH AT THE END; OTHERS HAVE RICE INSTEAD OF PASTA. FOR *MINESTRONE ALLA MILANESE*, ADD 200 GRAMS (7 OUNCES) ARBORIO RICE INSTEAD OF THE PASTA.

225 g (8 oz) dried borlotti beans
50 g (1¾ oz) lard or butter
1 large onion, finely chopped
1 garlic clove, finely chopped
15 g (½ oz) parsley, finely chopped
2 sage leaves
100 g (3½ oz) pancetta, cubed
2 celery stalks, halved then sliced
2 carrots, sliced
3 potatoes, peeled but left whole
1 teaspoon tomato paste (purée)
400 g (14 oz) tin chopped tomatoes
8 basil leaves
3 litres (105 fl oz/12 cups) chicken or vegetable stock
2 zucchini (courgettes), sliced
220 g (8 oz) shelled peas
120 g (4 oz) green beans, cut into 4 cm (1½ inch) lengths
¼ cabbage, shredded
150 g (5 oz) ditalini, avemarie or other small pasta
pesto, to serve
grated parmesan cheese

SERVES 6

PUT dried beans in a large bowl, cover with cold water and leave to soak overnight. Drain and rinse under cold water.

TO MAKE the soffritto, melt the lard in a large saucepan and add the onion, garlic, parsley, sage and pancetta. Cook over low heat, stirring once or twice, for about 10 minutes, or until the onion is soft and golden.

ADD the celery, carrot and potatoes and cook for 5 minutes. Stir in the tomato paste, tomatoes, basil and borlotti beans. Season with plenty of pepper. Add the stock and bring slowly to the boil. Cover and leave to simmer for 2 hours, stirring once or twice.

IF the potatoes haven't already broken up, roughly break them up with a fork against the side of the pan. Taste for seasoning and add the zucchini, peas, runner beans, cabbage and pasta. Simmer until the pasta is al dente. Serve with a dollop of pesto and the parmesan.

Lyon is certainly the area of France most associated with the onion: 'à la lyonnaise' means a dish containing onions.

FROM FRANCE

FRENCH ONION SOUP

THE ORIGINS OF THIS ONION SOUP ARE UNCLEAR, SOME CLAIMING IT TO BE A LYONNAISE INVENTION AND OTHERS CREDITING IT TO PARIS. THERE IS ALSO MUCH DISPUTE OVER HOW THE DISH SHOULD BE MADE: WHEN TO ADD THE BREAD AND WHETHER THE ONIONS ARE COARSELY SLICED OR PURÉED.

60 g (2 oz) butter
750 g (1 lb 10 oz) onions, finely sliced
2 garlic cloves, finely chopped
45 g (1½ oz) plain (all-purpose) flour
2 litres (70 fl oz/8 cups) beef or chicken stock
250 ml (9 fl oz/1 cup) white wine
1 bay leaf
2 thyme sprigs
12 slices stale baguette
100 g (3½ oz) gruyère cheese, finely grated

SERVES 6

MELT the butter in a heavy-based saucepan and add the onion. Cook over low heat, stirring occasionally, for 25 minutes, or until the onion is deep golden brown and beginning to caramelise.

ADD the garlic and flour and stir continuously for 2 minutes. Gradually blend in the stock and wine, stirring all the time, and bring to the boil. Add the bay leaf and thyme and season. Cover pan and simmer for 25 minutes. Remove the bay leaf and thyme and check the seasoning. Preheat the grill.

TOAST the baguette slices, then divide among six warmed soup bowls and ladle the soup over the top. Sprinkle with the grated cheese and grill until the cheese melts and turns light golden brown. Serve immediately.

CAULIFLOWER SOUP

30 g (1 oz) butter
1 onion, finely chopped
1 small celery stalk, finely chopped
600 g (1 lb 5 oz) cauliflower, broken into florets
440 ml (15¼ fl oz/1¾ cups) chicken stock
315 ml (10¾ fl oz/1¼ cups) milk
1 bay leaf
1 thyme sprig
125 ml (4 fl oz/½ cup) cream
freshly grated nutmeg
2 tablespoons chopped chives

SERVES 4

MELT the butter in a large saucepan. Add the onion and celery. Cook over a low heat until the vegetables are softened but not browned. Add the cauliflower, stock, milk, bay leaf and thyme and bring to the boil. Cover the pan, reduce heat and simmer for 20 minutes, or until cauliflower is tender.

LEAVE soup to cool. Remove the bay leaf and thyme. Purée soup until smooth in a blender or food processor and return to the clean saucepan. Bring to the boil, stirring constantly, add cream and reheat without boiling. Season with salt, white pepper and nutmeg. Serve garnished with chives.

CAULIFLOWER SOUP

FRENCH ONION SOUP

FROM MOROCCO

BROAD BEAN SOUP

THE SERVING OF STREET FOOD BEGINS EARLY IN THE MORNING AND THIS DRIED BROAD (FAVA) BEAN SOUP IS A BREAKFAST STAPLE – WARMING, FILLING AND DELICIOUS. IT IS LADLED INTO BOWLS FROM A LARGE, BULBOUS EARTHENWARE JAR SET AT AN ANGLE OVER A CHARCOAL FIRE.

- 350g (12 oz/2 cups) dried, skinned and split broad (fava) beans or whole dried broad (fava) beans
- 2 garlic cloves, peeled
- 1 teaspoon cumin
- 1 teaspoon paprika
- extra virgin olive oil, cumin and paprika to serve

SERVES 6

PUT the broad beans in a large bowl, cover with 3 times their volume of cold water and leave to soak in a cool place for 12 hours. Drain and rinse before cooking. (If you are using whole beans, soak for 48 hours in a cool place. Change the water 3–4 times, then drain and remove skins.)

PLACE beans in a large soup pot, preferably of stainless steel. Add 1.25 litres (44 fl oz/ 5 cups) cold water, garlic and spices. Bring to the boil and simmer on low heat, covered, for 45–60 minutes, until beans are mushy; check and add a little more water if beans look dry. Do not add salt or stir the beans during cooking.

COOL slightly and then purée soup in batches in a blender, or use a stick blender and purée in the pot. Reheat soup and season to taste. Ladle into bowls and drizzle a little olive oil on each serve. Finish with a light dusting of paprika. Have extra olive oil on the table, and cumin and paprika in little bowls, to be added to suit individual tastes. Serve with bread.

Soak dried broad beans and then skin before cooking. Ready-skinned beans are more convenient.

FROM ITALY

LA RIBOLLITA

RIBOLLITA MEANS 'REBOILED' BECAUSE THIS TUSCAN BEAN SOUP IS BEST MADE A DAY IN ADVANCE TO LET THE FLAVOURS DEVELOP, THEN REHEATED. IT SHOULD THEN BE THICK ENOUGH TO EAT WITH A FORK RATHER THAN A SPOON.

4 tablespoons olive oil
1 onion, finely chopped
1 large carrot, finely chopped
3 celery stalks, finely chopped
2 large garlic cloves, crushed
250 g (9 oz) cavolo nero or savoy cabbage
1 zucchini (courgette), finely chopped
400 g (14 oz) cooked cannellini or borlotti beans
400 g (14 oz) tin tomatoes
185 ml (¾ cup) red wine
1 litre (35 fl oz/4 cups) chicken stock or water
75 g (2½ oz) stale 'country-style' bread, such as ciabatta or pugliese, crusts removed and broken into 2.5 cm (1 inch) cubes
drizzle of extra virgin olive oil

SERVES 4

TO MAKE the soffritto, pour the olive oil into a large saucepan and add the onion. Cook the onion gently – use this time to chop the carrot and celery and add them to the pan as you go along. Once you have added the garlic, leave to cook for a few minutes.

STRIP the leaves of the cavolo from the stems or cut away the thick stem of the savoy. Wash and finely chop the stems and roughly chop the leaves. Add the cabbage stems and zucchini to the soffritto and cook, stirring occasionally, for about 5 minutes, or until the vegetables have changed to an opaque colour and have soaked up some of the olive oil.

STIR in the beans and cook for 5 minutes more, then add the tomatoes and cook for a further 5 minutes to reduce the liquid.

ADD the cabbage leaves and mix into the soup, stirring until just wilted. Add the wine and stock or water and gently simmer for about 40 minutes.

ADD the bread to the pan (if the bread is very fresh, dry it out a little in the oven first to prevent it disintegrating into the soup). Mix briefly and remove the pan from the heat. Leave for about 30 minutes. This rests the soup and allows the flavours to merge. Serve hot but not boiling with a generous drizzle of extra virgin olive oil.

IF REHEATING the soup, make sure it comes to the boil, but then remove it from the heat and leave to cool for 5 minutes. Serve in cold bowls. The soup should be served warm, rather than piping hot.

Make sure the cabbage stems are thoroughly softened before adding the other vegetables – this gives the cabbage a chance to really soak up the flavour of the soffritto.

FROM FRANCE

CRAB BISQUE

ORIGINALLY BISQUES WERE MADE WITH POULTRY AND GAME BIRDS (IN PARTICULAR PIGEONS) AND WERE MORE OF A STEW. TODAY, THEY HAVE EVOLVED INTO RICH VELVETY SOUPS AND TEND TO USE CRUSTACEANS. YOU CAN RESERVE SOME OF THE CRABMEAT OR CLAWS FOR A GARNISH.

1 kg (2 lb 4 oz) live crabs
50 g (1¾ oz) butter
½ carrot, finely chopped
½ onion, finely chopped
1 celery stalk, finely chopped
1 bay leaf
2 thyme sprigs
2 tablespoons tomato purée
2 tablespoons brandy
150 ml (5 fl oz) dry white wine
1 litre (35 fl oz/4 cups) fish stock
60 g (2¼ oz) rice
60 ml (2 fl oz/¼ cup) thick (double/heavy) cream
¼ teaspoon cayenne pepper

SERVES 4

PUT the crabs in the freezer for 1 hour. Remove the top shell and bony tail flap from the underside of each crab, then remove gills from both sides of the crab and the grit sac. Detach claws and legs.

HEAT the butter in a large saucepan. Add the vegetables, bay leaf and thyme and cook over moderate heat for 3 minutes, without allowing the vegetables to colour. Add crab claws, legs and body and cook for 5 minutes, or until the crab shells turn red. Add tomato purée, brandy and white wine and simmer for 2 minutes, or until reduced by half.

ADD stock and 500 ml (17 fl oz/2 cups) water and bring to the boil. Reduce the heat and simmer for 5 minutes. Remove the shells and reserve the claws. Finely crush shells with a pestle and mortar (or in a food processor with a little of the soup).

RETURN the crushed shells to the soup with the rice. Bring to the boil, reduce the heat, cover the pan and simmer for 30 minutes, or until the rice is very soft.

STRAIN the bisque into a clean saucepan through a fine sieve lined with damp muslin, pressing down firmly on the solids to extract all the cooking liquid. Add the cream and season with salt and cayenne, then gently reheat to serve. Ladle into warmed soup bowls and garnish, if you like, with the crab claws or some of the meat.

You will need a large saucepan or stockpot for making crab bisque because crab shells take up a lot of room in the pan.

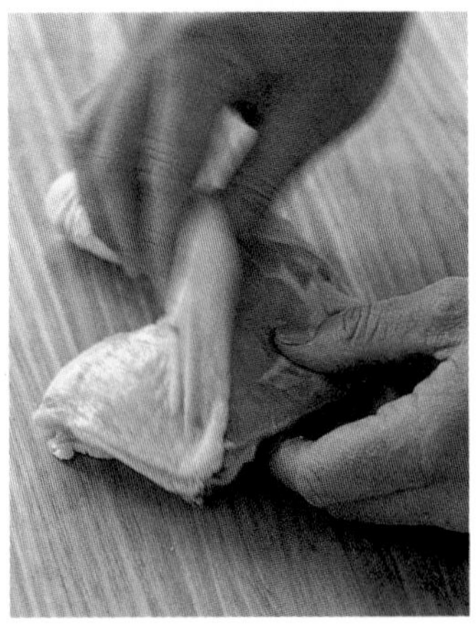

The skin is removed from the chicken before cooking as it is easier at this stage rather than when cooked.

FROM MOROCCO

CHICKEN SOUP WITH COUSCOUS

USE A WHOLE CHICKEN SUITABLE FOR STEWING AND CUT IT INTO EIGHTHS, OR USE CHICKEN PIECES FOR CONVENIENCE. WHEN COOKED, THE CHICKEN MUST BE TENDER ENOUGH FOR THE MEAT TO BE EASILY REMOVED FROM THE BONES.

1.5 kg (3 lb 5 oz) chicken
2 tablespoons olive oil
2 brown onions, finely chopped
½ teaspoon ground cumin
½ teaspoon paprika
½ teaspoon harissa, or to taste, or ¼ teaspoon cayenne pepper
2 tomatoes
1 tablespoon tomato paste (concentrated purée)
1 teaspoon caster (superfine) sugar
1 cinnamon stick
100 g (3½ oz/½ cup) couscous
2 tablespoons finely chopped flat-leaf (Italian) parsley
1 tablespoon finely chopped coriander (cilantro) leaves
2 teaspoons chopped fresh mint
lemon wedges, to serve

SERVES 4–6

RINSE chicken under cold running water and drain. Joint the chicken into eight pieces, first removing both legs and cutting through the joint of the drumstick and the thigh. Cut down each side of the backbone and lift it out. Turn chicken over and cut through the breastbone. Cut each breast in half, leaving the wing attached to the top half. Remove the skin and discard it.

HEAT olive oil in a large saucepan or stockpot, add the chicken and cook over high heat for 2–3 minutes, stirring often. Reduce the heat to medium, add the onion and cook for 5 minutes, or until the onion has softened. Stir in cumin, paprika and harissa or cayenne pepper. Add 1 litre (35 fl oz/4 cups) water. Bring to the boil.

HALVE tomatoes crossways and squeeze out the seeds. Coarsely grate the tomatoes over a plate, down to the skin, discarding the skin. Add grated tomato to the pan, along with the tomato paste, sugar, cinnamon stick, 1 teaspoon salt and some freshly ground black pepper. Bring to the boil, reduce the heat to low, then cover and simmer for 1 hour, or until the chicken is very tender.

REMOVE chicken to a dish using a slotted spoon. When cool enough to handle, remove the bones and tear chicken meat into strips. Return to the pan with an additional 500 ml (17 fl oz/2 cups) water and return to the boil. While it is boiling, gradually pour in the couscous, stirring constantly. Reduce the heat, then stir in the parsley, coriander and mint and simmer, uncovered, for 20 minutes. Adjust seasoning and serve with lemon wedges and crusty bread.

FROM ITALY

ZUPPA DI VERDURE

- 3 tablespoons olive oil
- 2 small onions, chopped
- 2 celery stalks, chopped
- 4 small carrots, chopped
- 2 large potatoes, diced
- 2 leeks, sliced
- 2 garlic cloves, crushed
- 125 g (4 oz) runner beans
- 125 g (4 oz) shelled green peas
- 1.75 litres (59 fl oz/7 cups) vegetable stock
- 150 g (5 oz) cavolo nero or cabbage
- 12 asparagus spears
- 6 slices 'country-style' bread, such as ciabatta, crusts removed
- 1 garlic clove, cut in half
- 30 g (1 oz/⅓ cup) grated parmesan cheese
- drizzle of extra virgin olive oil

SERVES 6

HEAT the olive oil in a large saucepan and add the onion, celery, carrot, potato, leek and crushed garlic. Cook over low heat for 5–6 minutes, or until the vegetables are softened but not browned. Season, add 375 ml (13 fl oz/1½ cups) water and bring to the boil. Reduce to low heat and simmer for 30 minutes.

SLICE the beans diagonally and add to the pan. Add the peas and stock and simmer for a further 30 minutes. Finely shred the cabbage and slice the asparagus diagonally. Add both to the pan and simmer for a further 5 minutes.

TOAST the bread and, while still hot, rub on both sides with the cut edge of the halved garlic clove.

STIR THE parmesan into the soup and taste for seasoning. Place a slice of toast in the bottom of each bowl and ladle soup over the top. Drizzle with a little olive oil and serve at once.

PAPPA AL POMODORO

PAPPA AL POMODORO IS A TUSCAN SOUP MADE, AS SO MANY GREAT ITALIAN DISHES ARE, TO USE UP LEFTOVERS – IN THIS CASE BREAD AND TOMATOES. *PAPPA* MEANS 'MUSH' AND THAT IS THE SOUP'S CONSISTENCY. PAPPA AL POMODORO IS A VARIETY OF *PANCOTTO,* BREAD SOUP.

- 2 tablespoons olive oil
- 3 garlic cloves, crushed
- 1 white onion, finely chopped
- 900 g (2 lb) ripe tomatoes, peeled and finely chopped
- 200 g (7 oz) stale 'country-style' bread, such as ciabatta, thickly sliced and crusts removed
- 850 ml (29 fl oz/3⅓ cups) hot chicken stock
- 20 basil leaves, shredded
- drizzle of extra virgin olive oil

SERVES 4

HEAT the olive oil in a large saucepan. Add garlic and onion and cook over a low heat for about 8 minutes, or until softened but not browned. Add tomatoes and season. Cover and simmer for 30 minutes. Break the bread into pieces and add to the saucepan. Simmer, stirring once or twice, for 5 minutes.

STIR in the stock gradually. Cook, stirring, until the bread has broken down and the soup is thick. Remove from the heat and add the basil. Cover and leave for 1 hour. Serve at room temperature or reheat. Drizzle extra virgin olive oil into each bowl before serving.

PAPPA AL POMODORO

ZUPPA DI VERDURE

FROM SPAIN

SEAFOOD SOUP WITH ALLÏOLI

ONE OF THE MANY WAYS TO CELEBRATE THE ABUNDANCE AND VARIETY OF SEAFOOD – INSPIRED BY THE SUQUET OF CATALONIA AND THE TIORO OF THE BASQUES. SIMPLE AND RELIANT ONLY ON THE FRESHEST MARISCOS – SEAFOOD – YOU CAN FIND. THIS HEARTY SOUP IS SURE TO PLEASE.

1 tablespoon olive oil
1 carrot, finely diced
1 white onion, finely diced
1 leek, finely diced
3 garlic cloves, chopped
1 small red chilli, seeded and finely chopped
1 celery stalk, finely diced
2 large all-purpose potatoes, peeled and cut into 2 cm (¾ inch) dice
500 g (1 lb 2 oz) skinless firm white fish fillets, cut into 2 cm (¾ inch) cubes (reserve bones and scraps)
1 bay leaf
250 ml (9 fl oz/1 cup) white wine
30 ml (1 fl oz/1½ tablespoon) brandy
400 g (14 oz) tinned chopped tomatoes, drained
60 ml (2 fl oz/¼ cup) tomato paste (concentrated purée)
12 black mussels, bearded and scrubbed
8 raw king prawns (shrimp), peeled and deveined, tails intact
2 tablespoons lemon juice
2 tablespoons chopped flat-leaf (Italian) parsley
fried bread, to serve (optional)
allïoli (see recipe on page 490), to serve (optional)

SERVES 4–6

HEAT oil in a large saucepan over medium heat. Add carrot, onion, leek, garlic, chilli and celery and cook for 5 minutes, or until onion is translucent. Add potato and 1.5 litres (52 fl oz/6 cups) of cold water. Bring to the boil, then reduce the heat and simmer for about 8 minutes, or until the potatoes are half cooked. Stir in the fish bones and scraps and bay leaf and simmer for 6–8 minutes, or until potatoes are soft. Strain the liquid and reserve. Remove the bones and bay leaf, and purée the remaining potato and vegetable mixture with the reserved liquid.

COMBINE the wine, brandy, chopped tomato and tomato paste in a separate saucepan and bring to the boil. Add the mussels and cook, covered, for 3–5 minutes, or until opened. Remove from the pan, discarding any that remain closed.

BLEND the mussel-cooking liquid with the potato purée. Transfer to a large saucepan and bring to the boil. Add the fish cubes and prawns, reduce the heat and simmer for 8 minutes, or until all the seafood is cooked.

STIR in the mussels and lemon juice and gently heat through. Season well and garnish with the parsley. This soup is delicious served with fried bread and allïoli.

Remove the mussels as they open and discard any that are still closed after 5 minutes.

FROM FRANCE

BOURRIDE

THIS RICH FISH SOUP CAN BE SERVED IN A VARIETY OF WAYS. THE BREAD CAN BE PUT IN A DISH WITH THE FISH PILED ON TOP AND THE SOUP LADLED OVER, OR THE BROTH MAY BE SERVED WITH CROUTONS AND THE FISH EATEN SEPARATELY WITH BOILED POTATOES AS A MAIN COURSE.

GARLIC CROUTONS
½ stale baguette, sliced
60 ml (2 fl oz/¼ cup) olive oil
1 garlic clove, halved

AÏOLI
2 egg yolks
4 garlic cloves, crushed
3–5 teaspoons lemon juice
250 ml (9 fl oz/1 cup) olive oil

STOCK
¼ teaspoon saffron threads
1 litre (35 fl oz/4 cups) dry white wine
1 leek, white part only, chopped
2 carrots, chopped
2 onions, chopped
2 long pieces orange zest
2 teaspoons fennel seeds
3 thyme sprigs
2.5 kg (5 lb 8 oz) whole firm white fish such as sea bass, cod, perch, sole or bream, filleted, skinned and cut into 4 cm (1½ inch) pieces (reserve the trimmings)
3 egg yolks

SERVES 4

PREHEAT the oven to 160°C (315°F/Gas 2–3). Brush the bread with oil and bake for 10 minutes until crisp. Rub one side of each slice with garlic.

TO MAKE the aïoli, put the egg yolks, garlic and 3 teaspoons of the lemon juice in a mortar and pestle or food processor and pound or mix until light and creamy. Add the oil, drop by drop from the tip of a teaspoon, whisking constantly until it begins to thicken, then add the oil in a very thin stream. (If you're using a processor, pour in the oil in a thin stream with the motor running.) Season, add the remaining lemon juice and, if necessary, thin with a little warm water. Cover and refrigerate.

TO MAKE stock, soak the saffron in a tablespoon of hot water for 15 minutes. Put the saffron, wine, leek, carrot, onion, orange zest, fennel seeds, thyme and fish trimmings in a large saucepan with 1 litre (35 fl oz/4 cups) water. Cover and bring to the boil, then simmer for 20 minutes, skimming occasionally. Strain through a sieve into a clean saucepan, pressing the solids with a wooden spoon to extract all the liquid. Bring the stock to a gentle simmer, add half the fish and poach for 5 minutes. Remove and keep warm while cooking the rest of the fish, then remove from the pan and bring the stock back to the boil. Boil for 5 minutes, or until slightly reduced, and remove from the heat.

PUT HALF the aïoli and the yolks in a bowl and mix until smooth. Whisk in a ladleful of hot stock, then gradually add 5 ladlefuls, stirring constantly. Pour back into the pan holding the rest of the stock and whisk over low heat for 3–5 minutes, or until the soup is hot and slightly thicker (don't let it boil or it will curdle). Season with salt and pepper.

TO SERVE, put two garlic croutons in each bowl, top with a few pieces of fish and ladle over the hot soup. Serve the remaining aïoli separately.

Use slightly stale bread for the croutons. Rubbing with the cut side of the garlic will give them a mild flavour. Buy whole fish and cut them up yourself, keeping the trimmings. A flavoursome stock, made with fresh trimmings, is the basis of a good fish soup.

FROM SPAIN

LENTEN SOUP

SEMANA SANTA (EASTER) IS AN IMPORTANT RELIGIOUS FESTIVAL IN SPAIN, AND FOR THE MANY CATHOLIC SPANIARDS WHO DON'T CONSUME MEAT DURING LENT, THIS IS A GOOD ALTERNATIVE. WITH THIS RICH PURÉE OF CHICKPEAS AND POTATOES, IT DOESN'T HAVE TO BE A HARDSHIP

250 g (9 oz) bacalao (salt cod)
250 g (9 oz) chickpeas
1 leek, white part only
1 red onion
2 carrots
1 green capsicum (pepper)
2 floury potatoes
4 tablespoons olive oil
2 garlic cloves, chopped
½ teaspoon sweet paprika (pimentón)

SERVES 4–6

PUT the bacalao in a large bowl and cover with cold water. Refrigerate for 20 hours, changing the water several times during the soaking process. Put the chickpeas in a separate bowl, cover with cold water and soak overnight.

ROUGHLY chop the leek, onion, carrots, capsicum and potatoes.

HEAT the oil in a large, heavy-based saucepan over medium heat. Sauté the onion, garlic, leek and carrot until softened, about 5 minutes. Add the drained chickpeas and bacalao and cover with 1.5 litres (52 fl oz/6 cups) of water. Bring to the boil, cover, reduce heat to a simmer and cook for 30 minutes. After 30 minutes carefully remove bacalao. When cool enough to handle, remove the skin and bones and return the flesh in large pieces back to the pan and continue simmering for a further 30 minutes. Add the potato, capsicum and paprika. Continue to cook for 30 more minutes or until potato is soft. Cool slightly then blend in a food processor, in batches, until smooth. Season to taste then gently reheat if necessary. Add more water if you prefer a thinner soup.

When the bacalao is cooked and cooled, separate the flesh from the skin and bones before returning the flesh to the pan.

FROM ITALY

ZUPPA DI PESCE

FOR A COUNTRY WHERE ALMOST EVERY REGION HAS A SEA COAST, IT IS HARDLY SURPRISING THAT ITALY HAS ALMOST AS MANY VERSIONS OF THIS SOUP AS THERE ARE FISH IN THE SEA. THIS RECIPE INCLUDES SUGGESTIONS FOR FISH VARIETIES, BUT ASK YOUR FISHMONGER WHAT'S BEST ON THE DAY.

FISH STOCK
300 g (10½ oz) firm white fish fillets, such as monkfish, red mullet, cod, deep sea perch, skinned and cut into large cubes, bones reserved
12 prawns (shrimp)
1 small onion, roughly chopped
1 carrot, roughly chopped
15 g (½ oz) parsley, roughly chopped, stalks reserved

200 g (7 oz) squid tubes
4 tablespoons olive oil
1 onion, finely chopped
1 celery stalk, finely chopped
1 carrot, finely chopped
2 garlic cloves, finely chopped
pinch of cayenne pepper
1 fennel bulb, trimmed and thinly sliced
125 ml (4 fl oz/½ cup) dry white wine
400 g (14 oz) tin chopped tomatoes
250 g (9 oz) scallops, cleaned

CROSTINI
3 tablespoons extra virgin olive oil
2 garlic cloves, crushed
4 slices 'country-style' bread, such as ciabatta

SERVES 4

TO MAKE the fish stock, rinse the fish bones in cold water, removing any blood or intestines. Peel and devein the prawns and put the fish bones and prawn shells in a large saucepan with just enough water to cover. Bring slowly to a simmer, skimming any froth from the surface. Add the onion, carrot and the stalks from the parsley, then simmer gently for 20 minutes. Strain through a fine colander and measure 1.5 litres (52 fl oz/6 cups) stock. If there is less than this, add a little water; if there is more, put the strained stock back into the saucepan and simmer until reduced to 1.5 litres (52 fl oz/6 cups).

LIE the squid out flat, skin side up, and score a crisscross pattern into the flesh, being careful not to cut all the way through. Slice diagonally into bite-sized strips.

Score a crisscross pattern into the squid to make it curl.

HEAT the oil in a large saucepan and cook the onion, celery, carrot, garlic and chopped parsley over moderately low heat for 5–6 minutes, or until softened but not browned. Add cayenne pepper and season well. Stir in fennel and cook for about 3 minutes. Add the white wine, increase the heat and cook until it has been absorbed. Stir in the tomatoes, then add the fish stock and bring to the boil. Reduce the heat and simmer for 20 minutes.

ADD the squid to the pan with the fish pieces and simmer for 1 minute. Add the scallops and prawns and simmer for a further 2 minutes. Taste and add more seasoning if necessary.

TO MAKE crostini, heat the olive oil and crushed garlic in a large frying pan over moderately low heat. Add the slices of bread and fry on both sides until golden. Place a slice of bread into each of four warmed serving bowls. Ladle the soup on top and serve immediately.

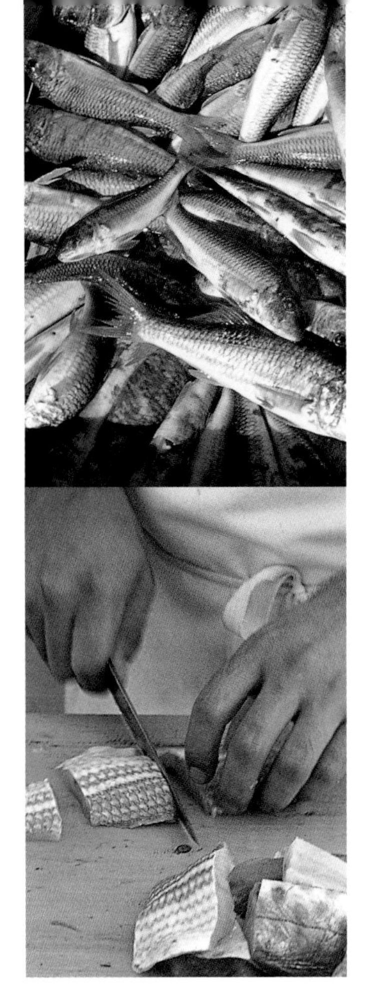

Leaving the skin on the fish is traditional as originally whole fish would have been used for this dish. The skin also helps the pieces hold together while the soup is cooking.

Fishermen selling their morning's catch on the Quai des Belges, in the old port of Marseille.

FROM FRANCE

BOUILLABAISSE

BOUILLABAISSE IS THE MOST FAMOUS FRENCH FISH SOUP AND IS ASSOCIATED WITH THE SOUTH OF THE COUNTRY, PARTICULARLY MARSEILLE. AS A FISHERMAN'S MEAL IT IS OFTEN MADE WITH WHOLE FISH, ESPECIALLY *RASCASSE* (SCORPION FISH). USING FILLETS IS MUCH SIMPLER.

ROUILLE
1 small red capsicum (pepper)
1 slice white bread, crusts removed
1 red chilli
2 garlic cloves
1 egg yolk
80 ml (2½ fl oz/⅓ cup) olive oil

SOUP
18 mussels
1.5 kg (3 lb 5 oz) firm white fish fillets such as red mullet, bass, snapper, monkfish, rascasse, John Dory or eel, skin on
2 tablespoons oil
1 fennel bulb, thinly sliced
1 onion, chopped
750 g (1 lb 10 oz) ripe tomatoes
1.25 (44 fl oz/5 cups) litres fish stock or water
pinch of saffron threads
bouquet garni
5 cm (2 inch) piece of orange zest

SERVES 6

TO MAKE the rouille, preheat the grill. Cut the capsicum in half, remove the seeds and membrane and place, skin side up, under the hot grill (broiler) until the skin blackens and blisters. Leave to cool before peeling away the skin. Roughly chop the capsicum.

SOAK bread in 3 tablespoons water, then squeeze dry with your hands. Put capsicum, chilli, bread, garlic and egg yolk in a mortar and pestle or food processor and pound or mix together. Gradually add the oil in a thin stream, pounding or mixing until rouille is smooth and has the texture of thick mayonnaise. Cover and refrigerate until needed.

TO MAKE the soup, scrub the mussels and remove their beards. Discard any mussels that are already open and don't close when tapped on the work surface. Cut the fish into bite-sized pieces.

HEAT oil in a large saucepan and cook the fennel and onion over medium heat for about 5 minutes, until golden.

SCORE a cross in the top of each tomato. Plunge into boiling water for 20 seconds, then drain and peel the skin away from the cross. Chop the tomatoes, discarding the cores. Add to the pan and cook for 3 minutes. Stir in the stock, saffron, bouquet garni and orange zest, bring to the boil and boil for 10 minutes. Remove bouquet garni and push the soup through a sieve. Return to the cleaned pan, season well and return to the boil.

REDUCE the heat to simmer and add the fish and mussels. Cook for 5 minutes or until the fish is tender and the mussels have opened. Throw out any mussels that haven't opened in this time. Serve the soup with rouille and bread. Or lift out the fish and mussels and serve separately.

You will probably eat this cold soup as a first course, just as they have been served for about thirty years in the restaurants and private homes of the large cities in Andalusia. But it is interesting to know that it is still customary in village homes to have gazpacho after the first course, and before dessert.

FROM SPAIN

CHILLED TOMATO SOUP

THE ANDALUCIANS HAVE DEVISED MANY WAYS TO DEAL WITH THE SEARING HEAT OF THEIR SUMMERS, NOT THE LEAST OF THEM, THE COLD SOUP. GAZPACHO, THE MOST FAMOUS OF THESE WONDERFULLY REFRESHING SOUPS IS SIMPLICITY ITSELF TO MAKE – AND EVEN EASIER TO EAT.

2 slices day-old white crusty bread, crusts removed, broken into pieces
1 kg (2 lb 4 oz) vine-ripened tomatoes, peeled, seeded and chopped
1 red capsicum (pepper), seeded, roughly chopped
2 garlic cloves, chopped
1 small green chilli, chopped (optional)
1 teaspoon caster (superfine) sugar
2 tablespoons red wine vinegar
2 tablespoons extra virgin olive oil

GARNISH
½ Lebanese (short) cucumber, seeded, finely diced
½ red capsicum (pepper), seeded, finely diced
½ green capsicum (pepper), seeded, finely diced
½ red onion, finely diced
½ ripe tomato, diced

SERVES 4

SOAK the bread in cold water for 5 minutes, then squeeze out any excess liquid. Put the bread in a food processor with the tomato, capsicum, garlic, chilli, sugar and vinegar, and process until combined and smooth.

WITH the motor running, gradually add the oil to make a smooth creamy mixture. Season to taste. Refrigerate for at least 2 hours. Add a little of the extra vinegar, if desired.

TO MAKE the garnish, mix together the ingredients. Spoon the chilled gazpacho into soup bowls, top with a little of the garnish and serve the remaining garnish in separate bowls on the side.

Use a teaspoon to scoop out the seeds. Squeeze excess water from the bread.

FROM SPAIN

CHILLED ALMOND SOUP

YOUR FIRST ENCOUNTER WITH THIS COOL, SILKY SMOOTH SOUP WITH PALE-GREEN GRAPES AND CROUTONS FLOATING ON TOP WILL ASTONISH AND DELIGHT YOU. ANOTHER VERSION OF GAZPACHO, AJO BLANCO IS A SURVIVOR OF THE MEDIEVAL MOORISH CUISINE OF THE MEDITERRANEAN.

200 g (7 oz) day-old white crusty bread, crusts removed
150 g (5 oz/1 cup) whole blanched almonds
3–4 garlic cloves, chopped
125 ml (4 fl oz/½ cup) extra virgin olive oil
80 ml (2½ fl oz/⅓ cup) sherry vinegar
310–375 ml (10–13 fl oz/1¼–1½ cups) vegetable or chicken stock
2 tablespoons olive oil
75 g (2¾ oz) day-old white crusty bread, extra, crusts removed, cut into 1 cm (½ inch) cubes
200 g (7 oz) small seedless green grapes
aged sherry vinegar, for serving

SERVES 4–6

SOAK the bread in cold water for 5 minutes, then squeeze out any excess liquid. Process the almonds and garlic in a food processor until well ground. Add the bread and process until smooth.

WITH the motor running, add the oil in a steady slow stream until the mixture is the consistency of thick mayonnaise (add a little water if the mixture is too thick). Slowly add the sherry vinegar and 310 ml (10¾ fl oz/1¼ cups) of the stock. Blend for 1 minute. Season with salt. Refrigerate for at least 2 hours. The soup thickens on refrigeration so you may need to add stock or water to thin it.

WHEN ready to serve, heat the olive oil in a frying pan, add bread cubes and toss over medium heat for about 3 minutes, or until golden. Drain on paper towels. Serve the soup very cold. Garnish with grapes and bread cubes and sprinkle with aged sherry vinegar if desired.

Sherry vinegar *(vinagre de Jerez)* is a gourmet wine vinegar made from Sherry. It is produced in the Spanish province of Cádiz and inside the triangular area between the city of Jerez de la Frontera and towns of Sanlúcar de Barrameda and El Puerto de Santa María, known as the 'sherry triangle'.

FROM FRANCE

SOUPE AU PISTOU

PISTOU IS A PROVENÇAL MIXTURE OF GARLIC, BASIL AND PARMESAN COMBINED WITH OLIVE OIL FROM THE SOUTH OF FRANCE. SIMILAR TO ITALIAN PESTO, IT IS THE TRADITIONAL ACCOMPANIMENT TO THIS SPRING VEGETABLE SOUP AND IS ADDED AT THE TABLE.

250 g (9 oz) dried haricot beans
2 teaspoons olive oil
1 onion, finely chopped
2 garlic cloves, crushed
1 celery stalk, chopped
3 carrots, diced
bouquet garni
4 potatoes, diced
150 g (5½ oz) small green beans, chopped
500 ml (17 fl oz/2 cups) chicken stock
3 tomatoes
4 zucchini (courgettes), diced
150 g (5 oz) vermicelli, broken into pieces
150 g (5 oz/1 cup) peas, fresh or frozen

PISTOU
6 garlic cloves
90 g (3 oz) basil leaves
90 g (3 oz) parmesan, grated
200 ml (7 fl oz) olive oil

SERVES 4

SOAK the haricot beans in cold water overnight, then drain, put in a saucepan and cover with cold water. Bring to the boil, lower the heat and simmer for 1 hour, or until the beans are tender. Drain well.

TO MAKE the pistou, put the garlic, basil and parmesan in a food processor or a mortar and pestle and process or pound until finely chopped. Slowly add the olive oil, with the motor running if you are using the food processor or pounding constantly with the mortar and pestle, and mix thoroughly. Cover with plastic wrap and set aside.

HEAT olive oil in a large saucepan, add onion and garlic and cook over low heat for 5 minutes until softened but not browned. Add celery, carrot and bouquet garni and cook for 10 minutes, stirring occasionally. Add potato, green beans, stock and 1.75 (6 fl oz) litres water. Simmer for 10 minutes.

SCORE a cross in the top of each tomato. Plunge into boiling water for 20 seconds, then drain and peel skin away. Chop tomatoes finely, discarding the cores. Add to the soup with zucchini, haricot beans, vermicelli and peas. Cook for 10 minutes or until tender (if you are using frozen peas, add them at the last minute just to heat through). Season and serve with pistou on top.

Basil is more usually associated with Italy than France but, in fact, the herb originated not in Italy, but in India. It was introduced to Europe in the sixteenth century and is often used in southern French cooking as a perfect match for Provençal tomatoes and olive oil. It can be bought in pots or as bunches, or you can grow your own.

VEGETABLE DISHES

Peeling hard pumpkin or winter squash can be hazardous if it is very firm. Use a heavy knife to cut pumpkin into large pieces. Place cut surface on a board and remove skin as shown.

FROM MOROCCO

PUMPKIN AND SWEET POTATO STEW

SELECT A PUMPKIN (SQUASH) WITH FIRM ORANGE FLESH SUCH AS QUEENSLAND BLUE, KENT, BUTTERNUT PUMPKIN OR OTHER WINTER SQUASH SUCH AS HUBBARD OR TURK'S CAP, BUT AVOID THE JACK'O'LANTERN-TYPE AS ITS FLESH BECOMES MUSH WHEN COOKED.

60 g (2 oz) butter
1 large brown onion, finely chopped
2 garlic cloves, finely chopped
1 teaspoon ground ginger
1 teaspoon ground turmeric
1 cinnamon stick
pinch of cayenne pepper, or ½ teaspoon harissa (see recipe on page 482), or to taste
500 ml (17 fl oz/2 cups) vegetable or chicken stock
⅛ teaspoon ground saffron threads
600 g (1 lb 5 oz) butternut pumpkin (squash) or other firm pumpkin (winter squash), peeled and cubed
500 g (1 lb 2 oz) orange sweet potato, peeled and cubed
60 g (2¼ oz/½ cup) raisins
1 tablespoon honey
coriander (cilantro) leaves, to serve

SERVES 4–6

MELT butter in a large saucepan over low heat. Add onion and cook gently, stirring occasionally for 5 minutes, until softened. Add garlic, ginger, turmeric, cinnamon stick and cayenne pepper or harissa. Stir over low heat for 1–2 minutes or until fragrant. Pour in the stock, add the saffron, then increase the heat to medium and bring to the boil.

ADD the pumpkin, sweet potato, raisins and honey and season with salt and freshly ground black pepper. Cover and simmer for a further 15 minutes, or until the vegetables are tender. Remove the cinnamon stick, transfer vegetables to a bowl and scatter with coriander leaves.

STEWS such as this are traditionally served as a hot or warm vegetable course after the appetiser salads, but can also be served as a vegetable accompaniment to a main meal.

FROM MOROCCO

TAGINE OMELETTE WITH TOMATOES

A TYPICAL DISH MADE IN THE REMOTE MIDDLE ATLAS, USUALLY COOKED IN A TAGINE. TOMATOES ARE KEY TO THE FLAVOUR, AND TO DUPLICATE THIS, ONE WOULD HAVE TO PEEL, SEED AND CHOP A KILO OF VINE-RIPENED TOMATOES. TINNED ROMA (PLUM) TOMATOES ARE JUST AS GOOD FOR THIS RECIPE.

2 tablespoons olive oil
1 white onion, finely chopped
1 teaspoon ground coriander
1 teaspoon paprika
pinch of cayenne pepper
2 x 400 g (14 oz) tins roma (plum) tomatoes, chopped
3 tablespoons chopped flat-leaf (Italian) parsley
3 tablespoons chopped coriander (cilantro) leaves, extra to serve
8 eggs

SERVES 4

USE a 25–28 cm (10–11¼ inch) non-stick frying pan with a domed lid. Place over low–medium heat and add oil and onion. Cook for 6 minutes or until onion is soft. Stir in ground coriander, paprika and cayenne and cook for a further 2 minutes, Add tomatoes and their liquid, and the parsley. Increase heat to medium, season and allow to simmer, uncovered until sauce is reduced and thick – about 10 minutes.

BREAK eggs into a bowl and add 2 tablespoons water. Season and beat lightly with a fork, just enough to amalgamate whites and yolks. Pour eggs over the back of a large spoon so that the mixture evenly covers the sauce. Cover with the domed lid and cook over medium heat for 15 minutes or until set and puffed. Scatter with fresh coriander leaves and serve immediately, either cut into wedges, or spooned onto plates. Serve with bread.

TO COOK in a tagine: Make tomato sauce in a frying pan or saucepan. Remove shelves in oven, leaving bottom shelf in place. Preheat oven to 180°C (350°F/Gas 4). Transfer hot, cooked sauce to the tagine. Cover, place in oven for 10 minutes to heat the sauce. Remove tagine from oven, immediately pour beaten eggs over sauce, replace lid and return to oven for 6 minutes until omelette is puffed and set. Serve from the tagine.

Cook the tomato sauce until reduced and thick. Pour the lightly beaten eggs over the back of a soup spoon to cover the sauce evenly.

Cook the roux for a couple of minutes without browning, then turn off the heat before adding the milk gradually. Removing the saucepan from the heat before adding each ingredient prevents the sauce becoming lumpy.

FROM FRANCE

BLUE CHEESE SOUFFLÉ

15 g (½ oz) butter, melted
30 g (1 oz) butter
30 g (1 oz) plain (all-purpose) flour
250 ml (9 fl oz/1 cup) milk
125 g (4 oz) blue cheese, mashed
4 egg yolks
grated nutmeg
5 egg whites

SERVES 4

PREHEAT the oven to 200°C (400°F/Gas 6). Cut a strip of baking paper long enough to fold around a 1.25 litre (44 fl oz/5 cups) soufflé dish, then fold in half and tie around the dish so it sticks 2–3 cm (¾-1¼ inch) above the top. Brush the inside of the dish and the collar with the melted butter and place the dish on a baking tray.

MELT the butter in a heavy-based saucepan and stir in the flour to make a roux. Cook, stirring, for 2 minutes over low heat without allowing the roux to brown. Remove from the heat and add the milk gradually, stirring after each addition until smooth. Return to the heat and bring to the boil. Simmer, stirring, for 3 minutes, then remove from the heat.

STIR the cheese into the sauce until it melts (it may separate but keep stirring – it will correct itself). Beat in the yolks, one at a time, beating well after each addition. Season with nutmeg, salt and pepper and pour into a large mixing bowl.

WHISK egg whites in a clean dry bowl until they form soft peaks. Spoon a quarter of the egg white onto the soufflé mixture and quickly but lightly fold it in, to loosen the mixture. Lightly fold in the remaining egg white. Pour into the soufflé dish.

BAKE for 20–25 minutes, or until the soufflé is well risen and wobbles slightly when tapped. Test with a skewer through a crack in the side of the soufflé. The skewer should come out clean or be slightly moist. If the skewer is slightly moist, by the time the soufflé is brought to the table, it will be cooked in the centre. Serve immediately.

FROM ITALY

EGGPLANT PARMIGIANA

PARMIGIANA IS A DECEPTIVE NAME FOR THIS DISH, AS THE RECIPE DOES NOT, IN FACT, HAIL FROM THAT CITY. INSTEAD ITS CREATION IS CLAIMED BY ALMOST EVERY REGION OF ITALY, BUT THE USE OF MOZZARELLA AND TOMATOES INDICATES A DISH FROM THE SOUTH.

1.5 kg (3 lb 5 oz) eggplants (aubergines)
plain (all-purpose) flour
330 ml (1 1/3 cups) olive oil
500 ml (2 cups) tomato passata (puréed tomatoes)
2 tablespoons roughly torn basil leaves
250 g (1 2/3 cups) grated mozzarella cheese
100 g (1 cup) grated parmesan cheese

SERVES 8

THINLY SLICE the eggplants lengthways. Layer the slices in a large colander, sprinkling salt between each layer. Leave for 1 hour to extract the bitter juices. Rinse and pat the slices dry on both sides with paper towels. Coat the eggplant slices lightly with flour.

PREHEAT the oven to 180°C (350°F/Gas 4) and grease a 32 x 20 cm (13 x 8 inch) shallow casserole or baking tray.

HEAT 125 ml (1/2 cup) of the olive oil in a large frying pan. Quickly fry the eggplant in batches over moderately high heat until crisp and golden on both sides. Add more olive oil as needed, and drain well on paper towels as you remove each batch from the pan.

MAKE a slightly overlapping layer of eggplant slices over the base of the dish. Season with pepper. Spoon 4 tablespoons of passata over the eggplant and scatter a few pieces of basil on top. Sprinkle with some mozzarella, followed by some parmesan. Continue with this layering until you have used up all the ingredients.

BAKE FOR 30 minutes. Remove from the oven and allow to cool for 30 minutes before serving.

Frying the eggplant (aubergine) slices first adds flavour to the finished dish.

FROM MOROCCO

SILVERBEET WITH RICE

CHARD (SILVERBEET) IS A POPULAR VEGETABLE THROUGHOUT THE MEDITERRANEAN REGION. IT IS A VEGETABLE THAT CHILDREN LOVE TO HATE, AND VEGETABLE GARDENERS INSIST ON PLANTING BECAUSE IT GROWS SO EASILY. THE FOLLOWING RECIPE IS AN EXCELLENT WAY TO PREPARE IT.

This leafy member of the silverbeet family has been favoured in the Mediterranean region for centuries; combining it with rice and herbs reveals Andalusian influences.

900 g (2 lb) silverbeet (Swiss chard)
80 ml (2½ fl oz/⅓ cup) olive oil
1 brown onion, chopped
1 teaspoon paprika
2 tablespoons chopped coriander (cilantro) leaves
2 tablespoons chopped flat-leaf (Italian) parsley
110 g (3¾ oz/½ cup) short-grain rice
1½ tablespoons lemon juice

SERVES 4

TRIM the ends of the stalks of the silverbeet. Wash well and cut the stalks from the leaves. Slice the stalks thickly and roughly shred the leaves.

HEAT the olive oil in a large saucepan and add the onion. Cook over low heat for 5 minutes, or until soft.

STIR in the silverbeet stalks and paprika and cook for 5 minutes more. Add the silverbeet leaves, coriander, parsley, rice and 125 ml (4 fl oz/½ cup) water. Increase the heat to medium and stir until the silverbeet begins to wilt.

REDUCE the heat to low, add the lemon juice and stir well. Cover and simmer for 25 minutes, or until the rice is tender, stirring occasionally. Season, to taste, and serve hot as a vegetable accompaniment.

FROM ITALY

PASTICCIO OF TORTELLINI, BROCCOLI AND RICOTTA

FILLING
650 g (1 lb 7 oz) ricotta cheese
pinch of ground nutmeg
100 g (1 cup) grated parmesan cheese
1 egg

600 g (1 lb 5 oz) broccoli, trimmed into florets
500 g (1 lb 2 oz) cheese-filled tortellini
3 eggs
1 quantity béchamel sauce (see recipe on page 489)
1½ tablespoons tomato paste (purée)
150 g (1 cup) grated mozzarella cheese
4 tablespoons grated parmesan cheese

SERVES 6

TO MAKE the filling, mash the ricotta with a fork, or pass through a food mill (do not use a blender or food processor). Mix in the nutmeg and salt and pepper. Add the parmesan, then mix in the egg. Set aside.

PREHEAT the oven to 180°C (350°F/Gas 4) and grease a large deep casserole dish. Bring a large saucepan of water to the boil. Add the broccoli florets and a teaspoon of salt and simmer for 3 minutes. Remove the broccoli with a slotted spoon and set aside. Stir the tortellini into the boiling water and then gently lower in the eggs. Cook until the pasta is *al dente*, drain and rinse under cold water. Take out the eggs after about 6 minutes when they are hard-boiled, remove the eggshells and slice thinly.

PUT HALF of the béchamel sauce into a large bowl and stir in the tomato paste. Add the tortellini and toss to coat. Pour half of this mixture into the casserole dish. Spread half of the ricotta filling over it, then top with half the egg slices. Layer all the broccoli on top of this, pressing it in firmly, then spoon the remaining plain béchamel sauce over the top. Sprinkle with the mozzarella. Finish with a final layer of tortellini, the remaining egg slices and finally the rest of the ricotta filling.

SPRINKLE the parmesan over the top and bake for 30–40 minutes. Remove from the oven and allow to rest for 10 minutes before serving.

Ricotta is made from the whey left over from cheese-making. These ricotta are made from the whey of parmesan cheese.

Bakeries and speciality shops make pasta daily. Here, tortellini and caramelle are made at Paolo Atti e Figli bakery in Bologna.

FROM ITALY

CHARGRILLED EGGPLANT SALAD

2 large eggplants (aubergines), thinly sliced lengthways
2 garlic cloves, crushed
170 ml (5½ fl oz/⅔ cup) extra virgin olive oil
juice of 1 small lemon
½ red chilli, finely chopped
1 large handful basil or mint leaves, roughly chopped

SERVES 4

HEAT a chargrill pan (griddle) on the stove and cook the eggplant, a few slices at a time, over moderately high heat, turning once until it is soft and cooked. (There is no need to add oil or to salt the eggplant first.) As you remove the eggplant slices from the pan, put them on a plate on top of each other – this helps them to steam a little and soften further.

IF you do not have a chargrill pan (griddle), preheat the oven to 200°C (400°F/Gas 6). Drizzle a couple of tablespoons of olive oil over a baking tray and place the eggplant slices on top. Drizzle with a little more oil and cook the eggplant until soft.

MIX TOGETHER the garlic, olive oil, lemon juice, chilli and herbs. (If you have baked the eggplant, use a little less oil.) Place the eggplant in a flat dish and pour over the marinade. Mix briefly without breaking up the eggplant and marinate for at least 30 minutes before serving.

CHARGRILLED VEGETABLE SALAD

4 long thin eggplants (aubergines)
4 zucchini (courgettes)
4 roma (plum) tomatoes
1 small red capsicum (pepper)
1 small green capsicum (pepper)
1 small yellow capsicum (pepper)
60 ml (2 fl oz/¼ cup) olive oil
2 garlic cloves, halved

DRESSING
60 ml (2 fl oz/¼ cup) extra virgin olive oil
1 tablespoon balsamic vinegar
1 garlic clove, crushed
3 tablespoons chopped parsley
¼ teaspoon caster (superfine) sugar

SERVES 4

SLICE the eggplants and zucchini diagonally into 1 cm (½ inch) thick pieces. Halve the tomatoes lengthways and slice the capsicums into short strips. Place all the vegetables in a bowl and add the olive oil and the garlic. Toss well.

PREHEAT a chargrill pan (griddle) or barbecue and brush with oil. Cook the eggplant and zucchini for 2–4 minutes on each side, or until browned. Transfer to a shallow serving dish. Cook the tomatoes and capsicums for 1–2 minutes on each side, or until the capsicums start to smell sweet and their skins blister. Transfer to the serving dish and set aside to cool.

TO MAKE the dressing, mix together all the ingredients and then season. Drizzle the dressing over the vegetables and toss lightly. Serve at room temperature.

CHARGRILLED VEGETABLE SALAD

CHARGRILLED EGGPLANT SALAD

FROM MOROCCO

TAGINE OF CHICKPEAS

AN ALTERNATIVE TO TINNED CHICKPEAS IS DRIED CHICKPEAS; FOR THIS RECIPE USE 1 CUP (220 G/8 OZ), SOAKED OVERNIGHT IN COLD WATER, DRAINED AND COOKED WITH WATER TO COVER FOR 1–1½ HOURS. IF PREFERRED, DO NOT SKIN THE CHICKPEAS.

- 3 tablespoons olive oil
- 1 brown onion, chopped
- 1 garlic clove, finely chopped
- 1 teaspoon harissa (see recipe on page 482), or to taste, or ¼ teaspoon cayenne pepper
- ½ teaspoon paprika
- ¼ teaspoon ground ginger
- ½ teaspoon ground turmeric
- 1 teaspoon ground cumin
- 1 teaspoon ground cinnamon
- 400 g (14 oz) tin chopped tomatoes
- 1 teaspoon caster (superfine) sugar
- 2 x 420 g (15 oz) tins chickpeas
- 3 tablespoons chopped flat-leaf (Italian) parsley
- 2 tablespoons chopped coriander (cilantro) leaves

SERVES 4

PUT the olive oil and onion in a large saucepan and cook over medium heat for 7–8 minutes, or until softened. Stir in the garlic, the harissa or cayenne pepper, and the spices and cook gently for 2 minutes or until fragrant. Add the tomatoes and sugar and season, to taste. Cover and simmer for 20 minutes.

MEANWHILE, drain the chickpeas and put them in a large bowl with enough cold water to cover well. Lift up handfuls of chickpeas and rub them between your hands to loosen the skins. Run more water into the bowl, stir well and let the skins float to the top, then skim them off. Repeat until all the skins have been removed.

DRAIN the chickpeas again and stir them into the tomato mixture. Cover and simmer for 20–25 minutes, adding a little more water if necessary. Stir through the parsley and coriander and season to taste. Serve with crusty bread or with couscous.

Chickpeas are traditionally skinned for tagines so that flavours can be absorbed. Place soaked, cooked or tinned chickpeas in a bowl of water, rub handfuls together, and remove floating skins.

FROM ITALY

RED WINE RISOTTO

THE SECRET TO A REALLY SPECTACULAR RED WINE RISOTTO IS TO USE ONLY THE VERY BEST INGREDIENTS. AS THE DISH IS SO SIMPLE, A GOOD-QUALITY WINE IS REQUIRED – TRADITIONALLY THE DRY RICH AMARONE OF VALPOLICELLA IS USED.

500 ml (17 fl oz/2 cups) chicken stock
100 g (3½ oz) butter
1 onion, finely chopped
1 large garlic clove, crushed
2 tablespoons chopped thyme
220 g (7¾ oz/1 cup) risotto rice (arborio, vialone nano or carnaroli)
500 ml (17 fl oz/2 cups) dry red wine
50 g (½ cup) grated parmesan cheese

SERVES 2

PUT the stock in a saucepan, bring to the boil and then maintain at a low simmer.

HEAT the butter in a large wide heavy-based saucepan. Add the onion and garlic and cook until softened but not browned. Add the thyme and rice and reduce the heat to low. Season and stir briefly to thoroughly coat the rice.

ADD HALF the red wine. Increase the heat and cook, stirring, until all the liquid has been absorbed. Stir in a ladleful of the simmering stock and cook over moderate heat, stirring continuously. When the stock has been absorbed, stir in another ladleful. Continue like this for about 10 minutes, until you have added half the stock.

ADD the remaining red wine to the risotto, stirring continuously until it has been absorbed. Stir in another ladleful of the stock and then continue for about 10 minutes until all the stock has been added and the rice is *al dente*. (You may not need to use all the stock, or you may need a little extra – every risotto will be slightly different.)

STIR IN half the parmesan just before serving with the remaining cheese to be sprinkled on top.

Stir the rice into the butter and onion mixture, making sure that you coat all the grains. Add the red wine and stir continuously so that the rice does not stick to the bottom of the pan and the grains are kept separate.

The history of wine in Italy stretches back thousands of years. The Etruscans may well have enjoyed wine, though it was the Greeks and later the Romans who saw the real potential in Italy for cultivating vines.

FROM ITALY

FAGIOLI ALL'UCCELLETTO

350 g (12 oz) dried cannellini beans
bouquet garni
125 ml (4 fl oz/½ cup) olive oil
2 garlic cloves
1 sprig of sage, or ½ teaspoon dried sage
4 ripe tomatoes, peeled and chopped
1 tablespoon balsamic vinegar

SERVES 6

SOAK the beans in cold water overnight, then drain. Place in a large saucepan of cold water with the bouquet garni and bring to the boil. Add 2 tablespoons of the olive oil, reduce the heat and simmer for 1 hour. Add 1 teaspoon of salt and 500 ml (17 fl oz/2 cups) boiling water and cook for a further 30 minutes, or until tender. Drain.

CUT the garlic cloves in half and put in a large saucepan with the sage and the remaining oil. Gently heat to infuse the flavours, but do not fry. Add the tomato and simmer for 10 minutes, then discard the garlic and the sprig of sage.

ADD the beans, season well and simmer for 15 minutes. Add a little boiling water at first to keep the pan moist, but then let the liquid evaporate towards the end of cooking. Stir the vinegar through just before serving. Serve hot.

The popularity of the bean has spread from its home region of Tuscany (whose inhabitants are affectionately known as the 'bean-eaters') to embrace the whole country. Many varieties of bean are bought dried and need to be soaked overnight before use.

BRAISED BORLOTTI BEANS

THESE BEANS ARE BEST EATEN WARM OR COLD RATHER THAN PIPING HOT STRAIGHT FROM THE STOVE. THEY KEEP WELL IN THE FRIDGE FOR UP TO SIX DAYS, BUT, IF YOU ARE MAKING THEM IN ADVANCE, DON'T ADD THE PARSLEY UNTIL YOU ARE READY TO SERVE.

350 g (12 oz) dried borlotti beans
440 ml (15¼ fl oz/1¾ cups) dry red wine
1 small onion, finely chopped
3 cloves
125 ml (4 fl oz/½ cup) olive oil
1 sprig of rosemary
3 garlic cloves, crushed
pinch of chilli flakes
3 tablespoons chopped parsley

SERVES 6

SOAK the beans in cold water overnight, then drain. Place in a large saucepan and add the wine, onion, cloves, half the olive oil and 875 ml (30 fl oz/3½ cups) water. Cover and bring to the boil. Reduce the heat and simmer, uncovered, for 1 hour.

HEAT the remaining oil in a small saucepan. Strip the leaves off the rosemary sprig and chop finely. Place in the oil with the garlic and chilli and cook for 1 minute. Add to the beans and simmer for 30 minutes to 1 hour, until the beans are tender.

DRAIN the beans, reserving the cooking liquid. Return the cooking liquid to the pan and simmer until it thickens. Season. Return the beans to the pan and simmer for a further 5 minutes. Stir in the parsley and cool for 15 minutes before serving.

BRAISED BORLOTTI BEANS

FAGIOLI ALL'UCCELLETTO

FROM ITALY

BAKED POLENTA WITH FOUR CHEESES

IF YOU HAVE TIME, USE 'PROPER' POLENTA INSTEAD OF THE QUICK-COOK VARIETY. IT MIGHT SEEM LABOUR INTENSIVE, AS YOU HAVE TO STIR CONSTANTLY, BUT THE FLAVOUR IS BETTER. IN ITALY THEY SOLVE THE PROBLEM BY HAVING SPECIAL 'SELF-STIRRING' POLENTA PANS WITH A REVOLVING SPOON.

Arrange the first layer of polenta carefully in the dish but don't worry if you break it – it will seal again as it cooks. Lay the cheese in an even layer on top of the polenta before finishing with the final layers.

POLENTA
1 tablespoon salt
300 g (10½ oz/2 cups) coarse-grain polenta
75 g (2½ oz) butter

TOMATO SAUCE
3 tablespoons olive oil
2 garlic cloves, thinly sliced
15 g (½ oz) rosemary or thyme, roughly chopped
800 g (1 lb 12 oz) tin tomatoes

200 g (7 oz) gorgonzola cheese, cubed
250 g (9 oz) taleggio cheese, cubed
250 g (9 oz) mascarpone cheese
100 g (1 cup) grated parmesan cheese

SERVES 6

BRING 1.5 litres (52 fl oz/6 cups) water to the boil in a heavy-based saucepan and add the salt. Add the polenta to the water in a gentle stream, whisking or stirring vigorously as you pour it in. Reduce the heat immediately so that the water is simmering. Stir continuously for the first 30 seconds to avoid any lumps appearing – the more you stir, the better the texture will be. Once you have stirred well at the beginning you can leave the polenta to mildly bubble away, stirring it every few minutes to prevent it sticking. Cook for 40 minutes. Add the butter and mix well.

POUR the polenta into a shallow casserole or baking tray about 5 cm (2 inches) deep (you want the polenta to come no more than halfway up the side of the dish). Leave to cool completely.

TO MAKE the tomato sauce, heat the olive oil in a saucepan and cook the garlic gently until light brown. Add half the rosemary or thyme and then the tomatoes. Season with salt and pepper and cook gently, stirring occasionally, until reduced to a thick tomato sauce.

PREHEAT the oven to 180°C (350°F/Gas 4). Turn the polenta out of the dish and onto a board, then slice it horizontally in two. Pour half the tomato sauce into the bottom of the empty dish. Place the bottom slice of the polenta on top of the sauce and season. Scatter the gorgonzola and taleggio over the top. Dot the mascarpone over the polenta with a teaspoon, and sprinkle with half the parmesan and the remaining herbs.

PUT the other layer of polenta on top and pour over the remaining tomato sauce. Sprinkle with the remaining parmesan and bake for 30 minutes. Leave to rest for 10 minutes before serving with a simple rocket (arugula) salad.

FROM ITALY

PIZZA SPINACI

- 2 tablespoons olive oil
- 2 garlic cloves, crushed
- 2 tablespoons pine nuts
- 1 kg (2 lb 4 oz) spinach, roughly chopped
- 1 x 30 cm (12 inch) pizza base (see recipe on page 469)
- cornmeal
- 1 quantity tomato sauce (see recipe on page 489)
- 220 g (7¾ oz) mozzarella cheese, chopped
- 15 very small black olives, such as Ligurian
- 3 tablespoons grated parmesan cheese

MAKES ONE PIZZA

PREHEAT the oven to 240°C (475°F/Gas 9). Heat the oil in a frying pan and fry the garlic and pine nuts over low heat until golden. Add the spinach, increase the heat and stir until wilted. Season.

PLACE the pizza base on a baking tray dusted with cornmeal and spoon the tomato sauce onto the base, spreading it up to the rim. Sprinkle with half the mozzarella. Spread the spinach and olives over the top, followed by the rest of the mozzarella and the parmesan.

BAKE for 12–15 minutes, or until golden and puffed. Brush the rim with a little extra olive oil before serving.

Naples in the shadow of Vesuvius.

PIZZA MARGHERITA

THIS CLASSIC PIZZA WAS SUPPOSEDLY INVENTED IN 1889 BY RAFFAELE ESPOSITO IN HONOUR OF QUEEN MARGHERITA. THE QUEEN HAD HEARD SO MUCH OF THE FABLED PIZZAS OF NAPLES THAT SHE REQUESTED ONE TO EAT WHEN SHE VISITED THE CITY.

- 1 x 30 cm (12 inch) pizza base (see recipe on page 469)
- cornmeal
- 1 quantity tomato sauce (see recipe on page 489)
- 150 g (5½ oz) mozzarella cheese, chopped
- 9 small basil leaves
- 1 tablespoon olive oil

MAKES ONE PIZZA

PREHEAT the oven to 240°C (475°F/Gas 9). Place the pizza base on a baking tray dusted with cornmeal and spoon the tomato sauce onto the base, spreading it up to the rim. Scatter with the mozzarella and basil and drizzle with the oil.

BAKE for 12–15 minutes, or until golden and puffed. Remove from the oven and brush the rim with a little extra olive oil before serving.

PIZZA MARGHERITA

PIZZA SPINACI

Fry the eggplant until golden on both sides then layer over the fried potato slices.

FROM SPAIN

BAKED LAYERED VEGETABLES

THE CLASSIC VEGETABLE DISH OF MALLORCA, TUMBET IS EATEN AS A MEAL IN ITS OWN RIGHT, EITHER HOT OR COLD, OR AS AN ACCOMPANIMENT TO DISHES LIKE BAKED LAMPUGA (IN ENGLISH, MAHI MAHI OR DOLPHIN FISH) ENJOYED DURING ITS SHORT MEDITERRANEAN AUTUMN SEASON.

TOMATO SAUCE
2 tablespoons olive oil
3 garlic cloves, crushed
1 red onion, finely chopped
1 kg (2 lb 4 oz) ripe tomatoes, peeled, seeded and chopped (see recipe on page 490)
2 teaspoons chopped thyme

250 ml (9 fl oz/1 cup) olive oil
500 g (1 lb 2 oz) all-purpose potatoes (such as desiree, kipfler or pontiac), cut into 5 mm (¼ inch) rounds
500 g (1 lb 2 oz) eggplants (aubergines), cut into 5 mm (¼ inch) rounds
500 g (1 lb 2 oz) green capsicums (peppers), seeded and cut into 3 cm (1¼ inch) pieces
1 handful flat-leaf (Italian) parsley, roughly chopped
allïoli (see recipe on page 490), to serve (optional)

SERVES 6–8

TO MAKE the tomato sauce, heat the oil in a heavy-based frying pan and cook the garlic and onion over low heat for 6–8 minutes, or until softened. Increase the heat to medium, add the tomato and thyme and cook for 20 minutes, or until thickened. Season to taste. Preheat the oven to 180°C (350°F/Gas 4).

WHILE the sauce is cooking, heat half the oil in a heavy-based frying pan over low heat and cook the potato in batches until tender but not brown. Remove with a slotted spoon or tongs and transfer to a casserole dish measuring about 27 x 21 x 5 cm (10¾ x 8¼ x 2 in). Season lightly.

INCREASE the heat to high and cook the eggplant for 3 minutes each side, or until golden, adding a little more oil as necessary. Drain the slices on paper towel, then arrange on top of the potatoes. Season lightly.

COOK the capsicum in the same pan until tender but not browned, about 5 minutes, adding a little more olive oil as needed. Remove with a slotted spoon, drain on paper towel and arrange over the eggplant. Season lightly. Pour the sauce over the top and bake for 20 minutes, or until hot and bubbling. Serve warm, sprinkled with parsley, to accompany fish or meat, or at room temperature with allïoli.

FROM MOROCCO

TOMATO AND PRESERVED LEMON SALAD

WITH ITS HOT CLIMATE AND FERTILE LAND, MOROCCO PRODUCES TOMATOES THAT ARE RICHLY RED AND LUSCIOUS. THIS SALAD TEMPTS THE PALATE WITH ITS VARIED FLAVOURS. SERVE IT AS AN APPETISER IN THE MOROCCAN MANNER, OR AS AN ACCOMPANIMENT TO CHICKEN OR LAMB.

750 g (1 lb 10 oz) tomatoes
1 red onion
1 preserved lemon (see recipe on page 485)
3 tablespoons olive oil
1 tablespoon lemon juice
½ teaspoon paprika
1 tablespoon finely chopped flat-leaf (Italian) parsley
2 tablespoons finely chopped coriander (cilantro) leaves

SERVES 4

PEEL the tomatoes. To do this, score a cross in the base of each one using a knife. Put the tomatoes in a bowl of boiling water for 20 seconds, then plunge them into a bowl of cold water to cool. Remove from the water and peel the skin away from the cross – it should slip off easily. Cut the tomatoes in half crossways and then squeeze out the seeds. Dice the tomatoes and put them in a bowl.

HALVE the onion lengthways, cut out the root end, slice into slender wedges and add to the bowl.

SEPARATE the preserved lemon into quarters, remove the pulp and membrane and discard them. Rinse the rind under cold running water, pat dry with paper towel and cut into strips. Add to the onion and tomato.

IN a small bowl, beat the oil, lemon juice and paprika, and add ½ teaspoon salt and a good grinding of black pepper. Pour the dressing over the salad, toss lightly, then cover and set aside for 30 minutes. Just before serving, add the parsley and coriander and toss again. If preparing this salad ahead of time, cover the bowl and place in the refrigerator, but bring to room temperature before adding the chopped herbs.

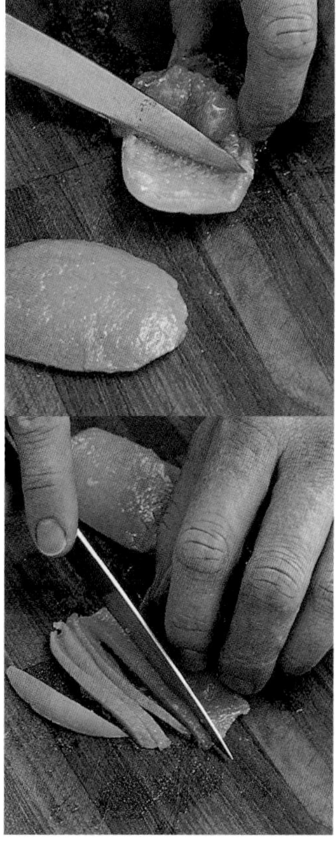

Remove pulp from preserved lemon, rinse rind, pat dry with paper towel and cut into strips.

FROM ITALY

ROMAN GNOCCHI

THESE GNOCCHI CAN BE PREPARED A DAY OR TWO IN ADVANCE, WRAPPED AND STORED IN THE REFRIGERATOR IN THE SLAB FORM OR AS CIRCLES. ROMAN GNOCCHI ARE MADE WITH SEMOLINA AND ARE QUITE DIFFERENT FROM THE MORE WELL-KNOWN POTATO GNOCCHI SERVED WITH PASTA SAUCE.

A biscuit cutter gives a good clean edge to the gnocchi. If you don't have one, use an upturned glass or teacup instead.

This cheesemaker has just opened a whole parmesan. Traditionally parmesan is 'flaked', as shown here, rather than cut.

45 g (1½ oz) unsalted butter, melted
35 g (⅓ cup) grated parmesan cheese
3 egg yolks
1 litre (35 fl oz/4 cups) milk
pinch of ground nutmeg
200 g (7 oz/1⅔ cups) semolina flour

TOPPING
40 g (1½ oz) butter, melted
80 ml (⅓ cup) thick (double/heavy) cream
35 g (⅓ cup) grated parmesan cheese

SERVES 4

LINE a 30 x 25 cm (12 x 10 inch) Swiss roll tin with baking paper. Beat together the butter, parmesan and egg yolks and season lightly. Set aside.

HEAT the milk in a large saucepan. Add the nutmeg, and season with salt and pepper. When the milk is just boiling, pour in the semolina in a steady stream, stirring as you pour. Reduce the heat and continue to cook, stirring, for about 10–12 minutes, or until all the milk has been absorbed and the mixture pulls away from the side of the pan in one mass.

REMOVE the pan from the heat and beat in the egg yolk mixture. When smooth, spoon quickly into the Swiss roll tin. Smooth the surface to give an even thickness, using a knife dipped in cold water. Set aside to cool.

PREHEAT the oven to 180°C (350°F/Gas 4) and grease a 25 x 18 cm (10 x 7 inch) shallow casserole or baking tray.

LIFT the semolina slab out of the tin and peel off the baking paper. Cut the semolina into circles, using a 4 cm (1½ inch) biscuit cutter dipped in cold water. Arrange the circles, slightly overlapping, in the greased casserole.

TO MAKE the topping, blend together the butter and cream. Pour this over the gnocchi and sprinkle the parmesan on top. Transfer to the oven and bake for about 25–30 minutes, or until golden. Serve at once.

FROM MOROCCO

TOMATO, ONION AND CAPSICUM SALAD

THIS SALAD IS MADE EVERY DAY IN HOUSEHOLDS FOR THE MIDDAY MEAL. MOROCCAN CAPSICUMS ARE NOT AS FLESHY AS THE POPULAR CAPSICUMS (SWEET BELL PEPPERS); THEY ARE ELONGATED AND HAVE A SLIGHT PIQUANCY. IF POSSIBLE, USE VINE-RIPENED TOMATOES.

2 green capsicums (peppers)
4 tomatoes
1 red onion
1 garlic clove, finely chopped
1 tablespoon finely chopped flat-leaf (Italian) parsley
80 ml (2½ fl oz/⅓ cup) olive oil
1 tablespoon red wine vinegar

SERVES 4

CUT the capsicums into large flattish pieces and remove the seeds and white membranes. Place the pieces, skin side up, under a grill (broiler) and grill (broil) until the skin blackens. Turn them over and cook for 2–3 minutes on the fleshy side. Remove the cooked capsicum and place in a plastic bag, tuck the end of the bag underneath and leave to steam in the bag until cool enough to handle. Remove the blackened skin and cut the flesh into short strips. Place in a bowl.

PEEL the tomatoes. To do this, score a cross on the base of each one using a knife. Put the tomatoes in a bowl of boiling water for 20 seconds, then plunge into a bowl of cold water to cool. Remove from the water and peel the skin away from the cross – it should slip off easily. Cut the tomatoes in half crossways and squeeze out the seeds. Dice the tomatoes and add to the capsicum. Halve the onion lengthways and remove the root. Cut into slender wedges. Add to the bowl, along with the garlic and parsley.

BEAT the olive oil with the red wine vinegar and add ½ teaspoon salt and a good grinding of black pepper. Pour the dressing over the salad ingredients and toss well.

To peel a tomato, score a cross in the base, plunge into a bowl of boiling water. After 20 seconds, transfer to cold water, then peel off skin and remove stem end as shown. To seed, cut crossways and squeeze out seeds.

FROM ITALY

POTATO AND LEEK GRATIN

- 3 tablespoons butter
- 400 g (14 oz) leeks, trimmed, halved and sliced
- 3 garlic cloves, thinly sliced
- 1 tablespoon chopped thyme
- 1 kg (2 lb 4 oz) all-purpose potatoes, thinly sliced
- 350 g (12 oz) mascarpone cheese
- 250 ml (9 fl oz/1 cup) vegetable stock

SERVES 4

PREHEAT the oven to 180°C (375°F/Gas 4). Heat the butter in a saucepan and cook the leeks for 10 minutes until soft. Season, add the garlic and thyme and cook for a couple of minutes. Grease a 20 cm (8 inch) round gratin dish with butter.

ARRANGE a layer of potato in the base of the dish and season with salt and pepper. Scatter with 3 tablespoons of leek and a few dollops of mascarpone. Continue the layers, finishing with a layer of potato and some mascarpone. Pour the stock over the top and cover with foil.

BAKE for 45 minutes, then remove the foil and bake for a further 15 minutes to brown the top.

POTATO AND PUMPKIN GRATIN

- 450 g (1 lb) all-purpose potatoes, thinly sliced
- leaves from 3 large sprigs of thyme or rosemary, finely chopped
- 700 g (1 lb 9 oz) pumpkin (squash), thinly sliced
- 1 large garlic clove, crushed
- 500 ml (17 fl oz/2 cups) thick (double/heavy) cream

SERVES 4

PREHEAT the oven to 180°C (375°F/Gas 4). Lightly grease a 25 x 23 cm (10 x 9 inch) gratin dish with a little butter. Arrange a layer of potato in the dish, season with salt, pepper and herbs, then top with a layer of pumpkin. Continue the layers, finishing with pumpkin. Mix the garlic with the cream and pour over the top. Cover the dish with buttered foil and bake for about 45 minutes.

TEST TO see if the gratin is cooked by inserting a knife into the centre. If the slices seem soft, it is cooked. Remove the foil and increase the oven temperature to 190°C (375°F/Gas 5). Cook for a further 15 minutes, until there is a good brown crust on top. Leave to rest for at least 10 minutes before serving. Delicious with grilled (broiled) meats or on its own with just a green salad.

POTATO AND PUMPKIN GRATIN

POTATO AND LEEK GRATIN

FROM SPAIN

POOR MAN'S POTATOES

THIS DISH OF CRISP POTATOES AND TENDER CAPSICUM IS SIMPLE TO MAKE AND DELICIOUS, THIS IS ANOTHER RECIPE FROM LA COCINA POBRE – THE CUISINE OF THE POOR – THAT WOULD BE AT HOME ON EVEN THE RICHEST OF TABLES. PARTICULARLY WONDERFUL WHEN SERVED WITH BAKED LAMB.

4 large all-purpose potatoes, such as desiree, approx. 800g (1 lb 12 oz)
250 ml (9 fl oz/1 cup) light olive oil
250 ml (9 fl oz/1 cup) extra virgin olive oil
1 green capsicum (pepper), diced into 2 cm (¾ inch) cubes
1 red onion, diced into 2 cm (¾ inch) cubes

SERVES 4–6

PEEL and cut the potatoes into 1 cm (½ inch) thick slices and soak in cold water for 20 minutes. Drain well and dry on paper towels.

HEAT the oils in a large, deep heavy-based frying pan over medium–high heat. When the oil is hot, add the potatoes and 1 teaspoon salt. Fry on high heat for 10 minutes, rotating and turning potatoes regularly until lightly golden. Reduce heat to low, cover with a lid and cook for 10 minutes or until starting to soften. Add the capsicum and onion, stirring well. Cover and cook a further 10 minutes, stirring occasionally to prevent sticking. Increase heat to high and cook uncovered for another 15 minutes. When cooked the potatoes will be tender and have broken up slightly but will be a little crispy on the edges. Drain well. Season to taste and serve hot.

Add the onion and capsicum to the potatoes when lightly golden.

Chickpeas are grown in the south of Italy but appear in the cuisines of all regions, either whole or ground into *farinata* (flour).

FROM ITALY

PASTA WITH BORLOTTI BEANS

200 g (7 oz/1 cup) dried borlotti beans
2 tablespoons olive oil
100 g (3½ oz) pancetta, diced
1 celery stalk, chopped
1 onion, finely chopped
1 carrot, diced
1 garlic clove, crushed
3 tablespoons chopped parsley
1 bay leaf
400 g (14 oz) tin chopped tomatoes, drained
1.5 litres (52 fl oz/6 cups) vegetable stock
150 g (5½ oz) ditalini or macaroni
drizzle of extra virgin olive oil
grated parmesan cheese

SERVES 4

PLACE the beans in a large saucepan, cover with cold water and soak overnight. Drain and rinse under cold water.

HEAT the olive oil in a large saucepan and add the pancetta, celery, onion, carrot and garlic and cook over moderately low heat for 5 minutes until golden. Season with black pepper. Add the parsley, bay leaf, tomatoes, stock and borlotti beans and bring slowly to the boil. Reduce the heat and simmer for 1–1½ hours, or until the beans are tender, adding a little boiling water every so often to maintain the level.

ADD the pasta and simmer for about 6 minutes, or until the pasta is just *al dente*. Remove from the heat and leave to rest for 10 minutes. Serve warm with a drizzle of extra virgin olive oil over each bowl. Serve the parmesan separately.

PASTA WITH CHICKPEAS

PASTA WITH CHICKPEAS

250 g (9 oz) dried chickpeas
3 tablespoons olive oil
1 large onion, finely chopped
1 celery stalk, finely chopped
1 carrot, finely chopped
2 garlic cloves, crushed
1 sprig of rosemary
pinch of crushed dried chilli
2 tablespoons tomato paste (purée)
1.5 litres (52 fl oz/6 cups) vegetable concentrated stock
125 g (4½ oz) small pasta shells
drizzle of extra virgin olive oil
grated parmesan cheese

SERVES 4

PUT the chickpeas in a large saucepan, cover with cold water and soak overnight. Drain and rinse under cold water.

HEAT the olive oil in a large saucepan, add the chopped vegetables, garlic and rosemary and cook over moderately low heat for 8 minutes. Add the chilli and season. Stir in the tomato paste and stock, then add the chickpeas. Bring to the boil. Reduce the heat and simmer for 1–1½ hours, or until the chickpeas are tender, adding a little boiling water every so often to maintain the level.

ADD the pasta and continue cooking until it is *al dente*. Remove the rosemary sprig. Drizzle with extra virgin olive oil and sprinkle with parmesan.

PASTA WITH BORLOTTI BEANS

H.G.

FROM ITALY

POLENTA WITH WILD MUSHROOMS

POLENTA, MADE FROM COARSE-GROUND CORN, WAS KNOWN AS THE FOOD OF THE POOR IN ROMAN TIMES. TODAY, ESPECIALLY AMONG ITALIANS LIVING ABROAD, IT HAS A WIDE AND LOVING AUDIENCE. SOMETIMES POLENTA IS SO FINE IT IS ALMOST WHITE; MORE OFTEN IT IS GOLDEN YELLOW.

POLENTA
1 tablespoon salt
300 g (10½ oz/2 cups) coarse-grain polenta
50 g (1¾ oz) butter
75 g (2½ oz/¾ cup) grated parmesan cheese

60 ml (2 fl oz/¼ cup) olive oil
400 g (14 oz) selection of wild mushrooms, particularly fresh porcini, sliced if large, or chestnut mushrooms
2 garlic cloves, crushed
1 tablespoon chopped thyme
150 g (5½ oz) mascarpone cheese

SERVES 6

BRING 1.5 litres (52 fl oz/6 cups) water to the boil in a heavy-based saucepan and add the salt. Add the polenta to the water in a gentle stream, whisking or stirring vigorously as you pour it in. Reduce the heat immediately so that the water is simmering. Stir continuously for the first 30 seconds to avoid any lumps appearing – the more you stir, the better the texture will be. Once you have stirred well at the beginning you can leave the polenta to mildly bubble away, stirring it every few minutes to prevent it sticking. Cook for 40 minutes.

MEANWHILE, prepare the mushrooms. Heat the olive oil in a large saucepan or frying pan. When the oil is hot, add just enough mushrooms to cover the base of the pan and cook at quite a high heat, stirring frequently. Season with salt and pepper. Sometimes the mushrooms can become watery when cooked: just keep cooking until all the liquid has evaporated. Add a little of the garlic at the last minute to prevent it burning and then add a little thyme.

REMOVE THIS batch of mushrooms from the pan and repeat the process until they are all cooked. Return all the mushrooms to the pan (if the polenta isn't yet cooked, leave all the mushrooms in the pan and then reheat gently). Add the mascarpone and let it melt into the mushrooms.

ADD the butter and 50 g (1¾ oz/½cup) of the grated parmesan to the cooked polenta and season with pepper. Spoon the polenta onto plates and then spoon the mushrooms on top. Sprinkle with the remaining parmesan and serve immediately.

The fresh porcini is considered the king of mushrooms. Several different varieties are available and appear during the summer and autumn. Porcini are also dried and preserved in oil for the months they are not available.

Cook the onion for the tart slowly to bring out the sweetness.

FROM FRANCE

ONION TART

- 1 quantity tart pastry (see recipe on page 477)
- 50 g (1¾ oz) butter
- 550 g (1 lb 4 oz) onions, finely sliced
- 2 teaspoons thyme leaves
- 3 eggs
- 275 ml (9½ fl oz) thick (double/heavy) cream
- 60 g (2¼ oz) gruyère cheese, grated
- grated nutmeg

SERVES 6

PREHEAT the oven to 180°C (350°F/Gas 4). Line a 23 cm (9½ inch) fluted loose-based tart tin with the pastry. Line the pastry shell with a crumpled piece of baking paper and baking beads (use dried beans or rice if you don't have beads). Blind bake the pastry for 10 minutes, remove the paper and beads and bake for a further 3–5 minutes, or until the pastry is just cooked but still very pale.

MEANWHILE, melt the butter in a small frying pan and cook the onion, stirring, for 10–15 minutes or until tender and lightly browned. Add the thyme leaves and stir well. Leave to cool. Whisk together the eggs and cream and add the cheese. Season with salt, pepper and nutmeg.

SPREAD the onion into the pastry shell and pour the egg mixture over the top. Bake for 35–40 minutes, or until golden brown. Leave in the tin for 5 minutes before serving.

FLAMICHE

A SPECIALITY OF THE PICARDIE REGION, FLAMICHE IS MADE BOTH AS AN OPEN TART AND A CLOSED PIE. YOU WILL USUALLY COME ACROSS IT WITH A LEEK FILLING, AS HERE, BUT IT CAN ALSO BE MADE WITH ONION, PUMPKIN OR SQUASH.

FLAMICHE

- 1 quantity tart pastry (see recipe on page 477)
- 500 g (1 lb 2 oz) leeks, white part only, finely sliced
- 50 g (1¾ oz) butter
- 180 g (6 oz) Maroilles (soft cheese), Livarot or Port-Salut, chopped
- 1 egg
- 1 egg yolk
- 60 ml thick (double/heavy) cream
- 1 egg, lightly beaten

SERVES 6

PREHEAT the oven to 180°C (350°F/Gas 4) and put a baking tray on the top shelf. Use three-quarters of the pastry to line a 23 cm (9½ inch) fluted loose-based tart tin.

COOK the leek for 10 minutes in boiling salted water, then drain. Heat the butter in a frying pan, add the leek and cook, stirring, for 5 minutes. Stir in the cheese. Tip into a bowl and add the egg, egg yolk and cream. Season and mix well.

POUR the filling into the pastry shell and smooth. Roll out the remaining pastry to cover the pie. Pinch the edges together and trim. Cut a hole in the centre and brush egg over the top. Bake for 35–40 minutes on the baking tray until browned. Leave in the tin for 5 minutes before serving.

FROM SPAIN

BARBECUED VEGETABLE SALAD

ESCALIVAR IS A CATALAN VERB MEANING TO COOK IN HOT ASHES OR EMBERS, WHICH IS HOW ESCALIVADA, THIS FLAVOURSOME VEGETABLE SALAD, IS BEST PREPARED. LACKING ASHES OR EMBERS, IT WORKS WELL WHEN COOKED ON A BARBECUE AND ASSEMBLED WITH FRIED CAPERS.

1 red onion
6 small eggplants (aubergines), about 16 cm (6¼ inch) long
4 red capsicums (peppers)
4 orange capsicums (peppers)
1 tablespoon baby capers, rinsed and drained
80 ml (2½ fl oz/⅓ cup) olive oil
1 tablespoon chopped flat-leaf (Italian) parsley
2 garlic cloves, finely chopped

SERVES 4

WITHOUT slicing through the base, cut the red onion from top to bottom into six sections. Put on a barbecue, or over an open-flamed grill or gas stovetop with the eggplants and capsicums. Cook over medium heat for 10 minutes, turning occasionally, until the eggplant and capsicum skins are blackened and blistered. Put the capsicums in a plastic bag for 10 minutes to cool. Set aside the onion and eggplant.

DRY-FRY the capers with a pinch of salt until crisp. Separate the onion into its six sections and discard the charred outer skins. Peel the skins off the eggplants and remove the stalks. Cut the eggplants from top to bottom into slices. Peel the capsicums and remove the seeds. Cut the capsicums into wide slices. Arrange all the vegetables on a large serving platter. Drizzle the olive oil over the top and season with salt and pepper. Scatter the parsley, garlic and capers over the top. Serve cold as a salad or warm as an accompaniment to barbecued meats.

Without cutting right through, section the onion before charring over an open flame.

FROM ITALY

VEGETABLE TORTE

150 g (5½ oz) asparagus
4 tablespoons olive oil
1 onion, chopped
1 zucchini (courgette), halved lengthways and finely sliced
2 large garlic cloves, crushed
100 g (3½ oz) spinach, stalks removed if necessary
1 tablespoon chopped basil
75 g (2½ oz/¾ cup) grated parmesan cheese
250 g (9 oz/1 cup) ricotta cheese
250 g (9 oz) mascarpone cheese
4 eggs

SERVES 4

WASH the asparagus and remove the woody ends (hold each spear at both ends and bend it gently – it will snap at its natural breaking point). Remove the spear tips of the asparagus and slice the remaining stems. Bring a small saucepan of salted water to the boil and cook the asparagus stems for about 2 minutes. Add the tips and cook for 1 minute. Drain the asparagus and set aside.

PREHEAT the oven to 180°C (375°F/Gas 4). Heat the olive oil in a saucepan and cook the onion until soft. Increase the heat and add the zucchini. Cook until the zucchini is soft and golden brown, stirring occasionally. Add garlic and cook for 1 minute more. Finally, add the spinach and mix briefly until just wilted.

REMOVE the pan from the heat, add the asparagus and the basil, season with salt and pepper and set aside to cool.

GREASE a 20 cm (8 inch) springform tin with butter and dust with about 1 tablespoon of the parmesan. Mix together the ricotta, mascarpone, eggs and 50 g (½ cup) of the Parmesan and add it to the cooled vegetables. Mix well and taste for seasoning.

SPOON the mixture into the tin and scatter with the remaining parmesan. Place in the oven, on a tray to catch any drips, and cook for about 30 minutes. The top should be light golden brown and the mixture should still wobble slightly in the centre. Leave to cool for 30 minutes, then chill in the fridge for about 3 hours, until the torte has set. Serve with a simple rocket (arugula) or mixed leaf salad.

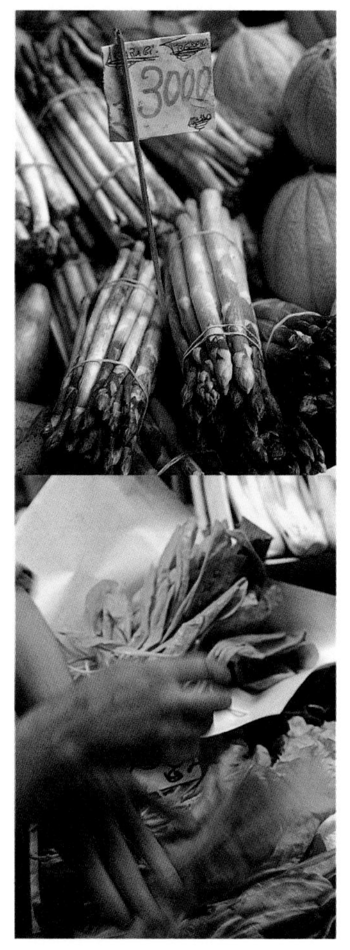

FROM ITALY

RAVIOLI APERTO

FILLING
30 g (1 oz) butter
1 small onion, finely chopped
85 g (3 oz) baby English spinach
250 g (9 oz/1 cup) ricotta cheese
3 tablespoons thick (double/heavy) cream

1 quantity pasta (see recipe on page 470), rolled out
100 g (3½ oz) frozen spinach, thawed
250 ml (9 fl oz/1 cup) chicken stock

SERVES 4

TO MAKE the filling, melt the butter in a frying pan and add the onion. Cook, stirring, for 5 minutes, or until softened. Add the baby spinach leaves and cook for 4 minutes. Remove from the heat, cool to room temperature and then chop. Add the ricotta and 2 tablespoons of the cream and stir well. Season with salt and pepper.

TO MAKE the ravioli, cut the rolled out pasta into sixteen 8 cm (3 inch) squares and cook in a large saucepan of boiling salted water until *al dente*. Drain. Preheat the oven to 180°C (350°F/Gas 4).

LINE a baking tray with baking paper and lay out half the pieces of pasta on the tray. Divide the filling into eight portions and spoon into the centre of each square. Place the other eight pasta sheets on top to enclose the filling and cover with a damp tea towel (dish towel).

TO MAKE a sauce, blend the spinach with a little of the chicken stock until smooth. Transfer to a saucepan with the remaining stock and heat for 2 minutes. Add the remaining cream, stir well, season and remove from the heat.

HEAT the ravioli in the oven for 5 minutes, or until just warm. Place two ravioli on each plate, reheat the sauce gently, pour over the ravioli and serve immediately.

Take time to place the filling carefully in the middle of each pasta square, so it doesn't ooze out of the sides when it cooks.

Combine the tomato and the chickpea mixtures before stirring in the silverbeet.

FROM SPAIN

CHICKPEAS AND SILVERBEET

THIS QUICK AND EASY RECIPE IS GREAT AS AN ACCOMPANIMENT TO A HEAVIER MAIN DISH, OR AS A TASTY, NUTRITIOUS VEGETARIAN ALTERNATIVE, WITH SILVERBEET ADDING A DISTINCTIVE FLAVOUR. POPULAR IN CÁDIZ, ON THE ANDALUCÍAN ATLANTIC COAST, DURING SEMANA SANTA, EASTER.

- 250 g (9 oz) dried chickpeas, soaked in water overnight
- 1 carrot, diced
- 1 sprig flat-leaf (Italian) parsley
- 1 bay leaf
- 2 brown onions, chopped
- 80 ml (2½ fl oz/⅓ cup) extra virgin olive oil
- 1 garlic clove, chopped
- 2 tomatoes, chopped
- 250 g (9 oz) silverbeet (Swiss chard), washed well and chopped
- 2 hard-boiled eggs, peeled and chopped

SERVES 4

DRAIN and rinse the chickpeas and put in a large saucepan with the carrot, parsley, bay leaf and half the chopped onion. Cover with 750 ml (26 fl oz/ 3 cups) of water, bring to the boil and cook for about 20 minutes, or until almost tender. Add 2 teaspoons salt and half the oil and cook for a further 10 minutes.

HEAT the remaining oil in a frying pan over medium heat and cook the remaining onion and the garlic for 5 minutes, or until softened. Add the tomato and cook for 5 minutes. Stir the tomato mixture into the chickpea mixture (it should be wet enough to be saucy but not too soupy). Stir in the silverbeet. Cook for 5 minutes, or until the silverbeet is tender. Season well and serve garnished with the boiled egg.

FROM MOROCCO

CUCUMBER AND OLIVE SALAD

4 Lebanese (short) cucumbers
1 red onion
3 teaspoons caster (superfine) sugar
1 tablespoon red wine vinegar
3 tablespoons olive oil
½ teaspoon finely crumbled dried za'atar, or 1 teaspoon finely chopped lemon thyme
90 g (3¼ oz/½ cup) black olives
flat bread, to serve

SERVES 4

WASH the cucumbers and dry with paper towel. Do not peel the cucumbers if the skins are tender. Coarsely grate the cucumbers, mix the grated flesh with ½ teaspoon salt and leave to drain well.

HALVE the onion and chop it finely. Add to the cucumber, along with the sugar and toss together.

IN A small bowl, beat the red wine vinegar with the olive oil, then add the za'atar, and freshly ground black pepper, to taste. Whisk the ingredients together and pour over the cucumber. Cover and chill for 15 minutes. Scatter with olives and serve with flat bread.

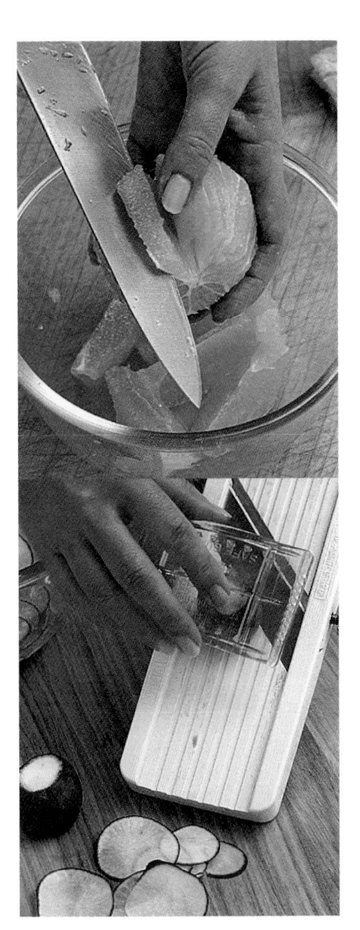

Segment an orange by cutting between membranes. Slice radishes on a mandolin (vegetable slicer).

ORANGE AND RADISH SALAD

3 sweet oranges
12 red radishes
1 tablespoon lemon juice
2 teaspoons caster (superfine) sugar
2 tablespoons olive oil
1 tablespoon orange flower water
ground cinnamon, to serve
small mint leaves, to serve

SERVES 4

CUT off the peel from the oranges using a sharp knife, removing all traces of pith and cutting through the outer membranes to expose the flesh. Holding the oranges over a small bowl to catch the juice, segment them by cutting between the membranes. Remove the seeds from the orange segments, then put the segments in the bowl. Squeeze the remains of the orange into the bowl.

DRAIN the orange segments, reserving the orange juice, and return the drained oranges to the bowl. Set the juice aside.

WASH the radishes and trim off the roots. Slice thinly using a mandolin (vegetable slicer). Add to the orange segments.

PUT 2 tablespoons of the reserved orange juice in a small bowl, add the lemon juice, sugar, olive oil and a pinch of salt. Beat well and pour over the salad. Sprinkle with orange flower water, toss lightly, then cover and chill for 15 minutes. Transfer to a serving bowl, sprinkle the top lightly with cinnamon and scatter with the mint leaves.

ORANGE AND RADISH SALAD

CUCUMBER AND OLIVE SALAD

Arabs were involved in the spice trade for centuries before their foray across North Africa in the late Seventh Century. The spicing skills of Moroccan cooks is the essence of their unique cuisine.

FROM MOROCCO

SPICED LENTILS WITH PUMPKIN

THERE ARE FEW TRULY VEGETARIAN RECIPES IN MOROCCAN COOKING, BUT THIS IS ONE OF THEM, AND A DELICIOUS AND NUTRITIOUS ONE AT THAT. THE EARTHY FLAVOUR OF LENTILS COMBINES WITH THE SWEETNESS OF THE PUMPKIN, THE FLAVOURS MELDING WITH TRADITIONAL HERBS AND SPICES.

275 g (9¾ oz/1½ cups) green lentils
2 tomatoes
600 g (1 lb 5 oz) firm pumpkin (winter squash) or butternut pumpkin (squash)
3 tablespoons olive oil
1 brown onion, finely chopped
3 garlic cloves, finely chopped
½ teaspoon ground cumin
½ teaspoon ground turmeric
¼ teaspoon cayenne pepper, or 1 teaspoon harissa (see recipe on page 482), or to taste
1 teaspoon paprika
3 teaspoons tomato paste (concentrated purée)
½ teaspoon caster (superfine) sugar
1 tablespoon finely chopped flat-leaf (Italian) parsley
2 tablespoons chopped coriander (cilantro) leaves

SERVES 4–6

PICK over the lentils and discard any damaged lentils and any stones. Put the lentils in a sieve and rinse under cold running water. Tip into a saucepan and add 1 litre (35 fl oz/4 cups) cold water. Bring to the boil, skim the surface if necessary, then cover and simmer over low heat for 20 minutes.

MEANWHILE, halve the tomatoes crossways and squeeze out the seeds. Coarsely grate the tomatoes into a bowl down to the skin, discarding the skin. Set the grated tomato aside. Peel and seed the pumpkin and cut into 3 cm (1¼ inch) dice. Set aside.

HEAT the oil in a large saucepan over low heat, add the onion and cook until softened. Add the garlic, cook for a few seconds, then stir in the cumin, turmeric and cayenne pepper or harissa. Cook for 30 seconds, then add the paprika, grated tomato, tomato paste, sugar, half of the parsley and coriander, 1 teaspoon salt and freshly ground black pepper, to taste.

ADD the lentils and the prepared pumpkin, stir well, then cover and simmer for about 20 minutes, or until the pumpkin and lentils are tender. Adjust the seasoning and transfer to a serving bowl. Sprinkle with the remaining parsley and coriander leaves and serve hot or warm with crusty bread.

FROM SPAIN

GREEN BEANS IN TOMATO SAUCE

300 g (10½ oz) green beans, trimmed
1 tablespoon olive oil
1 brown onion, finely chopped
2 garlic cloves, finely chopped
1 tablespoon sweet paprika (pimentón)
¼ teaspoon chilli flakes
1 bay leaf, crushed
400 g (14 oz) tinned chopped tomatoes
2 tablespoons chopped flat-leaf (Italian) parsley

SERVES 4

COOK the beans in boiling water for 3–5 minutes, or until tender. Drain and set aside.

HEAT the olive oil in a frying pan, add the onion and cook over medium heat for 5 minutes, or until soft. Add the garlic and cook for 1 minute. Add the paprika, chilli flakes and bay leaf, cook for 1 minute, then stir in the tomato. Simmer over medium heat for 15 minutes, or until reduced and pulpy. Add the beans and parsley and cook for 1 minute, or until warmed through. Season to taste. Serve warm or at room temperature.

SILVERBEET WITH RAISINS AND PINE NUTS

500 g (1 lb 2 oz) silverbeet (Swiss chard) or English spinach
2 tablespoons pine nuts
1 tablespoon olive oil
1 small red onion, halved and sliced
1 garlic clove, thinly sliced
2 tablespoons raisins
pinch of ground cinnamon

SERVES 6

TRIM the stalks from the silverbeet, then wash the leaves and shred them.

PUT the pine nuts in a frying pan and stir over medium heat for 3 minutes, or until lightly brown. Remove from the pan.

HEAT the oil in the pan, add the onion and cook over low heat, stirring occasionally, for 10 minutes, or until softened. Increase the heat to medium, add the garlic and cook for 1 minute. Add the silverbeet with the water clinging to it, the raisins and cinnamon. Cover and cook for 2 minutes, or until the silverbeet wilts. Stir in the pine nuts, season to taste and serve.

SILVERBEET WITH RAISINS AND PINE NUTS

GREEN BEANS IN TOMATO SAUCE

SEAFOOD

FROM ITALY

SEAFOOD RISOTTO

AS WITH MOST SEAFOOD DISHES, DON'T SERVE THIS RISOTTO WITH PARMESAN. IN LOMBARDIA AND PIEMONTE, RISOTTO IS CREAMY BUT THE GRAINS RETAIN A 'BITE'. VENETIANS MAKE THEIR RISOTTOS ALL'ONDA, ALMOST LIQUID LIKE SOUPS, TO BE EATEN WITH A SPOON. YOU CAN CHOOSE EITHER STYLE.

175 g (6 oz) squid tubes
200 g (7 oz) prawns (shrimp)
4 tablespoons olive oil
2 garlic cloves, crushed
175 g (6 oz) firm white fish fillets, such as monkfish, sea bass or fresh haddock, skinned and cut into bite-sized pieces
16 scallops, cleaned
1 litre (35 fl oz/4 cups) fish stock
1 leek, white part only, thinly sliced
360 g (13 fl oz/1⅔ cups) risotto rice (arborio, vialone nano or carnaroli)
125 ml (4 fl oz/½ cup) dry white wine
3 roma (plum) tomatoes, chopped
1 tablespoon butter
1½ tablespoons finely chopped parsley
1½ tablespoons finely chopped dill

SERVES 4

CUT the squid tubes into thinner rings. Peel and devein the prawns.

HEAT HALF the olive oil in a large wide heavy-based saucepan. Add the garlic and cook gently without browning for 20–30 seconds. Add the squid and prawns and season lightly. Increase heat and cook until they turn opaque. Remove squid and prawns from the pan and set aside.

ADD the fish and scallops to the pan and cook until they change colour. Remove from the pan and set aside.

PUT stock in a saucepan, bring to the boil and then maintain at a low simmer.

ADD the remaining olive oil to the large wide pan. Add the leek and cook for 3–4 minutes, or until softened but not browned. Add rice and reduce heat to low. Season and stir briefly to thoroughly coat the rice, then add the white wine. Increase the heat and cook, stirring, until all the liquid has been absorbed.

STIR IN a ladleful of simmering stock. Cook over a moderate heat, stirring continuously. When the stock has been absorbed, stir in another ladleful. Continue like this for about 20 minutes, until all the stock has been added and the rice is just tender. (You may not need to use all the stock, or you may need a little extra. Every risotto is slightly different. If you prefer, add more stock to make the risotto more liquid.) Add the tomato and cooked seafood and toss lightly.

REMOVE the saucepan from the heat and gently stir in the butter and chopped herbs. Season with salt and black pepper. Spoon into warm serving bowls and serve at once.

Cooking the seafood quickly over a high heat keeps it tender.

FROM ITALY

LIGURIAN FISH STEW

THE FISH SUGGESTIONS BELOW ARE MERELY A GUIDELINE. TAKE YOUR FISHMONGER'S ADVICE ON WHAT IS FRESH AND SEASONAL. ASK FOR THE FISH TO BE PREPARED AND CUT INTO LARGE CHUNKS, THOUGH YOU WILL NEED THE BONES FOR YOUR STOCK (THIS CAN BE MADE IN ADVANCE AND FROZEN).

Skim the froth from the surface of the fish stock as it simmers.

FISH STOCK

250 g (9 oz) red mullet or red snapper fillet, cut into chunks, bones reserved
250 g (9 oz) cod, halibut or turbot fillet, cut into chunks, bones reserved
250 g (9 oz) monkfish fillet, or other firm white fish, cut into chunks, bones reserved
6 large prawns (shrimp) or langoustines
1 small onion, roughly chopped
1 carrot, roughly chopped
15 g (½ oz) flat-leaf (Italian) parsley, roughly chopped, stalks reserved

125 ml (4 fl oz/½ cup) olive oil
1 red onion, halved and thinly sliced
1 large fennel bulb, thinly sliced
3 garlic cloves, thinly sliced
800 g (1 lb 12 oz) tin tomatoes
310 ml (11 fl oz/1¼ cups) dry white vermouth or wine
large pinch of saffron threads
450 g (1 lb) waxy potatoes, quartered lengthways
450 g (1 lb) mussels

SERVES 6

TO MAKE fish stock, rinse the fish bones in cold water, removing any blood or intestines. Peel and devein the prawns and put the fish bones and prawn shells in a large saucepan with just enough water to cover. Bring slowly to a simmer, skimming any froth from the surface. Add the onion, carrot and the stalks from the parsley, then simmer gently for 20 minutes. Strain through a fine colander and measure 1 litre (35 fl oz/4 cups) stock. If there is more, put strained stock back into the saucepan and simmer until reduced to 1 litre (35 fl oz/4 cups).

TO MAKE the soup base, heat the olive oil in a large saucepan and cook the onion and fennel for about 5 minutes to soften. Add the garlic and tomatoes. Bring to the boil, then reduce the heat and simmer until the tomatoes have reduced to a thick sauce. Season and add 200 ml (7 fl oz) of the vermouth, the saffron and potatoes. Increase the heat and boil for about 5 minutes, then add the fish stock, reduce the heat and simmer for 10 minutes, or until the potatoes are cooked.

SCRUB the mussels, pull off the beards and discard any that are broken or cracked or don't close when tapped on the work surface. Bring the remaining vermouth to the boil in another saucepan and add the mussels. Cover with a lid and cook quickly for about 1 minute, or until the shells have just opened (discard any that stay closed). Remove mussels from their shells and place in a bowl. Pour over the remaining cooking liquid, discarding any sediment left in the pan.

ADD the prawns and fish to the soup. Stir briefly, season and simmer for 5 minutes, until the fish is cooked. Add the mussels at the last moment to reheat. Remove from the heat and leave for at least 10 minutes before serving. Add the parsley and serve in hot bowls with bread or crostini.

Monkfish being skinned in the Vucciria market in Palermo.

FROM MOROCCO

SAFFRON FISH BALLS IN TOMATO SAUCE

THIS RECIPE WAS DEVISED BY MOROCCAN JEWS, WHO WERE ALSO THE PRINCIPAL GATHERERS OF THE SAFFRON CROCUS WHEN IT WAS INTRODUCED FROM MOORISH SPAIN. IT IS BASED ON THEIR TRADITIONAL RECIPE FOR FISH BALLS, BUT WITH DISTINCTIVE MOROCCAN FLAVOURS.

500 g (1 lb 2 oz) boneless firm white fish fillets
1 egg
2 spring onions (scallions), chopped
1 tablespoon chopped flat-leaf (Italian) parsley
1 tablespoon chopped coriander (cilantro) leaves
55 g (2 oz/2⁄3 cup) fresh breadcrumbs
small pinch saffron threads

TOMATO SAUCE
500 g (1 lb 2 oz) tomatoes
1 brown onion, coarsely grated
3 tablespoons olive oil
2 garlic cloves, finely chopped
1 teaspoon paprika
½ teaspoon harissa (see recipe on page 482), or to taste, or ¼ teaspoon cayenne pepper
½ teaspoon ground cumin
1 teaspoon caster (superfine) sugar

SERVES 4

CUT the fish fillets into rough pieces and put in a food processor bowl, along with the egg, spring onion, parsley, coriander and breadcrumbs. Soak the saffron in 1 tablespoon warm water for 5 minutes and add to the other ingredients with ¾ teaspoon salt and some freshly ground black pepper. Process to a thick paste, scraping down the sides of the bowl occasionally.

WITH moistened hands, shape the fish mixture into balls the size of a walnut. Put on a tray, cover and set aside in the refrigerator.

TO MAKE the tomato sauce, first peel tomatoes by scoring a cross in the base of each one. Put them in a bowl of boiling water for 20 seconds, then plunge into a bowl of cold water to cool. Remove from the water and peel the skin away from the cross – it should slip off easily. Halve the tomatoes crossways and squeeze out the seeds. Chop the tomatoes and set aside.

PUT the onion and olive oil in a saucepan and cook over medium heat for 5 minutes. Add the garlic, paprika, harissa and cumin. Stir for a few seconds, then add the tomato, sugar, 250 ml (9 fl oz/1 cup) water, and salt and freshly ground black pepper, to taste. Bring to the boil, cover, reduce heat and simmer for 15 minutes.

ADD the fish balls to the tomato sauce, shaking the pan occasionally as they are added so that they settle into the sauce. Return to a gentle boil over medium heat, then cover and reduce heat to low. Simmer for 20 minutes. Serve hot with crusty bread.

A small pinch of saffron is all that is required to impart the spice's flavour and aroma to these delicious fish balls.

FROM FRANCE

LOBSTER THERMIDOR

LOBSTER THERMIDOR WAS CREATED FOR THE FIRST-NIGHT CELEBRATIONS OF A PLAY CALLED 'THERMIDOR' IN PARIS IN 1894. TRADITIONALLY THE LOBSTER IS CUT IN HALF WHILE ALIVE, BUT FREEZING IT FIRST IS MORE HUMANE.

- 2 live lobsters
- 250 ml (9 fl oz/1 cup) fish stock
- 2 tablespoons white wine
- 2 shallots, finely chopped
- 2 teaspoons chopped chervil
- 2 teaspoons chopped tarragon
- 125 g (4 oz) butter
- 2 tablespoons plain (all-purpose) flour
- 1 teaspoon dry mustard
- 250 ml (9 fl oz/1 cup) milk
- 60 g (3¼ oz) parmesan grated, grated

SERVES 4

PUT lobsters in the freezer an hour before you want to cook them. Bring a large pan of water to the boil, drop in the lobsters and cook for 10 minutes. Drain and cool slightly before cutting off the heads. Cut lobster tails in half lengthways. Use a spoon to ease the lobster meat out of the shells and cut it into bite-sized pieces. Rinse the shells, pat dry and keep for serving.

PUT the stock, wine, shallot, chervil and tarragon into a small saucepan. Boil until reduced by half and then strain.

MELT 60 g (2 oz) of the butter in a heavy-based saucepan and stir in the flour and mustard to make a roux. Cook, stirring, for 2 minutes over low heat without allowing the roux to brown.

REMOVE from the heat and add the milk and the reserved stock mixture gradually, stirring after each addition until smooth. Return to the heat and stir constantly until sauce boils and thickens. Simmer, stirring occasionally, for 3 minutes. Stir in half the parmesan. Season with salt and freshly ground black pepper.

HEAT the remaining butter in a frying pan and fry the lobster over moderate heat for 2 minutes until lightly browned. Take care not to overcook. Preheat the grill (broiler).

DIVIDE half the sauce among the lobster shells, top with the lobster meat and then finish with the remaining sauce. Sprinkle with the remaining parmesan and place under the grill until golden brown and bubbling. Serve immediately.

Fry the lobster in butter until it is lightly browned. Take care not to overcook or it will toughen. Spoon lobster and sauce into the cleaned shells for serving.

FROM SPAIN

CLAMS IN WHITE WINE

WHAT COULD BE SIMPLER AND MORE DELICIOUS THAN FRESH CLAMS STEAMED OPEN IN WHITE WINE AND GARLIC, THE FLAVOURS MINGLING WITH THE CLAMS' OWN JUICES OF THE SEA? TRY THIS MODERN VERSION OF ALMEJAS A LA MARINERA FROM CANTABRIA, ON THE NORTHERN COAST.

1 kg (2 lb 4 oz) clams (vongole)
2 tablespoons olive oil
1 small onion, finely chopped
2 garlic cloves, crushed
2 large ripe tomatoes, peeled, seeded and chopped (see recipe on page 490)
1 tablespoon chopped flat-leaf (Italian) parsley
pinch of ground nutmeg
80 ml (2½ fl oz/⅓ cup) dry white wine

SERVES 4

SOAK the clams in salted water for 2 hours to release any grit. Rinse under running water and discard any open clams.

HEAT the oil in a large flameproof casserole dish and cook the onion over low heat for 8 minutes, or until softened. Add the garlic and tomato and cook for 5 minutes. Stir in parsley and nutmeg and season with salt and pepper. Add 80 ml (2½ fl oz/⅓ cup) of water.

ADD the clams and cook, covered, over low heat for 5–8 minutes or until they open (discard any that do not open). Add the wine and cook for about 3 minutes, or until sauce thickens, gently moving the dish back and forth a few times, rather than stirring, so that the clams stay in their shells. Serve immediately, with bread.

In the Rias Baixas region of Galicia, the classic white wine of Spain is made using the Albariño grape.

FROM SPAIN

SARDINES MURCIA STYLE

ALL ALONG THE MURCIAN COAST, IN SPAIN'S SOUTH-EAST, SARDINES ARE LANDED AND TRANSPORTED, STILL FLAPPING, TO KITCHENS ALONG THE SEAFRONT. WITH SEAFOOD, FRESHNESS IS PARAMOUNT, BUT THIS IS ESPECIALLY SO FOR SPAIN'S MUCH-LOVED SARDINA.

- 24 fresh large sardines, cleaned, with backbones, heads and tails removed
- 1 kg (2 lb 4 oz) ripe tomatoes, peeled and seeded (see recipe on page 490)
- 2 green capsicums (peppers), cored, seeded and cut into thin rings
- 1 white onion, sliced into thin rings
- 2 all-purpose potatoes, cut into 5 mm (¼ inch) slices
- 2 tablespoons chopped flat-leaf (Italian) parsley
- 3 garlic cloves, crushed
- ¼ teaspoon saffron threads, lightly toasted
- 2 tablespoons olive oil
- chopped flat-leaf (Italian) parsley, extra, to garnish

SERVES 6

PREHEAT oven to 180°C (350°F/Gas 4). Lightly oil a large, shallow earthenware or ceramic baking dish wide enough for the length of the sardines. Open out the sardines. Lightly sprinkle the insides with salt. Fold them back into their original shape.

CUT each prepared tomato into thin slices. Cover base of dish with a third of the tomato slices. Layer half the sardines on top. Follow with a layer of half the capsicum, then half the onion, then half the potato. Sprinkle on half the parsley and garlic, and season with freshly ground black pepper. Crumble half the saffron over the top.

LAYER the remaining sardines, half the remaining tomatoes and then the other ingredients as before. Finish with the last of the tomatoes. Season well with salt and freshly ground black pepper. Drizzle oil over the surface and cover with foil. Bake for 1 hour, or until potatoes are cooked. Spoon off any excess liquid, sprinkle with parsley and serve straight from the dish.

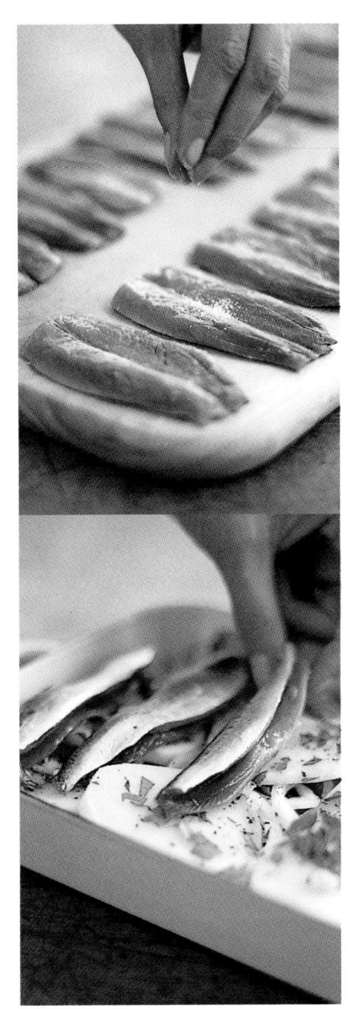

Sprinkle the salt over the cleaned sardines before layering with the vegetables.

FROM SPAIN

ALMOND-CRUSTED FISH WITH PRUNES

NORMALLY THIS RECIPE USES WHOLE FISH STUFFED WITH PRUNES, COATED WITH A GROUND-ALMOND MIXTURE AND BAKED. FISH PIECES PAN-FRIED WORKS JUST AS WELL, PROVIDING CARE IS TAKEN THAT THE CRUST DOES NOT BURN.

- 4 x 200 g (7 oz) firm white fish fillets, such as blue eye, snapper, hake or sea bass
- 24 pitted prunes
- 24 blanched almonds, lightly toasted
- 30 g (1 oz) butter
- 2 brown onions, sliced
- ¾ teaspoon ground ginger
- ¾ teaspoon ground cinnamon
- ⅛ teaspoon freshly ground black pepper
- ⅛ teaspoon ground saffron threads
- 1½ teaspoons caster (superfine) sugar
- 3 teaspoons lemon juice
- 3 teaspoons orange flower water
- 1 egg
- 100 g (3½ oz/1 cup) ground almonds
- 4 tablespoons ghee (clarified butter)
- lemon wedges, to serve

SERVES 4

CHOOSE centre-cut fish fillets no more than 3 cm (1¼ inch) thick at the thickest part. Remove the skin (if present) and season lightly with salt. Cover and refrigerate until ready to use. Stuff each prune with a whole toasted almond and set aside.

MELT the butter in a frying pan and add the onion. Cook for 10 minutes over low heat, stirring often, until the onion is soft and golden. Add ½ teaspoon each of the ground ginger and cinnamon, a pinch of salt and the black pepper. Stir for 30 seconds or until fragrant. Pour in 250 ml (9 fl oz/1 cup) water and stir in the saffron. Cover and simmer gently for 5 minutes, then add the stuffed prunes, sugar, lemon juice and orange flower water. Stir gently. Cover and simmer for 15 minutes, or until prunes are plump.

MEANWHILE, beat the egg in a shallow dish with ¼ teaspoon each of ground ginger, cinnamon and salt. Spread the ground almonds in a flat dish. Dip the fish into the beaten egg, drain briefly, and coat on all sides with the ground almonds. Place on a tray lined with baking paper.

MELT the ghee in a large non-stick frying pan over medium–high heat (the depth of the ghee should be about 5 mm/¼ inch). Add coated fish, reduce the heat to medium and cook for 2 minutes, then turn and cook for a further 2 minutes, or until golden and just cooked through. Do not allow the almond coating to burn. If you have to remove the fish before it is cooked through, place it on top of the onion and prune mixture, cover and simmer gently for 2–3 minutes, taking care that the coating does not become too moist on top. Serve the fish immediately with the onion and prune sauce, with lemon wedges to squeeze over the fish.

Prunes are stuffed with whole almonds for the sauce. The fish is coated with ground almonds.

FROM SPAIN

PRAWNS WITH ROMESCO SAUCE

THIS CLASSIC CATALAN SAUCE IS FROM THE TOWN OF TARRAGONA, BEST MADE WITH THE ROMESCO OR NYORA CAPSICUM (PEPPER), THOUGH ANCHO CHILLIES OR ANY DRIED CAPSICUM WILL ALSO WORK WELL. ROMESCO SAUCE IS FAMED AS THE BASIS OF CATALAN SEAFOOD STEW.

30 raw large prawns (shrimp)
1 tablespoon olive oil

ROMESCO SAUCE
4 garlic cloves, unpeeled
1 roma (plum) tomato, halved and seeded
2 long red chillies
2 tablespoons whole blanched almonds
2 tablespoons hazelnuts
60 g (2 oz) sun-dried capsicums (peppers) in oil
1 tablespoon olive oil
1 tablespoon red wine vinegar

SERVES 6–8

PEEL prawns, leaving the tails intact. Cut down the back and gently pull out the dark vein, starting at the head end. Mix the prawns with ¼ teaspoon salt and refrigerate for 30 minutes.

TO MAKE the romesco sauce, preheat the oven to 200°C (400°F/Gas 6). Wrap the garlic cloves in foil, put on a baking tray with the tomato and chillies and bake for about 12 minutes. Spread almonds and hazelnuts on the tray and bake for another 3–5 minutes. Leave to cool for 15 minutes. Peel the skin off the tomato.

TRANSFER the almonds and hazelnuts to a small blender or food processor and blend until finely ground. Squeeze the garlic, and the tomato flesh, into the blender, discarding the skins. Split chillies and remove the seeds. Scrape the flesh into the blender, discarding the skins. Pat capsicums dry with paper towel, then chop them and add to the blender with the oil, vinegar, some salt and 2 tablespoons water. Blend until smooth, adding more water, if necessary, to form a soft dipping consistency. Set aside for 30 minutes.

HEAT the olive oil in a frying pan over high heat and cook the prawns for 5 minutes, or until curled up and slightly pink. Serve with the sauce.

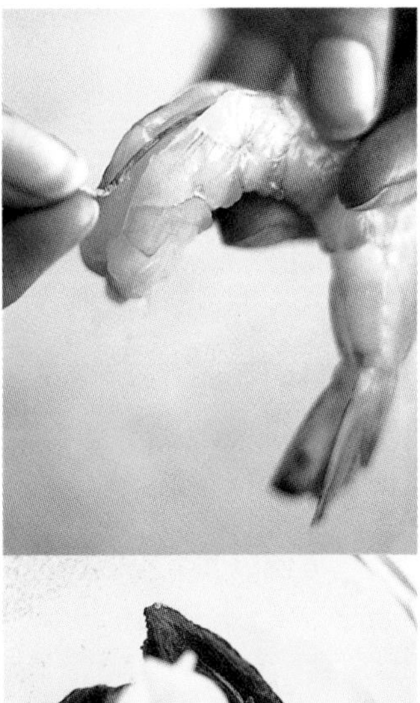

Make sure the skins are removed from the tomato and chillies for a smoother sauce.

Brushing the fish with oil prevents the skin from drying out while it bakes and helps the seasoning to stick to the fish skin.

FROM ITALY

RED MULLET WITH FENNEL

2 fennel bulbs
2 tablespoons butter
2 tablespoons olive oil
1 onion, chopped
1 garlic clove, crushed
4 red mullet, gutted and scaled
extra virgin olive oil
1 lemon, quartered
2 teaspoons chopped oregano, or ½ teaspoon dried oregano
lemon wedges

SERVES 4

PREHEAT the oven to 190°C (375°F/Gas 5) and grease a large shallow ovenproof dish. Finely slice the fennel, keeping the green fronds.

HEAT the butter and olive oil in a large frying pan and gently cook the fennel, onion and garlic for 12–15 minutes until softened but not browned. Season with salt and pepper.

STUFF EACH fish with a heaped tablespoon of the fennel mixture and a quarter of the fennel fronds. Brush with extra virgin olive oil, squeeze a lemon quarter over each one and season well.

SPOON the remainder of the cooked fennel into the dish and sprinkle with half of the oregano. Arrange the fish, side by side, on top. Sprinkle the remaining oregano over the fish and cover the dish loosely with foil. Bake for 25 minutes, or until just cooked through. Serve with lemon wedges.

BAKED SWORDFISH SICILIANA

BAKED SWORDFISH SICILIANA

FISHED MAINLY OFF THE COAST OF SICILY, SWORDFISH HAS A FIRM MEATY TEXTURE. WHILE MANY MORE DELICATE FISH WOULD BE OVERPOWERED BY THE STRONG MEDITERRANEAN FLAVOURS OF THIS DISH, THE MORE ROBUST FLESH OF THE SWORDFISH CAN HOLD ITS OWN. YOU CAN ALSO USE TUNA.

80 ml (2½ fl oz/⅓ cup) olive oil
2 tablespoons lemon juice
2½ tablespoons finely chopped basil
4 swordfish steaks
60 g (2 oz) pitted black olives, chopped
1 tablespoon baby capers
¼ teaspoon finely chopped anchovies in olive oil
400 g (14 oz) tomatoes, peeled, seeded and chopped
2 tablespoons dried breadcrumbs

SERVES 4

MIX half the olive oil with the lemon juice and 1 tablespoon of the basil. Season and pour into a shallow ovenproof dish, large enough to hold the swordfish in a single layer. Place swordfish in the dish and leave to marinate for 15 minutes, turning once. Preheat oven to 230°C (450°F/Gas 8) and preheat the grill (broiler).

COMBINE olives, capers, anchovies and tomatoes with the remaining olive oil and basil and season well. Spread over the swordfish and sprinkle the breadcrumbs over the top. Bake for 20 minutes, or until the fish is just opaque. Finish off by placing briefly under the hot grill (broiler) until breadcrumbs are crisp. Serve with bread to soak up the juices.

FROM SPAIN

BACALAO WITH RED CAPSICUM

CERTAIN COMBINATIONS OF INGREDIENTS NATURALLY WORK WELL TOGETHER. ONE SUCH COMBINATION IS THAT OF BACALAO (SALT COD) AND RED CAPSICUM (PEPPER) AND TOMATOES, AS THIS DISH HAPPILY PROVES. IT'S FOUND, IN VARIOUS FORMS, ON TABLES RIGHT THROUGHOUT SPAIN.

800 g (1 lb 12 oz) bacalao (salt cod)
2 tablespoons olive oil
1 large white onion, chopped
3 garlic cloves, crushed
½ teaspoon dried chilli flakes
2 teaspoons sweet paprika (pimentón)
125 ml (4 fl oz/½ cup) dry white wine
4 ripe tomatoes, finely chopped
2 tablespoons tomato paste (concentrated purée)
2 red capsicums (pepper), roasted and cut into strips (see recipe on page 490)
2 tablespoons chopped flat-leaf (Italian) parsley

SERVES 6

SOAK the bacalao in plenty of cold water for about 20 hours in the fridge, changing the water four or five times to remove excess saltiness.

ADD the cod to a saucepan of simmering water and poach it gently for 35 minutes. Drain and leave for 10 minutes, or until cool enough to handle. Remove the skin and flake the fish into large pieces, removing any bones. Transfer to a bowl.

HEAT the oil in a saucepan over medium heat, add the onion and cook, stirring occasionally, for 5 minutes, or until softened. Add the garlic, chilli flakes and paprika and cook for 1 minute. Increase the heat to high, add the white wine and simmer for 30 seconds. Reduce the heat, add the tomato and tomato paste and cook, stirring occasionally, for 5 minutes, or until thick.

ADD the bacalao, cover and simmer for about 5 minutes to heat through. Gently stir in the sliced capsicum and parsley and taste before seasoning with salt. Serve hot.

FROM FRANCE

CRAB SOUFFLÉS

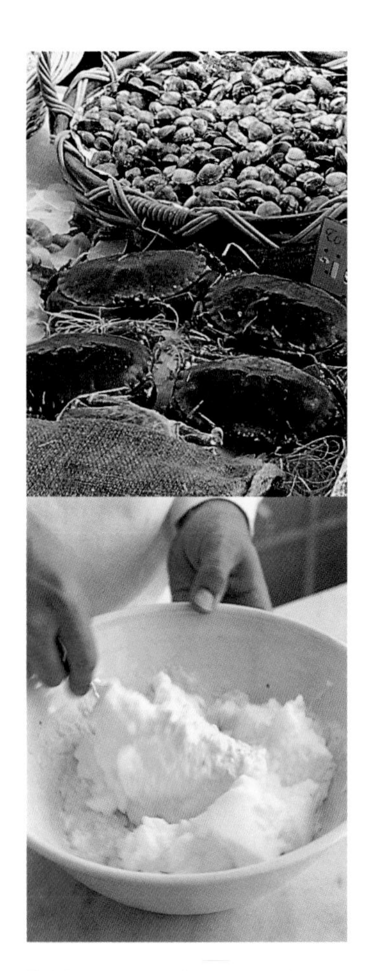

Fold a quarter of the egg white into the soufflé mixture to loosen it up before you add the rest.

Unloading the catch in Marseille.

15 g (½ oz) butter, melted
2 cloves
1/4 small onion
1 bay leaf
6 black peppercorns
250 ml (9 fl oz/1 cup)milk
15 g (½ oz) butter
1 shallot, finely chopped
15 g (½ oz) plain (all-purpose) flour
3 egg yolks
250 g (9 oz) cooked crabmeat
pinch of cayenne pepper
5 egg whites

SERVES 6

PREHEAT the oven to 200°C (400°F/Gas 6). Brush six 125 ml (4 fl oz/½ cup) ramekins with the melted butter.

PRESS the cloves into the onion, then put in a small saucepan with the bay leaf, peppercorns and milk. Gently bring to the boil, then remove from the heat and leave to infuse for 10 minutes. Strain the milk.

MELT butter in a heavy-based saucepan, add the shallot and cook, stirring, for 3 minutes until softened but not browned. Stir in the flour to make a roux and cook, stirring, for 3 minutes over low heat without allowing the roux to brown.

REMOVE from the heat and add the infused milk gradually, stirring after each addition until smooth. Return to the heat and simmer for 3 minutes, stirring continuously. Beat in the egg yolks, one at a time, beating well after each addition. Add the crabmeat and stir over the heat until the mixture is hot and thickens again (do not let it boil). Pour into a large heatproof bowl, then add the cayenne and season well.

WHISK the egg whites in a clean dry bowl until they form soft peaks. Spoon a quarter of the egg white onto the soufflé mixture and quickly but lightly fold it in, to loosen the mixture. Lightly fold in the remaining egg white. Pour into the ramekins and then run your thumb around the inside rim of each ramekin. This ridge helps the soufflés to rise evenly without sticking.

PUT ramekins on a baking tray and bake for 12–15 minutes, or until the soufflés are well risen and wobble slightly when tapped. Test with a skewer through a crack in the side of a soufflé. The skewer should come out clean or slightly moist. If the skewer is slightly moist, by the time the soufflés make it to the table they will be cooked in the centre. Serve immediately.

FROM ITALY

STUFFED SARDINES

TO MAKE A SARDINE DISH MEMORABLE THE FISH MUST BE REALLY FRESH. SARDINES, LIKE MACKEREL, DO NOT LAST LONG OUT OF THE WATER SO DON'T ATTEMPT THIS RECIPE IF THE FISH LOOK TIRED. THIS RECIPE WILL SERVE TWO AS A MAIN COURSE OR FOUR AS AN ANTIPASTO.

8 medium-sized sardines, heads removed, scaled and gutted
4 tablespoons olive oil
1 small onion, thinly sliced
1 fennel bulb, thinly sliced
50 g (1¾ oz/½ cup) pine nuts
4 tablespoons parsley, roughly chopped
20 g (¾ oz/¼ cup) fresh breadcrumbs
1 large garlic clove, crushed
juice of ½ lemon
extra virgin olive oil
lemon wedges, to serve

SERVES 4

BUTTERFLY the sardines by pressing your fingers on either side of the backbone and gently easing it away from the flesh, following the line of the bone. Remove the bone, leaving the tail attached to the flesh for a more attractive look. The fresher the fish, the harder this is to do, so you might want to ask your fishmonger to butterfly the sardines for you. (Alternatively, use fillets and put them back together to form a whole after cooking, although the result will not be as neat.) Rinse fish in cold water and drain on paper towels. Leave in the fridge until needed.

PREHEAT the oven to 200°C (400°F/Gas 6). To prepare stuffing, heat olive oil in a frying pan and add the onion, fennel and pine nuts. Cook over moderately high heat until soft and light brown, stirring frequently. Mix 1 tablespoon of parsley with 1 tablespoon of breadcrumbs. Set aside. Add garlic and remaining breadcrumbs to the pan. Cook for a few minutes more. Add the rest of the parsley, season and set aside. (Mixture can be made in advance and kept in the fridge. Bring back to room temperature before cooking.)

DRIZZLE a little olive oil in an ovenproof dish that will fit eight sardines in a single layer. Arrange the fish in the dish, skin side down, and season with salt and pepper. Spread stuffing over the sardines and fold over to encase. (If you are using fillets, spread half of them with stuffing, then place the other fillets on top, skin side up, tail to tail like a sandwich.) Season again and sprinkle with the parsley and breadcrumb mixture. Drizzle with the lemon juice and a little extra virgin olive oil.

BAKE for 5–10 minutes, depending on the size of the sardines. (If filling is still warm, the sardines will cook faster.) Serve immediately or at room temperature with lemon wedges.

Outdoor fish stall in Palermo, Sicily.

FROM MOROCCO

SPICY PRAWNS

M'HAMMAR IS ONE OF THE FOUR BASIC FLAVOURING COMBINATIONS OF MOROCCAN CUISINE, WITH ITS MAIN INGREDIENTS BEING GARLIC, PAPRIKA AND CUMIN. WITH THE ADDITION OF CHOPPED RED CHILLI, THIS PRAWN DISH IS A WORTHY RIVAL TO THE POPULAR GARLIC PRAWNS.

375 g (13 oz) raw prawns (shrimp)
3 tablespoons olive oil
½ teaspoon ground cumin
½ teaspoon cumin seeds
1 teaspoon ground ginger
2 teaspoons chopped red chilli
3 garlic cloves, finely chopped
½ teaspoon ground turmeric
1 teaspoon paprika
2 tablespoons finely chopped coriander (cilantro) leaves
lemon wedges, to serve

SERVES 4

PEEL the prawns, leaving the tails intact. To devein the prawns, cut a slit down the back and remove any visible vein. Put the prawns in a colander and rinse under cold running water. Shake colander to remove any excess water, sprinkle the prawns with ½ teaspoon salt, toss through and set aside.

POUR the olive oil into a large frying pan and place over medium heat. Stir in the ground cumin, cumin seeds, ginger and chilli. Cook until fragrant and the cumin seeds start to pop. Add the garlic, turmeric and paprika. Cook, stirring, for a few seconds, then add the prawns. Increase heat a little and fry prawns, tossing frequently, for 3–4 minutes until they firm up and turn pink. Stir in the coriander and 3 tablespoons water. Bring to a simmer, then remove from the heat. Serve with lemon wedges.

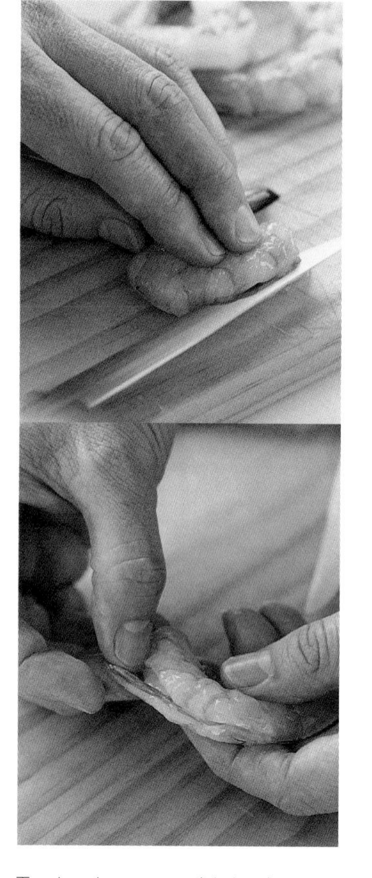

To devein prawns (shrimp), cut a shallow slit along the back to expose the vein and pull it out very gently.

FROM ITALY

SPAGHETTI WITH PRAWNS, CLAMS AND SCALLOPS

SEAFOOD PASTA IN MANY RESTAURANTS AROUND THE WORLD IS ERRONEOUSLY TERMED *MARINARA*. MARINARA IS TRADITIONALLY THE SAUCE MADE BY FISHERMEN (OR THEIR WIVES), TO WHICH THE DAY'S CATCH WOULD BE ADDED. SO THE NAME, IN FACT, REFERS TO THE SAUCE, NOT THE SEAFOOD.

250 ml (9 fl oz/1 cup) dry white wine
pinch of saffron threads
1 kg (2 lb 4 oz) clams (vongole)
4 baby octopus
200 g (7 oz) small squid tubes
500 g (1 lb 2 oz) prawns (shrimp)
6 tomatoes
400 g (14 oz) spaghetti
4 tablespoons olive oil
3 garlic cloves, crushed
8–10 scallops, cleaned
6 tablespoons chopped parsley
lemon wedges, to serve

SERVES 4

PUT the wine and saffron in a bowl and leave to infuse. Clean clams by scrubbing them thoroughly and scraping off any barnacles. Rinse well under running water and discard any that are broken or open and don't close when tapped on the work surface. Place in a large saucepan with 185 ml (6 fl oz/¾ cup) water. Cover pan and cook over high heat for 1–2 minutes, or until the clams open (discard any that stay closed after that time). Drain, reserving the liquid. Remove the clams from their shells and set aside.

CLEAN octopus by slitting the head and pulling out the innards. Cut out the eyes and hard beak and rinse. Lay squid out flat, skin side up, and score a crisscross pattern into the flesh, taking care not to cut all the way through. Slice squid diagonally into 2 x 4 cm (¾ x 1½ inch) strips. Peel and devein the prawns.

SCORE a cross in the top of each tomato, plunge them into boiling water for 20 seconds, then drain and peel the skin away from the cross. Core and chop. Cook pasta in a large saucepan of boiling salted water until al dente.

MEANWHILE, heat the oil in a large frying pan and add the garlic and tomato. Stir over moderate heat for 10–15 seconds, then pour in saffron-infused wine and the reserved clam liquid. Season and simmer for 8–10 minutes, or until reduced by half. Add squid, prawns and octopus and cook until the squid turns opaque. Add scallops, clam meat and parsley and cook until scallops turn opaque.

DRAIN spaghetti and return to the pan. Add two-thirds of the sauce, toss well, then transfer to a large serving platter. Spoon the remaining sauce over the top and serve with lemon wedges.

The prawns (shrimp), squid and octopus are added first as they take marginally longer to cook than the scallops and clams (vongole).

FROM SPAIN

STUFFED SQUID WITH RICE

THIS IS ANOTHER EXAMPLE OF THE GLORIOUS RICE DISHES TO BE FOUND IN SPAIN. HERE, SHORT-GRAIN RICE IS TEAMED WITH SWEET, PLUMP LITTLE SQUID STUFFED WITH CURRANTS AND PINE NUTS, PROVIDING NOT ONLY A GREAT TASTE, BUT A PLEASING COMBINATION OF TEXTURES.

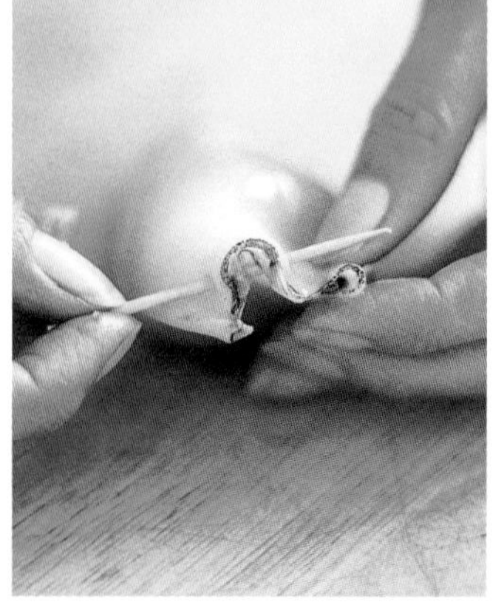

Carefully spoon filling into each squid and seal with a toothpick.

8 small squid, cleaned, tentacles reserved
1 small red onion
2 tablespoons olive oil
2 tablespoons currants
2 tablespoons pine nuts
25 g (1 oz/⅓ cup) fresh breadcrumbs
1 tablespoon chopped mint
1 tablespoon chopped flat-leaf (Italian) parsley
1 egg, lightly beaten
2 teaspoons plain (all-purpose) flour

SAUCE
1 tablespoon olive oil
1 small onion, finely chopped
1 garlic clove, crushed
60 ml (2 fl oz/¼ cup) dry white wine
400 g (14 oz) tinned chopped tomatoes
1 bay leaf
½ teaspoon caster (superfine) sugar

RICE
1¼ litres (44 fl oz/5 cups) fish stock
60 ml (2 fl oz/¼ cup) olive oil
1 brown onion, finely chopped
3 garlic cloves, crushed
275 g (9¾ oz/1¼ cups) short-grain rice
¼ teaspoon cayenne pepper
3 teaspoons squid ink
60 ml (2 fl oz/¼ cup) dry white wine
60 ml (2 fl oz/¼ cup) tomato paste (concentrated purée)
2 tablespoons chopped flat-leaf (Italian) parsley

SERVES 4

FINELY chop the squid tentacles and the onion in a processor. Heat oil in a saucepan and cook the currants and pine nuts over low heat for 5 minutes until the nuts are browned. Remove to a bowl. Add the onion mix to the pan and cook gently for 5 minutes, then stir into the pine nut mixture with the breadcrumbs, herbs and egg. Season. Stuff squid bodies with the mixture, close openings and secure with toothpicks. Dust with flour.

TO MAKE the sauce, heat the oil for 8 minutes in a frying pan and cook the onion over low heat until soft. Stir in the garlic, wine and 125 ml (4 fl oz/½ cup) water. Cook over high heat for 1 minute, then add the tomato, bay leaf and sugar. Season, reduce heat and simmer for 5 minutes. Add the squid to pan in a single layer. Simmer, covered, for 20 minutes, or until tender.

MEANWHILE, to make the rice, bring the stock to a simmer in a saucepan. Heat the oil in a large saucepan and cook the onion over low heat until soft. Add the garlic, rice and cayenne. Mix the ink, if using, with 80 ml (2½ fl oz/⅓ cup) of the stock, add to the rice with the wine and tomato paste and stir until the liquid has almost evaporated. Add 250 ml (9 fl oz/1 cup) of stock, simmer until this evaporates. Add remaining stock, a cup at a time, until the rice is tender and creamy. Cover and leave off the heat for 5 minutes. Season. Stir in the parsley. Put rice on a serving plate, arrange the squid on top and spoon on the sauce.

FROM FRANCE

MOULES MARINIÈRE

GROWN ALL ALONG THE COAST OF FRANCE ON WOODEN POSTS, MUSSELS ARE REGIONAL TO MANY AREAS BUT ARE PARTICULARLY ASSOCIATED WITH BRITTANY, NORMANDY AND THE NORTHEAST. THIS IS ONE OF THE SIMPLEST WAYS TO SERVE THEM.

Wash the mussels, taking care to discard any that are already open and don't close when they are tapped.

2 kg (4 lb 8 oz) mussels
45 g (1½ oz) butter
1 large onion, chopped
½ celery stalk, chopped
2 garlic cloves, crushed
410 ml (14 fl oz) white wine
1 bay leaf
2 thyme sprigs
220 ml (7 fl oz) thick (double/heavy) cream
2 tablespoons chopped parsley

SERVES 4

SCRUB the mussels and remove their beards. Discard any that are open already and don't close when tapped on the work surface. Melt the butter in a large saucepan and cook the onion, celery and garlic, stirring occasionally, over moderate heat until the onion is softened but not browned.

ADD wine, bay leaf and thyme to the saucepan and bring to the boil. Add the mussels, cover the pan tightly and simmer over low heat for about 3 minutes, shaking the pan occasionally. Lift out the mussels as they open, using tongs, putting them into a warm dish. Throw away any mussels that have not opened after 3 minutes.

STRAIN the liquid through a fine sieve into a clean saucepan, leaving behind any grit or sand. Bring to the boil and boil for 2 minutes. Add the cream and reheat the sauce without boiling. Season well. Serve mussels in individual bowls with the liquid poured over. Sprinkle with the parsley and serve with plenty of bread.

GRILLED SARDINES

8 sardines
2 tablespoons olive oil
3 tablespoons lemon juice
½ lemon, halved and thinly sliced
lemon wedges, to serve

SERVES 4

SLIT the sardines along their bellies and remove the guts. Rinse well and pat dry. Use scissors to cut out the gills.

COMBINE the oil and lemon juice and season generously with salt and black pepper. Brush the inside and outside of each fish with the oil, then place a few lemon slices into each cavity.

PUT the sardines onto a preheated hotplate (chargrill pan) and cook, basting frequently with the remaining oil, for about 2–3 minutes each side until cooked through. They can also be cooked under a very hot grill (broiler). Serve with lemon wedges.

GRILLED SARDINES

FROM ITALY

RISOTTO NERO

YOU CAN SOMETIMES BUY THE INK SAC OF THE SQUID FROM YOUR FISHMONGER, ALTHOUGH MOST ARE LOST OR BURST BY THE TIME THE SQUID REACHES THE SHOP. THE LITTLE SACHETS OF INK ARE MORE EASILY FOUND. SQUID INK QUALIFIES AS SEAFOOD, SO DON'T SERVE THIS RISOTTO WITH PARMESAN.

2 medium-sized squid
1 litre (4 cups) fish stock
100 g (3½ oz) butter
1 red onion, finely chopped
2 garlic cloves, crushed
360 g (13 oz/1⅔ cups) risotto rice (arborio, vialone nano or carnaroli)
3 sachets of squid or cuttlefish ink, or the ink sac of a large cuttlefish
170 ml (5½ fl oz/⅔ cup) white wine
2 teaspoons olive oil

SERVES 6 AS A STARTER

PREPARE squid by pulling heads and tentacles out of the bodies along with any innards. Cut the heads off below the eyes, leaving the tentacles. Discard heads and set tentacles aside. Rinse the bodies, pulling out the transparent quills. Finely chop the bodies.

PUT the stock in a saucepan, bring to the boil and then maintain at a low simmer.

HEAT the butter in a large, wide heavy-based saucepan and cook the onion until softened but not browned. Increase heat and add chopped squid. Cook for 3–5 minutes, or until the squid turns opaque. Add the garlic and stir briefly. Add the rice and reduce the heat to low. Season and stir briefly to thoroughly coat the rice.

SQUEEZE OUT the ink from the sachets and add to the rice with the wine. Increase the heat and stir until all the liquid has been absorbed.

STIR IN a ladleful of the simmering stock and cook over moderate heat, stirring continuously. When stock has been absorbed, stir in another ladleful. Continue like this for about 20 minutes, until all the stock has been added and the rice is just tender. (You may not need to use all the stock, or you may need a little extra. Every risotto is slightly different.)

HEAT olive oil in a frying pan and fry the squid tentacles quickly. Garnish the risotto with the tentacles and serve immediately.

Adding the wine to the ink and rice helps the ink dissolve and spread evenly through the risotto.

FROM FRANCE

COQUILLES SAINT JACQUES MORNAY

SCALLOPS IN FRANCE ARE NAMED AFTER SAINT JAMES. THEIR SHELLS WERE ONCE WORN BY PILGRIMS WHO FOUND THEM AS THEY WALKED ALONG THE SPANISH COAST ON THEIR PILGRIMAGE TO A CATHEDRAL IN SPAIN DEDICATED TO THE SAINT.

COURT BOUILLON
250 ml (9 fl oz/1 cup) white wine
1 onion, sliced
1 carrot, sliced
1 bay leaf
4 black peppercorns

24 scallops on their shells
50 g (1¾ oz) butter
3 shallots, finely chopped
3 tablespoons plain (all-purpose) flour
400 ml (14 fl oz) milk
125 g (4 oz) gruyère cheese, grated

SERVES 6

TO MAKE the court bouillon, put the wine, onion, carrot, bay leaf, peppercorns and 500 ml (17 fl oz/2 cups) water into a deep frying pan. Bring to the boil. Simmer for 20 minutes. Strain court bouillon and return to the clean frying pan.

REMOVE the scallops from their shells and pull away the white muscle and digestive tract from each one, leaving the roes intact. Clean shells and keep for serving.

BRING the court bouillon to a gentle simmer, add scallops and poach over low heat for 2 minutes. Remove scallops from the court bouillon, drain and return to their shells. Pour away court bouillon.

MELT the butter in a heavy-based saucepan, add the shallot and cook, stirring, for 3 minutes. Stir in the flour to make a roux and cook, stirring, for 3 minutes over low heat without allowing the roux to brown.

REMOVE from the heat and add the milk gradually, stirring after each addition until smooth. Return to the heat and simmer, stirring, for about 3 minutes, until sauce has thickened. Remove from the heat and stir in the cheese until melted. Season with salt and freshly ground black pepper. Preheat the grill (broiler). Spoon sauce over the scallops, place under the grill until golden brown and serve.

Poach scallops in court bouillon first, so that they are thoroughly cooked before grilling. The heat of the grill alone isn't enough to cook them.

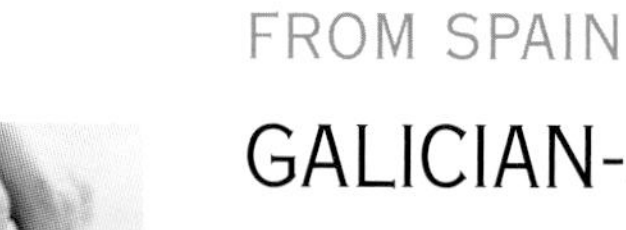

FROM SPAIN

GALICIAN-STYLE OCTOPUS

MELT-IN-THE-MOUTH OCTOPUS, RED WITH PIMENTÓN AND GLISTENING WITH EXTRA VIRGIN OLIVE OIL, MAKES PULPO GALLEGO A LONG-STANDING FAVOURITE. IT IS USUALLY SERVED ON A WOODEN PLATTER, FRESH OFF THE GRILL. SERVE WITH A GALICIAN RIBEIRO OR SIMILAR YOUNG WINE.

2 medium octopus, approximately 500 g (1 lb 2 oz) each
1 bay leaf
10 black peppercorns
smoked or sweet paprika (pimentón), for sprinkling
2 tablespoons extra virgin olive oil
lemon wedges, to serve

SERVES 4

WASH octopus. Using a small knife, carefully cut between the head and tentacles of the octopus, just below the eyes. Grasp the body and push the beak out and up through the centre of the tentacles with your finger. Cut the eyes from the head of the octopus by slicing a small disc off with a sharp knife. Discard the eye section.

TO CLEAN the octopus head, carefully slit through one side (taking care not to break the ink sac) and scrape out any guts from inside, then rinse under running water to remove any remaining guts.

BRING a large saucepan of water to the boil. Add the bay leaf, peppercorns, 1 teaspoon salt and the octopus. Reduce the heat and simmer for 1 hour, or until tender. Remove the octopus from the water, drain well and leave for 10 minutes.

CUT the tentacles into 1 cm (½ inch) thick slices and cut the head into bite-sized pieces. Arrange on a serving platter and sprinkle with paprika and salt. Drizzle with olive oil. Garnish with lemon wedges.

Cut just beneath the eye to separate the head from the tentacle. Pop out the beak, and carefully clean the head without piercing the ink sac.

FROM FRANCE

MARMITE DIEPPOISE

THIS RICH SOUPY STEW OF SHELLFISH AND FISH GIVES AWAY ITS ORIGINS IN THE NORMANDY REGION BY ITS USE OF CIDER AND CREAM. TRADITIONALLY TURBOT AND SOLE ARE USED, BUT THE SALMON ADDS A CHEERFUL SPLASH OF COLOUR.

16 mussels
12 large prawns (shrimp)
450 ml (16 fl oz) cider or dry white wine
50 g (1¾ oz) butter
1 garlic clove, crushed
2 shallots, finely chopped
2 celery stalks, finely chopped
1 large leek, white part only, thinly sliced
250 g (9 oz) small chestnut mushrooms, sliced
1 bay leaf
300 g (10½ oz) salmon fillet, skinned and cut into chunks
400 g (14 oz) sole fillet, skinned and cut into thick strips widthways
300 ml (10 fl oz) thick (double/heavy) cream
3 tablespoons finely chopped parsley

SERVES 6

SCRUB the mussels and remove their beards. Throw away any that are already open and don't close when tapped on the work surface. Peel and devein the prawns.

POUR cider or white wine into a large saucepan and bring to a simmer. Add mussels, cover the pan and cook for 3–5 minutes, shaking the pan every now and then. Place a fine sieve over a bowl and tip the mussels into the sieve. Transfer the mussels to a plate, throwing away any that haven't opened in the cooking time. Strain the cooking liquid again through the sieve, leaving behind any grit or sand.

ADD butter to the cleaned saucepan and melt over moderate heat. Add the garlic, shallot, celery and leek and cook for 7–10 minutes, or until the vegetables are just soft. Add the mushrooms and cook for a further 4–5 minutes, until softened. While the vegetables are cooking, remove the mussels from their shells.

ADD strained liquid to the vegetables in saucepan, add the bay leaf and bring to a simmer. Add the salmon, sole and prawns and cook for about 4 minutes until the fish is opaque and the prawns have turned pink. Stir in the cream and cooked mussels and simmer gently for 2 minutes. Season to taste and stir in the parsley.

Tip the cooked mussels into a sieve and throw away any that haven't opened. Make a sauce of the vegetables and poaching liquid, then add the seafood to cook quickly at the end.

FROM SPAIN

STUFFED CRABS

THE BASQUE WORD FOR CRAB IS THE NAME GIVEN TO THIS JUSTLY CELEBRATED DISH OF CRAB STUFFED WITH ITS OWN MEAT, WINE AND GARLIC. IT IS A DELICIOUS ILLUSTRATION OF THE BASQUE GENIUS FOR DEVISING DISHES THAT COMPLEMENT THE FLAVOUR OF THE CENTRAL INGREDIENT.

- 4 live large-bodied crabs (such as centollo or spider), about 750 g (1 lb 10 oz) each
- 80 ml (2½ fl oz/⅓ cup) olive oil
- 1 white onion, finely chopped
- 1 garlic clove
- 125 ml (4 fl oz/½ cup) dry white wine
- 250 ml (9 fl oz/1 cup) tomato passata (purèed tomato)
- ¼ teaspoon finely chopped tarragon
- 2 tablespoons dry breadcrumbs
- 2 tablespoons chopped flat-leaf (Italian) parsley
- 40 g (1½ oz) chilled butter, chopped into small pieces

SERVES 4

PUT crabs in the freezer an hour before you want to cook them. Bring a large saucepan of water to the boil. Stir in 3 tablespoons of salt, then add the crabs. Return to the boil and simmer, uncovered, for 15 minutes. Remove crabs from the water and cool for 30 minutes. Extract the meat from the legs. Open the body without destroying the upper shell, which is needed for serving, reserving any liquid in a bowl. Take out the meat and chop finely with the leg meat. Scoop out all the brown paste from the shells and mix with the chopped meat.

HEAT olive oil in a frying pan over medium heat and cook onion and garlic clove for 5–6 minutes, or until softened. Stir in the wine and tomato passata. Simmer for 3–4 minutes, then add any reserved crab liquid. Simmer for 3–4 minutes, then add the crabmeat and tarragon, and season with salt and freshly ground black pepper. Simmer for about 5 minutes, or until thick. Discard the garlic.

PREHEAT the oven to 210°C (415°F/Gas 6–7). Rinse out and dry the crab shells. Spoon crab mixture into the shells, levelling the surface. Combine the breadcrumbs and parsley and sprinkle over the top. Dot with butter and bake for 6–8 minutes, or until the butter melts and the breadcrumbs brown. Serve hot.

The breadcrumb mixture forms a crunchy crust for the tender crab filling below.

FROM MOROCCO

PRAWNS WITH HERBS AND PRESERVED LEMON

THERE ARE VARIOUS VERSIONS OF CHERMOULA. IT IS USED WIDELY IN COOKING SEAFOOD, WITH THE PRESERVED LEMON IN THIS VERSION ADDING A DELICATE PIQUANCY. IF YOU DO NOT HAVE PRESERVED LEMON ON HAND, ADD THE ZEST OF HALF A LEMON AND LEMON JUICE TO TASTE.

1 kg (2 lb 4 oz) raw large prawns (shrimp)
2 tablespoons olive oil
lemon wedges, to serve
saffron rice, to serve

CHERMOULA
½ preserved lemon (see recipe on page 485)
2 garlic cloves, roughly chopped
3 tablespoons chopped flat-leaf (Italian) parsley
3 tablespoons chopped coriander (cilantro) leaves
⅛ teaspoon ground saffron threads (optional)
½ teaspoon paprika
⅛ teaspoon cayenne pepper or ½ teaspoon harissa (see recipe on page 482)
½ teaspoon ground cumin
2 tablespoons lemon juice
3 tablespoons olive oil
lemon wedges, to serve

SERVES 4

PEEL the prawns, leaving the tails intact. To devein the prawns, cut a slit down the back and remove any visible vein. Place prawns in a colander and rinse under cold running water. Shake colander to remove any excess water, sprinkle the prawns with ½ teaspoon salt toss through and set aside.

TO MAKE the chermoula, remove the pulp and membrane from the preserved lemon, rinse the rind and pat dry with paper towel. Chop roughly and place in a food processor bowl, along with the garlic, parsley, coriander, saffron (if using), paprika, cayenne pepper, cumin and lemon juice. Process to a coarse paste, gradually adding the olive oil while processing.

HEAT oil in a large frying pan over medium–high heat, then add the prawns and cook, stirring often, until they begin to turn pink. Reduce the heat to medium, add the chermoula and continue to cook, stirring often, for 3 minutes, or until the prawns are firm. Season to taste. Serve hot with lemon wedges and saffron rice.

In a frying pan, cook the prawns in olive oil, stirring or tossing often, until they stiffen and change colour.

The most famous of Morocco's preserves is 'Hamed Markad' (preserved lemons). The transformation of whole lemons into a new ingredient. Unique in taste and silken in texture – achieved by preserving them with salt, lemon juice and boiled water.

FROM SPAIN

SEAFOOD RICE

PAELLA IS THE DISH BY WHICH SPANISH FOOD IS DEFINED INTERNATIONALLY. IT ORIGINATED IN THE RICE-GROWING EBRO RIVER DELTA AREA, INLAND FROM THE CITY OF VALENCIA IN THE EAST OF THE COUNTRY, BUT NOW FIRMLY BELONGS, WITH DELICIOUS SEAFOOD ADDED, TO THE WHOLE COUNTRY.

125 ml (4 fl oz/½ cup) white wine
1 red onion, chopped
12 black mussels, bearded and scrubbed
125 ml (4 fl oz/½ cup) olive oil
½ red onion, extra, finely chopped
1 thick slice of jamón, finely chopped
4 garlic cloves, crushed
1 red capsicum (pepper), finely chopped
1 ripe tomato, peeled, seeded and chopped (see recipe on page 490)
90 g (3 oz) chorizo, thinly sliced
pinch of cayenne pepper
220 g (7 oz/1 cup) paella or medium-grain rice
¼ teaspoon saffron threads
500 ml (17 fl oz/2 cups) chicken stock, heated
85 g (3 oz/½ cup) fresh or frozen peas
12 raw prawns (shrimp), peeled and deveined
2 squid tubes, cleaned and cut into rings
115 g (4 oz) skinless firm white fish fillets, cut into pieces
2 tablespoons finely chopped flat-leaf (Italian) parsley

SERVES 4

HEAT the wine and onion in a saucepan over high heat. Add the mussels, cover and gently shake the pan for 5–8 minutes. Remove from the heat, discard any closed mussels and drain, reserving the liquid.

HEAT the oil in a large heavy-based frying pan, add the extra onion, jamón, garlic and capsicum, and cook for about 5 minutes. Add the chopped tomato, chorizo and cayenne pepper. Season. Stir in the reserved liquid, then add rice and stir again.

BLEND the saffron with the hot stock, then stir into the rice mixture. Bring to the boil, then reduce the heat to low and simmer, uncovered, for 15 minutes without stirring.

PUT the peas, prawns, squid and fish on top of the rice. Push them in, cover and cook over low heat for 10 minutes, turning over halfway through, until the rice is tender and the seafood is cooked through. Add the mussels for the last 5 minutes to heat through. If the rice is not quite cooked, add a little extra stock and cook for a few more minutes. Leave to rest for 5 minutes, then add the parsley and serve.

Stir the paella rice into the flavoursome base sauce.

FROM ITALY

CHARGRILLED SHELLFISH

THIS RECIPE CALLS FOR DUBLIN BAY PRAWNS (SHRIMP) BUT, IF YOU CAN'T FIND THEM, ANY PRAWNS (SHRIMP) WILL DO. USING A ROSEMARY TWIG FOR BASTING GIVES THE MARINADE A SUBTLE HERB FLAVOUR, WITHOUT ALLOWING IT TO BECOME OVERPOWERING.

125 ml (4 fl oz/½ cup) extra virgin olive oil
2 garlic cloves
1 tablespoon finely chopped basil
80 ml (2 fl oz/⅓ cup) lemon juice
12 Dublin Bay prawns (scampi or gamberoni)
12 scallops in the half shell
16 prawns (shrimp)
long sturdy twig of rosemary, for basting
16 large clams (sea dates, warty venus shells, pipis or vongole)

SERVES 4

COMBINE the oil, garlic cloves, basil and lemon juice in a bowl and season well. Set aside to infuse for 15–20 minutes.

REMOVE the claws and heads from Dublin Bay prawns. To butterfly, split them down the underside with a sharp knife and open them out.

REMOVE the scallops from their shells, reserving the shells, and pull away the white muscle and digestive tract around each one, leaving the roes intact if you like. Peel and devein the prawns, leaving the tails intact.

PREHEAT a chargrill pan (griddle) or barbecue until hot. Using the rosemary twig as a brush, lightly brush the cut surfaces of the Dublin Bay prawns with the oil dressing. Brush chargrill pan (griddle) or barbecue plate with the dressing (be careful of the flame flaring) and place the Dublin Bay prawns on to cook, shell sides down.

AFTER 30 seconds, brush the scallops with the dressing and add them to the chargrill pan with the prawns and clams (discard any clams that are broken or don't close when tapped). Turn Dublin Bay prawns over and cook for another minute. Turn the prawns once. Baste with more dressing once or twice. All the shellfish should be ready within 3–4 minutes – the clams can be moved to the side and brushed with a little dressing as they open. Put the scallops back on their shells.

DISCARD the garlic cloves and pour the oil dressing into a small serving bowl. Transfer the shellfish to a warm serving platter. Serve at once with the dressing, bread and finger bowls.

Butterflying allows the flesh to cook through the shell and take on the flavour of the rosemary.

FROM MOROCCO

TROUT STUFFED WITH DATES

THE MARRIAGE OF DATES WITH FISH IS A TIME-HONOURED PRACTICE IN MOROCCO. TRADITIONALLY THE STUFFED FISH WOULD BE COOKED IN A TAGINE, BUT WITH DOMESTIC OVENS NOW MORE WIDELY AVAILABLE, IT IS OFTEN OVEN-BAKED. THE FOIL WRAPPING KEEPS THE FISH MOIST.

4 medium-sized trout, scaled and cleaned
140 g (5 oz/¾ cup) stoned, chopped dried dates
40 g (1½ oz/¼ cup) cooked rice
4 tablespoons chopped coriander (cilantro) leaves
¼ teaspoon ground ginger
¼ teaspoon ground cinnamon
50 g (1¾ oz/⅓ cup) roughly chopped blanched almonds
1 white onion, finely chopped
40 g (1½ oz) butter, softened
ground cinnamon, to serve (optional)

SERVES 4

PREHEAT the oven to 180°C (350°F/Gas 4). Rinse the trout under cold running water and pat them dry with paper towel. Season lightly with salt and freshly ground black pepper.

COMBINE dates, cooked rice, coriander, ginger, cinnamon, almonds, half the onion and half the butter in a bowl to make the stuffing. Season well with salt and freshly ground black pepper.

SPOON the stuffing into the fish cavities and place each fish on a well-greased double sheet of foil. Brush the fish with the remaining butter, season with salt and freshly ground black pepper and divide the remaining onion among the four parcels. Wrap the fish neatly and seal the edges of the foil. Place the parcels on a large baking tray and bake for 15–20 minutes, or until flesh is opaque and flakes easily with a fork. Dust with cinnamon.

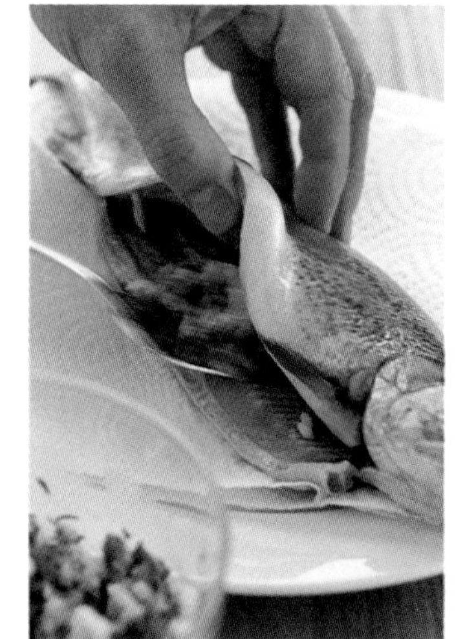

Spoon the stuffing into the fish cavities before sealing in foil panels to keep moist during cooking.

According to a Moroccan saying, date palms must have their heads in fire and their feet in water – the hot Moroccan sun to bring the fruit to succulent sweetness, and groundwater for their roots to maintain growth.

FROM SPAIN

SCALLOPS WITH CAVA SAUCE

THIS DELICATE AND DELICIOUS DISH IS ANOTHER WELCOME MODERN ADDITION TO THE SPANISH TABLE. JUICY SCALLOPS ARE LIGHTLY COOKED IN THE FRUITY SPANISH SPARKLING WINE OF CATALONIA, CAVA. IT CAN BE SERVED AS A STARTER OR A MAIN COURSE FOR A LIGHT SUMMER MEAL.

20 large white scallops
60 g (2¼ oz) butter
2 tablespoons thinly sliced French shallots
375 ml (13 fl oz/1½ cups) cava or other sparkling white wine
250 ml (9 fl oz/1 cup) cream (whipping)
2–3 teaspoons lemon juice
1 tablespoon chopped flat-leaf (Italian) parsley

SERVES 4

REMOVE and discard the vein, membrane or hard white muscle from the scallops. Remove the roe.

MELT the butter in a large heavy-based frying pan over medium–high heat. Sauté the scallops for 1–2 minutes each side, or until almost cooked through. Transfer to a plate.

ADD shallots to the pan and cook for 3 minutes, or until soft. Add the cava and simmer for 6–8 minutes, or until reduced by half. Stir in the cream and simmer for about 10 minutes, or until reduced to a sauce consistency. Stir in the lemon juice and season. Return scallops to the sauce to reheat gently. Serve garnished with the chopped parsley.

Spain's coastline stretches from France to Africa, and is lapped by the Mediterranean, the Atlantic and the Cantabrian Sea – providing an abundance of seafood.

SCALLOPS WITH CAVA SAUCE

POULTRY

FROM MOROCCO

CHICKEN WITH ONIONS AND CHICKPEAS

A K'DRA IS A BERBER METHOD OF COOKING CHICKEN, CHARACTERISED BY THE LARGE AMOUNT OF HERBED SMEN (CLARIFIED BUTTER) AND ONIONS USED, AS WELL AS CHICKPEAS AND SAFFRON. THE AMOUNT OF BUTTER HAS BEEN REDUCED IN THIS RECIPE.

60 g (2¼ oz) clarified butter (ghee) or herbed butter
3 brown onions, thinly sliced
½ teaspoon ground ginger
½ teaspoon freshly ground black pepper
1.5 kg (3 lb 5 oz) chicken, quartered
⅛ teaspoon ground saffron threads
1 cinnamon stick
2 x 420 g (15 oz) tins chickpeas
3 tablespoons finely chopped flat-leaf (Italian) parsley, plus extra, to serve
lemon wedges, to serve

SERVES 4

MELT the butter in a large frying pan. Add a third of the onion. Cook over medium heat for 5 minutes, or until softened. Add the ginger, black pepper and chicken pieces and cook without browning for 2–3 minutes, turning chicken occasionally. Add remaining onion, 310 ml (10¾ fl oz/1¼ cups) water, the saffron, cinnamon stick and 1 teaspoon salt. Bring to a slow boil, reduce the heat to low, then cover and simmer gently for 45 minutes.

MEANWHILE, drain chickpeas. Place in a large bowl with cold water to cover. Lift up handfuls of chickpeas and rub them between your hands to loosen the skins, dropping them back into the bowl. Run more water into the bowl, stir well and let the skins float to the top, then skim them off. Repeat until skins have been removed. Add the skinned chickpeas to the chicken, along with the parsley, stir gently, then cover and simmer for 15 minutes, or until the chicken is tender.

TILT saucepan and spoon off some of the fat from the surface and put it into a frying pan. Lift out the chicken pieces, allowing sauce to drain back into the saucepan. Heat the fat in the frying pan and brown chicken pieces quickly over high heat. Meanwhile, boil the sauce to reduce it a little.

SERVE chicken with the chickpeas and the sauce spooned over. Sprinkle with the extra parsley and serve with lemon wedges and crusty bread.

The browning of both chicken and lamb after braising is a characteristic of Berber cooking. This gives an appealing golden crust on the chicken, improving presentation and flavour.

FROM SPAIN

CHICKEN IN BEER

THE USE OF BEER IN THIS POPULAR DISH GIVES IT A UNIQUE, STEW-LIKE CONSISTENCY. A TASTY, FLAVOURSOME DISH, POLLO A LA CERVEZA IS A COMMON WEEKNIGHT MEAL FOR MANY SPANISH FAMILIES AND IS FINE FOR CHILDREN AS THE ALCOHOL CONTENT IS ELIMINATED DURING COOKING.

- 350 ml (12 fl oz) bottle of beer (Spanish if possible)
- 1 tablespoon dijon mustard
- 1 teaspoon sweet paprika (pimentón)
- 2 brown onions, diced
- 2 garlic cloves, crushed
- 1½ kg (2 lb 12 oz) chicken, cut into pieces
- 2 tablespoons olive oil
- 1 green capsicum (pepper), diced
- 400 g (14 oz) tinned chopped tomatoes
- 1 onion, extra, diced
- 1 garlic clove, extra, crushed

SERVES 4

COMBINE the beer, mustard, paprika, half the onion, half the garlic and a large pinch of salt in a large bowl. Add the chicken, toss until well coated and marinate overnight covered in the refrigerator.

PREHEAT the oven to 180°C (350°F/Gas 4). Heat the olive oil in a large flameproof casserole dish over medium heat, add the capsicum and remaining onion and garlic and cook for 10 minutes, or until softened.

STIR in the chicken, marinade and tomatoes and season well. Cover and bake for 45–60 minutes, or until the chicken is tender.

Overnight refrigeration helps the flavour to permeate and tenderise the chicken.

Adding the orange juice to the caramel sauce.

A butcher's shop in Paris.

FROM FRANCE

DUCK A L'ORANGE

DUCK CAN BE FATTY, WHICH IS WHY IT SHOULD BE PRICKED ALL OVER AND COOKED ON A RACK TO LET THE FAT DRAIN AWAY. THE REASON THAT DUCK A L'ORANGE WORKS SO PERFECTLY AS A DISH, IS THAT THE SWEET ACIDITY OF THE CITRUS FRUIT CUTS THROUGH THE RICH DUCK FAT.

5 oranges
1 x 2 kg (4 lb 8 oz) duck
2 cinnamon sticks
1 handful mint leaves
95 g (3¼ oz) soft brown sugar
125 ml (4 fl oz/½ cup) cider vinegar
80 ml (2½ fl oz/⅓ cup) Grand Marnier
30 g (1 oz) butter

SERVES 4

PREHEAT the oven to 150°C (300°F/Gas 2). Halve two of the oranges and rub them all over the duck. Place them in the duck cavity with the cinnamon sticks and mint. Tie the legs together and tie the wings together. Prick all over with a fork so that the fat can drain out as the duck cooks.

PUT the duck on a rack, breast side down, and put the rack in a shallow roasting tin. Roast for 45 minutes, turning the duck halfway through.

MEANWHILE, zest and juice the remaining oranges (if you don't have a zester, cut orange peel into thin strips with a sharp knife). Heat the sugar in a saucepan over low heat until it melts and then caramelises: swirl pan gently to make sure it caramelises evenly. When the sugar is a rich brown, add the vinegar (be careful as it will splutter) and boil for 3 minutes. Add the orange juice and Grand Marnier and simmer for 2 minutes.

BLANCH the orange zest in boiling water for 1 minute three times, changing the water each time. Refresh under cold water, drain and reserve.

REMOVE the excess fat from the tin. Increase the oven temperature to 180°C (350°F/Gas 4). Spoon some of the orange sauce over the duck and roast for 45 minutes, spooning the remaining sauce over the duck every 5–10 minutes and turning the duck to baste all sides.

REMOVE the duck from the oven, cover with foil and strain the juices back into a saucepan. Skim off any excess fat and add the orange zest and butter to the saucepan. Stir to melt the butter. Reheat the sauce and serve over the duck.

FROM ITALY

CHICKEN CACCIATORA

JUST LIKE THE FRENCH *CHASSEUR*, CACCIATORA MEANS 'HUNTER'S STYLE'. THE DISH IS ORIGINALLY FROM CENTRAL ITALY, BUT LIKE SO MUCH ITALIAN FARE, EVERY REGION HAS PUT ITS OWN TWIST ON THE RECIPE. THIS ONE, WITH TOMATOES, IS PROBABLY THE MOST WIDELY TRAVELLED.

3 tablespoons olive oil
1 large onion, finely chopped
3 garlic cloves, crushed
1 celery stalk, finely chopped
150 g (5 oz) pancetta, finely chopped
125 g (4½ oz) button mushrooms, thickly sliced
4 chicken drumsticks
4 chicken thighs
80 ml (2½ fl oz/⅓ cup) dry vermouth or dry white wine
2 x 400 g (14 oz) tins chopped tomatoes
¼ teaspoon soft brown sugar
1 sprig of oregano, plus 4–5 sprigs to garnish
1 sprig of rosemary
1 bay leaf

SERVES 4

HEAT half the oil in a large casserole. Add the onion, garlic and celery and cook, stirring from time to time, over moderately low heat for about 8 minutes, until the onion is golden.

ADD the pancetta and mushrooms, increase the heat and cook, stirring occasionally, for 4–5 minutes. Spoon onto a plate and set aside.

ADD the remaining olive oil to the casserole and lightly brown the chicken pieces, a few at a time. Season them as they brown. Spoon off excess fat and return all the pieces to the casserole. Add the vermouth, increase the heat and cook until the liquid has almost evaporated.

ADD the tomatoes, sugar, oregano, rosemary, bay leaf and 80 ml (2½ fl oz/⅓ cup) cold water. Bring to the boil then stir in reserved pancetta mixture. Cover and leave to simmer for 20 minutes, or until the chicken is tender but not falling off the bone.

IF the liquid is too thin, remove the chicken from the casserole, increase the heat and boil until thickened. Discard the sprigs of herbs and taste for salt and pepper. Toss in the additional oregano sprigs and the dish is ready to serve.

FROM FRANCE

COQ AU VIN

A DISH ALLEGEDLY PREPARED BY CAESAR WHEN BATTLING THE GAULS, WHO SENT HIM A SCRAWNY CHICKEN AS A MESSAGE OF DEFIANCE. CAESAR COOKED IT IN WINE AND HERBS AND INVITED THEM TO EAT, THUS DEMONSTRATING THE OVERWHELMING SOPHISTICATION OF THE ROMANS.

2 x 1.6 kg (3 lb 8 oz) chickens
1 bottle red wine
2 bay leaves
2 thyme sprigs
250 g (9 oz) bacon, diced
60 g (2¼ oz) butter
20 pickling or pearl onions
250 g (9 oz) button mushrooms
1 teaspoon oil
30 g (1 oz) plain (all-purpose) flour
1 litre (35 fl oz/4 cups) chicken stock
125 ml (4 fl oz/½ cup) brandy
2 teaspoons tomato purée
1½ tablespoons softened butter
1 tablespoon plain (all-purpose) flour
2 tablespoons chopped parsley

SERVES 8

JOINT EACH chicken into eight pieces by removing both legs and cutting between the joint of the drumstick and the thigh. Cut down either side of the backbone and lift it out. Turn chicken over and cut through the cartilage down the centre of the breastbone. Cut each breast in half, leaving the wing attached to the top half.

PUT the wine, bay leaves, thyme and some salt and pepper in a bowl. Add the chicken, cover and leave to marinate, preferably overnight.

BLANCH the bacon in boiling water, then drain, pat dry and sauté in a frying pan until golden. Lift out onto a plate. Melt a quarter of the butter in the pan, add onions and sauté until browned. Lift out and set aside.

MELT another quarter of the butter, add the mushrooms, season with salt and pepper and sauté for 5 minutes. Remove and set aside.

DRAIN the chicken, reserving the marinade, and pat the chicken dry. Season. Add the remaining butter and the oil to the frying pan, add the chicken and sauté until golden. Stir in the flour.

TRANSFER the chicken to a large saucepan or casserole and add the stock. Pour the brandy into the frying pan and boil, stirring, for 30 seconds to deglaze the pan. Pour over the chicken. Add the marinade, onions, mushrooms, bacon and tomato purée. Cook over moderate heat for 45 minutes, or until the chicken is cooked through.

IF the sauce needs thickening, lift out the chicken and vegetables and bring the sauce to the boil. Mix together the butter and flour to make a *beurre manié* and whisk into the sauce. Boil, stirring, for 2 minutes until thickened. Add the parsley and return the chicken and vegetables to the sauce.

Cooking the chicken with the skin on keeps the flesh moist.

FROM MOROCCO

SPICED GRILLED CHICKEN

THE MOROCCAN SPICES AND SUGAR-DIPPED, GRILLED LEMON QUARTERS ADD AN EXOTIC TOUCH TO BARBECUED CHICKEN. PUMPKIN AND SWEET POTATO STEW (PAGE 154) GOES WELL AS AN ACCOMPANIMENT AND CAN BE COOKED ON THE BARBECUE ALONGSIDE THE CHICKEN.

2 x 750 g (1 lb 10 oz) chickens
pinch of saffron threads
1 teaspoon coarse salt
2 garlic cloves, chopped
1½ teaspoons paprika
¼ teaspoon cayenne pepper
2 teaspoons ground cumin
½ teaspoon freshly ground black pepper
1 tablespoon lemon juice
1 tablespoon olive oil
2 lemons
2 tablespoons icing (confectioners') sugar
watercress, picked over, to serve

SERVES 4

TO PREPARE chickens, cut them on each side of the backbone using poultry shears or kitchen scissors. Rinse the chickens and dry with paper towels. Open out on a board, skin side up, and press down with the heel of your hand on the top of each breast to break the breastbone and to flatten it. Cut deep slashes diagonally in each breast and on the legs. Using two long metal skewers for each chicken, push skewers from the tip of each breast through to the underside of the legs, which should be spread outwards so that the thickness of the chicken is as even as possible.

PUT saffron in a mortar with the salt and pound with a pestle to pulverise the threads. Add the garlic and pound to a paste. Work in the paprika, cayenne pepper, cumin, black pepper, lemon juice and olive oil. Rub the spice mix into the chickens, rubbing it into the slashes. Cover. Marinate in the refrigerator for at least 2 hours, or overnight. Bring to room temperature 1 hour before cooking.

PREPARE a charcoal fire or preheat the barbecue and place the chickens on the grill, skin side up. Cook over medium heat for 20 minutes, continually turning the chicken as it cooks and brushing with any remaining marinade. The chicken is cooked if the juices run clear when the thigh is pierced. Cooking time can be shortened on a barbecue if a roasting tin is inverted over the chickens to act as a mini oven – reduce the heat to low to prevent burning. Transfer the chickens to a platter, remove the skewers, cover with a foil tent and leave to rest for 5 minutes before cutting in half to serve.

QUARTER the lemons and dip the cut surfaces in the sifted icing sugar. Place on the barbecue hotplate. Cook briefly on the cut surfaces until golden and caramelised. Serve the chickens with the lemon quarters and watercress.

The opened-out (spatchcocked) chicken cooks more quickly on the barbecue grill, with skewers helping to keep it flat. Pound the garlic–spice mix in a mortar with a pestle as they do in Morocco.

FROM SPAIN

CHICKEN WITH RAISINS AND PINE NUTS

SOME INGREDIENTS, PINE NUTS AND RAISINS FOR EXAMPLE, TURN UP IN SPANISH FOOD TIME AND TIME AGAIN. OFTEN TOGETHER, LIKE CHORIZO AND GARBANZOS (CHICKPEAS), AND ALWAYS GOOD. IN THIS SIMPLE DISH THEY ADD RICHNESS AND SWEETNESS TO THE CHICKEN.

1¼ kg (2 lb 12 oz) chicken
½ lemon, cut into 2 wedges
2 bay leaves
60 ml (2 fl oz/¼ cup) olive oil
1 brown onion, thinly sliced
3 garlic cloves, crushed
400 g (14 oz) tinned chopped tomatoes
170 ml (5½ fl oz/⅔ cup) white wine
2 tablespoons sun-dried tomato purée or tomato paste (concentrated purée)
1 red or green capsicum (pepper), cut into thin strips
40 g (1½ oz/⅓ cup) pitted black olives
3 tablespoons raisins
2 tablespoons pine nuts, toasted

SERVES 4

PREHEAT oven to 200°C (400°F/Gas 6). Wash and pat dry the chicken, then season with salt and pepper. Put lemon wedges and bay leaves in the cavity, drizzle with 2 tablespoons of the oil and roast in the oven for 1 hour. Pierce the chicken between the thigh and body through to the bone and check that the juices run out clear; if they are pink, cook for another 15 minutes.

MEANWHILE, heat remaining oil in a large frying pan over medium heat and cook the onion and garlic for 5 minutes, or until softened. Add the tomato and cook for 2 minutes. Stir in the wine, tomato purée, capsicum, olives and raisins and simmer for 6–8 minutes, or until mixture reaches a sauce consistency. Cut chicken into 8 portions, tipping the juice from the chicken cavity into the sauce. Spoon the sauce over the chicken and garnish with the pine nuts.

Add the chicken juices to the capsicum mixture for extra flavour.

Pistachios ripen on a tree in Sicily.

FROM ITALY

ROAST TURKEY WITH PISTACHIO STUFFING

ITALIAN ROAST TURKEY IS TRADITIONALLY SERVED WITH *MOSTARDA DI CREMONA*, A TYPE OF ITALIAN CHUTNEY, MADE FROM CANDIED FRUIT SUCH AS PEAR, APRICOT, MELON AND ORANGE PRESERVED WITH MUSTARD, HONEY, WINE AND SPICES. YOU CAN ALSO USE THIS RECIPE TO ROAST GUINEA FOWL.

STUFFING
45 g (1½ oz) shelled pistachio nuts
100 g (3½ oz) prosciutto, finely chopped
225 g (8 oz) minced (ground) pork
225 g (8 oz) minced (ground) chicken
1 egg
80 ml (2½ fl oz/⅓ cup) thick (double/heavy) cream
150 g (5½ oz) chestnut purée
½ teaspoon finely chopped sage or ¼ teaspoon dried sage
pinch of cayenne pepper

1 x 3 kg (6 lb 8 oz) turkey
300 g (10½ oz) butter, softened
1 onion, roughly chopped
4 sage leaves
1 sprig of rosemary
½ celery stalk, cut into 2–3 pieces
1 carrot, cut into 3–4 pieces
250 ml (9 fl oz/1 cup) dry white wine
125 ml (4 fl oz/½ cup) dry Marsala
250 ml (9 fl oz/1 cup) chicken stock

SERVES 8

TO MAKE the stuffing, preheat the oven to 170°C (325°F/Gas 3). Spread the pistachio nuts on a baking tray and toast for 6–8 minutes. Place in a bowl with the other stuffing ingredients, season well and mix together thoroughly.

FILL the turkey cavity with the stuffing and sew up the opening with kitchen string. Cross the legs and tie them together, and tuck the wings behind the body. Rub skin with 100 g (3½ oz) of the butter. Put the onion in the centre of a roasting tin and place the turkey on top, breast up. Add another 100 g (3½ oz) of butter to the tin with the sage, rosemary, celery and carrot. Pour white wine and Marsala over the top. Roast for 2½–3 hours, basting several times. Cover with buttered baking paper when the skin becomes golden brown.

TRANSFER the turkey to a carving plate and leave to rest in a warm spot. Put the vegetables from the pan into a food processor and blend, or push them through a sieve. Add the pan juices and scrapings from the bottom of the tin and blend until smooth. Transfer the mixture to a saucepan, add the remaining 100 g (3½ oz) of butter and the chicken stock and bring to the boil. Season and cook until thickened to a good gravy consistency. Transfer to a gravy boat.

CARVE turkey and serve with stuffing and gravy, and, preferably, *mostarda di Cremona*.

Marsala is a fortified wine that takes its name from the town in Sicily where the grapes are grown. It was created by an English wine shipper in 1773, who added grape spirit to wine to prevent it spoiling at sea.

FROM ITALY

VINEGAR-POACHED CHICKEN

The chickens are simmered in liquid to keep the flesh moist and infuse it with the vinegar flavour.

The home of balsamic vinegar is Modena, where authentic vinegars aged for at least 12 years (usually much more) are labelled *aceto balsamico tradizionale di Modena*. Originally made only by wealthy families who could afford to wait for their vinegar to mature, a version is now produced commercially and sold without the *'tradizionale'* label.

LIKE A LOT OF ITALIAN FOOD, THE SIMPLICITY OF THIS DISH MEANS YOU REALLY DO NEED TO USE THE BEST-QUALITY INGREDIENTS. BUY A FREE-RANGE BIRD. YOU'LL FIND IT HAS A GREAT DEAL MORE FLAVOUR FOR JUST A LITTLE MORE EXPENSE. USE ANY LEFTOVER POACHING LIQUID FOR SOUP STOCK.

4 x 500 g (1 lb 2 oz) small chickens or spatchcocks (poussin)
1 large carrot, chopped
1 large onion, chopped
1 celery stalk, chopped
bouquet garni
1½ tablespoons sugar
500 ml (17 fl oz/2 cups) white wine vinegar
3 tablespoons balsamic vinegar
1 tablespoon butter
1 tablespoon plain (all-purpose) flour
170 ml (5½ fl oz/⅔ cup) chicken stock
4 sprigs of rosemary

SERVES 4

TRIM ANY fat from the chickens and season well with salt and pepper, both inside and out. Tie legs together and tuck the wings behind the chicken. Spread out the carrot, onion and celery in a casserole large enough to take the chickens side by side (don't add the chickens yet). Add bouquet garni, sugar, white wine vinegar and balsamic vinegar and bring to the boil. Reduce the heat and simmer for 5 minutes.

PLACE the chickens on top of the vegetables, breast up. Add enough boiling water to cover the birds, put the lid on the casserole and simmer for 25 minutes, or until they are just cooked. Turn off the heat and leave the chickens in the casserole for 10 minutes.

MELT the butter in a small saucepan. Add flour and cook, stirring, for 30 seconds. Gradually stir in the chicken stock and simmer until smooth and thickened. Stir in 3–4 tablespoons of the chicken poaching liquid and then taste. Continue adding a little poaching liquid, probably about 125 ml (4 fl oz/½ cup) in total, until sauce is to your taste. Increase the heat and boil until slightly thickened. Season with salt and pepper.

REMOVE the chickens from the casserole, drain well and arrange on a warm serving platter. Spoon just enough sauce over the chickens to glaze the skin, garnish with the rosemary sprigs and serve.

FROM FRANCE

TARRAGON CHICKEN

TARRAGON HAS A DELICATE, BUT DISTINCTIVE, LIQUORICE FLAVOUR AND IS ONE OF THE HERBS THAT GOES INTO THE FRENCH *FINES HERBES* MIXTURE. IT IS KNOWN AS A PARTICULARLY GOOD PARTNER FOR CHICKEN, WITH A TARRAGON CREAM SAUCE MAKING A CLASSIC COMBINATION.

1½ tablespoons chopped tarragon
1 small garlic clove, crushed
50 g (1¾ oz) butter, softened
1 x 1.6 kg (3 lb 8 oz) chicken
2 teaspoons oil
150 ml (5 fl oz) chicken stock
30 ml (1 fl oz) white wine
1 tablespoon plain (all-purpose) flour
1 tablespoon tarragon leaves
150 ml (5 fl oz) thick (double/heavy) cream

SERVES 4

PREHEAT the oven to 200°C (400°F/Gas 6). Combine the chopped tarragon, garlic and half the butter. Season with salt and pepper and place in the cavity of the chicken. Tie the legs together and tuck the wing tips under.

HEAT the remaining butter with the oil in a large casserole dish over low heat and brown the chicken on all sides. Add the chicken stock and wine. Cover the casserole and bake in the oven for 1 hour 20 minutes, or until the chicken is tender and the juices run clear when the thigh is pierced with a skewer. Remove the chicken, draining all the juices back into the casserole. Cover with foil and a tea towel (dish towel). Leave chicken to rest.

SKIM a tablespoon of the surface fat from the cooking liquid and put it in a small bowl. Skim the remainder of the fat from the surface and throw this away. Add the flour to the reserved fat. Mix until smooth, then whisk quickly into the cooking liquid and stir over moderate heat until the sauce boils and thickens.

STRAIN the sauce into a clean saucepan and add the tarragon leaves. Simmer for 2 minutes, stir in the cream and reheat without boiling. Season with salt and freshly ground black pepper. Carve the chicken and spoon the sauce over the top.

Brown the chicken to seal before adding the stock and wine.

Buying cooked chickens and meat from a market rotisserie.

FROM MOROCCO

CHICKEN WITH PRESERVED LEMON AND OLIVES

ONE OF THE CLASSIC DISHES OF MOROCCO, THIS COMBINATION OF SUBTLY SPICED CHICKEN, PRESERVED LEMON AND OLIVES IS USUALLY SERVED AT BANQUETS. USE UNPITTED GREEN OLIVES; IF BITTER, BLANCH THEM IN BOILING WATER FOR 5 MINUTES BEFORE ADDING TO THE CHICKEN.

¼ preserved lemon (see recipe on page 485)
3 tablespoons olive oil
1.6 kg (3 lb 8 oz) chicken
1 brown onion, chopped
2 garlic cloves, chopped
625 ml (21½ fl oz/2½ cups) chicken stock
½ teaspoon ground ginger
1½ teaspoons ground cinnamon
pinch of saffron threads
100 g (3½ oz/½ cup) green olives
2 bay leaves
2 chicken livers
3 tablespoons chopped coriander (cilantro) leaves

SERVES 4

RINSE the preserved lemon quarter under cold running water, remove and discard the pulp and membranes. Drain the rind, pat dry with paper towel and cut into strips. Set aside.

PREHEAT the oven to 180°C (350°F/Gas 4). Heat 2 tablespoons of the olive oil in a large frying pan, add the chicken and brown on all sides. Place in a deep baking dish.

HEAT the remaining oil in the pan over medium heat, add onion and garlic and cook for 5 minutes, or until the onion has softened. Add the chicken stock, ginger, cinnamon, saffron, olives, bay leaves and preserved lemon strips. Stir well, then pour the sauce around the chicken in the dish. Bake for 1½ hours, or until cooked through, adding a little more water or stock if the sauce gets too dry. Baste the chicken during cooking.

REMOVE the chicken from the dish, cover with foil and leave to rest. Pour the contents of the baking dish into a frying pan and place over medium heat. Add the chicken livers and mash them into the sauce as they cook. Cook for 5–6 minutes, or until the sauce has reduced and thickened. Add the chopped coriander. Cut the chicken into pieces and serve with the sauce.

Brown the chicken in a non-stick frying pan so that the chicken skin remains intact. Use the same pan for completing the sauce after chicken is cooked.

FROM SPAIN

DUCK WITH PEARS

THIS CATALAN FAVOURITE WOULD MOST LIKELY BE MADE USING THE DUCK FARMED IN THE AMPURDÁN REGION, THE BARBARY, OR MUSCOVY, DUCK, WHICH ARE LARGE AND HAVE RICH-TASTING MEAT. FOR BEST RESULTS, USE AMONTILLADO SHERRY AND VERY FIRM, RIPE PEARS.

¼ teaspoon ground nutmeg
½ teaspoon smoked paprika (pimentón)
pinch of ground cloves
2 kg (4 lb 8 oz) duck, jointed into 8 pieces
1 tablespoon olive oil
1 bay leaf
8 French shallots, peeled
8 baby carrots, trimmed
2 garlic cloves, sliced
80 ml (2½ fl oz/⅓ cup) rich sweet sherry such as amontillado
1 thyme sprig
1 cinnamon stick
1 litre (38 fl oz/4 cups) chicken stock
4 firm ripe pears, peeled, halved and cored
60 g (2¼ oz) whole almonds, toasted
25 g (1 oz) dark bittersweet chocolate, grated

SERVES 4

PREHEAT the oven to 180°C (350°F/Gas 4). In a small bowl, mix together the nutmeg, paprika, cloves and a little salt and pepper. Dust the duck pieces with the spice mixture. Heat oil in a large flameproof casserole dish and, when hot, brown the duck in batches. Remove from the dish.

LEAVING a tablespoon of fat in the dish, drain off the excess. Add the bay leaf, shallots and carrots. Cook over medium heat for 3–4 minutes, or until lightly browned. Stir in the garlic and cook for a further minute. Pour in the sherry and boil for 1 minute to deglaze the casserole dish. Stir in thyme, cinnamon stick and stock and return the duck to the dish.

BRING to the boil, then transfer the casserole to the oven and bake, covered, for 1 hour 10 minutes, turning the duck halfway through. Put the pears on top of the duck and bake for a further 20 minutes.

MEANWHILE, finely grind the almonds in a food processor, then combine with the chocolate.

WHEN the duck is cooked, lift the duck pieces and the pears out of the liquid using a slotted spoon and transfer to a serving dish with the carrots, shallots and cinnamon. Keep warm.

PUT the casserole dish on the stovetop over medium heat and bring liquid to the boil. Boil for 7–10 minutes, or until the liquid has reduced by half. Add 60 ml (2 fl oz/¼ cup) of the hot liquid to the ground almonds and chocolate and stir to combine. Whisk the paste into the rest of the sauce to thicken. Season to taste, pour over the duck and serve.

Combine a little of the cooking juices with the almonds and chocolate to make a paste before returning to the casserole.

FROM FRANCE

POULET VALLÉE D'AUGE

THIS IS ONE OF THE CLASSIC DISHES OF NORMANDY AND BRITTANY, THE APPLE-GROWING REGIONS OF FRANCE. IF YOU HEAR IT REFERRED TO AS *POULET AU CIDRE*, THIS MEANS THE CHICKEN HAS BEEN COOKED IN CIDER RATHER THAN STOCK.

Fry the chopped apple with the chicken and its sauce, to give flavour and then fry the apple wedges separately.

1 x 1.6 kg (3 lb 8 oz) chicken
2 dessert apples
1 tablespoon lemon juice
60 g (2¼ oz) butter
½ onion, finely chopped
½ celery stalk, finely chopped
10 g (¼ oz) plain (all-purpose) flour
80 ml (2½ fl oz/⅓ cup) Calvados or brandy
375 ml (13 fl oz/1½ cups) chicken stock
100 ml (3½ fl oz) crème fraîche

SERVES 4

JOINT the chicken into eight pieces by removing both legs and cutting between the joint of the drumstick and the thigh. Cut down either side of the backbone and lift it out. Turn the chicken over and cut through the cartilage down the centre of the breastbone. Cut each breast in half, leaving the wing attached to the top half.

PEEL and core the apples. Finely chop half of one apple and cut the rest into 12 wedges. Toss the apple in the lemon juice.

HEAT half the butter in a large frying pan, then add the chicken pieces, skin side down, and cook until golden. Turn over and cook for another 5 minutes. Lift the chicken out of the pan and tip away the fat.

HEAT 20 g (¾ oz) more butter in the same pan, add onion, celery and chopped apple and fry over moderate heat for 5 minutes without browning.

REMOVE from the heat. Sprinkle the flour over the vegetables and stir in. Add the Calvados and return to the heat. Gradually stir in the chicken stock. Bring to the boil, return the chicken to the pan, cover and simmer gently for 15 minutes, or until the chicken is tender and cooked through.

MEANWHILE, heat remaining butter in a small frying pan. Add the apple wedges and fry over moderate heat until browned and tender. Remove from the pan and keep warm.

REMOVE chicken from the pan and keep it warm. Skim excess fat from the cooking liquid. Add the crème fraîche and bring to the boil. Boil for about 4 minutes, or until the sauce is thick enough to lightly coat the back of a spoon. Season and pour over the chicken. Serve with the apple wedges.

FROM SPAIN

CHICKEN IN SAFFRON STEW

THIS DISH IS TYPICAL TO THE CASTILLA – LA MANCHA AREA, IN THE CENTRE OF THE IBERIAN PENINSULA. TYPICAL OF THE LOCAL CUISINE, THIS DISH IS FLAVOURED WITH SAFFRON AND THICKENED AND ENRICHED WITH ALMONDS AND EGG YOLKS. A REGULAR FAMILY WEEKNIGHT DISH.

60 ml (2 fl oz/¼ cup) olive oil
50g (1¾ oz/⅓ cup) blanched almonds
1 thick slice bread, crusts removed, cut into pieces
½ teaspoon ground cinnamon
pinch of saffron threads
2 garlic cloves
2 tablespoons chopped flat-leaf (Italian) parsley
1½ kg (3 lb 5 oz) chicken, cut into 8 pieces and seasoned with salt
2 brown onions, finely chopped
125 ml (4 fl oz/½ cup) fino sherry
375 ml (13 fl oz/1½ cups) chicken stock
1 bay leaf
2 thyme sprigs
2 tablespoons lemon juice
2 egg yolks

SERVES 4

HEAT 1 tablespoon of the oil in a heavy-based flameproof casserole dish over medium–high heat. Add the almonds and bread and fry for 3 minutes, or until golden. Remove and drain on paper towel. When cooled slightly, put in a mortar and pestle or food processor, add the cinnamon, saffron, garlic and half the parsley, and grind or process to a coarse, crumbly consistency.

HEAT the rest of the oil in the casserole dish over medium heat and brown the chicken pieces for about 5 minutes. Remove to a plate. Add the onion and cook gently for 5 minutes, or until softened.

RETURN the chicken pieces to the casserole dish with the sherry, stock, bay leaf and thyme and simmer, covered, over medium heat for 1 hour, or until the chicken is tender. Remove the chicken and cover to keep warm. Add the almond paste to the dish and cook for 1 minute. Remove from the heat and whisk in the lemon juice, egg yolks and remaining parsley. Return the casserole dish to the stovetop and stir over very low heat until just thickened slightly (do not allow it to boil or the sauce will separate). Season to taste, return the chicken to the casserole and gently warm through before serving.

Once the egg is added, do not boil or the sauce will separate.

Wild chillies have been eaten in Mexico since 7000 BC. It is likely that the plants were brought to Europe by Columbus. The chilli reached southern Italy in 1526 and, as in many other countries, was absorbed into local dishes.

FROM ITALY

POLLO ALLA DIAVOLA

DEVIL'S CHICKEN ORIGINATED IN THE TUSCAN KITCHEN. THE CHICKEN IS BUTTERFLIED, THEN MARINATED IN OLIVE OIL AND CHILLI. TRADITIONALLY, THE BIRD WOULD BE COOKED ON A GRILL OVER AN OPEN FIRE – THE FLAMES LICKING UP FROM BELOW LIKE THE FIRES OF THE DEVIL.

2 x 900 g (2 lb) chickens
170 ml (6 fl oz/⅔ cup) olive oil
juice of 1 large lemon
2 sage leaves
3–4 very small red chillies, finely minced, or ½ teaspoon dried chilli flakes
2 French shallots
2 garlic cloves
4 tablespoons chopped parsley
2½ tablespoons softened butter
lemon slices, to serve

SERVES 4

SPLIT EACH chicken through the breastbone and press open to form a butterfly, joined down the back. Flatten with your hand to give a uniform surface for cooking. Place in a shallow dish large enough to take both chickens side by side.

MIX TOGETHER the olive oil, lemon juice, sage and chilli in a bowl and season well with salt and pepper. Pour over the chicken and leave to marinate in the fridge for 30 minutes. Turn the chickens and leave for a further 30 minutes.

MEANWHILE, chop the shallots, garlic, parsley and butter in a blender or food processor until fine and paste-like. (To do this by hand, chop the vegetables and then mix them into the softened butter.) Season with salt and pepper. Preheat the grill (broiler).

PLACE the chickens, skin side down, on a grill (broiler) tray. Position about 10 cm (4 inches) below the heat. Grill (broil) for 10 minutes, basting with marinade once or twice. Turn the chickens and grill, basting occasionally, for about another 10 minutes, or until the juices run clear when a thigh is pierced deeply with a skewer.

SPREAD the butter paste over the skin of the chickens with a knife. Reduce the heat and grill for about 3 minutes until the coating is lightly browned. Serve hot or cold, with lemon slices.

FROM SPAIN

QUAILS IN VINE LEAVES

A WIDE VARIETY OF BIRDS ARE USED IN SPANISH COOKING, FROM WELL-FED FARM CHICKENS TO WILD PHEASANTS AND EVEN PARTRIDGES, WHICH ARE OFTEN SERVED WITH A RICH CHOCOLATE SAUCE. QUAILS, WITH THEIR DELICATE-TASTING FLESH, ARE GENERALLY TREATED MORE SIMPLY.

8 quails
2 lemons
8 slices jamón or prosciutto
16 vine leaves in brine, rinsed in cold water
1 tablespoon olive oil
60 ml (2 fl oz/¼ cup) veal or chicken stock
100 ml (3½ fl oz) sweet sherry, such as oloroso
50 g (1¾ oz) chilled butter, diced

SERVES 4

PREHEAT the oven to 200°C (400°F/Gas 6). Wash the quails and pat dry with paper towels. Cut the lemons into quarters and put a quarter inside each quail cavity. Season and wrap each quail with a slice of jamón. Put a quail on top of two overlapping vine leaves, fold the leaves around the bird and secure with kitchen twine. Repeat with the remaining quails and leaves.

PUT the wrapped quails in a roasting tin, drizzle with the oil and bake for 30 minutes. Remove from the oven and pierce one bird between the thigh and body through to the bone and check that the juices run clear. If they are pink, cook for another 5 minutes. Transfer the quails to a separate plate to rest for 10 minutes, removing the twine and vine leaves.

POUR the remaining juices in the roasting tin into a small saucepan and add the stock and sherry. Bring to the boil and gradually whisk in the butter for 3 minutes, or until the sauce is slightly glazy. Serve the quail drizzled with the sauce.

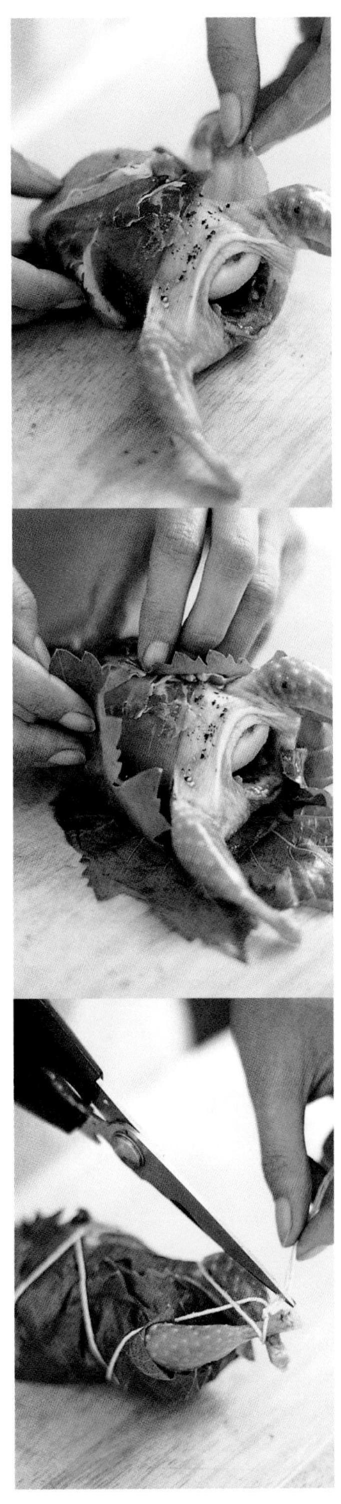

Wrap the quails in the jamón and vine leaves before trussing with kitchen string to help hold their shape.

FROM SPAIN

CHICKEN IN SAMFAINA SAUCE

EVERYONE ELSE IN SPAIN DESCRIBES SAMFAINA AS THE CATALAN RATATOUILLE, WHILE THE CATALANS SAY THAT RATATOUILLE IS THE PROVENÇAL SAMFAINA. EITHER WAY, IT WORKS WONDERS WITH POULTRY, AS HERE IN THIS WONDERFUL, MODERN DISH WITH FRIED CHICKEN.

1½ kg (3 lb 5 oz) chicken, cut into 8 pieces
60 ml (2 fl oz/¼ cup) olive oil
2 large brown onions, chopped
400 g (14 oz) eggplant (aubergine), peeled and cut into 2 cm (¾ inch) cubes
3 garlic cloves, crushed
350 g (12 oz) zucchini (courgettes), cut into strips
2 green or red capsicums (peppers), cut into 1 cm (½ inch) strips
2 x 400 g (14 oz) tins chopped tomatoes
1 bay leaf
2 tablespoons chopped herbs (such as thyme, oregano and flat-leaf (Italian) parsley)
125 ml (4 fl oz/½ cup) white wine

SERVES 4

SEASON the chicken pieces with salt and pepper. Heat the oil in a large heavy-based saucepan over medium heat, add the chicken in batches and brown well on all sides. Remove from the pan and reduce the heat to low–medium.

ADD the onion and cook for about 10 minutes, or until softened. Add the eggplant, garlic, zucchini and capsicum and cook for 10 minutes, or until the vegetables are softened.

STIR in the tomato, bay leaf, herbs and wine, and return the chicken pieces to the pan. Bring to the boil, then cover and simmer over low heat for about 45 minutes, or until the chicken is tender and the eggplant is soft. Season well with salt and pepper before serving.

FROM FRANCE

DUCK CONFIT

A CONFIT IS THE TRADITIONAL METHOD OF PRESERVING MEAT FOR USE THROUGHOUT THE YEAR. TODAY IT IS STILL A DELICIOUS WAY TO COOK AND EAT DUCK. THE THIGHS AND LEGS ARE USUALLY PRESERVED, WITH THE BREAST BEING SERVED FRESH.

8 large duck legs
8 tablespoons coarse sea salt
12 bay leaves
8 thyme sprigs
16 juniper berries, lightly crushed
2 kg (4 lb 8 oz) duck or goose fat, cut into pieces

SERVES 8

PUT the duck legs in a bowl or dish in which they fit snuggly. Scatter salt over the top, season with black pepper and tuck half the bay leaves, thyme sprigs and juniper berries into the dish. Cover and leave in the fridge overnight.

PREHEAT the oven to 180°C (350°F/Gas 4). Put duck legs in a large roasting tin, leaving behind the herbs and any liquid that has formed in the bottom of the bowl. Add the duck or goose fat to the tin and roast for 1 hour. Reduce the oven to 150°C (300°F/Gas 2) and roast the duck for a further 2 hours, basting occasionally, until the duck is very well cooked.

WASH one large (or two small) kilner jars. Dry in the hot oven for 5 minutes to sterilise them. Use tongs to put the hot duck legs into the hot jar and add the remaining bay leaves, thyme sprigs and juniper berries. Strain the cooking fat through a sieve and into a large jug. Now pour the fat into the jar to cover the duck. Close the lid and leave to cool. The fat will solidify on cooling.

DUCK CONFIT will keep for several months in a cool larder or fridge. To use, remove as much duck as you need from the jar, returning any excess fat to cover the remaining duck. The meat can be roasted in a very hot oven until very crisp and served with lentils, beans or salad. Or the duck can be used to make cassoulet.

Use tongs to push the duck legs into the jars, then cover with the strained hot fat to seal.

Confit de canard is used to add richness to cassoulet.

Loosely pack the stuffing into the cavity using very clean hands.

FROM SPAIN

STUFFED CHICKEN

UNTIL NOT SO LONG AGO, THE CHICKENS OF SPAIN COULD BE FOUND PECKING AROUND UNDER ORANGE AND OLIVE TREES, THE OPEN GRAZING WORKING THEIR MUSCLES, FLAVOURING THEIR MEAT. TO MAKE THIS SIMPLE MEAL, BE SURE TO USE AN ORGANIC OR AT LEAST FREE-RANGE CHICKEN.

100 g (3½ oz) ham or bacon, chopped
100 g (3½ oz) minced (ground) pork
2 tablespoons chopped flat-leaf (Italian) parsley
1 garlic clove, crushed
pinch of ground nutmeg
½ red onion, finely diced
1 teaspoon finely chopped oregano
2 tablespoons lemon juice
1 egg, beaten
1.6 kg (3 lb 8 oz) chicken
2 tablespoons olive oil

SERVES 4

PREHEAT oven to 200°C (400°F/Gas 6). To make the stuffing, mix together the ham, pork, parsley, garlic, nutmeg, onion, oregano and lemon juice. Add the beaten egg and mix with your hands until thoroughly combined. Season well.

WASH and pat dry the chicken inside and out, then loosely fill the cavity with the stuffing. Tie the legs together and put the chicken in a roasting tin. Rub with the oil, season with salt and pepper and roast for 30 minutes.

REDUCE heat to 180°C (350°F/Gas 4) and cook for a further 35–40 minutes, or until the juices run clear when the chicken is pierced between the thigh and body. Allow to rest for 10–15 minutes before carving. Serve a little of the stuffing with each portion of chicken.

FROM MOROCCO

SPICED CHICKEN WITH PRUNES

THE SPECIAL MOROCCAN SPICE MIX, RAS EL HANOUT, TOGETHER WITH ROSEWATER, ADDS FRAGRANCE TO THIS DISH OF CHICKEN AND PRUNES. WITH MODERN PROCESSING, PRUNES DO NOT REQUIRE PRE-SOAKING; USE PITTED PRUNES RATHER THAN HAVING TO PIT THEM YOURSELF – A STICKY TASK.

30 g (1 oz) butter
1½ teaspoons ras el hanout (see recipe on page 482)
4 x 175 g (6 oz) chicken breast
1 brown onion, sliced
250 ml (9 fl oz/1 cup) chicken stock
150 g (5½ oz/⅔ cup) pitted prunes
3 teaspoons honey
3 teaspoons lemon juice
3 teaspoons rosewater
couscous, to serve (see recipe on page 473)

SERVES 4

MELT butter in a large, lidded frying pan. Add the ras el hanout, stirring briefly over alow heat. Increase the heat to medium, add the chicken breast and cook for 1 minute on each side, taking care that the spices don't burn. Remove chicken from the pan.

ADD the onion to the pan and cook over medium heat for 5 minutes or until softened. Pour in the chicken stock and add pitted prunes, honey, lemon juice and rosewater. Cover and simmer over low heat for 10 minutes.

RETURN chicken to the pan, cover and simmer gently for 15 minutes or until the chicken is just cooked through and tender. Slice the chicken breasts on the diagonal and serve with the prune sauce and steamed couscous.

Heat the butter and *ras el hanout* until fragrant before adding the chicken; do not allow the spices to burn. The spices complement the prunes.

Each spice shop has it own *ras el hanout*, which translates as 'top of the shop', or 'shopkeeper's choice'. This ground mixture may contain as many as 26 different spices and herbs, depending on the expertise of the shopkeeper.

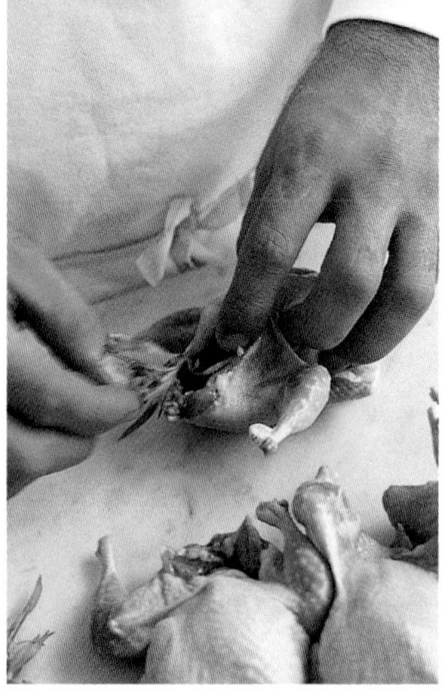

Push a fresh tarragon sprig into each quail before cooking, so that the flavour infuses the flesh.

FROM FRANCE

QUAILS WITH GRAPES AND TARRAGON

8 tarragon sprigs
8 x 150 g (5 oz) quails
2 tablespoons clarified butter
150 ml (5 fl oz) wine
400 ml (14 fl oz) chicken stock
150 g (5½ oz) seedless green grapes

SERVES 4

PUT a sprig of tarragon in the cavity of each quail and season well. Heat clarified butter in a sauté pan or deep frying pan and brown the quails on all sides. Add the wine and boil for 30 seconds, then add the stock and grapes.

COVER the pan and simmer for 8 minutes or until the quails are cooked through. Lift out the quails and grapes and keep warm. Boil the sauce until it has reduced by two-thirds and become syrupy. Strain the sauce and pour over the quails and grapes to serve.

PRUNE AND WALNUT-STUFFED POUSSINS

FRENCH AGEN PRUNES ARE SAID TO BE THE BEST IN THE WORLD AND THE COMBINATION OF PRUNES WITH WALNUTS IS A CLASSIC ONE, WITH BOTH THE FRUIT AND THE NUTS COMING FROM THE SAME AREA OF SOUTHWEST FRANCE.

PRUNE AND WALNUT-STUFFED POUSSINS

STUFFING
10 g (¼ oz) butter
4 shallots, finely chopped
1 large garlic clove, crushed
70 g (2½ oz) shelled walnuts, chopped
14 prunes, pitted and chopped

4 poussins
4 bay leaves
4 slices streaky bacon
50 g (1¾ oz) butter
juice of 1 small lemon
2 tablespoons honey
50 ml (1½ fl oz) thick (double/heavy) cream or crème fraîche

SERVES 4

To make the stuffing, heat the butter in a frying pan, add the shallot and cook for 10–15 minutes. Add the garlic and cook for 1 minute. Remove the pan from the heat and stir in the walnuts and prunes. Season and leave to cool. Preheat the oven to 180°C (350°F/Gas 4).

SPOON an equal amount of stuffing into each poussin, then add a bay leaf. Tie the legs together and tuck the wing tips under. Arrange the poussins in a roasting tin and wrap a rasher of bacon around each poussin breast.

Place the butter in a small pan with the lemon juice and honey. Melt together, then pour over the poussins. Roast, basting often, for 45 minutes, or until a skewer pushed into the centre of the stuffing comes out too hot to touch.

LIFT the poussins out of the tin, cover and keep warm. Put the roasting tin on the stovetop, heat until the juices bubble and stir in the cream or crème fraîche. Season the sauce, pour a little over the poussins and serve the rest separately.

MEAT

SALAME

FROM MOROCCO

MEATBALLS WITH HERBS AND LEMON

THE MEATBALLS IN THIS DISH, TAGINE KEFTA 'MCHERMEL, DO NOT NEED TO BE BROWNED. SPICES, COMBINED WITH FRESH FLAT-LEAF PARSLEY AND CORIANDER, AND THE HEAT OF FRESH CHILLI, ARE USED WITH LEMON TO MAKE A DELICIOUS SAUCE IN WHICH TO COOK THEM.

A food processor makes short work of the meatball mix. The combination of both lemon juice and preserved lemon adds to the appeal of this dish.

½ brown onion, roughly chopped
2 tablespoons roughly chopped flat-leaf (Italian) parsley
2 slices white bread, crusts removed
1 egg
500 g (1 lb 2 oz) minced (ground) lamb or beef
½ teaspoon ground cumin
½ teaspoon paprika
½ teaspoon freshly ground black pepper

HERB AND LEMON SAUCE
1 tablespoon butter or oil
½ brown onion, finely chopped
½ teaspoon paprika
½ teaspoon ground turmeric
¼ teaspoon ground cumin
1 red chilli, seeded and sliced, or ¼ teaspoon cayenne pepper
375 ml (13 fl oz/1½ cups) chicken stock or water
2 tablespoons chopped coriander (cilantro) leaves
2 tablespoons chopped flat-leaf (Italian) parsley
2 tablespoons lemon juice
½ preserved lemon (see recipe on page 485) (optional)

SERVES 4

PUT the onion and parsley in the food processor bowl and process until finely chopped. Tear the bread into pieces, add to the bowl with the egg and process briefly. Add the meat, cumin, paprika, black pepper and 1 teaspoon salt and process to a thick paste, scraping down the side of the bowl occasionally. Alternatively, grate the onion, chop the parsley, crumb the bread and add to the mince in a bowl with the egg, spices and seasoning. Knead until paste-like in consistency.

WITH moistened hands, shape the mixture into walnut-sized balls and place on a tray. Cover and refrigerate until required.

TO MAKE the herb and lemon sauce, heat the butter or oil in a saucepan and add the onion. Cook over low heat for 8 minutes until softened. Add the paprika, turmeric, cumin and chilli or cayenne pepper and cook, stirring, for 1 minute. Add the stock and coriander and bring to the boil.

ADD meatballs, shaking the pan so that they settle into the sauce. Cover and simmer for 45 minutes. Add most of the parsley and the lemon juice and season, if necessary. Simmer a further 2 minutes. If using preserved lemon, rinse well under running water, remove and discard pulp and membrane and cut the rind into strips. Add to the meatballs. Transfer to a tagine or bowl, scatter with the remaining parsley and serve with crusty bread.

FROM SPAIN

MADRID HOTPOT

A COCIDO CAN CONTAIN ANY TYPE OF MEAT TO HAND, PLUS CHICKPEAS. THE ONE CONSTANT, ACCORDING TO THE OLD SONG, 'COCIDITO MADRILEÑO' (LITTLE STEW FROM MADRID), IS '... ALL THE CHARM AND THE SPICE/THAT A WOMAN'S LOVE PUTS RIGHT/INTO THE COCIDITO MADRILEÑO'.

220 g (7¾ oz/1 cup) dried chickpeas
1 kg (2 lb 4 oz) chicken, trussed
500 g (1 lb 2 oz) beef brisket, in one piece
250 g (9 oz) piece smoke-cured bacon
125 g (4 oz) tocino, streaky bacon or speck
1 pig's trotter
200 g (7 oz) chorizo
1 brown onion, studded with 2 cloves
1 bay leaf
1 morcilla blood sausage (optional)
250 g (9 oz) green beans, trimmed and sliced lengthways
250 g (9 oz) green cabbage, cut into sections through the heart
300 g (10 oz) silverbeet (Swiss chard) leaves, washed well, stalks removed
8 small potatoes
3 leeks, white part only, cut into 10 cm (4 inch) lengths
pinch of saffron threads
75 g (2¾ oz) dried rice vermicelli

SERVES 6

SOAK the chickpeas in cold water overnight. Drain and rinse. Tie loosely in a muslin (cheesecloth) bag.

PUT 3 litres (105 fl oz/12 cups) of cold water in a very large deep saucepan. Add the chicken, beef, bacon and tocino and bring to the boil. Add the chickpeas, pig's trotter and chorizo, return to the boil, then add the onion, bay leaf and ½ teaspoon salt. Simmer, partially covered, for 2½ hours (skim the surface, if necessary) or until meats are tender.

AFTER 2 hours, bring a saucepan of water to the boil, add the morcilla and gently boil for 5 minutes. Drain and set aside. Tie green beans loosely in a muslin bag. Pour 1 litre (35 fl oz/4 cups) water into the pan and bring to the boil. Add cabbage, silverbeet, potatoes, leek and saffron with 1 teaspoon salt. Return to the boil and simmer for 30 minutes. Add green beans in the last 10 minutes.

STRAIN stock from both the meat and vegetable pans and combine in a large saucepan. Bring to the boil, adjust the seasoning and stir in the vermicelli. Simmer for 6–7 minutes. Release the chickpeas and pile them in the centre of a large warm platter. Discard the tocino, then slice the meats and sausages. Arrange in groups around the chickpeas at one end of the platter. Release the beans. Arrange vegetables in groups around the other end. Spoon a little of the simmering broth (minus the vermicelli) over the meat, then pour the rest into a soup tureen, along with the vermicelli. Serve at once. It is traditional to serve both dishes together; the broth is eaten first.

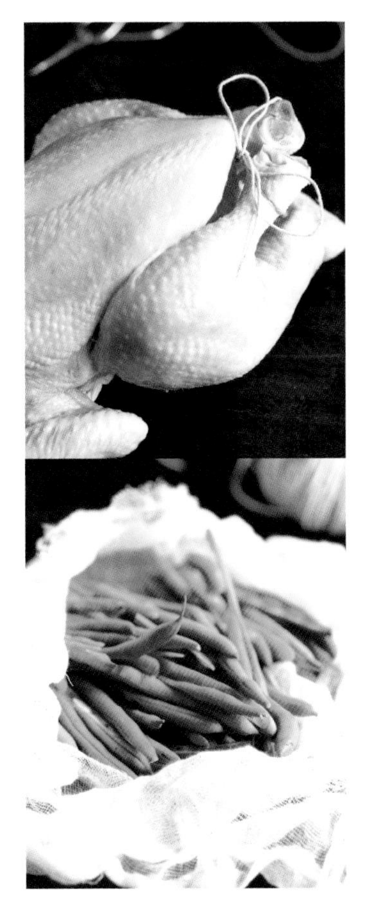

Truss the chicken with kitchen string and tie the beans up in muslin before adding to the pot.

FROM FRANCE

PORK CHOPS WITH BRAISED RED CABBAGE

Braise the red cabbage slowly to bring out the sweetness.

BRAISED RED CABBAGE
30 g (1 oz) clarified butter
1 onion, finely chopped
1 garlic clove, crushed
1 small red cabbage, shredded
1 dessert apple, peeled, cored and finely sliced
75 ml (2¼ fl oz) red wine
1 tablespoon red wine vinegar
¼ teaspoon ground cloves
1 tablespoon finely chopped sage

15 g (½ oz) clarified butter
4 x 200 g (7 oz) pork chops, trimmed
75 ml (2¼ fl oz) white wine
400 ml (14 fl oz) chicken stock
3 tablespoons thick (double/heavy) cream
1¼ tablespoons dijon mustard
4 sage leaves

SERVES 4

TO BRAISE the cabbage, put the clarified butter in a large saucepan, add the onion and garlic and cook until softened but not browned. Add the cabbage, apple, wine, vinegar, cloves and sage and season with salt and pepper. Cover pan and cook for 30 minutes over very low heat. Uncover the pan and cook, stirring, for a further 5 minutes to evaporate any liquid.

MEANWHILE, heat the clarified butter in a frying pan, season the chops and brown well on both sides. Add the wine and stock, cover and simmer for 20 minutes, or until the pork is tender.

REMOVE the chops from the frying pan and strain the liquid. Return the liquid to the pan, bring to the boil and cook until reduced by two-thirds. Add the cream and mustard and stir over very low heat without allowing to boil, until sauce has thickened slightly. Pour over the pork chops and garnish with sage. Serve with the red cabbage.

PORK CHOPS WITH CALVADOS

PORK CHOPS WITH CALVADOS

60 g (2¼ oz) butter
2 dessert apples, cored, each cut into 8 wedges
½ teaspoon sugar
1½ tablespoons oil
4 x 200 g (7 oz) pork chops, trimmed
45 ml (1½ fl oz) Calvados
2 shallots, finely chopped
250 ml (9 fl oz/1 cup) dry cider
125 ml (4 fl oz/½ cup) chicken stock
150 ml (5 fl oz) thick (double/heavy) cream

SERVES 4

MELT half the butter in a frying pan, add the apple and sprinkle with the sugar. Cook over low heat, turning occasionally, until tender and glazed.

HEAT oil in a frying pan and sauté pork chops until cooked, turning once. Pour the excess fat from the pan, add the Calvados and flambé by lighting the pan with a match (stand well back when you do this and keep a pan lid handy for emergencies). Transfer pork to a plate. Keep warm.

ADD remaining butter to the pan and cook the shallot until soft but not brown. Add the cider, stock and cream and bring to the boil. Reduce the heat and simmer for 15 minutes, or until reduced enough to coat the back of a spoon.

SEASON the sauce, add the pork and simmer for 3 minutes to heat through. Serve with the apple.

FROM SPAIN

LAMB CALDERETA

THIS LAMB STEW IS FROM THE HUELVA DEHESA, THE SPARSE MEDITERRANEAN WOODLANDS OF THE HUELVA REGION. FOR HUNDREDS OF YEARS THE IBERIAN PIGS AND SHEEP HAVE ROAMED HERE AND THIS DISH CAN BE TRACED BACK TO THE TRADITIONAL FOOD OF THE SHEPHERDS OF THE REGION.

2 tablespoons olive oil
1 brown onion, roughly diced
1 carrot, roughly diced
1 red capsicum (pepper), cut into large dice
2 garlic cloves, chopped
1 kg (2 lb 4 oz) lamb leg, boned and cut into 2 cm (¾ inch) cubes
1 ham bone or trimmings
400 g (14 oz) tinned chopped tomatoes
2 tablespoons chopped flat-leaf (Italian) parsley
2 tablespoons chopped mint
2 tablespoons tomato paste (concentrated purée)
2 bay leaves
250 ml (9 fl oz/1 cup) white wine
1 teaspoon ground cumin
1 teaspoon sweet paprika (pimentón)
25 g (1 oz/¼ cup) dry breadcrumbs
½ teaspoon ground cinnamon

SERVES 4

PREHEAT the oven to 180°C (350°F/Gas 4). Heat olive oil in a large flameproof casserole dish over medium heat and cook onion, carrot, capsicum and garlic until softened, about 8 minutes. Add the lamb cubes, ham bone or trimmings, tomato, parsley, mint, tomato paste, bay leaves, white wine and 185 ml (6 fl oz/¾ cup) water. Bring to the boil, then cover and bake for 1–1½ hours, or until the lamb is tender.

MEANWHILE, combine the cumin, paprika, breadcrumbs, cinnamon and a pinch of pepper.

REMOVE the lamb from the casserole dish with a slotted spoon or tongs and set aside. Discard bay leaves and ham bone. Purée the remaining liquid and vegetables, then stir in the breadcrumb mixture. Cook, stirring, for about 10 minutes, or until the sauce has thickened. Return lamb to the casserole and gently warm through. Season to taste. Serve with green beans.

Remove the lamb from the casserole. The breadcrumb mixture helps to thicken the vegetable purée.

FROM FRANCE

VENISON CASSEROLE

THIS WINTER CASSEROLE IS SERVED UP DURING THE HUNTING SEASON IN POPULAR GAME AREAS SUCH AS THE ARDENNES, AUVERGNE AND ALSACE. VENISON BENEFITS FROM BEING MARINATED BEFORE COOKING, OTHERWISE IT CAN BE A LITTLE TOUGH.

The easiest way to mix the venison with the marinade is to toss together with your hands.

MARINADE
½ onion
4 cloves
8 juniper berries, crushed
8 black peppercorns, crushed
250 ml (9 fl oz/1 cup) red wine
1 carrot, roughly chopped
½ celery stalk
2 bay leaves
2 garlic cloves
2 pieces lemon zest
5 rosemary sprigs

1 kg (2 lb 4 oz) venison, cubed
30 g (1 oz) plain (all-purpose) flour
1 tablespoon vegetable oil
15 g (½ oz) clarified butter
8 shallots
500 ml (17 fl oz/2 cups) brown stock
2 tablespoons redcurrant jelly
rosemary sprigs, to garnish

SERVES 4

TO MAKE the marinade, cut the half onion into four pieces and stud each one with a clove. Combine in a large bowl with the rest of the marinade ingredients. Add the venison, toss well and leave overnight in the fridge to marinate.

LIFT the venison out of the marinade (reserving the marinade), drain and pat dry with paper towels. Season the flour and use to coat the venison (the cleanest way to do this is to put the flour and venison in a plastic bag and toss well).

PREHEAT the oven to 160°C (315°F/Gas 2–3). Heat the oil and clarified butter in a large casserole dish, brown the shallots and then remove from the dish. Brown the venison in the oil and butter, then remove from the casserole.

STRAIN the marinade liquid through a sieve into the casserole and boil, stirring, for 30 seconds to deglaze. Pour in the stock and bring to the boil.

TIP the remaining marinade ingredients out of the sieve onto a piece of muslin and tie up in a parcel to make a bouquet garni. Add to the casserole with the venison. Bring liquid to simmering point, then put the casserole in the oven. Cook for 45 minutes and then add the shallots. Cook for a further 1 hour.

DISCARD the bouquet garni, remove the venison and shallots from the cooking liquid and keep warm. Add the redcurrant jelly to the liquid and boil on the stovetop for 4–5 minutes to reduce by half. Strain the sauce and pour over the venison. Serve garnished with sprigs of rosemary.

FROM ITALY

VEAL SALTIMBOCCA

8 small veal escalopes
8 slices prosciutto
8 sage leaves
2 tablespoons olive oil
60 g (2¼ oz) butter
185 ml (¾ cup) dry white wine or dry Marsala

SERVES 4

PLACE the veal between two sheets of plastic wrap and pound with a meat mallet until an even thickness. Season lightly. Cut the prosciutto slices to the same size as the veal. Cover each piece of veal with a slice of prosciutto and place a sage leaf on top. Secure in place with a cocktail stick.

HEAT the oil and half the butter in a large frying pan. Add the veal in batches and fry, prosciutto up, over moderately high heat for 3–4 minutes, or until the veal is just cooked through. Transfer each batch to a warmed plate as it is done.

POUR OFF the oil from the pan and add the wine. Cook over high heat until reduced by half, scraping up the bits from the bottom of the pan. Add the remaining butter and, when it has melted, season. Spoon over the veal to serve.

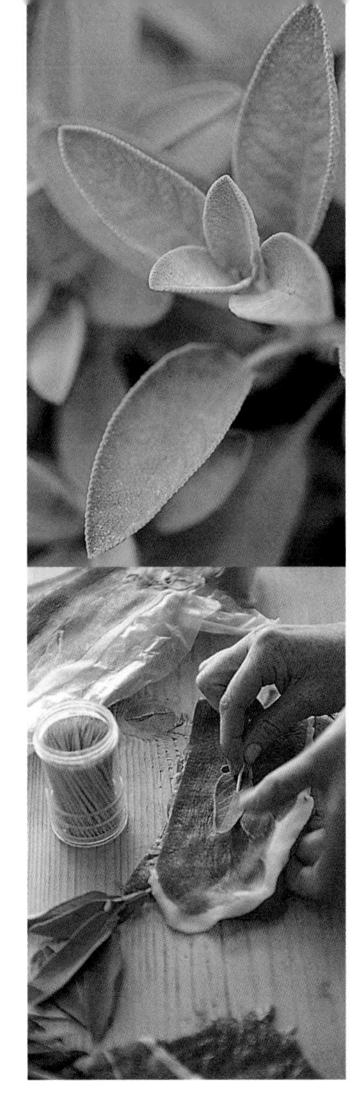

The cocktail stick will hold together the sage, prosciutto and veal. Take it out just before serving.

VEAL ALLA MILANESE

8 veal chops
2 eggs
50 g (1¾ oz/½ cup) fine dried breadcrumbs
3 tablespoons grated parmesan cheese
3 tablespoons butter
1 tablespoon oil
4 lemon wedges dipped in finely chopped parsley

SERVES 4

CUT ALL the fat from the veal chops and trim the lower rib bone until it is clean of all fat and flesh. Place each chop between two sheets of plastic wrap and pound the flesh with a meat mallet until it is half its original thickness.

LIGHTLY BEAT the eggs with salt and pepper and pour into a dish. Combine the breadcrumbs and parmesan and place in another dish. Dip each chop into the egg, coating it on both sides. Shake off excess egg. Coat the chop with breadcrumb mix, pressing each side firmly into the crumbs. Place chops on a plate and chill for 30 minutes.

HEAT butter and oil in a large frying pan. As soon as the butter stops foaming, add the chops and fry gently for 4 minutes on each side, until the breadcrumbs are deep golden. Serve immediately with the lemon wedges.

VEAL ALLA MILANESE

VEAL SALTIMBOCCA

FROM MOROCCO

LAMB TAGINE WITH SWEET TOMATO JAM

TOMATO JAM IS SERVED AS AN APPETISER, LIKE A DIP, BUT THE SAME INGREDIENTS COMBINE WITH LAMB TO GIVE A BEAUTIFULLY FLAVOURED TAGINE, REDOLENT OF CINNAMON AND HONEY. IT IS PREFERABLE TO USE FRESH TOMATOES RATHER THAN TINNED.

1.5 kg (3 lb 5 oz) ripe tomatoes
1 kg (2 lb 4 oz) lamb shoulder or leg steaks
2 tablespoons olive oil
2 brown onions, coarsely grated
2 garlic cloves, finely chopped
1 teaspoon ground ginger
¼ teaspoon freshly ground black pepper
1 cinnamon stick
⅛ teaspoon ground saffron threads
3 tablespoons tomato paste (concentrated purée)
2 tablespoons honey
1½ teaspoons ground cinnamon
30 g (1 oz) butter
40 g (1½ oz/¼ cup) blanched almonds

SERVES 4

HALVE the tomatoes crossways and squeeze out the seeds. Coarsely grate the tomatoes into a bowl down to the skin, discarding the skin. Set aside.

TRIM the lamb steaks and cut into 3 cm (1¼ inch) pieces. Heat half the olive oil in a heavy-based saucepan over high heat and brown the lamb on each side, in batches. Set aside on a plate.

REDUCE heat to low, add remaining olive oil and the onion and cook gently, stirring occasionally, for 10 minutes, or until the onion has softened. Stir in the garlic, ginger, black pepper and cinnamon stick and cook for 1 minute. Add the saffron and the tomato paste and cook for a further 1 minute. Return the lamb to the pan, along with the grated tomato, stir and season with salt and pepper. Cover and simmer gently for 1¼ hours. After this time, set the lid slightly ajar so that the pan is partly covered. Continue to simmer for 15 minutes, stirring occasionally, then remove lid and simmer for 25 minutes, or until the sauce has thickened. When it is very thick and almost jam-like with the oil beginning to separate, stir in the honey and ground cinnamon and simmer for 2 minutes.

MELT the butter in a small frying pan, add the almonds and cook over medium heat, stirring onto a plate at once to stop them from burning.

REMOVE the cinnamon stick from the lamb, transfer to a serving dish and sprinkle with the almonds. Serve with crusty bread or couscous.

Moroccans love their honey – this most ancient of sweeteners; it adds a special flavour to this tagine when combined with spices and tomatoes. The fried almonds add crunch.

FROM SPAIN

PORK IN MILK

AS UNLIKELY AS THIS ANDALUCÍAN DISH SOUNDS, IT RESULTS IN WONDERFUL, TENDER MEAT WITH A RICH, CREAMY SAUCE DEMONSTRATING A MIXTURE OF FLAVOURS AND DELIGHTFUL AROMAS – YOUR GUESTS ARE SURE TO GRAVITATE TO THE KITCHEN TO INHALE THE SMELLS AS IT IS BEING COOKED.

- 1 garlic clove, sliced thinly
- 1 kg (2 lb 4 oz) boned, rolled pork loin, skin off
- 2 tablespoons olive oil
- 500 ml (17 fl oz/2 cups) milk
- ¼ teaspoon ground cinnamon
- ground white pepper
- 2 tablespoons fresh breadcrumbs

SERVES 4

PREHEAT the oven to 200°C (400°F/Gas 4). Push the garlic into each rolled end of the pork.

IN A heavy-based, flameproof casserole dish, heat the olive oil over high heat until very hot. Add the pork and brown evenly on each side. Add milk and cinnamon and season with salt and white pepper. Bring to the boil on the stovetop, then place in the oven, uncovered. Reduce the oven temperature to 150°C (300°F/Gas 2). Cook for about 1½ hours, basting regularly.

REMOVE the pork from the casserole, cover with foil topped with a folded tea towel (dish towel) to keep warm and set aside. Place the casserole on the stovetop over a high heat and bring to the boil. Reduce to a simmer. Cook for about 30 minutes or until about half the liquid remains. The sauce will look split or curdled but this is normal. Stir in the breadcrumbs which will bind and slightly thicken the sauce. Slice the pork and pour the hot sauce over the top. Season to taste.

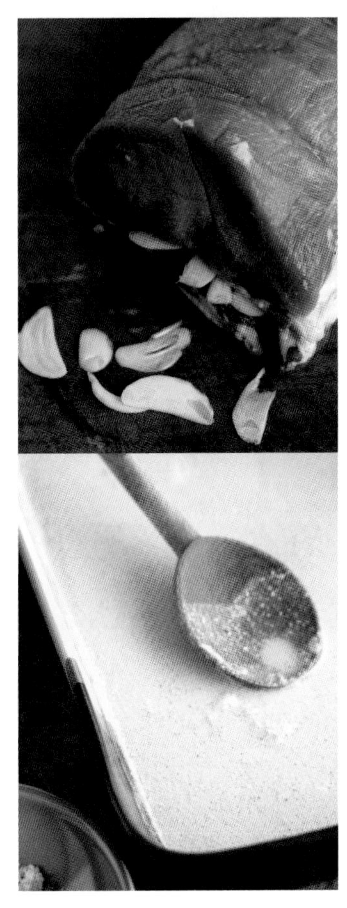

Insert the garlic slices into each end of the skinless pork loin. Thicken the sauce by stirring in breadcrumbs.

FROM FRANCE

BOEUF BOURGUIGNON

ALMOST EVERY REGION OF FRANCE HAS ITS OWN STYLE OF BEEF STEW, BUT BURGUNDY'S VERSION IS THE MOST WELL KNOWN. IF YOU CAN, MAKE IT A DAY IN ADVANCE TO LET THE FLAVOURS DEVELOP. SERVE WITH A SALAD OF ENDIVE, CHICORY AND WATERCRESS AND BREAD OR NEW POTATOES.

If you have time, leave the beef to marinate overnight to deepen the flavours of this dish.

1.5 kg (3 lb 5 oz) beef blade or chuck steak
750 ml (26 fl oz/3 cups) red wine (preferably Burgundy)
3 garlic cloves, crushed
bouquet garni
70 g (2½ oz) butter
1 onion, chopped
1 carrot, chopped
2 tablespoons plain (all-purpose) flour
200 g (7 oz) bacon, cut into short strips
300 g (10 oz) shallots, peeled but left whole
200 g (7 oz) small button mushrooms

SERVES 6

CUT the meat into 4 cm (1½ inch) cubes and trim away any excess fat. Put the meat, wine, garlic and bouquet garni in a large bowl, cover with plastic wrap and leave in the fridge for at least 3 hours and preferably overnight.

PREHEAT the oven to 160°C (315°F/Gas 2–3). Drain the meat, reserving the marinade and bouquet garni. Dry the meat on paper towels. Heat 30 g (1 oz) of the butter in a large casserole dish. Add the onion, carrot and bouquet garni and cook over low heat, stirring occasionally, for 10 minutes. Remove from the heat.

HEAT 20 g (¾ oz) of the butter in a large frying pan over high heat. Fry the meat in batches for about 5 minutes or until well browned. Add to the casserole dish.

POUR the reserved marinade into the frying pan and boil, stirring, for 30 seconds to deglaze the pan. Remove from the heat. Return the casserole to high heat and sprinkle the meat and vegetables with the flour. Cook, stirring constantly, until the meat is well coated with the flour. Pour in the marinade and stir well. Bring to the boil, stirring constantly, then cover and cook in the oven for 2 hours.

HEAT the remaining butter in the clean frying pan and cook the bacon and shallots, stirring, for about 10 minutes, or until the shallots are softened but not browned. Add the mushrooms and cook, stirring occasionally, for about 3 minutes, or until browned. Drain on paper towels. Add the shallots, bacon and mushrooms to the casserole.

COVER the casserole and return to the oven for 30 minutes, or until the meat is soft and tender. Discard the bouquet garni. Season and skim any fat from the surface before serving.

FROM MOROCCO

SLOW-COOKED BEEF WITH HERBS

TANGIA IS A BACHELOR'S DISH, NAMED FOR THE EARTHENWARE AMPHORA IN WHICH IT IS COOKED. INGREDIENTS ARE PLACED IN THE POT, THE TOP SEALED WITH PARCHMENT AND STRING, THEN TAKEN TO THE LOCAL BATHHOUSE FURNACE ROOM AND COOKED IN THE EMBERS FOR HOURS.

- 1 kg (2 lb 4 oz) chuck steak or boneless beef shin
- 1½ brown onions, finely chopped
- 4 garlic cloves, finely chopped
- 2 tablespoons olive oil
- 2 teaspoons ras el hanout (see recipe on page 482)
- ½ teaspoon harissa (see recipe on page 482), or to taste, or ⅛ teaspoon cayenne pepper
- ¼ teaspoon freshly ground black pepper
- 3 ripe tomatoes
- 1½ preserved lemons (see recipe on page 485)
- 2 teaspoons honey
- 1 tablespoon chopped coriander (cilantro) leaves
- 2 tablespoons chopped flat-leaf (Italian) parsley

SERVES 4

TRIM the beef and cut into 2.5 cm (1 inch) pieces. Place the beef in a deep casserole dish. Add the onion, garlic, oil, ras el hanout, harissa and the black pepper and season with salt. Toss the meat with the marinade. Preheat the oven to 140°C (275°F/Gas 1).

HALVE the tomatoes crossways and squeeze out the seeds. Coarsely grate the tomatoes down to the skins, grating them straight into the casserole. Discard the skins. Rinse the preserved lemons and remove the pulp and membranes. Chop the rind into chunks, reserving some for garnish, and add to the meat, along with the honey, coriander and 1 tablespoon of the parsley. Stir well, then cover and cook in the oven for 3½ hours. Juices from the meat should keep the dish moist, but check after 1½ hours and add a little water, if necessary.

WHEN the meat is very tender, transfer it to a serving dish, scatter over the reserved lemon rind and garnish with the remaining parsley.

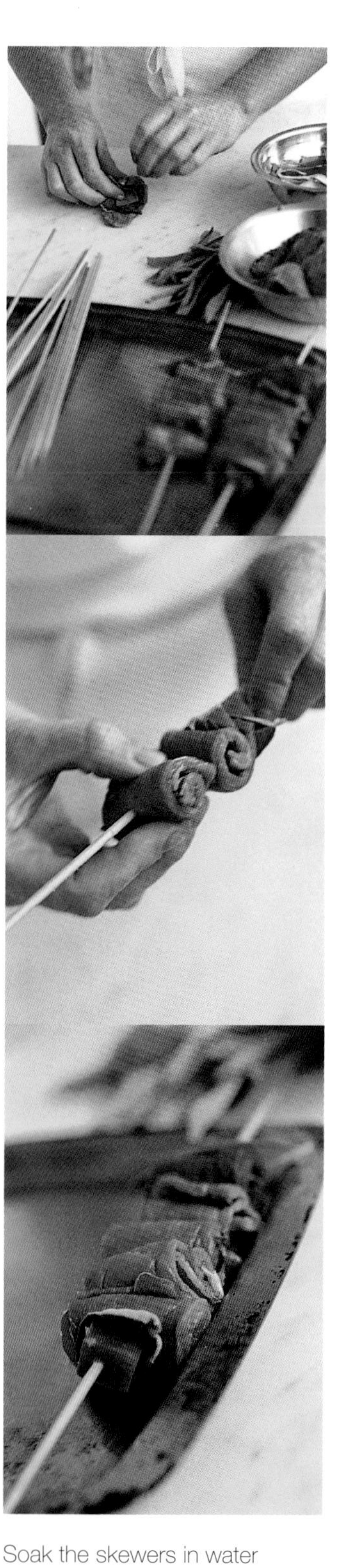

Soak the skewers in water before you start to prevent them scorching (unless you're using metal skewers). Roll up the tiny bundles of veal, pancetta and sage and thread onto the skewers so they can't unroll. Wedge them in place at either end with a sage leaf and pancetta cube.

FROM ITALY

UCCELLETTI SCAPPATI

THE NAME MEANS LITERALLY 'LITTLE BIRDS THAT GOT AWAY', EITHER BECAUSE IT IS FLAVOURED WITH SAGE AS BIRDS TRADITIONALLY WERE, OR BECAUSE IT LOOKS LIKE BIRDS ON A SKEWER. YOU CAN ALSO GRILL (BROIL) THE SKEWERS IF YOU PREFER, BASTING FREQUENTLY WITH MELTED BUTTER.

650 g (1 lb 7 oz) sliced leg of veal
90 g (3¼ oz) pancetta, thinly sliced
50–60 sage leaves
90 g (3¼ oz) pancetta, cubed
75 g (2½ oz) butter

SERVES 6

SOAK 12 bamboo skewers in cold water for 1 hour.

PLACE the veal between two sheets of plastic wrap and pound with a meat mallet until an even thickness. Cut into 6 x 3 cm (2½ x 1¼ inch) rectangles and trim the pancetta slices to the same size.

WORKING in batches, lie the veal pieces out flat on a board and season with pepper. Place a slice of pancetta on each rectangle of veal and then half a sage leaf on top. Roll each veal slice up, starting from one of the shortest ends.

THREAD a cube of pancetta onto a skewer, then a sage leaf. Thread the skewer through a veal roll to prevent it unrolling. Thread four more veal rolls onto the skewer, followed by a sage leaf and, finally, another cube of pancetta. Continue with more skewers until all the ingredients are used.

HEAT the butter in a large frying pan. When it is foaming, add skewers in batches and cook over high heat for about 12 minutes, or until cooked through, turning several times during cooking. Season lightly and serve with fried polenta.

FROM FRANCE

VEAL PAUPIETTES

PAUPIETTES ARE SLICES OF MEAT, WRAPPED AROUND A SAVOURY STUFFING AND ROLLED UP TO MAKE LITTLE PARCELS. IN FRANCE, THEY ARE ALSO REFERRED TO AS '*OISEAUX SANS TÊTES*', WHICH MEANS LITERALLY 'BIRDS WITHOUT HEADS'.

STUFFING
30 g (1 oz) butter
2 shallots, finely chopped
1 garlic clove, crushed
200 g (7 oz) minced (ground) pork
200 g (7 oz) minced (ground) veal
1 egg
2 tablespoons dry white wine
3 tablespoons fresh white breadcrumbs
2 tablespoons finely chopped parsley

4 x 150 g (5 oz) veal escalopes, pounded flat

SAUCE
30 g (1 oz) clarified butter
1 onion, diced
1 carrot, diced
1 celery stalk, diced
100 ml (3½ fl oz) white wine
2 teaspoons tomato purée
1 bay leaf
350 ml (12 fl oz) beef or veal stock

SERVES 4

TO MAKE the stuffing, melt the butter in a small saucepan and cook the shallots over gentle heat until softened but not browned. Add garlic and cook for a further 2 minutes, then set aside to cool. Mix with the other stuffing ingredients and season with salt and pepper.

LAY the veal escalopes flat and spread evenly with the stuffing, leaving a narrow border around the edge. Roll up the paupiettes, then tie up with string as you would a parcel.

TO MAKE the sauce, melt half the clarified butter in a large frying pan. Add the onion, carrot and celery and soften over low heat. Increase heat to brown the vegetables, stirring occasionally. Remove from the pan.

HEAT the remaining clarified butter in the sauté pan and brown the paupiettes, turning once. Remove from the pan, pour in the white wine and boil, stirring, for 30 seconds to deglaze the pan. Add the tomato purée and bay leaf. Pour in the stock and bring to a simmer before adding the vegetables and paupiettes.

COVER the pan and cook for 12–15 minutes, or until a skewer poked into the centre of a paupiette comes out too hot to touch. Remove paupiettes from the pan and keep warm.

STRAIN sauce, pressing down on the vegetables with a spoon to extract as much liquid as possible. Return the sauce to the pan and boil until reduced by half and syrupy. Slice each paupiette into five pieces and serve with a little sauce poured over.

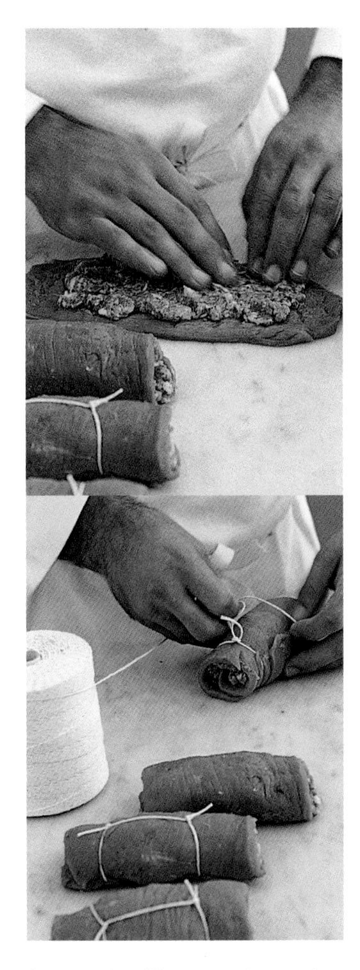

Spread the filling over the veal escalopes, then roll up and tie into parcels with string.

Pavement tables in Paris.

FROM MOROCCO

VEGETABLES WITH LAMB STUFFING

HERE IS ONE VERSION OF MOROCCAN STUFFED VEGETABLES. MOROCCAN COOKS TAKE THE TIME TO HOLLOW OUT THE WHOLE ZUCCHINI (COURGETTE) BEFORE FILLING THEM, BUT IT'S ACCEPTABLE TO HALVE THEM, SCOOP OUT THE CENTRES, FILL THEM WITH THE STUFFING AND RE-ASSEMBLE.

4 zucchini (courgettes)
2 small capsicums (peppers)
6 tomatoes

LAMB STUFFING
2 tablespoons olive oil
1 brown onion, finely chopped
2 garlic cloves, finely chopped
½ teaspoon ground ginger
½ teaspoon ground cinnamon
¼ teaspoon freshly ground black pepper
500 g (1 lb 2 oz) minced (ground) lamb or beef
2 tablespoons chopped flat-leaf (Italian) parsley
1 tablespoon chopped coriander (cilantro) leaves
2 teaspoons chopped mint
55 g (2 oz/¼ cup) short-grain rice

TOMATO SAUCE
1 tablespoon olive oil
1 brown onion, coarsely grated
1 garlic clove, finely chopped
½ teaspoon paprika
¼ teaspoon ground cumin
1 large tomato, peeled, seeded and chopped
2 tablespoons tomato paste (concentrated purée)
1 teaspoon caster (superfine) sugar
1 tablespoon lemon juice

SERVES 4

HALVE the zucchini lengthways. Scoop out the centres, leaving a 1 cm (½ inch) border. Halve the capsicums lengthways; remove the seeds and membranes. Slice the tops from four tomatoes (reserve the tops), scoop out the centres and rub the pulp through a sieve into a bowl. Remove the skin from the remaining tomatoes, slice them thinly and set aside.

TO MAKE the stuffing, put the oil and onion in a saucepan over medium heat and cook for 5 minutes. Stir in the garlic, ginger, cinnamon, pepper and add meat, stirring well to break up lumps. Add 250 ml (9 fl oz/1 cup) water, the parsley, coriander and mint and 1 teaspoon salt. Bring to the boil. Cover and simmer over low heat for 20 minutes. Stir in the rice, cover, and cook for 10 minutes, or until most of the liquid is absorbed.

TO MAKE the sauce, add all the sauce ingredients and 125 ml (4 fl oz/½ cup) water to the tomato pulp. Season. Preheat the oven to 180°C (350°F/Gas 4).

LOOSELY fill vegetables with the stuffing: fill four zucchini halves and top with an unfilled half, then secure with wooden cocktail sticks; fill capsicums and arrange tomato slices over the top; fill the tomatoes and replace the tops. Arrange in an ovenproof dish. Pour in the sauce, cover with foil and bake for 50 minutes. Remove the foil, baste with sauce and cook for 10 minutes, or until tender. Remove picks from zucchini and serve.

Scoop out zucchini, fill and re-assemble. For capsicums, fill and top with sliced tomato.

FROM FRANCE

BOEUF EN CROÛTE

FOR THIS DISH TO WORK REALLY WELL, YOU NEED TO ASK THE BUTCHER FOR A PIECE OF CENTRE-CUT BEEF FILLET THAT IS AN EVEN THICKNESS ALL THE WAY ALONG. THE PASTRY CAN BE PUFF, FLAKY OR EVEN BRIOCHE DOUGH. BEEF WELLINGTON IS THE ENGLISH EQUIVALENT.

PÂTÉ
180 g (6 oz) butter
3 shallots, chopped
1 garlic clove, chopped
360 g (12 oz) chicken livers
1 tablespoon brandy or Cognac

1 x 1 kg (2 lb 4 oz) thick beef fillet
30 g (1 oz) dripping or butter
1 quantity puff pastry (see recipe on page 474)
1 egg, lightly beaten

SERVES 6

PREHEAT oven to 220°C (425°F/Gas 7). To make the pâté, melt half the butter in a frying pan and add the shallots and garlic. Cook until softened but not browned.

REMOVE any discoloured spots from the chicken livers, wash and pat dry. Add chicken livers to the frying pan and sauté for about 5 minutes, or until cooked but still a little pink in the middle. Let the livers cool completely. Process in a food processor with the rest of the butter and the brandy. Or, push the chopped livers through a sieve and mix with butter and brandy. Season.

TIE the beef four or five times along its length to keep it in shape. Heat the dripping in a roasting tin and brown the beef on all sides, then put in the oven and roast for 20 minutes. Allow to cool and remove the string.

REDUCE the oven temperature to 200°C (400°F/Gas 6). Roll the pastry into a rectangle just big enough to cover the beef fillet completely. Trim the edges and keep them for decoration. Spread pâté over the pastry, leaving a border around the edge. Brush the border with beaten egg.

LAY the fillet on the pastry and wrap it up tightly like a parcel, pressing the seams together firmly and tucking the ends under. Put the parcel, seam side down, on a baking tray and brush all over with beaten egg. Cut pieces from the trimmings to decorate pastry and brush with beaten egg. Bake for 25–30 minutes for rare and 35–40 minutes for medium. Allow the beef to rest for 5 minutes before carving.

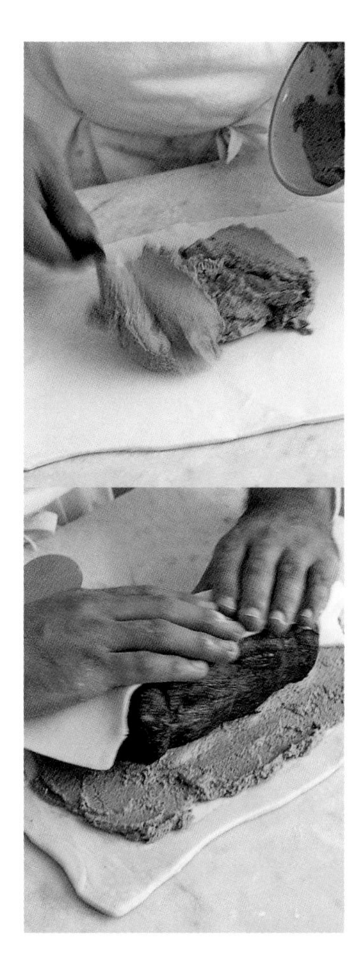

Fold the beef tightly into the pastry parcel as the meat will shrink slightly when cooked.

Cattle farming is a major industry of the Alpine areas.

FROM ITALY

POTATO GNOCCHI WITH PANCETTA AND SAGE

WHEN COOKING THE POTATOES FOR GNOCCHI YOU WANT TO KEEP THEM AS DRY AS POSSIBLE – TOO MUCH MOISTURE WILL RESULT IN A HEAVY DOUGH. FLOURY POTATOES HAVE A LOW MOISTURE CONTENT AND BAKING THE POTATOES IN THEIR SKINS KEEPS THEM DRIER THAN BOILING.

Knead enough to just bring the dough together and make it smooth. Keep the work surface, your hands and storage trays well floured. Roll and shape the dough quickly to stop it drying out.

GNOCCHI
1 kg (2 lb 4 oz) floury potatoes, unpeeled
2 egg yolks
2 tablespoons grated parmesan cheese
125–185 g (1–1½ cups) plain (all-purpose) flour

SAUCE
1 tablespoon butter
75 g (2½ oz) pancetta or bacon, cut into thin strips
8 very small sage or basil leaves
125 ml (4 fl oz/½ cup) thick (double/heavy) cream
50 g (1¾ oz/½ cup) grated parmesan cheese

SERVES 4

PRICK the potatoes all over, then bake for 1 hour, or until tender. Leave to cool for 15 minutes, then peel and mash, or put through a ricer or a food mill (do not use a blender or food processor).

MIX IN egg yolks and parmesan, then gradually stir in the flour. When the mixture gets too dry to use a spoon, work with your hands. Once a loose dough forms, transfer to a lightly floured surface and knead gently. Work in enough extra flour to give a soft, pliable dough that is damp to the touch but not sticky.

DIVIDE dough into six portions. Working with one portion at a time, roll out on the floured surface to make a rope about 1.5 cm (⅝ inch) thick. Cut the rope into 1.5 cm (⅝ inch) lengths. Take one piece of dough and press your finger into it to form a concave shape, then roll outer surface over the tines of a fork to make deep ridges. Fold outer lips in towards each other to make a hollow in the middle. Continue with the remaining dough.

BRING a large saucepan of salted water to the boil. Add the gnocchi in batches, about 20 at a time. Stir gently and return to the boil. Cook for 1–2 minutes, or until they rise to the surface. Remove with a slotted spoon, drain and put in a greased shallow casserole or baking tray. Preheat the oven to 200°C (400°F/Gas 6).

TO MAKE the sauce, melt the butter in a small frying pan and fry the pancetta until crisp. Stir in the sage leaves and cream. Season and simmer for 10 minutes, or until thickened.

POUR sauce over the gnocchi, toss gently and sprinkle parmesan on top. Bake for 10 minutes, or until parmesan melts and turns golden.

FROM SPAIN

VENISON IN SHERRY WITH CABRALES CHEESE

MODERN SPANISH COOKS ARE TAKING ADVANTAGE OF THE COUNTRY'S ARRAY OF WONDERFUL CHEESES AND DEFYING A TRADITION THAT RARELY COOKED WITH THEM. THIS RECIPE IS TYPICAL OF SUCH INVENTIONS AND A TRULY LOVELY DISH.

1 kg (2 lb 4 oz) venison leg meat, cut into 2½ cm (1 inch) cubes
250ml (9 fl oz/1 cup) Pedro Ximénez (or other rich sweet Spanish sherry)
1 carrot
1 leek, white part only
1 stalk celery
1 red onion
2 tablespoons olive oil
12 garlic cloves, roughly chopped
100 g (3½ oz) jamón, diced
2 tablespoons tomato paste (concentrated purée)
250 ml (9 fl oz/1 cup) beef stock
a few sprigs thyme, chopped
2 tablespoons chopped marjoram
100 g (3½ oz) cabrales cheese (or roquefort)
3 tablespoons cream
1 tablespoon Pedro Ximénez sherry, extra

SERVES 4

PLACE the venison into a bowl, pour over the sherry and toss to combine. Cover and marinate in the refrigerator for 24 hours; stir occasionally.

HEAT oven to 180°C (350°F/Gas 4). Drain venison, reserving marinade. Cut carrot, leek, celery and onion into 1 cm (½ inch) dice.

PUT the olive oil in a heavy-based flameproof casserole over medium heat. Add the diced vegetables, garlic and jamón. Stir for 5 minutes or until softened. Reduce heat to medium–high and add drained venison and stir for about 2 minutes until sealed and light brown in colour. Add the reserved marinade, tomato paste, beef stock and herbs. Cover and place in oven for 2 hours, stirring occasionally until the venison is tender and the sauce reduced and thickened.

MEANWHILE place the cheese into a bowl with 1 tablespoon of the cream and mash together well. In a small saucepan over low heat, combine the remaining cream and sherry. When warm, stir in the cheese until melted and smooth.

REMOVE venison from oven. Serve drizzled with cheese mixture.

Mash the cheese together with a little cream before melting into the remaining cream and sherry.

The pig's trotter will give a gelatinous texture to the daube, as well as adding extra flavour.

Speciality award-winning meats for sale at a Paris butcher shop.

FROM FRANCE

BOEUF EN DAUBE

DAUBES ARE TRADITIONALLY COOKED IN SQUAT EARTHENWARE DISHES CALLED DAUBIÈRES, BUT A CAST-IRON CASSEROLE DISH WITH A TIGHT-FITTING LID WILL WORK JUST AS WELL. DAUBES HAIL FROM PROVENCE AND ARE USUALLY SERVED WITH BUTTERED MACARONI OR NEW POTATOES.

MARINADE
2 cloves
1 onion, cut into quarters
500 ml red wine
2 strips of orange zest
2 garlic cloves
½ celery stalk
2 bay leaves
a few parsley stalks

1.5 kg beef topside, blade or rump, cut into large pieces
2 tablespoons oil
3 strips pork fat
1 pig's trotter or 225 g piece streaky bacon
700 ml beef stock

SERVES 6

TO MAKE the marinade, push the cloves into a piece of onion and mix together in a large bowl with the remaining marinade ingredients. Season the beef with salt and pepper, add to the marinade and leave to marinate overnight.

HEAT the oil in a saucepan. Lift beef out of the marinade and pat dry, then brown in batches in the oil and remove to a plate. You might need to use a little of the marinade liquid to deglaze the pan between batches to prevent bits sticking to the bottom of the pan and burning.

STRAIN marinade through a sieve into a bowl and tip the contents of the sieve into the pan to brown. Remove from the pan. Add marinade liquid to the pan and boil, stirring, for 30 seconds to deglaze the pan.

PLACE the pork fat in a large casserole, then add the pig's trotter, beef and marinade ingredients. Pour in the marinade liquid and stock. Bring to the boil, then cover, reduce the heat and simmer gently for 2–2½ hours or until the meat is tender.

LIFT the meat out of the casserole into a serving dish, cover and keep warm. Discard the garlic, onion, pork fat and pig's trotter. Pour the liquid through a fine sieve and skim off as much fat as possible, then return to the casserole. Bring to the boil and boil until reduced by half and syrupy. Pour the gravy over the meat to serve.

FROM ITALY

RAVIOLI

FILLING
30 g (1 oz) butter
½ small onion, finely chopped
2 garlic cloves, crushed
90 g (3 oz) prosciutto, finely chopped
125 g (4 oz) finely minced (ground) pork
125 g (4 oz) finely minced (ground) veal
½ teaspoon finely chopped fresh oregano, or 1/8 teaspoon dried
1 teaspoon paprika
½ tablespoon tomato paste (purée)
125 ml (4 fl oz/½ cup) chicken stock
2 egg yolks

1 quantity pasta (see recipe on page 470), rolled out
semolina
1 egg, beaten

SERVES 4

TO MAKE the filling, heat the butter in a frying pan. Cook onion, garlic and prosciutto over moderately low heat for 5–6 minutes without browning. Add the pork and veal, increase the heat and lightly brown, breaking up the lumps. Add the oregano and paprika, season well and stir in the tomato paste and chicken stock.

COVER pan and cook for 50 minutes. Uncover, increase the heat and cook for another 10 minutes until the filling is quite dry. Cool, then chop to get rid of any lumps. Stir in the egg yolks.

TO MAKE the ravioli, divide the rolled out pasta into four sheets: two 30 x 20 cm (12 x 8 inch) sheets and two slightly larger. Dust work surface with semolina and lay out one of the smaller sheets (keep the rest of the pasta covered with a damp tea towel (dish towel) to prevent it drying out). Lightly score the pasta sheet into 24 squares. Place a scant teaspoon of filling in the centre of each square and flatten it slightly with the back of the spoon.

BRUSH beaten egg along the score lines around the filling. Take one of the larger pasta sheets and cover the first, starting at one end. Match edges and press the top sheet onto the beaten egg as you go. Avoid stretching the top sheet, rather let it settle into place. Run your finger firmly around the filling and along the cutting lines to seal well. Use a sharp knife to cut into 24 ravioli squares.

(IF YOU are not using the ravioli immediately, place them, well spaced out, on baking paper dusted with cornmeal and cover with a tea towel. They can be left for 1–2 hours before cooking – don't refrigerate or they will become damp.)

COOK ravioli, in small batches, in a large saucepan of boiling salted water until al dente. Remove and drain with a slotted spoon. Serve on their own or with melted butter, olive oil or grated parmesan.

Making ravioli by scoring the pasta, adding the filling, covering it and then cutting it is much easier than cutting the pasta first. You can also use a special fluted ravioli wheel to cut the edges, giving a crimped effect.

FROM MOROCCO

COUSCOUS WITH LAMB AND SEVEN VEGETABLES

THE NUMBER SEVEN IS CONSIDERED AUSPICIOUS, HENCE THE SEVEN VEGETABLES IN THIS POPULAR DISH. THE CORRECT TRANSLATION OF 'BIDAWI' IS 'IN THE STYLE OF CASABLANCA' (DAR-EL-BEIDA IN ARABIC). IN MOROCCAN HOUSEHOLDS, COUSCOUS IS SERVED ON FRIDAYS.

1 kg (2 lb 4 oz) lamb shoulder, boned
3 tablespoons olive oil
2 brown onions, quartered
2 garlic cloves, finely chopped
½ teaspoon ground turmeric
½ teaspoon paprika
¼ teaspoon ground saffron threads
1 cinnamon stick
4 coriander (cilantro) sprigs and 4 flat-leaf (Italian) parsley sprigs, tied in a bunch
400 g (14 oz) tin chopped tomatoes
1½ teaspoons freshly ground black pepper
3 carrots, peeled and cut into thick sticks
3 small turnips, peeled and quartered
30 g (1 oz/¼ cup) raisins
4 zucchini (courgettes), cut into sticks
400 g (14 oz) firm pumpkin (winter squash) or butternut pumpkin (squash), peeled and cut into 2.5 cm (1 inch) chunks
420 g (15 oz) tin chickpeas, rinsed and drained
1 quantity couscous (see recipe on page 473)
2–3 teaspoons harissa (see recipe on page 482), to taste

SERVES 6

TRIM the lamb of excess fat if necessary, then cut into 2 cm (¾ inch) cubes.

HEAT the oil in a large saucepan or the base of a large couscoussier and add the lamb, onion and garlic. Cook over medium heat, turning the lamb once, just until the lamb loses its red colour. Stir in the turmeric, paprika and saffron, add 750 ml (26 fl oz/3 cups) water, then add the cinnamon stick, the bunch of herbs, tomatoes, pepper and 1½ teaspoons salt, or to taste. Bring to a gentle boil, then cover and simmer over low heat for 1 hour. Add the carrots and turnips and cook for a further 20 minutes.

ADD raisins, zucchini, pumpkin and chickpeas to the saucepan, adding a little water if necessary to almost cover the ingredients. Cook for a further 20 minutes, or until meat and vegetables are tender.

WHILE the stew is cooking, prepare the couscous. Steam it either over the stew or over a saucepan of boiling water.

PILE the couscous in a deep, heated platter and make a dent in the centre. Remove the herbs and cinnamon stick from the stew and ladle the meat and vegetables into the hollow and on top of the couscous, letting some tumble down the sides. Moisten with a little broth from the stew, then pour 250 ml (9 fl oz/1 cup) of the remaining broth into a bowl and stir in the harissa. The harissa-flavoured broth is added to the couscous to keep it moist, and according to individual taste.

In Morocco, couscous comes in three different sized grains; medium or regular grains are preferred.

FROM ITALY

VITELLO TONNATO

THERE ARE TWO VERSIONS OF THIS NORTH ITALIAN DISH, BOTH FEATURING A SAUCE OF MASHED TUNA AND ANCHOVIES. IN THE OLDER, MILANESE, VERSION THE SAUCE IS THINNED WITH CREAM; THIS RECIPE IS FOR THE PIEMONTESE DISH, WHICH USES MAYONNAISE RATHER THAN CREAM.

1 x 1.25 kg (2 lb 12 oz) boneless rolled veal roast
500 ml (17 fl oz/2 cups) dry white wine
500 ml (17 fl oz/2 cups) chicken stock
2 garlic cloves
1 onion, quartered
1 carrot, roughly chopped
1 celery stalk, roughly chopped
2 bay leaves
3 cloves
10 peppercorns

SAUCE
100 g (3½ oz) tin tuna in olive oil
15 g (½ oz) anchovy fillets
2 egg yolks
2 tablespoons lemon juice
125 ml (4 fl oz/½ cup) olive oil

sprigs of parsley
capers
thin lemon slices

SERVES 4

PUT the veal, wine, stock, garlic, onion, carrot, celery, bay leaves, cloves and peppercorns in a stockpot or very large saucepan. Add enough water to come two-thirds of the way up the veal and bring to the boil. Reduce the heat, cover the saucepan and simmer for 1¼ hours, or until tender. Leave to cool for 30 minutes, then remove veal from the pan and strain the stock. Pour stock into a saucepan and boil rapidly until reduced to about 250 ml (8 fl oz/1 cup).

TO MAKE the sauce, purée the tuna and its oil with the anchovy fillets in a blender or small food processor. Add the egg yolks and 1 tablespoon of the lemon juice and process until smooth. With the motor running, slowly pour in the oil. Gradually add the reduced stock until the sauce has the consistency of a thin mayonnaise. (If you're doing this by hand, chop the tuna and anchovy finely, mix in the egg yolks and lemon juice and whisk in the oil and stock.) Blend in the remaining lemon juice and season well.

TO SERVE, thinly slice the cold veal and arrange in overlapping slices down the centre of a serving platter. Spoon the sauce over the top and garnish with the parsley, capers and lemon slices.

Capers are usually available preserved in vinegar (these are best rinsed before use) but you will find that those preserved in salt are of a superior quality. Rinse well and pat dry before using.

The veal can be cooling in the stock while you make the sauce.

While the rabbit is simmering, deep-fry the sage until crispy.

FROM FRANCE

RABBIT FRICASSÉE

THE NAME OF THE DISH COMES FROM AN OLD FRENCH WORD, FRICASSER, TO FRY. A FRICASSÉE IS A DISH OF WHITE MEAT, USUALLY CHICKEN, VEAL OR RABBIT, IN A VELOUTÉ SAUCE WITH EGG YOLKS AND CREAM. WILD RABBIT, IF YOU CAN GET IT, HAS A BETTER FLAVOUR THAN FARMED.

60 g (2 oz) clarified butter
1 x 1.5 kg (3 lb) rabbit, cut into 8 pieces
200 g (7 oz) button mushrooms
90 ml (3 fl oz) white wine
150 ml (5 fl oz) chicken stock
bouquet garni
90 ml (3 fl oz) oil
small bunch of sage
150 ml (5 fl oz) thick (double/heavy) cream
2 egg yolks

SERVES 4

HEAT half the clarified butter in a large saucepan, season the rabbit and brown in batches, turning once. Remove from the saucepan and set aside. Add the remaining butter to the saucepan and brown the mushrooms.

PUT the rabbit back into the saucepan with the mushrooms. Add the wine and boil for a couple of minutes before adding the stock and bouquet garni. Cover the pan tightly and simmer gently over very low heat for 40 minutes.

MEANWHILE, heat the oil in a small saucepan. Remove the leaves from the bunch of sage and drop them, a few at a time, into the hot oil. The leaves will immediately start to bubble around the edges. Cook them for 30 seconds, or until bright green and crispy. Make sure you don't overheat the oil or cook the leaves for too long or they will turn black and taste burnt. Drain the leaves on paper towels and sprinkle with salt.

LIFT the cooked rabbit and mushrooms out of the saucepan and keep warm. Discard the bouquet garni. Remove the pan from the heat, mix together the cream and egg yolks and stir quickly into the stock. Return to very low heat and cook, stirring, for about 5 minutes to thicken slightly (don't let the sauce boil or the eggs will scramble). Season with salt and pepper.

TO SERVE, pour the sauce over the rabbit and mushrooms and garnish with crispy sage leaves.

FROM MOROCCO

STEAMED LAMB WITH CUMIN

THIS IS A DISH OF SIMPLE BUT DELICIOUS FLAVOURS. WHEN SERVED AS PART OF A MOROCCAN MEAL, MORSELS OF LAMB ARE GENTLY PULLED FROM THE BONE WITH THE FINGERS. HOWEVER, LAMB CAN BE SLICED AND SERVED WITH BEETROOT AND CUMIN SALAD AND TINY BOILED POTATOES.

- 1.25 kg (2 lb 12 oz) lamb shoulder on the bone
- 1½ teaspoons ground cumin, plus extra to serve (optional)
- 1 teaspoon coarse salt, plus extra to serve (optional)
- ½ teaspoon freshly ground black pepper
- pinch of ground saffron threads
- 6 garlic cloves, bruised
- 10–12 flat-leaf (Italian) parsley stalks
- 1 tablespoon olive oil

SERVES 4

TRIM the excess fat from the whole shoulder of lamb if necessary. Wipe the meat with damp paper towel and then cut small incisions into the meat on each side.

COMBINE cumin, salt, black pepper and saffron and rub mixture into the lamb, pushing it into the incisions. Cover and leave for 30 minutes to allow the flavours to penetrate. Place the lamb, fat side up, on a piece of muslin (cheesecloth), top with half the garlic cloves and tie the muslin over the top.

USING a large saucepan onto which a steamer will fit, or the base of a couscoussier, fill it three-quarters full with water. If using a saucepan and steamer, check that the base of the steamer is at least 3 cm (1¼ inch) above the surface of the water. Cover and bring to the boil. Line the base of the steamer with the parsley stalks and the remaining garlic cloves. Place lamb on top, put folded strips of foil around the rim of the steamer and put the lid on firmly to contain the steam. Keeping the heat just high enough to maintain a boil, steam for 2–2½ hours – do not lift the lid for the first 1½ hours of cooking. The lamb should easily pull away from the bone when cooked. Lift it out of the steamer. Remove the muslin.

HEAT the oil in a large frying pan and quickly brown lamb on each side for a more attractive presentation. This dish is traditionally served as part of a Moroccan meal, with the lamb taken from the bone with the fingers. It is accompanied with little dishes of coarse salt and ground cumin for extra seasoning.

Rub spices into the incisions and wrap in muslin (cheesecloth) to contain the flavourings.

FROM ITALY

CANNELLONI

Roll the pasta around the filling fairly tightly, then lay the cannelloni seam side down in the dish.

MEAT SAUCE
3 tablespoons olive oil
1 onion, finely chopped
2 garlic cloves, crushed
120 g (4 oz) bacon, finely chopped
60 g (2 oz) button mushrooms, finely chopped
¼ teaspoon dried basil
225 g (8 oz) minced (ground) pork
225 g (8 oz) minced (ground) veal
1 tablespoon finely chopped parsley
200 g (7 oz) tin chopped tomatoes
250 ml (9 fl oz/1 cup) beef stock
3 tablespoons dried breadcrumbs
1 egg

TOMATO SAUCE
2 tablespoons olive oil
1 small onion, finely chopped
2 garlic cloves, crushed
2 x 400 g (14 oz) tins chopped tomatoes
1 teaspoon chopped basil

10 sheets fresh lasagne, about 17 x 12 cm (7 x 5 inches) (the grain of the pasta should run with the width not the length, or the pasta will split when rolled up), or 1½ quantities pasta (see recipe on page 470) rolled and cut into 10 sheets as above
4 large slices prosciutto, cut in half
60 g (2 oz/½ cup) grated fontina cheese
185 ml (6 fl oz/¾ cup) thick (double/heavy) cream
65 g (2 oz/⅔ cup) grated parmesan cheese

SERVES 4

TO MAKE the meat sauce, heat the oil in a frying pan and cook the onion, garlic and bacon over moderate heat for 6 minutes, or until the onion is soft and golden. Stir in the mushrooms and basil, cook for 2–3 minutes, then add the pork and veal. Cook, stirring often to break up the lumps, until the mince has changed colour. Season well, add parsley, tomatoes and stock. Partially cover the pan. Simmer for 1 hour. Remove lid and simmer for another 30 minutes to reduce the liquid. Cool slightly, then stir in the breadcrumbs, then the egg.

TO MAKE the tomato sauce, heat oil in a frying pan and cook the onion and garlic for 6 minutes, or until the onion has softened but not browned. Stir in tomatoes and basil. Add 250 ml (9 fl oz/ 1 cup) water and season well. Simmer for about 30 minutes, or until you have a thick sauce.

COOK lasagne in batches in a large saucepan of boiling salted water until al dente. Scoop out each batch with a slotted spoon and drop into a bowl of cold water. Spread the sheets out in a single layer on a tea towel (dish towel), turning them over once to blot dry each side. Trim away any torn edges. (We have allowed two extra sheets of fresh lasagne in case of tearing.)

PREHEAT oven to 190°C (375°F/Gas 5). Grease a shallow 30 x 18 cm (12 x 7 inch) ovenproof dish and spoon the tomato sauce over the base.

PLACE a half slice of prosciutto over each pasta sheet. Top with a sprinkling of fontina. Spoon an eighth of the meat filling across one end of the pasta sheet. Starting from this end, roll the pasta up tightly to enclose the filling. Place the filled rolls, seam side down, in a row in the dish.

BEAT TOGETHER the cream and parmesan and season well. Spoon over the cannelloni so that it is covered. Bake for 20 minutes, or until lightly browned on top. Leave to rest for 10 minutes before serving.

FROM FRANCE

STEAK AU POIVRE

- 4 x 200 g (7 oz) fillet steaks
- 2 tablespoons oil
- 6 tablespoons black peppercorns, crushed
- 40 g (1½ oz) butter
- 3 tablespoons Cognac
- 60 ml (2 fl oz/¼ cup) white wine
- 125 ml (4 fl oz/½ cup) double (thick/heavy) cream

SERVES 4

RUB steaks on both sides with the oil and press the crushed peppercorns into the meat. Melt the butter in a large frying pan and cook the steaks for 2–4 minutes on each side, depending on how you like your steak.

ADD the Cognac and flambé by lighting the pan with your gas flame or a match (stand well back when you do this and keep a pan lid handy for emergencies). Put steaks on a hot plate. Add wine to the pan and boil, stirring, for 1 minute to deglaze the pan. Add the cream and stir for 1–2 minutes. Season and pour over the steaks.

Press the peppercorns firmly into the steaks, so they don't come off while you are frying.

STEAK BÉARNAISE

- 1 shallot, finely chopped
- 2 tablespoons white wine vinegar or tarragon vinegar
- 2 tablespoons white wine
- 3 tarragon sprigs
- 1 teaspoon dried tarragon
- 3 egg yolks
- 200 g (7 oz) clarified butter, melted
- 1 tablespoon chopped tarragon leaves
- 4 x 200 g (7 oz) fillet steaks
- 1 tablespoon oil

SERVES 4

PUT the shallot, vinegar, wine, tarragon sprigs and dried tarragon in a saucepan. Bring to the boil and cook until reduced to 1 tablespoon. Remove from the heat and cool slightly.

WHISK the egg yolks with 1½ tablespoons water, and add to the saucepan. Place the pan over very low heat or over a simmering bain-marie and continue to whisk until the sauce is thick. Do not boil or the eggs will scramble.

REMOVE the sauce from the heat, continue to whisk and slowly add the butter in a thin steady stream. Pass through a fine strainer. Stir in the chopped tarragon. Season with salt and pepper and keep warm while cooking the steaks.

RUB the steaks with oil, season them with salt and pepper and cook for 2–4 minutes on each side, depending on how you like your steak. Serve with the sauce.

STEAK BÉARNAISE

STEAK AU POIVRE

FROM ITALY

TAGLIATELLE WITH RAGU

SPAGHETTI BOLOGNESE IS ONE OF THE MOST POPULAR AND WELL-KNOWN ITALIAN DISHES AROUND THE WORLD. HOWEVER, THE ITALIANS THEMSELVES WOULD NEVER DREAM OF SERVING THEIR TRADITIONAL BOLOGNESE SAUCE ON SPAGHETTI. TAGLIATELLE IS THE USUAL ACCOMPANIMENT.

60 g (2 oz) butter
1 onion, finely chopped
1 celery stalk, finely chopped
1 carrot, finely chopped
90 g (3 oz) pancetta or bacon, finely chopped
225 g (8 oz) minced (ground) beef
225 g (8 oz) minced (ground) pork
2 sprigs of oregano, chopped, or ¼ teaspoon dried oregano
pinch of ground nutmeg
120 g (4 oz) chicken livers, trimmed and finely chopped
125 ml (4 fl oz/½ cup) dry white wine
185 ml (6 fl oz/¾ cup) milk
400 g (14 oz) tin chopped tomatoes
250 ml (9 fl oz/1 cup) beef stock
400 g (14 oz) tagliatelle
grated parmesan cheese, to serve

SERVES 4

HEAT the butter in a saucepan and add the onion, celery, carrot and pancetta. Cook over moderate heat for 6–8 minutes, stirring from time to time.

ADD the minced beef, pork and oregano to the saucepan. Season with salt and pepper and the nutmeg. Cook for about 5 minutes, or until the mince has changed colour but not browned. Add chicken liver and cook until it changes colour.

POUR IN the wine, increase heat and boil over high heat for 2–3 minutes, or until the wine has been absorbed. Stir in 125 ml (4 fl oz/½ cup) of the milk, reduce heat and simmer for 10 minutes. Add the tomatoes and half the stock, partially cover the pan and leave to simmer gently over very low heat for 3 hours. Add more of the stock as it is needed to keep the sauce moist.

MEANWHILE, cook the pasta in a large saucepan of boiling salted water until al dente. Stir remaining milk into the sauce 5 minutes before serving. Taste the sauce for seasoning, then drain the tagliatelle, toss with the sauce and serve with the parmesan.

The backstreets of Bologna.

FROM SPAIN

CATALAN NOODLES

THERE ARE NUMEROUS RECIPES FOR THIS NOODLE DISH, A CURIOSITY OF CATALAN CUISINE. UNLIKE MOST ITALIAN PASTAS, FIDEOS ARE VERY SHORT – HALF THE LENGTH OF YOUR LITTLE FINGER – AND THIN, MORE NOODLE THAN SPAGHETTI. BELOW IS A CLASSIC COMBINATION OF FIDEOS WITH PORK.

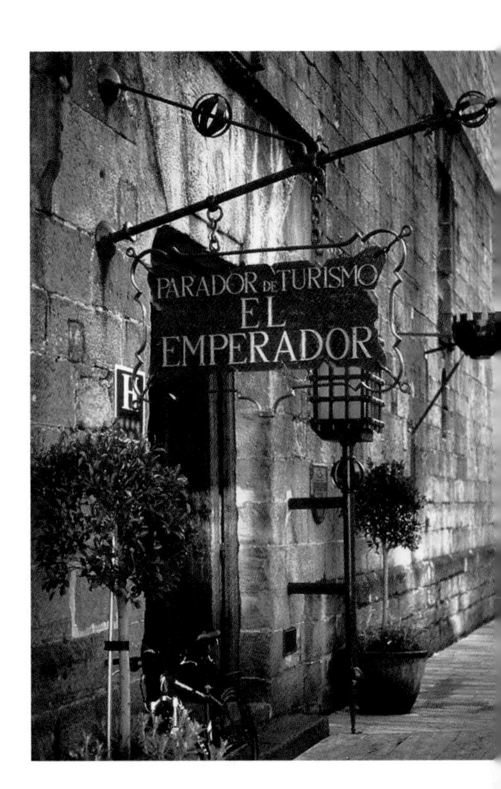

80 ml (2½ fl oz/⅓ cup) olive oil
250 g (9 oz) pork spare ribs, cut into 1 cm (½ inch) thick slices
1 brown onion, chopped
125 ml (4 fl oz/½ cup) tomato passata (puréed tomato)
1 teaspoon sweet paprika (pimentón)
100 g (3½ oz) fresh spicy pork sausages, thickly sliced
100 g (3½ oz) chorizo, sliced
1½ litres (52 fl oz/6 cups) beef or chicken stock
500 g (1 lb 2 oz) spaghettini, broken into 2½ cm (1 inch) pieces

PICADA
50 g (1¾ oz/⅓ cup) nuts (either hazelnuts, pine nuts or almonds)
2 garlic cloves, crushed
2 tablespoons chopped flat-leaf (Italian) parsley
¼ teaspoon ground cinnamon
1 slice bread, toasted and crusts removed
¼ teaspoon saffron threads

SERVES 4

HEAT the oil in a large heavy-based saucepan over medium–high heat and cook the ribs in batches until golden. Add the onion and cook for 5 minutes, or until softened. Stir in puréed tomato and paprika and cook for a few minutes more.

ADD pork sausages, chorizo and stock (reserving 2 tablespoons) and bring to the boil. Reduce to a simmer and add the spaghettini. Cook, covered, for 15 minutes, or until the pasta is al dente.

MEANWHILE, to make the picada, in a mortar and pestle or a food processor, crush the nuts with the garlic, parsley, cinnamon and bread to make a paste. Stir in the saffron. If the mixture is too dry, add 1–2 tablespoons of the reserved stock. Stir into the casserole and simmer for 5 minutes, or until the casserole has thickened slightly. Season well before serving.

Stir picada through the noodles towards the end of cooking to thicken and add flavour.

FROM ITALY

SPICY LAMB CASSEROLE

THE PINCH OF CHILLI SIGNIFIES THIS AS A SOUTHERN DISH, PROBABLY FROM BASILICATA, WHERE SHEEP WERE THE MAIN SOURCE OF INCOME. SUCH DISHES OFTEN ORIGINATED WITH SHEPHERDS, WHO USED WILD HERBS AND VEGETABLES FOUND AROUND THEIR CAMP.

3 tablespoons olive oil
1.25 kg (2 lb 12 oz) lamb leg or shoulder, cut into 4 cm (1½ inch) cubes
1 small onion, finely chopped
1 celery stalk, finely chopped
3 garlic cloves, crushed
125 ml (4 fl oz/½ cup) dry Marsala
¾ teaspoon chilli flakes
1 tablespoon crushed juniper berries
2 tablespoons tomato paste (purée)
250 ml (9 fl oz/1 cup) chicken stock
1 sprig of rosemary
12 small onions, such as cipolline or pearl onions
2 all-purpose potatoes, cut into cubes
2 tablespoons finely chopped parsley

SERVES 4

PREHEAT the oven to 180°C (350°F/Gas 4).

HEAT the olive oil in a large casserole. Add lamb in batches, taking care not to overcrowd the pan. Season with salt and pepper and brown lightly over a high heat. Remove each batch from the casserole as it browns. Once all the lamb has been browned and removed from the casserole, add the onion, celery and garlic, reduce the heat and cook for 4–5 minutes until softened.

RETURN the lamb to the casserole. Pour in the Marsala and cook over high heat until it is dark brown and reduced by half. Add the chilli flakes and juniper berries and cook, stirring, for just 10–15 seconds. Add the tomato paste, chicken stock, rosemary and about 250 ml (9 fl oz/1 cup) water, or enough to just cover.

COVER the casserole with a lid and bake in the oven for 45 minutes. Add the onions and potato and cook for another 45 minutes. Stir the parsley through just before serving.

A butcher trims a leg of lamb in a Sicilian market.

FROM FRANCE

PORK NOISETTES WITH PRUNES

PORK WITH PRUNES IS A TYPICAL DISH OF THE ORCHARD-RICH TOURAINE REGION. IT IS SOMETIMES SAID THAT THE FRENCH GENERALLY DO NOT COMBINE FRUIT WITH MEAT, SWEET FLAVOURS WITH SAVOURY, BUT PRUNES AND APPLES ARE BOTH ENTHUSIASTICALLY COMBINED WITH PORK.

8 pork noisettes or 2 x 400 g (14 oz) pork fillets
16 prunes, pitted
1 tablespoon oil
45 g (1½ oz) butter
1 onion, finely chopped
155 ml (5 fl oz) white wine
280 ml (9½ fl oz) chicken or beef stock
1 bay leaf
2 thyme sprigs
250 ml (9 fl oz/1 cup) thick (double/heavy) cream

SERVES 4

TRIM any excess fat from the pork, making sure you get rid of any membrane that will cause the pork to shrink. If you are using pork fillet, cut each fillet into four diagonal slices. Put the prunes in a small saucepan, cover with cold water and bring to the boil. Reduce heat and simmer prunes for 5 minutes. Drain well.

HEAT oil in a large heavy-based frying pan and add half the butter. When butter starts foaming, add the pork, in batches, if necessary, and sauté on both sides until cooked. Transfer the pork to a warm plate, cover and keep warm.

POUR OFF excess fat from the pan. Melt the remaining butter, add the onion and cook over a low heat until softened but not browned. Add wine, bring to the boil and simmer for 2 minutes. Add the stock, bay leaf and thyme and bring to the boil. Reduce heat and simmer for 10 minutes or until reduced by half.

STRAIN the stock into a bowl and rinse the frying pan. Return the stock to the pan, add the cream and prunes and simmer for 8 minutes, or until the sauce thickens slightly. Tip the pork back into the pan and simmer until heated through.

Sauté the pork on both sides, then keep it warm while you make the sauce.

Streets behind the Bay of Naples.

FROM ITALY

PICCATA AL LIMONE

- 4 large veal escalopes
- plain (all-purpose) flour, seasoned with salt and pepper
- 1 tablespoon olive oil
- 2 tablespoons butter
- 80 ml (2½ fl oz/⅓ cup) dry white wine
- 250 ml (9 fl oz/1 cup) chicken stock
- 3 tablespoons lemon juice
- 2 tablespoons capers, rinsed and chopped, if large
- 1 tablespoon finely chopped parsley
- 8 caperberries

SERVES 4

PLACE the veal between two sheets of plastic wrap and pound with a meat mallet until an even thickness. Lightly dust each side with flour.

HEAT the olive oil and butter in a large frying pan. Fry the escalopes over moderately high heat for about 2 minutes on each side, or until golden. Season and transfer to a warm plate.

ADD the wine to the pan, increase the heat to high and boil until there are just 3–4 tablespoons of liquid left. Pour in the stock and boil for about 5 minutes, or until it has reduced and slightly thickened. Add the lemon juice and capers and cook, stirring, for 1 minute. Taste for seasoning, then return the escalopes to the pan and heat through for 30 seconds. Sprinkle with parsley and serve at once, garnished with caperberries.

BISTECCA ALLA PIZZAIOLA

BISTECCA ALLA PIZZAIOLA

- 4 rib or rump steaks
- 4 tablespoons olive oil
- 550 g (1 lb 4 oz) tomatoes
- 3 garlic cloves, crushed
- 3 basil leaves, torn into pieces
- 1 teaspoon finely chopped parsley

SERVES 4

BRUSH the steaks with 1 tablespoon of the olive oil and season well. Put on a plate and set aside.

SCORE a cross in the top of each tomato. Plunge into boiling water for 20 seconds, drain and peel the skin. Chop tomatoes, discarding the cores.

HEAT 2 tablespoons of the olive oil in a saucepan over low heat and add the garlic. Soften without browning for 1–2 minutes, then add the tomato and season. Increase the heat, bring to the boil and cook for 5 minutes. Stir in the basil.

HEAT the remaining oil in a large frying pan with a tight-fitting lid. Brown the steaks over moderately high heat for 2 minutes on each side (cook in batches rather than overcrowding the pan). Place in a slightly overlapping row down the centre of the pan and spoon the sauce over the top, covering the steaks completely. Cover pan and cook over low heat for about 5 minutes, or until steaks are cooked to your taste. Serve, sprinkled with parsley.

PICCATA AL LIMONE

FROM SPAIN

LAMB STEW

WHAT MOST SPANISH PEOPLE EAT TODAY IS VERY MUCH WHAT THEY HAVE EATEN FOR HUNDREDS OF YEARS. A BOWL OF FILLING, TASTY COCHIFRITO, SERVED ON A WINTER'S NIGHT IN FRONT OF A WARM FIRE WITH BREAD AND A GLASS OF LOCALLY MADE WINE, IS AS APPEALING NOW AS IT EVER WAS.

The flavours in this stew rely heavily on browning the lamb and onions well.

- 80 ml (2½ fl oz/⅓ cup) olive oil
- 1 kg (2 lb 4 oz) lamb shoulder, diced
- 1 large brown onion, finely chopped
- 4 garlic cloves, crushed
- 2 teaspoons sweet paprika (pimentón)
- 100 ml (3½ fl oz) lemon juice
- 2 tablespoons chopped flat-leaf (Italian) parsley

SERVES 4

HEAT the oil in a large, deep heavy-based frying pan over high heat and cook the lamb in two batches for 5 minutes each batch, or until well browned. Remove all the lamb from the pan.

ADD the onion to the pan and cook for 5 minutes, or until soft and golden. Stir in the garlic and paprika and cook for 1 minute. Return the lamb to the pan and add 80 ml (2½ fl oz/⅓ cup) of the lemon juice and 1¾ litres (61 fl oz/7 cups) water. Bring to a boil, then reduce to a simmer and cook, stirring occasionally, for about 2 hours, or until the liquid has almost evaporated and the oil starts to reappear. Stir in the parsley and remaining lemon juice, season with salt and freshly ground black pepper, and serve.

Ravida Estate in Menfi, Sicily.

A metal pie tin will give your pastry a good crisp finish and help it brown nicely on the outside. When putting in the filling, make sure you squash out any air bubbles so the pie is packed full.

FROM ITALY

PIZZA RUSTICA

THE NAME IS MISLEADING, BECAUSE PIZZA RUSTICA IS A PIE, NOT A PIZZA. THIS MEDIEVAL RECIPE IS UNUSUAL IN ITS COMBINATION OF A SWEET PASTRY CASE WITH A SAVOURY FILLING AND, LIKE MANY RICH PIES, PROBABLY BEGAN ITS LIFE AS A CELEBRATION DISH FOR COUNTRY FESTIVALS.

PASTRY
220 g (8 oz/1¾ cups) plain (all-purpose) flour
½ teaspoon baking powder
pinch of salt
100 g (3½ oz) butter, chilled
55 g (2 oz/¼ cup) caster (superfine) sugar
1 egg yolk
60 ml (2 fl oz/¼ cup) cream

FILLING
500 g (1 lb 2 oz) ricotta cheese
3 eggs
50 g (1½ oz/½ cup) grated pecorino romano cheese
100 g (3½ oz/⅔ cup) grated mozzarella cheese
125 g (4 oz) prosciutto, finely shredded
2 tablespoons finely chopped parsley

SERVES 6

TO MAKE the pastry, sift the flour, baking powder and salt into a large bowl. Cut butter into cubes and add to the bowl. Rub it in with your fingertips until mixture resembles fine breadcrumbs. Stir in the sugar.

COMBINE the egg yolk and cream and pour this into the pastry mixture. Combine and then knead once or twice to make a soft dough. Refrigerate until needed.

TO MAKE the filling, mix the ricotta with the eggs, cheese, prosciutto and parsley and season well with pepper – you probably won't need to add any salt if the prosciutto is salty. Preheat the oven to 200°C (400°F/Gas 6).

CUT off one-third off the pastry and roll out the remainder on a floured surface. Line a 20 x 4 cm (8 x 1½ inch) pie tin and trim off any excess pastry. Fill the pastry case with the filling and smooth the top.

ROLL OUT the remaining pastry and cover the pie. Trim edges and bake for 20 minutes, then reduce the temperature to 180°C (350°F/Gas 4). Bake for a further 20 minutes, or until the filling is cooked.

FROM MOROCCO

LAMB TAGINE WITH PEAS AND LEMONS

PRESERVED LEMONS ADD A WONDERFUL FLAVOUR TO THIS DELICIOUS COMBINATION OF LAMB, GREEN PEAS, FRESH HERBS AND GROUND SPICES. WHILE SHELLED FRESH GREEN PEAS ARE PREFERRED, FROZEN PEAS ALSO GIVE GOOD RESULTS.

- 1 kg (2 lb 4 oz) boneless lamb shoulder or leg
- 2 tablespoons olive oil
- 1 brown onion, finely chopped
- 2 garlic cloves, finely chopped
- 1 teaspoon ground cumin
- ½ teaspoon ground ginger
- ½ teaspoon ground turmeric
- 3 tablespoons chopped coriander (cilantro) leaves
- 3 tablespoons chopped flat-leaf (Italian) parsley
- 1 teaspoon dried za'atar or 2 teaspoons chopped fresh lemon thyme
- 1½ preserved lemons (see recipe on page 485)
- 235 g (8½ oz/1½ cups) shelled fresh or frozen green peas
- 2 teaspoons chopped mint
- ½ teaspoon caster (superfine) sugar

SERVES 6

TRIM the lamb and cut into 3 cm (1¼ inch) pieces. Heat olive oil in a large saucepan over high heat and brown lamb in batches, removing to a dish when cooked. Add more oil if required.

REDUCE the heat to low, add the onion and cook for 5 minutes until softened. Add the garlic, cumin, ginger and turmeric and cook for a few seconds. Add 375 ml (13 fl oz/1½ cups) water and stir well to lift the browned juices off the base of the pan, then return the lamb to the pan with a little salt and a good grinding of black pepper. Add coriander, parsley and za'atar, then cover and simmer over low heat for 1½ hours, or until the lamb is tender.

SEPARATE the preserved lemons into quarters and rinse well under cold running water, removing and discarding the pulp and membranes. Cut the rind into strips and add to the lamb, along with the peas, mint and sugar. Return to a simmer, cover and simmer for a further 10 minutes, or until the peas are cooked. Serve hot.

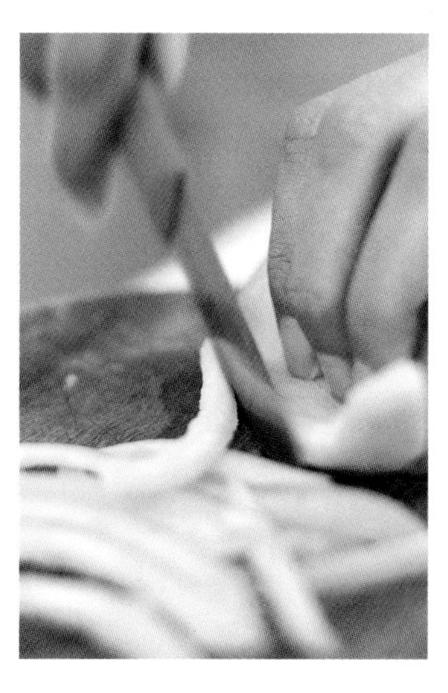

Preserved lemon is essential for this delicious dish. Cut rinsed rind into strips and add towards end of cooking.

A greengrocer at Saint-Rèmy.

FROM FRANCE

NAVARIN A LA PRINTANIÈRE

NAVARIN A LA PRINTANIÈRE IS TRADITIONALLY MADE TO WELCOME SPRING AND THE NEW CROP OF YOUNG VEGETABLES. NAVARINS, OR STEWS, CAN ALSO BE MADE ALL YEAR ROUND, USING OLDER WINTER ROOT VEGETABLES SUCH AS POTATOES, CARROTS AND TURNIPS.

1 kg (2 lb 4 oz) lean lamb shoulder
30 g (1 oz) butter
1 onion, chopped
1 garlic clove, crushed
1 tablespoon plain (all-purpose) flour
500 ml (17 fl oz/2 cups) beef or veal stock
bouquet garni
18 baby carrots
8 large-bulb spring onions (scallions)
200 g (7 oz) baby turnips
175 g (6 oz) small all-purpose potatoes
150 g (5 oz) peas, fresh or frozen

SERVES 6

TRIM the lamb of any fat and sinew and then cut it into bite-sized pieces. Heat the butter over high heat in a large casserole. Brown lamb in two or three batches, then remove from the casserole.

ADD the onion to the casserole and cook, stirring occasionally, over moderate heat for 3 minutes or until softened but not browned. Add the garlic and cook for a further minute or until aromatic.

RETURN the meat and any juices to the casserole and sprinkle with the flour. Stir over high heat until the meat is well coated and the liquid is bubbling, then gradually stir in the stock. Add the bouquet garni and bring to the boil. Reduce the heat to low, cover the casserole and cook for 1¼ hours.

TRIM the carrots, leaving a little bit of green stalk, and do the same with the spring onions and baby turnips. Cut the potatoes in half if they are large.

ADD vegetables to the casserole dish, bring to the boil and simmer, covered, for 15 minutes or until the vegetables are tender. (If you are using frozen peas, add them right at the end so they just heat through.) Season with plenty of salt and pepper before serving.

Brown the lamb in a couple of batches so that you don't lower the temperature by overcrowding. Once all the meat is browned and coated with flour, slowly stir in the stock.

FROM ITALY

VENISON CASSEROLE

A DARK GAMEY MEAT LIKE VENISON NEEDS STRONG FLAVOURS TO BALANCE IT. THIS CASSEROLE CONTAINS CLOVES, JUNIPER AND ALLSPICE, ALL OF WHICH ARE ROBUST FLAVOURINGS IN THEIR OWN RIGHT. SERVE WITH CREAMY POLENTA OR POTATOES TO MOP UP THE RICH GRAVY.

1 sprig of rosemary
1 large onion
1 garlic clove
85 g (3 oz) prosciutto
100 g (3½ oz) butter
1 kg (2 lb 4 oz) venison, cut into large cubes
1 litre (35 fl oz/4 cups) beef stock
80 ml (2½ fl oz/⅓ cup) red wine vinegar
80 ml (2½ fl oz/⅓ cup) robust red wine
2 cloves
4 juniper berries
pinch of allspice
1 bay leaf
3 tablespoons plain (all-purpose) flour
2 tablespoons dry Marsala or brandy
1½ teaspoons grated lemon zest
1½ tablespoons finely chopped parsley

SERVES 4

STRIP the leaves off the rosemary and chop them finely with the onion, garlic and prosciutto. Heat half the butter in a large heavy saucepan with a lid. Add chopped mixture and soften over moderately low heat for 5 minutes. Season with pepper. Increase the heat, add the venison and cook for 10 minutes, or until brown on all sides.

PUT the stock in another saucepan and bring to the boil, then reduce the heat and keep at a low simmer.

INCREASE the heat under the venison, add the vinegar and cook until the liquid becomes thick and syrupy. Pour in red wine. When that becomes syrupy, stir in half of the simmering stock. Add the cloves, juniper berries, allspice and bay leaf and simmer for 1 hour, covered, stirring occasionally and adding hot water, if necessary, to maintain the liquid level.

MEANWHILE, melt remaining butter in a saucepan. Stir in the flour and cook over moderately low heat for 1 minute. Slowly stir in the remaining stock and cook until the sauce thickens slightly.

STIR sauce into the venison casserole, then add the Marsala. Uncover pan and simmer for a further 20 minutes. Taste for salt and pepper. Combine the lemon zest and parsley and sprinkle over the top before serving.

La Kalsa, Palermo.

FROM SPAIN

VALENCIAN LAMB AND RICE

A TRADITIONAL MEAL, ORIGINALLY DESIGNED TO USE UP THE LEFT-OVER MEAT AND BROTH FROM A COCIDO (A STEW USUALLY COMPRISED OF MEAT AND CHICKPEAS) AND FINISHED IN THE OVEN – ANOTHER SPANISH DISH PROVING THERE'S MORE TO RICE THAN PAELLA.

- 100 g (3½ oz/½ cup) chickpeas
- 1 red onion
- 1 parsnip
- 1 celery stick
- 1 turnip
- 200 g (7 oz) diced lamb leg
- 1 pig's ear, about 150–200 g (5½–7 oz), salted if possible
- 100 g (3½ oz) minced (ground) pork
- 4 tablespoons fine fresh breadcrumbs
- 50 g (1¾ oz) jamón, finely chopped
- 1 egg
- pinch of ground cinnamon
- 3 tablespoons chopped flat-leaf (Italian) parsley
- 1 morcilla or other blood sausage, about 200 g (7 oz)
- 1 white catalan sausage, butifarra or other mild pork sausage, about 200 g (7 oz)
- 2 tablespoons olive oil
- 1 garlic clove, finely chopped
- 300 g (10½ oz/1⅓ cups) short-grain rice

SERVES 5

SOAK the chickpeas in water for 3–4 hours, then drain.

MEANWHILE, chop the onion, parsnip, celery and turnip into 2 cm (¾ inch) dice and set aside. Bring 2 litres (70 fl oz/8 cups) of water to the boil in a large pot. Add diced lamb and pig's ear (whole). Bring water back to boil then reduce to a steady simmer and cook for 30 minutes. Next, add the drained chickpeas, diced onion, parsnip, celery and turnip and season to taste – if the pig's ear was salted you may not need any more salt. Continue to simmer for another 20 minutes.

MEANWHILE combine the pork mince with the breadcrumbs, jamón, egg, cinnamon and 1 tablespoon of the chopped parsley. Season well. Take heaped teaspoons of the mixture and roll them into balls.

ADD the whole sausages and the meatballs to the pot. Return to a simmer and cook for a further 10 minutes, or until the meatballs are firm to the touch and cooked through. Cover. Turn off heat.

PREHEAT oven to 180°C (350°F/Gas 4). Place a heavy based flameproof casserole on stovetop over medium–high heat. Add the oil and chopped garlic and cook, stirring for 2 minutes or until the garlic is lightly golden. Add the rice and stir for a further 1 minute. Stir in 600 ml (21 fl oz) of the cooking liquid from the stew. Bring to the boil, cover and place in oven for 20 minutes or until rice is cooked. Gently reheat the stew and serve the rice, garnished with the remaining parsley.

Roll the mince mixture into small balls. Slightly brown the garlic before stirring into the rice.

FROM MOROCCO

BEEF TAGINE WITH OKRA AND TOMATOES

TO PREVENT THE OKRA FROM BREAKING UP DURING COOKING, COOKS PASS A NEEDLE AND THREAD THROUGH THE CONICAL STEMS OF THE PODS, TYING THE THREAD TO FORM A 'NECKLACE'. WHEN THE TAGINE HAS TO BE STIRRED OR REMOVED, THIS IS LIFTED WITH THE END OF A WOODEN SPOON.

1 kg (2 lb 4 oz) beef chuck steak
3 tablespoons olive oil
1 brown onion, finely chopped
3 garlic cloves, finely chopped
½ teaspoon ground cumin
½ teaspoon ground turmeric
400 g (14 oz) tin chopped, peeled tomatoes
½ teaspoon caster (superfine) sugar
1 cinnamon stick
2 tablespoons chopped flat-leaf (Italian) parsley
1 tablespoon chopped coriander (cilantro) leaves, plus extra leaves, to serve
500 g (1 lb 2 oz) small fresh okra

SERVES 6

TRIM the steak and cut into 2.5 cm (1 inch) pieces. Heat half the olive oil in a large saucepan over a medium heat and brown beef in batches, adding a little more oil as needed. Set aside in a dish.

REDUCE heat to low, add the onion and remaining oil to the pan and cook gently for 10 minutes, or until softened. Add the garlic, cumin and turmeric, cook for a few seconds, then add the tomatoes, sugar, cinnamon stick, 1 teaspoon salt and a good grinding of black pepper. Return beef to the pan, add parsley, coriander and 250 ml (9 fl oz/1 cup) water. Cover the pan and simmer over low heat for 1½ hours, or until the meat is almost tender.

MEANWHILE, trim the very ends of the okra stems, avoiding cutting into the pods. Rinse okra in a colander under cold running water. Check that there is sufficient liquid in the saucepan, add a little more water if necessary so that the meat is almost covered, and place okra on top. Lightly sprinkle with salt, then cover and simmer for 30 minutes. Do not stir during this stage of cooking.

SCATTER with the extra coriander leaves and serve with crusty bread.

Is it the shape of the okra that appeals to Moroccans, or the taste? Certainly they make the most of the shape when presenting a cooked dish.

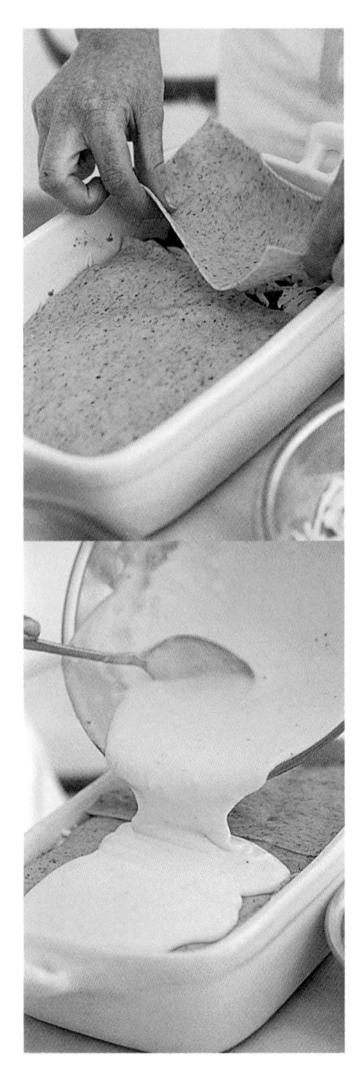

Lasagne is traditionally made with lasagne verde. Make sure the layers fit without overlapping too much or the lasagne will be stodgy. Leave enough béchamel for a good thick layer on top.

FROM ITALY

LASAGNE AL FORNO

MEAT SAUCE
30 g (1 oz) butter
1 onion, finely chopped
1 small carrot, finely chopped
½ celery stalk, finely chopped
1 garlic clove, crushed
125 g (4 oz) pancetta, sliced
500 g (1 lb 2 oz) minced (ground) beef
¼ teaspoon dried oregano
pinch of ground nutmeg
90 g (3 oz) chicken livers, trimmed and finely chopped
80 ml (2½ fl oz/⅓ cup) dry vermouth or dry white wine
330 ml (11 fl oz/1⅓ cups) beef stock
1 tablespoon tomato paste (purée)
2 tablespoons thick (double/heavy) cream
1 egg, beaten

1 quantity béchamel sauce (see recipe on page 489)
125 ml (4 fl oz/½ cup) thick (double/heavy) cream
100 g (3½ oz) fresh lasagne verde or 6 sheets dried lasagne
150 g (5 oz/1 cup) grated mozzarella cheese
65 g (2¼ oz/⅔ cup) grated parmesan cheese

SERVES 6

TO MAKE the meat sauce, heat the butter in a frying pan and add the chopped vegetables, garlic and pancetta. Cook over moderately low heat for 5–6 minutes, or until softened and lightly golden. Add the minced beef, increase the heat a little and cook for 8 minutes, or until coloured but not browned, stirring to break up the lumps. Add the oregano and nutmeg and season well.

STIR IN chicken livers and cook until they change colour. Pour in vermouth, increase the heat and cook until it has evaporated. Add the beef stock and tomato paste and simmer for 2 hours. Add a little hot water, if necessary, during this time to keep the mixture moist, but towards the end, ensure all the liquid is absorbed. Stir in the cream. Remove from heat. Leave to cool for 15 minutes. Stir in the egg.

PUT the béchamel in a saucepan, heat gently and stir in the cream. Remove from the heat and cool slightly. Preheat the oven to 180°C (350°F/Gas 4) and grease a 22 x 15 x 7 cm (9 x 6 x 2¾ inch) ovenproof dish.

IF USING fresh pasta, cut it into manageable sheets and cook in batches in a large saucepan of boiling salted water until al dente. Scoop out each batch with a slotted spoon as it is done and drop into a bowl of cold water. Spread the sheets out in a single layer on a tea towel (dish towel), turning them over once to blot dry each side. Trim away any torn edges.

SPREAD HALF the meat sauce in the dish. Scatter with half the mozzarella, cover with a slightly overlapping layer of pasta sheets and spread half the béchamel on top. Sprinkle with half the parmesan. Repeat layers, finishing with a layer of béchamel and parmesan.

BAKE for about 40 minutes until golden brown and leave to rest for 10 minutes before serving.

FROM SPAIN

STEWED LENTILS WITH CHORIZO

LENTILS ARE A PULSE WIDELY USED AROUND THE MEDITERRANEAN, IN SOUPS, STEWS AND SALADS, ALTHOUGH THE SPANISH DON'T OFTEN USE THEM. HOWEVER, THEY DO TEAM THEM WITH SWEET AND SMOKY CHORIZO AND ADDED PIMENTÓN, CREATING A DISH THAT IS A SIMPLE HEARTY WINTER MEAL.

400 g (14 oz) green lentils
100 ml (3½ fl oz) olive oil
2 garlic cloves, crushed
1 green capsicum (pepper), seeded and diced
2 brown onions, chopped
2 teaspoons sweet paprika (pimentón)
1 bay leaf
2 slices bacon, cut into thin strips
200 g (7 oz) chorizo, sliced
1 tomato, chopped
extra virgin olive oil, for drizzling

SERVES 4

RINSE the lentils, then cover with cold water and soak for 2 hours.

HEAT 1 tablespoon of the olive oil in a large saucepan over medium heat and cook the garlic, capsicum and half the onion for 5 minutes, or until the onion is softened. Add the drained lentils, paprika, bay leaf and most of the remaining oil. Cover with water, bring to the boil, then reduce heat and simmer for 30 minutes, or until tender.

MEANWHILE, heat the remaining oil in a frying pan. Add the bacon, chorizo and remaining onion and fry for 10 minutes until golden on medium heat. Add to the lentil mixture with the tomato and a large pinch of salt, and cook for 5 minutes. Drizzle a little extra virgin olive oil over the top and serve.

Sangria (meaning 'bloody') is a wine punch typical of Spain. It normally consists of red wine, chopped or sliced fruit (often orange, lemon, apple, and/or peach), a sweetener such as honey, sugar, or orange juice, a small amount of added brandy, triple sec, or other spirits, and gaseosa (carbonated water).

Scoring the pork all over and pressing the fennel, garlic and rosemary into the cuts ensures that the flavour infuses the meat while it cooks. Cook the chopped fennel separately until it is creamy.

FROM ITALY

FLORENTINE ROAST PORK

3 large fennel bulbs
½ tablespoon finely chopped rosemary
4 garlic cloves, crushed
1 x 1.5 kg (3 lb 5 oz) pork loin, chined and skinned
3 white onions
80 ml (2½ fl oz/⅓ cup) olive oil
185 ml 6 fl oz/¾ cup) dry white wine
80 ml (2½ fl oz/⅓ cup) extra virgin olive oil
250 ml (9 fl oz/1 cup) chicken stock
3–4 tablespoons thick (double/heavy) cream

SERVES 6

PREHEAT the oven to 200°C (400°F/Gas 6). Cut the green fronds from the tops of the fennel and chop to give 2 tablespoons. Mix with rosemary, garlic and plenty of salt and black pepper. Make deep incisions with a sharp knife all over the pork and rub this mixture in the incisions and the splits in the pork bone. Cut two onions in half and place in a roasting tin. Put the pork on top of the onion and drizzle the olive oil over the top.

ROAST in the oven for 30 minutes. Baste pork with the pan juices, then reduce temperature to 180°C (350°F/Gas 4). Roast for 30 minutes. Baste and lightly salt the surface of the pork. Pour in half the white wine. Roast for another 30–45 minutes, basting once or twice.

MEANWHILE, remove the tough outer leaves of the fennel and discard. Slice the bulbs vertically into 1 cm (½ inch) sections and place in a large saucepan. Thinly slice the remaining onion and add to the saucepan with the extra virgin olive oil and a little salt. Add enough water to cover, put the lid on and bring to the boil. Simmer for about 45 minutes, or until the fennel is creamy and soft and almost all the liquid has evaporated.

REMOVE pork from the tin and leave to rest in a warm spot. Spoon off the excess oil from the tin and discard the onion. Place tin over high heat on the stovetop and stir in the remaining wine to deglaze. Add the stock and boil the sauce until slightly thickened. Remove from the heat, season with salt and pepper and stir in the cream. Slice the pork and serve on the fennel, with the sauce.

FROM SPAIN

SPANISH PORK AND VEGETABLE STEW

PERFECT ON A WINTRY NIGHT WITH A BIG GLASS OF RIOJA, THIS RUSTIC AND COMFORTING STEW IS A VARIATION ON THE STYLE POPULAR IN CENTRAL SPAIN. USING DELICIOUS PRODUCTS LOCAL TO THE AREA, IT IS PACKED FULL OF FLAVOUR: SMOKY CHORIZO, SWEET PEPPERS AND RICH TOMATOES.

600 g (1 lb 5 oz) boneless pork shoulder (hand/collar butt)
4 (100 g/3½ oz each) all-purpose potatoes, peeled
1 red capsicum (pepper)
1 green capsicum (pepper)
2 tablespoons olive oil
1 large red onion, chopped
2 garlic cloves, crushed
100 g (3½ oz) jamón
1 chorizo, sliced
2 x 400g (14 oz) tins tomatoes, chopped
10 g (¼ oz) thyme
2 tablespoons sherry vinegar
100 ml (3½ fl oz) white wine
1 bay leaf
250 ml (9 fl oz/1 cup) chicken stock

SERVES 6

CUT the pork into 2 cm (¾ inch) pieces. Peel the potatoes and cut into same size. Seed and chop capsicums into 2 cm (¾ inch) squares.

PREHEAT oven to 180°C (350°F/Gas 4). Place a large fryingpan over medium heat. Heat the oil then add the pork, onions and garlic. Cook for 5 minutes until onion is softened and the meat is lightly browned all over. Next, add capsicums, chorizo and jamón. Continue to cook, stirring occasionally, for another 5 minutes or until the liquid is slightly reduced.

PLACE in a large, deep ovenproof pan or casserole. Add the remaining ingredients and season with salt and pepper. Place in oven and cook for 2 hours or until meat is very tender.

When the liquid has reduced slightly, transfer to an ovenproof cooking dish.

The pan for osso buco must be large enough to fit the shank pieces in a single layer so that they cook through evenly.

FROM ITALY

OSSO BUCO ALLA MILANESE

OSSO BUCO IS A MILANESE DISH AND TRADITIONALLY TOMATOES ARE NOT USED IN THE COOKING OF NORTHERN ITALY. THE ABSENCE OF THE ROBUST TOMATO ALLOWS THE MORE DELICATE FLAVOUR OF THE GREMOLATA TO FEATURE IN THIS CLASSIC OSSO BUCO. SERVE WITH *RISOTTO ALLA MILANESE*.

12 pieces veal shank, about 4 cm (1½ inches) thick
plain (all-purpose) flour, seasoned with salt and pepper
60 ml (2 fl oz/¼ cup) olive oil
60 g (2¼ oz) butter
1 garlic clove
250 ml (9 fl oz/1 cup) dry white wine
1 bay leaf or lemon leaf
pinch of allspice
pinch of ground cinnamon

GREMOLATA
2 teaspoons grated lemon zest
6 tablespoons finely chopped parsley
1 garlic clove, finely chopped

thin lemon wedges, to serve

SERVES 4

TIE each piece of veal shank around its girth to secure the flesh. Dust with the seasoned flour. Heat the oil, butter and garlic in a large heavy saucepan big enough to hold the shanks in a single layer. Put shanks in the pan and cook for 12–15 minutes until well browned. Arrange the shanks, standing them up in a single layer, pour in the wine and add the bay leaf, allspice and cinnamon. Cover the saucepan.

COOK at a low simmer for 15 minutes, then add 125 ml (4 fl oz/½ cup) warm water. Continue cooking, covered, for about 45 minutes to 1 hour (the timing will depend on the age of the veal) until the meat is tender and you can cut it with a fork. Check the volume of liquid once or twice and add more warm water as needed. Transfer the veal to a plate and keep warm. Discard the garlic clove and bay leaf.

TO MAKE the gremolata, mix together the lemon zest, parsley and garlic. Increase the heat under the saucepan and stir for 1–2 minutes until the sauce is thick, scraping up any bits off the bottom of the saucepan as you stir. Stir in the gremolata. Season with salt and pepper, if necessary, and return the veal to the sauce. Heat through, then serve with the lemon wedges.

DESSERTS & BAKING

Scrape the vanilla seeds from the pod. Whisk into the warm milk mixture, and stir until creamy.

FROM SPAIN

CATALAN CUSTARD

THOSE UNFAMILIAR WITH CATALAN CUISINE MAY LOOK AT THIS DISH AND SAY, 'BUT THIS IS THE FRENCH DESSERT CALLED CRÈME BRÛLÉE (BURNT CREAM)'. WHILE ON THE OTHER HAND, A CATALAN WILL INDIGNANTLY LOOK AT A CRÈME BRÛLÉE, AND SAY, 'THEY'VE STOLEN OUR CREMA CATALANA'.

1 litre (35 fl oz/4 cups) milk
1 vanilla bean, split
1 cinnamon stick
zest of 1 small lemon, cut into strips
2 strips orange zest, 4 x 2 cm (1½ x ¾ inch)
8 egg yolks
115 g (4 oz/½ cup) caster (superfine) sugar
40 g (1½ oz/⅓ cup) cornflour (cornstarch)
45 g (1½ oz/¼ cup) soft brown sugar

SERVES 6

PUT the milk, scraped vanilla bean, cinnamon stick and lemon and orange zests in a saucepan and bring to the boil. Simmer for 5 minutes, then strain and set aside.

WHISK the egg yolks with the sugar in a bowl for 5 minutes, or until pale and creamy. Add the cornflour and mix well. Slowly add the warm milk mixture to the egg while you whisk continuously. Return to the saucepan and cook over low–medium heat, stirring constantly, for 5–10 minutes, or until the mixture is thick and creamy. Do not allow it to boil as it will curdle. Pour into six 185 ml (6 fl oz/ ¾ cup) ramekins and refrigerate for 6 hours, or overnight.

WHEN ready to serve, sprinkle the top evenly with brown sugar and grill (broil) for 3 minutes, or until it caramelises.

FROM MOROCCO

FIGS WITH ROSEWATER, ALMONDS AND HONEY

FRESH FIGS ARE ONE OF THE DELIGHTS OF LATE SUMMER AND AUTUMN. WHILE PERFECT ON THEIR OWN, THEY ARE SOMETIMES PREPARED IN THIS WAY AND LOOK VERY ATTRACTIVE SERVED AT THE END OF A BANQUET, WITH THEIR PINK FLOWER INTERIOR EXPOSED.

- 12 fresh purple-skinned figs
- 50 g (1¾ oz/⅓ cup) blanched almonds, lightly toasted
- 3–4 teaspoons rosewater
- 1–2 tablespoons honey

SERVES 6

WASH the figs gently and pat them dry with paper towel. Starting from the stem end, cut each fig into quarters, almost to the base, then gently open out and put on a serving platter. Cover and chill in the refrigerator for 1 hour, or until needed.

ROUGHLY chop the toasted almonds and set aside.

CAREFULLY drizzle about ¼ teaspoon of the rosewater onto the exposed centres of each of the figs, and sprinkle the chopped almonds over the top. Drizzle a little honey over the nuts. Serve immediately.

WATERMELON WITH ROSEWATER AND MINT

IN SUMMER, CHILLED WATERMELON IS A GREAT WAY TO FINISH A MEAL. FOR A SPECIAL MEAL OR BANQUET, IT IS OFTEN PRESENTED CUBED AND SEEDED FOR EASE OF EATING. ROSEWATER AND MINT COMPLEMENT THE CRISP, SWEET MELON WITH THEIR FRESH AND FLORAL TONES.

- 2 kg (4 lb 8 oz) wedge of watermelon
- 3 teaspoons rosewater
- small, fresh mint leaves, to serve

SERVES 4

WORKING over a plate to catch any juice, remove the skin and the rind from the watermelon and cut the flesh into 2.5 cm (1 inch) cubes, removing any visible seeds. Pile the cubes in a bowl. Pour the watermelon juice into a small jug and stir in rosewater. Sprinkle over the watermelon, cover and chill in refrigerator for 1 hour or until required. Scatter with small fresh mint leaves and serve chilled.

WATERMELON WITH ROSEWATER AND MINT

FIGS WITH ROSEWATER, ALMONDS AND HONEY

FROM FRANCE

CHOCOLATE MOUSSES

300 g (10½ oz) dark chocolate, chopped
30 g (1 oz) unsalted butter
2 eggs, lightly beaten
3 tablespoons Cognac
4 egg whites
5 tablespoons caster (superfine) sugar
500 ml (17 fl oz/2 cups) whipping cream

SERVES 8

PUT the chocolate in a heatproof bowl over a saucepan of simmering water, making sure the base of the bowl isn't touching the water. Leave the chocolate until it looks soft and then stir until melted. Add the butter and stir until melted. Remove the bowl from the saucepan and cool for a few minutes. Add the eggs and Cognac and stir.

USING electric beaters or balloon whisk, beat the egg whites in a clean dry bowl until soft peaks form, adding the sugar gradually. Whisk one-third of the egg white into the chocolate mixture to loosen it and then fold in the remainder with a large metal spoon or spatula.

WHIP the cream and fold into the mousse. Pour into glasses or a large bowl, cover and refrigerate for at least 4 hours.

PETITS POTS DE CRÈME

THE FLAVOUR OF THESE PETITS POTS COMES FROM THE VANILLA POD USED TO INFUSE THE MILK. FOR CHOCOLATE POTS, ADD A TABLESPOON OF COCOA AND 60 GRAMS (2¼ OZ) MELTED DARK CHOCOLATE TO THE MILK INSTEAD OF THE VANILLA. FOR COFFEE POTS, ADD A TABLESPOON OF GRANULATED COFFEE.

400 ml (14 fl oz) milk
1 vanilla pod
3 egg yolks
1 egg
80 g (2¾ oz) caster (superfine) sugar

SERVES 4

PREHEAT the oven to 140°C (275°F/Gas 1). Put the milk in a saucepan. Split the vanilla pod in two, scrape out the seeds and add the whole lot to the milk. Bring the milk just to the boil.

MEANWHILE, mix together the egg yolks, egg and sugar. Strain the boiling milk over the egg mixture and stir well. Skim off the surface to remove any foam.

LADLE INTO four 25 ml (¾ fl oz) ramekins and place in a roasting tin. Pour enough hot water into the tin to come halfway up the sides of the ramekins. Bake for 30 minutes, or until the custards are firm to the touch. Leave the ramekins on a wire rack to cool, then refrigerate until ready to serve.

PETITS POTS DE CRÈME

FROM ITALY

TIRAMISU

TIRA MI SU MEANS 'PICK ME UP' IN ITALIAN AND THIS IS HOW THE DESSERT STARTED LIFE – AS A NOURISHING DISH TO BE EATEN WHEN FEELING LOW. YOU CAN ALSO MAKE A FRUIT VERSION, USING FRAMBOISE AND PUREED RASPBERRIES INSTEAD OF BRANDY AND COFFEE.

- 5 eggs, separated
- 170 g (5¾ oz/¾ cup) caster (superfine) sugar
- 300 g (10½ oz) mascarpone cheese
- 250 ml (9 fl oz/1 cup) cold strong coffee
- 3 tablespoons brandy or sweet Marsala
- 36 small sponge fingers
- 80 g (3 oz) dark chocolate, finely grated

SERVES 4

BEAT the egg yolks with the sugar until the sugar has dissolved and the mixture is light and fluffy and leaves a ribbon trail when dropped from the whisk. Add the mascarpone and beat until the mixture is smooth.

WHISK the egg whites in a clean dry glass bowl, using a wire whisk or hand beaters, until soft peaks form. Fold into the mascarpone mixture.

POUR the coffee into a shallow dish and add the brandy. Dip enough biscuits to cover the base of a 25 cm (10 inch) square dish into the coffee. The biscuits should be fairly well soaked but not so much so that they break up. Arrange the biscuits in one tightly packed layer in the base of the dish.

SPREAD half the mascarpone mixture over the layer of biscuits. Add another layer of soaked biscuits and then another layer of mascarpone, smoothing the top layer neatly.

DUST with the grated chocolate to serve.

Note: The flavours will be better developed if you can make the tiramisu a few hours in advance or even the night before. If you have time to do this, don't dust with the chocolate, but cover with plastic wrap and chill. Dust with chocolate at the last minute.

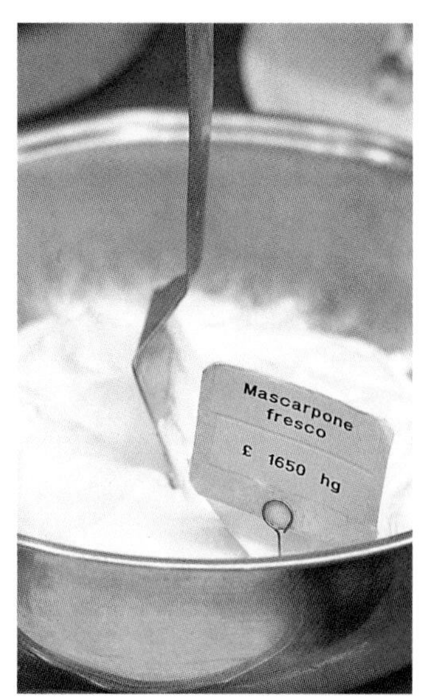

Made from cream rather than milk and a speciality of southern Lombardia, mascarpone is usually found as an ingredient in dishes rather than eaten as a cheese.

FROM SPAIN

HEAVEN'S BACON

TRANSLATED AS 'BACON FROM HEAVEN', THIS IS A POPULAR ANDALUCÍAN RECIPE, OFTEN MADE BY THE NUNS IN THEIR CONVENTS. IT IS INDEED HEAVENLY, BUT ALSO SATISFYINGLY WICKED. IT IS TRADITIONALLY DECORATED WITH TINY MERINGUES, WHICH SIT ON THE TOP.

Beat the cooled sugar mixture into the eggs then strain the toffee into the tin.

285 g (10 oz/1¼ cups) caster (superfine) sugar
1 vanilla bean, split
1 egg
6 egg yolks

MAKES ABOUT 18 PIECES

PREHEAT the oven to 180°C (350°F/Gas 4). Put 120 g (4¼ oz/½ cup) of the sugar and 2 tablespoons water in a small saucepan over low–medium heat. Stir with a metal spoon until all the sugar has dissolved. Bring to the boil and cook for a further 10 minutes, or until the toffee is a rich golden colour. Remove from the heat and, taking care not to burn yourself, pour into a 20 cm (8 inch) square cake tin, tilting to cover the base.

MEANWHILE, put 250 ml (9 fl oz/1 cup) water in a saucepan with the vanilla bean and remaining sugar. Stir until sugar is dissolved. Bring to the boil, then reduce the heat and simmer for 10 minutes, or until the liquid has reduced to a slightly syrupy consistency. Leave to cool a little. Remove the vanilla bean.

USING electric beaters, beat the whole egg and egg yolks until smooth. Slowly add a stream of the cooled sugar and vanilla mixture while beating on high. Once combined, strain the liquid onto the toffee mixture in the cake tin.

PUT the cake tin in a larger baking dish. Pour enough boiling water into the larger dish to come one-third of the way up the side of the cake tin. Bake for 35–40 minutes, or until just set. Cool slightly and then refrigerate until cold.

WHEN ready to serve, dip the tin into a hot water bath for 30 seconds to loosen the caramel. Run a knife around the custard and unmould onto a serving plate. Drizzle any remaining caramel over the top and cut into small squares to serve.

FROM MOROCCO

ALMOND CREAM PUDDING

THIS CREAMY MILK PUDDING IS MIDDLE EASTERN IN ORIGIN, THICKENED WITH CORNFLOUR, GROUND RICE AND GROUND ALMOND. ROSEWATER GIVES IT A SUBTLE FRAGRANCE. TOP WITH TOASTED SLIVERED ALMONDS AND A SPRINKLING OF POMEGRANATE SEEDS WHEN IN SEASON.

- 500 ml (17 fl oz/2 cups) milk
- 3 tablespoons caster (superfine) sugar
- 2 tablespoons cornflour (cornstarch)
- 1 tablespoon ground rice
- 70 g (2½ oz/⅔ cup) ground almonds
- 1 teaspoon rosewater
- 2 tablespoons slivered (or flaked) almonds, toasted
- 1 teaspoon caster (superfine) sugar, extra
- ½ teaspoon ground cinnamon

SERVES 4

PUT the milk and sugar in a heavy-based saucepan and heat over medium heat until the sugar has dissolved. Bring to the boil.

MEANWHILE, in a large bowl, combine the cornflour and ground rice with 3 tablespoons water and mix to a smooth paste. Pour in the boiling milk, stirring constantly with a balloon whisk, then return to the saucepan. Stir over medium heat until thickened and bubbling, then add the ground almonds and simmer over low heat for 5 minutes, stirring occasionally until thick and creamy. Add the rosewater and remove from the heat. Stir occasionally to cool a little, then spoon into serving bowls or glasses. Refrigerate for 1 hour.

MIX the toasted almonds with the extra sugar and the cinnamon and sprinkle over the top before serving.

For the best flavour, use freshly blanched almonds. Grind in a food processor and add to milk mixture.

Whisking the lemon filling for the tarte au citron.

FROM FRANCE

TARTE AU CITRON

1 quantity sweet pastry (see recipe on page 477)

FILLING
4 eggs
2 egg yolks
275 g (9¾ oz) caster (superfine) sugar
190 ml (6½ fl oz) thick (double/heavy) cream
275 ml (9½ fl oz) lemon juice
finely grated zest of 3 lemons

SERVES 8

PREHEAT the oven to 190°C (375°F/Gas 5). Roll out the pastry to line a 23 cm (9 inch) round loose-based fluted tart tin. Chill in the fridge for 20 minutes.

TO MAKE the filling, whisk together the eggs, egg yolks and sugar. Add the cream, whisking all the time, and then the lemon juice and zest.

LINE the pastry shell with a crumpled piece of baking paper and baking beads (use dried beans or rice if you don't have beads). Blind bake the pastry for 10 minutes, remove the paper and beads and bake for a further 3–5 minutes, or until the pastry is just cooked but still very pale. Remove from the oven and reduce the temperature to 150°C (300°F/Gas 2).

PUT the tin on a baking tray and carefully pour the filling into the pastry case. Return to the oven for 35–40 minutes, or until the filling has set. Leave to cool completely before serving.

APPLE TART

1 quantity sweet pastry (see recipe on page 477)
½ quantity crème pâtissière (see recipe on page 481)
4 dessert apples
80 g (2¾ oz) apricot jam

SERVES 8

PREHEAT the oven to 180°C (350°F/Gas 4). Roll out the pastry to line a 23 cm (9 inch) round loose-based fluted tart tin. Chill in the fridge for 20 minutes.

LINE the pastry shell with a crumpled piece of baking paper and baking beads (use dried beans or rice if you don't have beads). Blind bake the pastry for 10 minutes, remove the paper and beads and bake for a further 3–5 minutes, or until the pastry is just cooked but still very pale.

FILL the pastry with the crème pâtissière. Peel and core the apples, cut them in half and then into thin slices. Arrange over the top of the tart and bake for 25–30 minutes or until the apples are golden and the pastry is cooked. Leave to cool completely, then melt the apricot jam with 1 tablespoon water, sieve out any lumps and brush over the apples to make them shine.

APPLE TART

TARTE AU CITRON

FROM ITALY

PANFORTE

PANFORTE MEANS 'STRONG BREAD', AN APT DESCRIPTION FOR THIS DENSE, FRUITY LOAF THAT STILL RETAINS ITS MEDIEVAL FLAVOUR. PANFORTE IS ALSO KNOWN AS SIENA CAKE – SIENA POSSIBLY BEING THE FIRST ITALIAN CITY TO USE SUGAR AND SPICES SUCH AS WHITE PEPPER.(

105 g (3½ oz/¾ cup) hazelnuts
115 g (4 oz/¾ cup) almonds
125 g (4½ oz) candied mixed peel, chopped
100 g (3½ oz) candied pineapple, chopped
grated zest of 1 lemon
80 g (2¾ oz/⅔ cup) plain (all-purpose) flour
1 teaspoon ground cinnamon
¼ teaspoon ground coriander
¼ teaspoon ground cloves
¼ teaspoon grated nutmeg
pinch of white pepper
140 g (5 oz/⅔ cup) sugar
4 tablespoons honey
50 g (1¾ oz) unsalted butter
icing (confectioners') sugar

MAKES ONE 23 CM (9 INCH) CAKE

LINE a 23 cm (9 inch) springform tin with rice paper or baking paper and grease well with butter. Toast the nuts under a hot grill (broiler), turning them so they brown on all sides, then leave to cool. Put the nuts in a bowl with the mixed peel, pineapple, lemon zest, flour and spices and toss together. Preheat the oven to 150°C (300°F/Gas 2).

PUT the sugar, honey and butter in a saucepan and melt them together. Cook the syrup until it reaches 120°C (250°F) on a sugar thermometer, or a little of it dropped into cold water forms a soft ball when moulded between your finger and thumb.

POUR the syrup into the nut mixture and mix well, working fast before it stiffens too much. Pour straight into the tin, smooth the surface and bake for 35 minutes. (Unlike other cakes this will neither firm up as it cooks or colour at all so you need to time it carefully.)

COOL IN the tin until the cake firms up enough to remove the side of the tin. Peel off the paper and leave to cool completely. Dust the top heavily with icing sugar.

The hills around Siena.

FROM SPAIN

STUFFED FIGS

THE SEASON FOR FRESH FIGS IS SHORT AND INTENSE, BUT SO ABUNDANT ARE THE FIGS OF SPAIN THAT THEY CANNOT ALL BE EATEN, SO MANY ARE DRIED. INGENIOUS METHODS OF UTILISING THESE DRIED FIGS HAVE BEEN DEVISED, INCLUDING THIS SWEET, SYRUPY OFFERING.

175 g (6 oz/½ cup) honey
125 ml (4 fl oz/½ cup) oloroso sherry
¼ teaspoon ground cinnamon
18 large dried figs
18 whole blanched almonds
100 g (3½ oz) good-quality dark chocolate, cut into shards
thick (double/heavy) cream, for serving (optional)

SERVES 6

COMBINE the honey, sherry, cinnamon and figs with 375 ml (13 fl oz/1½ cups) of water in a large saucepan over high heat. Bring to the boil, then reduce the heat and simmer for 10 minutes. Remove the pan from the heat and set aside for 3 hours. Remove the figs with a slotted spoon, reserving the liquid.

PREHEAT the oven to 180°C (350°F/Gas 4).

RETURN the pan of liquid to the stove and boil over high heat for 5 minutes, or until syrupy, then set aside.

SNIP the stems from the figs with scissors, then cut a slit in the top of each fig with a small sharp knife. Push an almond and a few shards of chocolate into each slit. Put the figs in a lightly buttered ovenproof dish and bake for 15 minutes, or until the chocolate has melted.

SERVE three figs per person, with a little of the syrup and a dollop of cream.

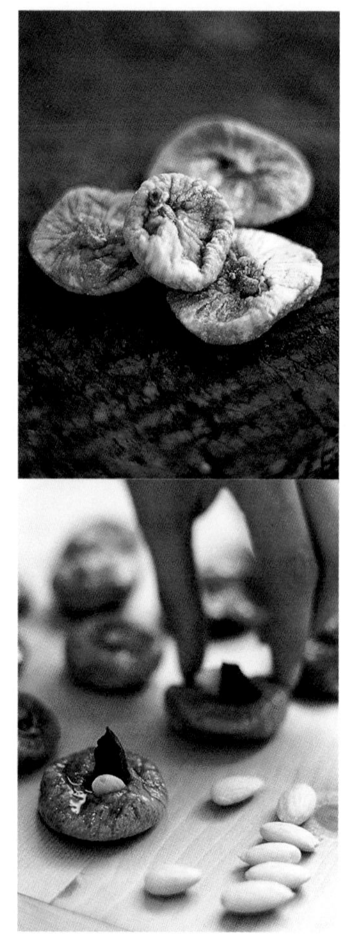

Stuff the figs with the almonds and dark chocolate shards.

FROM FRANCE

CINNAMON BAVAROIS

THE NAME OF THIS CREAMY DESSERT IS A PECULIARITY OF THE FRENCH LANGUAGE IN THAT IT CAN BE SPELT IN BOTH THE MASCULINE FORM, 'BAVAROIS' (FROM *FROMAGE BAVAROIS*), AND THE FEMININE 'BAVAROISE' (FROM *CRÈME BAVAROISE*). HOWEVER, ITS CONNECTION TO BAVARIA HAS BEEN LOST.

300 ml (10½ fl oz) milk
1 teaspoon ground cinnamon
50 g (1¾ oz) sugar
3 egg yolks
3 gelatine leaves or 1½ teaspoons powdered gelatine
½ teaspoon natural vanilla extract
175 ml (5½ fl oz) whipping cream
cinnamon, for dusting

SERVES 6

PUT the milk, cinnamon and half the sugar in a saucepan and bring to the boil. Whisk the egg yolks and remaining sugar until light and fluffy. Whisk the boiling milk into the yolks, then pour back into the saucepan and cook, stirring, until it is thick enough to coat the back of a wooden spoon. Do not let it boil or the custard will split.

SOAK the gelatine leaves in cold water until soft, drain and add to the hot custard with the vanilla. If using powdered gelatine, sprinkle it on to the hot custard, leave it to sponge for a minute, then stir it in. Strain the custard into a clean bowl and cool. Whip the cream, fold into the custard and pour into six 100 ml (3½ fl oz) oiled bavarois moulds. Set in the fridge.

UNMOULD by holding the mould in a hot cloth and inverting it onto a plate with a quick shake. Dust with the extra cinnamon.

Drape the warm tuiles over a rolling pin so that they set in a curved shape.

TUILES

2 egg whites
60 g (2¼ oz) caster (superfine) sugar
15 g (½ oz) plain (all-purpose) flour
60 g (2¼ oz) ground almonds
2 teaspoons peanut oil

MAKES 12

BEAT the egg whites in a clean dry bowl until slightly frothy. Mix in the sugar, then the flour, ground almonds and oil. Preheat the oven to 200°C (400°F/Gas 6).

LINE a baking tray with baking paper. Place one heaped teaspoon of tuile mixture on the tray and use the back of the spoon to spread it into a thin round. Cover the tray with tuiles, leaving 2 cm between them for spreading during cooking.

BAKE for 5–6 minutes or until lightly golden. Lift the tuiles off the tray with a metal spatula and drape over a rolling pin while still warm to make them curl (you can use bottles and glasses as well). Cool while you cook the rest of the tuiles. Serve with ice creams and other creamy desserts.

TUILES

FROM MOROCCO

ALMOND FILO COIL

M'HANNCHA, MEANING 'SNAKE', IS AN ALMOND PASTE-FILLED PASTRY MADE WITH MOROCCO'S WARKHA PASTRY (FILO PASTRY IS A GOOD SUBSTITUTE). THE PASTRY IS SERVED AT CELEBRATIONS, WITH GUESTS BREAKING OFF PIECES FROM THE COIL. SERVE WITH MINT TEA OR COFFEE.

1 small egg, separated
200 g (7 oz/2 cups) ground almonds
30 g (1 oz/⅓ cup) flaked almonds
125 g (4½ oz/1 cup) icing (confectioners') sugar
1 teaspoon finely grated lemon zest
¼ teaspoon almond extract
1 tablespoon rosewater
90 g (3¼ oz) unsalted butter or smen (see recipe on page 486), melted
9 sheets filo pastry
pinch of ground cinnamon
icing (confectioners') sugar, extra, to serve

SERVES 8

PREHEAT the oven to 180°C (350°F/Gas 4). Lightly grease a 20 cm (8 inch) round spring form tin.

PUT the egg white in a bowl and beat lightly with a fork. Add the ground almonds and flaked almonds, the icing sugar, lemon zest, almond extract and rosewater. Mix to a paste.

DIVIDE the mixture into four and roll each portion on a cutting board into a sausage shape about 5 cm (2 inches) shorter than the length of filo pastry – about 42 cm (16½ inches) long and 1 cm (½ inch) thick. If the paste is too sticky to roll, dust the cutting board with icing sugar.

KEEP the melted butter warm by placing the saucepan in another pan filled with hot water. Remove one sheet of filo pastry and place the rest in the folds of a dry tea towel (dish towel) or cover them with plastic wrap to prevent them from drying out. Brush the filo sheet with the butter, then cover with another sheet of filo, brushing the top with butter. Ease one almond 'sausage' off the board onto the buttered pastry, laying it along the length of the pastry, 2½ cm (1 inch) in from the base and sides. Roll up to enclose the filling. Form into a coil and sit the coil, seam side down, in the centre of the tin, tucking under the unfilled ends of the pastry to enclose the filling. Continue in this manner to make three more pastry 'snakes', shaping each around the smaller coil to make a large coil. If the coil breaks, cut small pieces of the remaining filo sheet, brush with a little egg yolk and press the filo onto the breaks.

ADD the cinnamon to the remaining egg yolk and brush over the coil. Bake for 30–35 minutes, or until golden brown. Dust with the extra icing sugar if desired and serve warm. This sweet pastry can be stored at room temperature for up to 2 days.

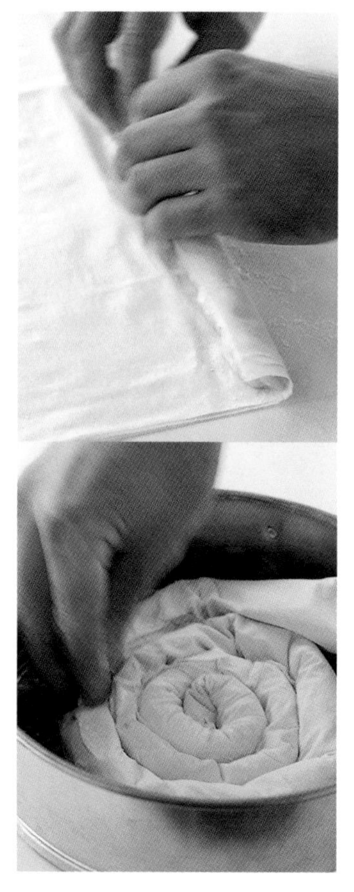

It is important to work quickly when making each roll to avoid the coils breaking.

FROM ITALY

BAKED PEACHES

THE PEACH IS ONE OF ITALY'S FAVOURITE FRUITS, WITH THE BEST BEING PRODUCED IN LE MARCHE, EMILIA-ROMAGNA AND CAMPANIA. THIS RECIPE ALSO WORKS WELL WITH FRESH APRICOTS. ALLOW THREE APRICOTS PER PERSON.

4 ripe peaches
40 g (1½ oz) amaretti biscuits
1 tablespoon sweet Marsala
20 g (¾ oz) ground almonds
1 egg yolk
1 tablespoon sugar
25 g (1 oz) unsalted butter
icing (confectioners') sugar

SERVES 4

PREHEAT the oven to 180°C (350°F/Gas 4). Halve the peaches and remove the stones. Crush the amaretti biscuits in a food processor or with the end of a rolling pin and mix them with the Marsala, almonds, egg yolk and sugar.

FILL the peaches with the biscuit mixture, spreading the filling in an even layer over the entire surface. Dot each peach with butter and arrange in a shallow ovenproof dish or baking tray. Bake for 20–30 minutes or until the peaches are tender right through. Dust lightly with icing sugar before serving.

ZABAIONE

ZABAIONE IS ONE OF THOSE HAPPY OCCURRENCES, A DISH CREATED PURELY BY ACCIDENT WHEN, IN SEVENTEENTH CENTURY TURIN, A CHEF POURED FORTIFIED SWEET WINE INTO EGG CUSTARD. IN RURAL AREAS ZABAIONE (ALSO KNOWN AS ZABAGLIONE) IS EATEN HOT FOR BREAKFAST.

6 egg yolks
3 tablespoons caster (superfine) sugar
125 ml (4 fl oz/½ cup) sweet Marsala
250 ml (9 fl oz/1 cup) thick (double/heavy) cream

SERVES 4

WHISK the egg yolks and sugar together in the top of a double boiler or in a heatproof bowl set over a saucepan of simmering water. When the mixture is tepid, add the Marsala and whisk for another 5 minutes, or until it has thickened.

Whip the cream until soft peaks form. Gently fold in the egg yolk mixture. Cover and refrigerate for 3–4 hours before serving.

ZABAIONE

BAKED PEACHES

FROM MOROCCO

GAZELLES' HORNS

THESE ARE THE MOST POPULAR PASTRIES IN MOROCCO, SOLD AT STREET STALLS AND IN PATISSERIES, AND, ON FESTIVE OCCASIONS, MADE IN ENORMOUS QUANTITIES BY GROUPS OF WOMEN. THE PASTRY SHRINKS AROUND THE FILLING DURING BAKING, ALLOWING THE FILLING TO DOMINATE.

This 'assembly line' method of filling and shaping pastries works well, especially if making large quantities.

PASTRY
- 300 g (10½ oz/2½ cups) plain (all-purpose) flour
- 1 egg yolk
- 30 g (1 oz) butter, melted
- 2 tablespoons orange flower water

ALMOND FILLING
- 300 g (10½ oz/3 cups) ground almonds
- 90 g (3¼ oz/¾ cup) icing (confectioners') sugar, plus extra to dust
- 1 tablespoon orange flower water
- 1 egg white, lightly beaten
- 30 g (1 oz) unsalted butter, melted
- ½ teaspoon ground cinnamon
- ¼ teaspoon almond extract

MAKES ABOUT 28

TO MAKE the pastry, sift the flour into a mixing bowl and make a well in the centre. Beat the egg yolk into 125 ml (4 fl oz/½ cup) water and pour into flour with the butter and the orange flower water. Mix to a soft dough, then knead in bowl for 5 minutes to form a smooth, elastic dough. Divide in half, wrap in plastic wrap and rest for 20 minutes.

TO MAKE the almond filling, mix filling ingredients to a stiff paste. Take 3 level teaspoons of filling, shape into a ball, then shape remaining almond paste into balls of the same size. Roll each ball between your palms into logs 7½ cm (3 in), tapering at each end. Place on baking paper and set aside. Preheat oven to 180°C (350°F/Gas 4).

ROLL out one ball of dough thinly on a lightly floured work surface, to a rectangle about 30 x 40 cm (12 x 16 in), with the shorter side towards you. Place three almond shapes 5 cm (2 inches) from edge of pastry closest to you and 2½ cm (1 inch) apart and half that from each end. Lightly brush pastry along edge and between almond shapes with cold water. Lift and stretch end of pastry over the filling and press firmly around filling to seal. Cut around filling with fluted pastry wheel, leaving a 1 cm (½ inch) border of pastry around filling. As each pastry is placed on the baking tray, bend it upwards on filling side into a crescent. Prick tops in four places with a cocktail pick. Straighten edge of pastry with a knife and repeat until all filling and pastry is used, including trimmings.

BAKE in oven for 12–15 minutes until cooked but still pale. Transfer to a wire rack and dust with sifted icing sugar while hot. Store in an airtight container when cool.

FROM SPAIN

FRIED BREAD WITH HONEY

AN IMPRESSIVE BUT SIMPLE-TO-MAKE DESSERT OF ANDALUCÍAN ORIGIN, ASSOCIATED WITH SEMANA SANTA. THIS DESSERT IS ENRICHED BY THE ADDITION OF THE SENSATIONAL SINGLE-ORIGIN SPANISH SWEET SHERRY, PEDRO XIMÉNEZ. BE SURE TO USE A GOOD-QUALITY WHITE BREAD.

4 thick slices of day-old bread
150–200 ml (5–7 fl oz) Pedro Ximénez or Malaga wine
60 ml (2 fl oz/¼ cup) vegetable oil
2 eggs, beaten with a dash of milk
1 teaspoon ground cinnamon
2 tablespoons caster (superfine) sugar, for dusting
honey, to serve (optional)

SERVES 4

DIP both sides of the bread slices in the sherry, then drizzle on any left-over liquid. Leave to sit for a few minutes to absorb the sherry.

HEAT the oil in a frying pan over medium heat. Dip the bread slices in the beaten egg, then fry on each side for 3–4 minutes, or until golden brown.

DRAIN on paper towel, then dust with the combined cinnamon and sugar and drizzle with honey.

Coat the slices of bread well in the egg mixture.

Pedro Ximénez (also known as PX) is the name of a white grape grown in certain regions of Spain, and also a varietal wine, an intensely sweet, dark, dessert sherry.

Once the crêpe starts to come away from the side of the pan, it is cooked enough to turn over.

FROM FRANCE

CRÊPES SUZETTE

THE ORIGIN OF THE NAME CRÊPES SUZETTE HAS BECOME A MYSTERY, BUT THEY SEEM TO HAVE APPEARED SOMETIME AT THE END OF THE NINETEENTH CENTURY. TRADITIONALLY FLAMBÉED AT THE TABLE IN RESTAURANTS, IN THIS RECIPE THE CRÊPES ARE QUICKLY SET ALIGHT ON THE STOVE TOP.

CRÊPES
2 tablespoons grated orange zest
1 tablespoon grated lemon zest
1 quantity crêpe batter (see recipe on page 478)

125 g caster (superfine) sugar
250 ml (9 fl oz/1 cup) orange juice
1 tablespoon grated orange zest
2 tablespoons brandy or Cognac
2 tablespoons Grand Marnier
50 g (1¾ oz) unsalted butter, diced

SERVES 6

TO MAKE the crêpes, stir the orange and lemon zest into the crêpe batter. Heat and grease a crêpe pan. Pour in enough batter to coat the base of the pan in a thin even layer and tip out any excess. Cook over moderate heat for about a minute, or until the crêpe starts to come away from the side of the pan. Turn the crêpe and cook on the other side for 1 minute or until lightly golden. Repeat with the remaining batter. Fold the crêpes into quarters.

MELT the sugar in a large frying pan over low heat and cook to a rich caramel, tilting the pan so the caramel browns evenly. Pour in the orange juice and zest and boil for 2 minutes. Put the crêpes in the pan and spoon the sauce over them.

ADD the brandy and Grand Marnier and flambé by lighting the pan with your gas flame or a match (stand well back when you do this and keep a pan lid handy for emergencies). Add the butter and shake the pan until it melts. Serve immediately.

CRÊPES SOUFFLÉS

CRÊPES SOUFFLÉS

1 quantity crème pâtissière (see recipe on page 481)
125 ml (4 fl oz/½ cup) orange juice
grated zest of 1 orange
2 tablespoons Grand Marnier
8 egg whites
2 tablespoons caster (superfine) sugar
½ quantity cooked crêpes (see recipe on page 478)
icing (confectioners') sugar

SERVES 6

PREHEAT the oven to 200°C (400°F/Gas 6). Warm the crème pâtissière in a bowl over a saucepan of simmering water and whisk in the orange juice, orange zest and Grand Marnier.

BEAT the egg whites in a clean dry bowl until firm peaks form. Whisk in the sugar gradually to make a stiff glossy meringue. Whisk half into the crème pâtissière to loosen the mixture, then fold in the rest with a large metal spoon or spatula. Place two big spoonfuls of soufflé on the centre of each crêpe. Fold in half with a spatula, without pressing. Bake on a buttered baking tray for 5 minutes. Dust with icing sugar and serve immediately.

CRÊPES SUZETTE

FROM ITALY

CANNOLI

IDEALLY YOU SHOULD USE METAL CANNOLI TUBES FOR THIS RECIPE. YOU'LL FIND THESE IN MAJOR DEPARTMENT STORES AND SPECIALITY KITCHEN SHOPS. ALTERNATIVELY, YOU COULD USE 2 CM (3/4 INCH) WIDE WOODEN OR CANE DOWELING, CUT INTO 12 CM (5 INCH) LENGTHS.

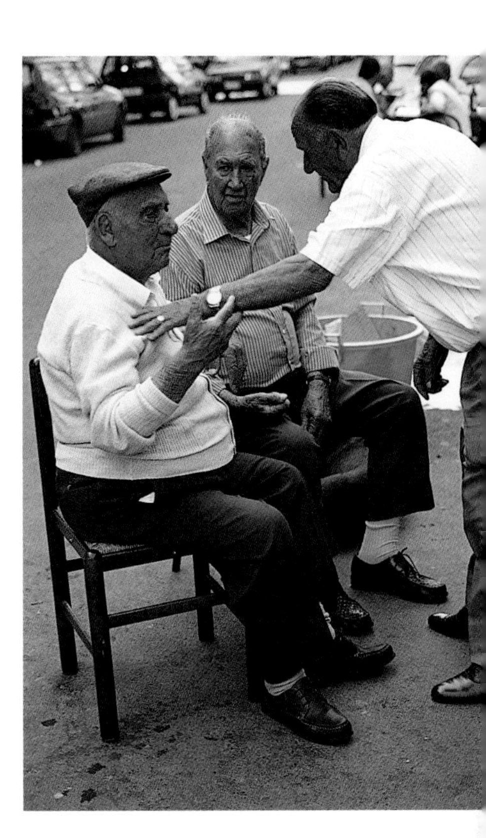

PASTRY
155 g (1¼ cups) plain (all-purpose) flour
2 teaspoons cocoa powder
1 teaspoon instant coffee
1 tablespoon caster (superfine) sugar
25 g (1 oz) unsalted butter, chilled and cut into small cubes
3 tablespoons dry white wine
1 teaspoon dry Marsala

1 egg, beaten
oil for deep-frying

FILLING
300 g (10½ oz) ricotta cheese
145 g (⅔ cup) caster (superfine) sugar
¼ teaspoon vanilla extract
½ teaspoon grated lemon zest
1 tablespoon candied peel, finely chopped
6 glacé cherries, chopped
15 g (½ oz) dark chocolate, grated
icing (confectioners') sugar

SERVES 6

TO MAKE the pastry, mix the flour, cocoa powder, coffee and sugar in a bowl. Rub in the butter, then add the wine and Marsala and mix until the dough gathers in a loose clump. Transfer dough to a lightly floured surface and knead until smooth (the dough will be quite stiff). Chill in a plastic bag for 30 minutes.

LIGHTLY DUST the work surface with flour and roll the pastry out to about 32 x 24 cm (13 x 9 inches). Trim the edges, then cut the pastry into twelve 8 cm (3 inch) squares. Lightly oil the metal cannoli tubes. Wrap a pastry square diagonally around each tube, securing the overlapping corners with beaten egg and pressing them firmly together.

HEAT the oil in a deep-fat fryer or deep frying pan to about 180°C (350°F), or until a scrap of pastry dropped into the oil becomes crisp and golden, with a slightly blistered surface, in 15–20 seconds. If the oil starts to smoke it is too hot. Add the cannoli, a couple at a time, and deep-fry until golden and crisp. Remove with tongs and drain on paper towels. As soon as the tubes are cool enough to handle, slide them out and leave the pastries on a rack to cool.

TO MAKE the filling, mash the ricotta with a fork. Blend in the sugar and vanilla extract, then mix in the lemon zest, candied peel, glacé cherries and chocolate. Fill the pastries, either with a piping bag or a spoon. Arrange on a plate and dust with icing sugar for serving. The cannoli should be eaten soon after they are filled.

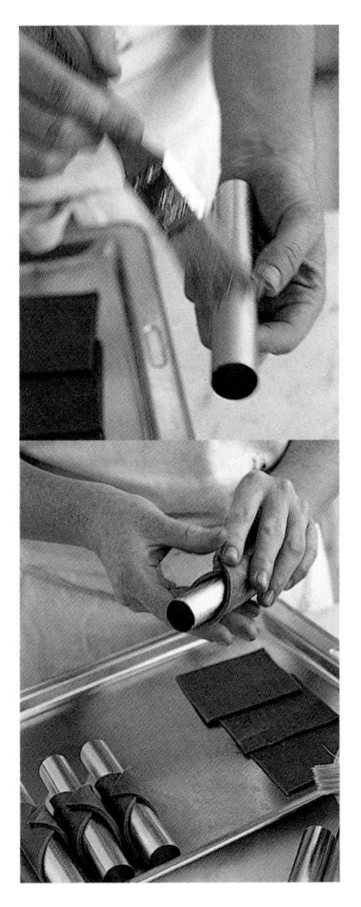

Traditional cannoli moulds need to be lightly greased before use. Wrap a pastry square around each tube, then deep-fry.

Carefully fold the egg whites into the rich chocolate mixture. Spread the cream over the cake and roll up carefully.

FROM SPAIN

GYPSY'S ARM CAKE

SIMILAR TO A SWISS ROLL, THIS RICH DESSERT, BRAZOS DE GITANO, AS IT IS KNOWN IN SPAIN, IS A FAVOURITE ON FEAST DAYS IN BARCELONA. FOR THE FULL SPANISH EFFECT, TRY PREPARING IT WITH PEDRO XIMENEZ. A TRADITIONAL SPANISH POSTRE THAT WILL LEAVE YOU LICKING YOUR LIPS!

200 g (7 oz) dark chocolate, broken into pieces
80 ml (2½ fl oz/⅓ cup) strong black coffee
7 eggs, at room temperature, separated
150 g (5½ oz/⅔ cup) caster (superfine) sugar
1 tablespoon icing (confectioners') sugar mixed with 2 tablespoons unsweetened cocoa powder
1 teaspoon rich sweet sherry, such as Pedro Ximénez or anís liqueur
300 ml (10½ fl oz) cream (whipping), whipped

SERVES 10

PREHEAT the oven to 180°C (350°F/Gas 4). Grease a 29 x 24 x 3 cm (11½ x 9½ x 1¼ inch) Swiss roll tin (jelly roll tin) and line with baking paper.

MELT the chocolate with the coffee in a bowl over a small saucepan of simmering water, stirring occasionally, until almost melted. Remove from the heat and stir until smooth. Set aside to cool a little.

BEAT the egg yolks and sugar in a large bowl until light and creamy, then stir in the chocolate mixture. Whisk the egg whites in a separate bowl until soft peaks form. Using a large metal spoon or rubber spatula, gently fold the whites into the chocolate mixture. Pour into the lined tin and bake on the middle shelf of the oven for 15 minutes, or until the cake springs back when lightly touched in the middle. Turn off the oven and open the door slightly.

AFTER 10 minutes, turn out the cake onto a clean tea towel (dish towel) that has been dusted with the icing sugar and cocoa mixture. Leave for 30 minutes, or until cool.

SPRINKLE the top of the sponge with the sherry and spread with the whipped cream. Roll the cake up, using the tea towel to help you but removing it as you go. Wrap in plastic wrap and refrigerate until ready to slice and serve.

FROM FRANCE

PITHIVIERS

ORIGINATING IN PITHIVIERS IN THE LOIRE VALLEY, THIS PASTRY IS TRADITIONALLY SERVED ON TWELFTH NIGHT, WHEN IT IS KNOWN AS *GALETTE DES ROIS* AND USUALLY CONTAINS A BEAN THAT BRINGS GOOD LUCK TO WHOEVER FINDS IT IN THEIR SLICE.

FILLING
140 g (5 oz) unsalted butter, at room temperature
140 g (5 oz) caster (superfine) sugar
2 large eggs, lightly beaten
2 tablespoons dark rum
finely grated zest of 1 small orange or lemon
140 g (5 oz) ground almonds
20 g (3⁄4 oz) plain (all-purpose) flour

1 quantity puff pastry (see recipe on page 474)
1 egg, lightly beaten
icing (confectioners') sugar

SERVES 6

TO MAKE the filling, beat the butter and sugar together until pale and creamy. Mix in the beaten eggs, little by little, beating well after each addition. Beat in the rum and the orange or lemon zest and then lightly fold in the almonds and flour. Put the filling in the fridge to firm a little while you roll out the pastry.

CUT the pastry in half and roll out one half. Cut out a 28 cm (11 1⁄4 inch) circle and place the circle on a large baking tray lined with baking paper. Spread the filling over the pastry, leaving a clear border of about 2 cm (3⁄4 inch) all the way round. Brush a little beaten egg over the clear border to help the two halves stick together.

ROLL OUT the other half of the pastry and cut out a second circle the same size as the first. Lay this circle on top of the filling and firmly press the edges of the pastry together. Cover and leave in the fridge for at least 1 hour (several hours or even overnight is fine).

PREHEAT the oven to 220°C (425°F/Gas 7). Brush all over the top of the pie with the beaten egg to give it a shiny glaze – be careful not to brush egg on the side of the pie or the layers won't rise properly. Working from the centre to the outside edge, score the top of the pithiviers with curved lines in a spiral pattern.

BAKE the pithiviers for 25–30 minutes, or until it is well risen and golden brown. Dust with icing sugar and allow to cool. Cut into slices to serve.

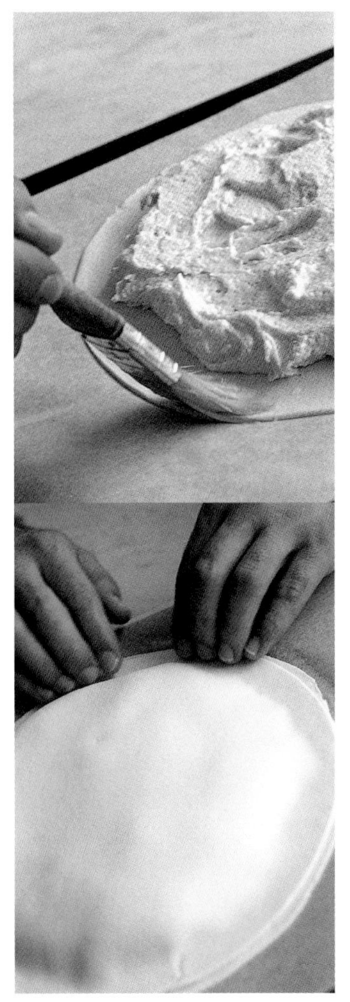

Leave a clear border around the filling, then brush it with egg to help the two halves of the pastry stick together.

FROM MOROCCO

HONEY-DIPPED BRIOUATS WITH ALMOND PASTE

THESE CRISP, HONEY-DIPPED PASTRIES ARE FILLED WITH A DELICIOUS ALMOND PASTE FRAGRANT WITH ORANGE FLOWER WATER. WHEN BOILING HONEY FOR DIPPING, IT IS IMPORTANT TO ADD WATER OTHERWISE THE HONEY BURNS.

Brush half the width of the filo strip with butter, then fold in half and butter top. Fold end of strip over filling to line up with side, then straight up and to the other side until end of strip is reached.

ALMOND FILLING
200 g (7 oz/2 cups) ground almonds
60 g (2¼ oz) unsalted butter
60 g (2¼ oz/½ cup) icing (confectioners') sugar
¼ teaspoon almond extract
1 tablespoon orange flower water

PASTRY WRAPPING
6 sheets filo pastry
125 g (4½ oz) smen (see recipe on page 486), melted

HONEY SYRUP
260 g (9¼ oz/¾ cup) honey
1 tablespoon orange flower water

MAKES 18

PLACE a heavy-based saucepan on medium heat, add ground almonds and stir constantly until lightly toasted – about 3–4 minutes. Quickly tip into a bowl, add the butter and stir until it melts. When cool, add remaining almond filling ingredients and mix thoroughly to a paste.

STACK the filo sheets on a cutting board with the longer side in front of you and, with a ruler and sharp knife, measure and cut into strips 12–14 cm (4½–5½ inches) wide and 28–30 cm (11¼–12 inches) long. Stack the strips and cover with a dry, folded cloth to prevent them from drying out.

PLACE a filo strip on a work surface, brush half the width with smen and fold in half to give a strip about 6 cm (2½ inches) wide. Brush over the top with smen and place a heaped teaspoon of the almond filling towards the end of the strip. Fold end diagonally across filling so that base lines up with side of strip, forming a triangle. Fold straight up once, then fold diagonally to opposite side; continue to end of strip, trimming excess pastry with scissors. Place, seam side down, on a lightly greased baking tray. Repeat with remaining ingredients and brush tops lightly with smen.

PREHEAT the oven to 180°C (350°F/Gas 4); do this after triangles are completed, so that the kitchen remains cool while shaping. Bake pastries for 20–25 minutes or until puffed and golden.

TOWARDS end of cooking, combine honey syrup ingredients with 60ml (2 fl oz/¼ cup) water in a 1.5 litre (52 fl oz/6 cup) saucepan. Bring to the boil and reduce heat to low. Dip hot pastries, two at a time, in the syrup, leave for 20 seconds and remove with two forks to a tray lined with baking paper. As pastries are dipped, honey boils up in pan, so take care. Cool and serve on the day of baking.

FROM ITALY

LEMON GELATO

GELATO IS THE ITALIAN NAME FOR AN ICE CREAM BASED ON AN EGG CUSTARD MIXTURE, THOUGH IT HAS NOW COME TO MEAN ALL ICE CREAMS, INCLUDING SORBETS. ITALIANS ARE DISCERNING ABOUT ICE CREAM AND FLAVOURS TEND TO BE FRESH AND AROMATIC, OFTEN BASED ON FRUIT.

5 egg yolks
110 g (3¾ oz/½ cup) sugar
500 ml (17 fl oz/2 cups) milk
2 tablespoons grated lemon zest
185 ml (6 fl oz/¾ cup) lemon juice
3 tablespoons thick (double/heavy) cream

SERVES 6

WHISK the egg yolks and half the sugar together until pale and creamy. Place the milk, lemon zest and remaining sugar in a saucepan and bring to the boil. Pour over the egg mixture and whisk to combine. Pour the custard back into the saucepan and cook over low heat, stirring continuously until the mixture is thick enough to coat the back of a wooden spoon – do not allow the custard to boil.

STRAIN the custard into a bowl, add the lemon juice and cream and then cool over ice. Churn in an ice-cream maker following the manufacturer's instructions. Alternatively, pour into a plastic freezer box, cover and freeze. Stir every 30 minutes with a whisk during freezing to break up the ice crystals and give a better texture. Keep in the freezer until ready to serve.

COFFEE GELATO

5 egg yolks
110 g (3¾ oz/½ cup) sugar
500 ml (17 fl oz/2 cups) milk
125 ml (4 fl oz/½ cup) freshly made espresso
1 tablespoon Tia Maria

SERVES 6

WHISK the egg yolks and half the sugar together until pale and creamy. Place the milk, coffee and remaining sugar in a saucepan and bring to the boil. Pour over the egg mixture and whisk to combine. Pour back into the saucepan and cook over low heat, stirring continuously until the mixture is thick enough to coat the back of a wooden spoon – do not allow the custard to boil.

STRAIN the custard into a bowl and cool over ice. Stir in the Tia Maria. Churn in an ice-cream maker following the manufacturer's instructions. Alternatively, pour into a plastic freezer box, cover and freeze. Stir every 30 minutes with a whisk during freezing to break up the ice crystals and give a better texture. Keep in the freezer until ready to serve.

COFFEE GELATO

LEMON GELATO

The pieces of cake need to be fitted into the mould as neatly as possible. Cut smaller pieces of cake to fill any gaps. Sprinkle the Marsala over the cake evenly so no one patch gets too moist. Fill the mould with ricotta and smooth any air bubbles as you go.

FROM ITALY

CASSATA

THERE ARE TWO DIFFERENT DISHES NAMED CASSATA, ONE A CAKE MADE WITH RICOTTA AND CANDIED FRUIT, THE OTHER AN ICE-CREAM DESSERT. THIS CASSATA IN ITS CAKE FORM IS A CLASSIC SICILIAN DISH DECORATED WITH BRIGHTLY COLOURED ICINGS, MARZIPAN AND CANDIED FRUIT.

400 g (14 oz) Madeira or pound cake
4 tablespoons sweet Marsala
350 g (12 oz) ricotta cheese
115 g (4 fl oz/½ cup) caster (superfine) sugar
½ teaspoon vanilla extract
150 g (5½ oz) mixed candied fruit (orange, lemon, cherries, pineapple, apricot), chopped
50 g (1¾ oz) dark chocolate, chopped
green food colouring
200 g (7 oz) marzipan
2 tablespoons apricot jam (jelly)
310 g (2½ cups) icing (confectioners') sugar

MAKES ONE 20 CM (8 INCH) CAKE

LINE a 20 cm (8 inch) round cake tin with sloping sides (a *moule à manqué* would be perfect) with plastic wrap. Cut the cake into thin slices to line the tin, reserving enough pieces to cover the top at the end. Fit the slices of cake carefully into the tin, making sure there are no gaps. Sprinkle the Marsala over the cake in the tin.

PUT the ricotta in a bowl and beat until smooth. Add the sugar and vanilla extract and mix well. Add the candied fruit and chocolate and mix well. Spoon into the mould, smooth the surface and then cover with the reserved slices of cake. Cover with plastic wrap and press the top down hard. Put the cassata in the fridge for at least 2 hours or preferably overnight, then unmould onto a plate.

KNEAD enough green food colouring into the marzipan to colour it light green. Roll out the marzipan in a circle until it is large enough to completely cover the cassata. Melt the jam in a saucepan with a tablespoon of water and brush over the cassata. Lift the marzipan over the top and trim it to fit around the edge.

MIX the icing sugar with a little hot water to make a smooth icing that will spread easily. Either pipe the icing onto the cassata in a decorative pattern, or drizzle it over the top in a crosshatch pattern.

FROM FRANCE

PARIS-BREST

THIS LARGE CHOUX PASTRY CAKE WAS NAMED AFTER THE PARIS-BREST BICYCLE RACE. IT WAS INVENTED IN 1891 BY A CANNY PARISIAN PASTRY CHEF WHO OWNED A SHOP ALONG THE ROUTE AND HAD THE IDEA OF PRODUCING THESE BICYCLE WHEEL-SHAPED CAKES.

1 quantity choux pastry (see recipe on page 478)
1 egg, lightly beaten
15 g flaked almonds
1 quantity crème pâtissière (see recipe on page 481)
icing (confectioners') sugar

PRALINE
100 g (3½ oz) caster (superfine) sugar
100 g (3½ oz) flaked almonds

SERVES 6

PREHEAT the oven to 200°C (400°F/Gas 4) and put the choux pastry in a piping bag fitted with a wide nozzle (about 18 mm wide). Draw a 20 cm (8 inch) circle on the back of a piece of baking paper in a dark pen so that the circle shows through onto the other side. Put the paper on a baking tray, pen side down.

PIPE a ring of pastry over the guide you have drawn. Now pipe another ring of pastry directly inside this one so that you have one thick ring. Pipe another two circles on top of the first two and continue until all the choux pastry has been used. Brush the choux ring with beaten egg and sprinkle with the flaked almonds.

BAKE the choux ring for 20–30 minutes, then reduce the oven to 180°C (350°F/Gas 4) and bake for a further 20–25 minutes. Remove from the baking tray and place on a wire rack. Immediately slice the ring in half horizontally, making the base twice as deep as the top. Lift off the top and scoop out any uncooked pastry from the base. Leave to cool completely.

TO MAKE the praline, grease a sheet of foil and lay it out flat on the work surface. Put the sugar in a small saucepan with 100 ml (3½ fl oz) water and heat gently until completely dissolved. Bring to the boil and cook until deep golden, then quickly tip in the flaked almonds and pour onto the oiled foil. Spread a little and leave to cool. When the praline has hardened, grind it to a fine powder in a food processor or with a mortar and pestle. Mix into the cold crème pâtissière.

SPOON the crème pâtissière into the base of the choux pastry ring and cover with the top. Dust with icing sugar to serve.

Pipe a double thickness ring of choux pastry over the guide.

ACCOMPANIMENTS & SIDE DISHES

Selles s/Cher
Berry 45%mg
35.60
Pièce
èvre au poivre
45%mg Provence
21.60
Pièce

This Moroccan way of preparing peeled and seeded tomatoes is well worth adopting. Halve them crossways, squeeze out seeds, then grate. The flavour rewards the effort.

FROM MOROCCO

SWEET TOMATO JAM

THIS CONFIT OF TOMATOES HAS A FANTASTIC FLAVOUR. IT IS WORTH THE EFFORT USING FRESH TOMATOES, AND PREPARING THEM IN THE MOROCCAN MANNER; HOWEVER, 2 X 400 G (14 OZ) TINS OF ROMA (PLUM) TOMATOES, UNDRAINED, MAY BE USED INSTEAD.

1.5 kg (3 lb 5 oz) ripe tomatoes
3 tablespoons olive oil
2 brown onions, coarsely grated
2 garlic cloves, crushed
1 teaspoon ground ginger
1 cinnamon stick
¼ teaspoon freshly ground black pepper
¼ teaspoon ground saffron threads (optional)
3 tablespoons tomato paste (concentrated purée)
2 tablespoons honey
1½ teaspoons ground cinnamon

MAKES 625 ML (21½ FL OZ/ 2½ CUPS)

HALVE the tomatoes crossways, then squeeze out the seeds. Coarsely grate the tomatoes into a bowl down to the skin, discarding the skin. Set aside.

HEAT the olive oil in a heavy-based saucepan over low heat and add the onion. Cook for 5 minutes. Stir in garlic, ginger, cinnamon stick and pepper and cook for about 1 minute. Add saffron, if using, the tomato paste and the tomatoes and season with ½ teaspoon salt.

SIMMER, uncovered, over medium heat for about 45 minutes, or until most of the liquid evaporates, stirring often when the sauce starts to thicken to prevent it catching on the base of the pan. When the oil begins to separate, stir in honey and ground cinnamon and cook over low heat for 2 minutes. Adjust the seasoning with salt if necessary.

SERVE the sweet tomato jam with other salads in the traditional Moroccan way – eaten with bread at the beginning of a meal. In Morocco, this is also used as a basis for some tagines, or as a stuffing for fish. Store in a clean, sealed jar in the fridge for up to 1 week.

FROM FRANCE

PURÉE OF SWEDES

IT IS EASIEST TO MAKE VEGETABLE PURÉES IN A FOOD PROCESSOR OR BLENDER BUT, IF YOU DON'T HAVE ONE, MASH THEM WITH A POTATO MASHER OR USE A FOODMILL. NEVER PURÉE POTATOES IN A PROCESSOR OR BLENDER BECAUSE THEY BECOME GLUEY.

- 1 kg (2 lb 4 oz) swedes (rutabagas), peeled and chopped
- 60 g (2 oz) butter
- 1 tablespoon crème fraîche

SERVES 4

PUT the swede in a saucepan, half-cover with water and add 1 teaspoon salt and 30 g (1 oz) of the butter. Bring to the boil and then reduce the heat, cover, and simmer for 30 minutes, or until tender. Drain, reserving the cooking liquid.

PROCESS swede in a food processor or blender with sufficient cooking liquid to make a purée. Spoon into a saucepan and stir in the remaining butter and the crème fraîche. Reheat gently for a couple of minutes, stirring all the time.

A vegetable stall in Lyon market.

Crème fraîche is regularly used in place of cream in French kitchens.

PURÉE OF JERUSALEM ARTICHOKES

- 750 g (1 lb 10 oz) jerusalem artichokes, peeled
- 250 g (9 oz) all-purpose potatoes, halved
- 30 g (1 oz) butter
- 2 tablespoons crème fraîche

SERVES 4

COOK the artichokes in boiling salted water for 20 minutes or until tender. Drain and then mix in a food processor or blender to purée.

COOK the potatoes in boiling salted water for 20 minutes, then drain and mash. Add to the artichoke with the butter and crème fraîche. Season, beat well and serve at once.

PURÉE OF SPINACH

- 1 kg (2 lb 4 oz) English spinach leaves or baby spinach
- 60 g (2 oz) butter, cubed
- 4 tablespoons crème fraîche
- ½ teaspoon nutmeg

SERVES 4

WASH the spinach and put in a large saucepan with just the water clinging to the leaves. Cover the pan and steam the spinach for 2 minutes, or until just wilted. Drain, cool and squeeze dry with your hands. Finely chop.

PUT the spinach in a small saucepan and gently heat through. Increase the heat and gradually add the butter, stirring all the time. Add the crème fraîche and stir into the spinach until it is glossy. Season well and stir in the nutmeg.

PURÉE OF SPINACH

Pushing the mashed potato through a sieve will ensure that the aligot is smooth.

FROM FRANCE

BOULANGÈRE POTATOES

1 kg (2 lb 4 oz) all-purpose potatoes
1 large onion
2 tablespoons finely chopped parsley
500 ml (17 fl oz/2 cups) hot chicken or vegetable stock
30 g (1 oz) butter, cubed

SERVES 6

PREHEAT the oven to 180°C (350°F/Gas 4).

THINLY SLICE the potatoes and onion with a mandolin or sharp knife. Build up alternate layers of potato and onion in a 20 x 10 cm (8 x 4 inch) deep dish, sprinkling parsley, salt and plenty of black pepper between each layer. Finish with a layer of potato. Pour the stock over the top and dot with butter.

BAKE, covered with foil, on the middle shelf of the oven for 30 minutes. Remove foil and lightly press down on the potatoes to keep them submerged in stock. Bake for a further 30 minutes, or until potatoes are tender and the top golden brown. Serve piping hot.

ALIGOT

THIS SPECIALITY OF THE AUVERGNE REGION IS A POTATO PURÉE BEATEN TOGETHER WITH CANTAL CHEESE TO MAKE A STRETCHY ELASTIC MIXTURE. CANTAL IS A SEMI-HARD SMOOTH CHEESE. USE MILD CHEDDAR IF YOU CAN'T FIND IT.

800 g (1 lb 12 oz) floury potatoes, cut into even-sized pieces
75 g (2½ oz) butter
2 garlic cloves, crushed
3 tablespoons milk
300 g (10 oz) cantal cheese (or mild cheddar), grated

SERVES 4

COOK potatoes in boiling salted water for about 25 minutes, or until tender. Meanwhile, melt the butter in a small saucepan over low heat and add the garlic. Mash potatoes and then sieve to give a very smooth purée (don't use a food processor or they will become gluey).

RETURN the potato purée to the saucepan over gentle heat and add the garlic butter and milk. Combine well and then add the cheese, handful by handful. Beat in the cheese; once it has melted, the mixture will be stretchy. Season with salt and pepper (preferably white) before serving.

ALIGOT

FROM ITALY

DEEP-FRIED ZUCCHINI FLOWERS

THOSE WHO GROW ZUCCHINI (COURGETTES) AT HOME CAN MAKE USE OF THE YELLOW FLOWERS THAT APPEAR IN STEADY SUPPLY THROUGHOUT THE SUMMER. IF FLOWERS AREN'T AVAILABLE, YOU CAN USE THE SAME BATTER AND METHOD TO DEEP-FRY SLICES OF ZUCCHINI AND EGGPLANT (AUBERGINE).

BATTER
50 g (1¾ oz) plain (all-purpose) flour
2 teaspoons olive oil
3 egg whites

8–12 zucchini (courgette) flowers
oil for deep-frying
lemon wedges, to serve

SERVES 4

TO MAKE the batter, sift the flour into a bowl and stir in 1/4 teaspoon salt. Mix in the oil with a wooden spoon. Slowly add 80–125 ml (⅓–½ cup) warm water, changing to a whisk when the mixture becomes liquid. Continue whisking until the batter is smooth and thick. Whisk the egg whites until stiff peaks form, then fold into the batter.

CHECK the zucchini flowers are clean and aren't hiding any stray insects. Trim the stem of each flower to 2 cm (¾ inch), to give you something to hold on to when dipping.

HEAT the oil in a deep-fat fryer or deep frying pan to about 180°C (350°F), or until a piece of bread fries golden brown in 15 seconds when dropped in the oil. If the oil starts to smoke, it is too hot.

DIP the zucchini flowers into the batter, coating both sides. Fry the flowers in batches until golden brown, turning once to cook on both sides. Drain on paper towels and serve with a sprinkling of salt and a lemon wedge. Don't let them sit around – serve and eat immediately, preferably with a glass of chilled white wine.

Zucchini (courgette) flowers can have a baby zucchini attached, while others are simply the male flowers of the plant and have a long stem instead of a zucchini. Choose fresh, firm flowers.

CIPOLLINE AGRODOLCE

1 kg (2 lb 4 oz) small onions (cipolline or pickling onions)
2 tablespoons soft brown sugar
2 tablespoons white wine vinegar
60 g (2 oz) butter

SERVES 8

PEEL onions, cut off the roots and remove the first layer of skin. Heat sugar in a large heavy-based saucepan until it melts and starts to caramelise. Remove from the heat, add the vinegar and butter and stir well. Return to the heat, bring to the boil and add the onions. Add enough water to just cover the onions. Simmer for 10 minutes. Cover pan and simmer for another 20 minutes, or until onions are tender. Serve hot or at room temperature.

CIPOLLINE AGRODOLCE

DEEP-FRIED ZUCCHINI FLOWERS

FROM FRANCE

POMMES ANNA

850 g (1 lb 14 oz) waxy potatoes
125 g (4 oz) clarified butter, melted

SERVES 4

PREHEAT the oven to 210°C (415°F/Gas 6–7). Grease a deep 20 cm (8 inch) round cake tin or ovenproof dish with melted butter.

PEEL the potatoes and cut into very thin slices with a mandolin or sharp knife. Lay potato slices on paper towels and pat dry. Starting from the centre of the dish, overlap one-fifth of the potato slices over the base. Drizzle one-fifth of the butter over the top. Season well.

REPEAT the layers four more times, drizzling the last bit of butter over the top. Cut out a circle of baking paper to fit over the top of the potato. Bake for 1 hour, or until cooked and golden and a knife blade slides easily into the centre. Remove from the oven and leave for 5 minutes, then pour off any excess butter. Run a knife around the edge to loosen and turn out onto a serving plate.

Floury potatoes will soak up the liquid in the gratin dauphinois and give a softer, fluffy texture.

GRATIN DAUPHINOIS

THERE ARE A NUMBER OF VERSIONS OF THIS REGIONAL DISH FROM DAUPHINÉ, SOME WITHOUT THE TOPPING OF GRILLED CHEESE. IN FACT, THE WORD GRATIN ORIGINALLY REFERRED NOT TO THE TOPPING, BUT TO THE CRISPY BITS AT THE BOTTOM OF THE PAN.

1 kg (2 lb 4 oz) floury potatoes
2 garlic cloves, crushed
75 g (2½ oz) gruyère cheese, grated
pinch of nutmeg
300 ml (10 fl oz) thick (double/heavy) cream
100 ml (3 fl oz) milk

SERVES 6

PREHEAT oven to 170°C (325°F/Gas 3). Thinly slice the potatoes with a mandolin or sharp knife. Butter a 23 x 16 cm (9 x 6 inch) ovenproof dish and layer the potatoes, sprinkling the garlic, grated cheese, nutmeg and seasoning between layers and leaving a little cheese for the top. Pour cream and milk over the top. Sprinkle with the cheese.

BAKE for 1 hour, or until potatoes are completely cooked and the liquid absorbed. If the top browns too much, cover loosely with foil. Leave to rest for 10 minutes before serving.

GRATIN DAUPHINOIS

Saint Cyprien in the Dordogne.

FROM FRANCE

PEAS WITH ONIONS AND LETTUCE

LETTUCE IS OFTEN THOUGHT OF AS PURELY A SALAD GREEN, BUT IN FACT UNTIL THE EIGHTEENTH CENTURY IT WAS MORE USUALLY COOKED THAN RAW, AND IN FRANCE IT IS STILL OFTEN EATEN THIS WAY, PARTICULARLY IN THIS DISH.

60 g (2 oz) butter
16 small pickling onions or shallots
500 g (1 lb 2 oz) shelled fresh peas
250 g (9 oz) iceberg lettuce heart, finely shredded
2 parsley sprigs
1 teaspoon caster (superfine) sugar
125 ml (4 fl oz/½ cup) chicken stock
1 tablespoon plain flour

SERVES 6

MELT 30 g (1 oz) of the butter in a large saucepan. Add onions and cook, stirring, for 1 minute. Add the peas, lettuce, parsley sprigs and sugar.

POUR in the stock and stir well. Cover pan and cook over moderately low heat for 15 minutes, stirring a couple of times, until the onions are cooked through. Remove the parsley.

MIX the remaining butter with the flour to make a *beurre manié*. Add in small amounts to the vegetables, stirring until the juices thicken a little. Season with salt and freshly ground black pepper.

VICHY CARROTS

500 g (1 lb 2 oz) carrots
½ teaspoon salt
1½ teaspoons sugar
45 g (1½ oz) butter
1½ tablespoons chopped parsley

SERVES 6

SLICE the carrots quite thinly, then put in a deep frying pan. Cover with cold water and add the salt, sugar and butter. Simmer until the water has evaporated. Shake the pan to glaze the carrot, then add the parsley, toss together and serve.

VICHY CARROTS

PEAS WITH ONIONS AND LETTUCE

FROM MOROCCO

PUMPKIN PURÉE

A BERBER SPECIALTY OF THE MIDDLE ATLAS, THIS IS MADE ON THE FIRST DAY AFTER RAMADAN AND SERVED WITH A CHICKEN TAGINE. THE PUMPKIN IS USUALLY BOILED, THEN FRIED, BUT AS SOME PUMPKINS CAN BECOME MUSHY VERY QUICKLY, USE THE FOLLOWING METHOD TO PREVENT THIS.

750 g (1 lb 10 oz) firm pumpkin (winter squash) or butternut pumpkin (squash)
¾ teaspoon ras el hanout (see recipe on page 482)
1 tablespoon lemon juice
½ teaspoon lemon zest, finely chopped
1–2 tablespoons honey
2 teaspoons toasted sesame seeds

SERVES 5

PEEL and remove the seeds from the pumpkin and cut into 2 cm (¾ inch) cubes. Put pumpkin in a roasting tin with 2 tablespoons oil. Toss to coat.

COMBINE the zest and juice and pour over the pumpkin. Sprinkle with the ras el hanout, season and drizzle with honey.

ROAST in a preheated 200°C (400°F/Gas 6) oven for 35 minutes, tossing occasionally with a spatula. Mash to a purée in the dish. Sprinkle with sesame seeds and serve warm.

WARM PUMPKIN SALAD WITH PRESERVED LEMON

THE COMBINATION OF SWEET-TASTING PUMPKIN AND TART PRESERVED LEMON, HERBED AND SPICED IN THE MOROCCAN MANNER, ILLUSTRATES THE INGENUITY OF MOROCCAN COOKS. SERVE IN THE TRADITIONAL WAY BEFORE THE MAIN MEAL, OR AS AN ACCOMPANIMENT TO SIMPLY COOKED CHICKEN.

1 kg (2 lb 4 oz) firm pumpkin (winter squash) or butternut pumpkin (squash)
1 preserved lemon (see recipe on page 485)
3 tablespoons olive oil
1 brown onion, grated
½ teaspoon ground ginger
½ teaspoon ground cumin
1 teaspoon paprika
2 tablespoons chopped flat-leaf (Italian) parsley
2 tablespoons chopped coriander (cilantro) leaves
1 tablespoon lemon juice

SERVES 4

PEEL pumpkin, remove seeds and cut into 2 cm (¾ inch) chunks. Set aside. Remove pulp from preserved lemon, rinse rind, dice and set aside.

HEAT the olive oil in a large, lidded frying pan on medium heat and add onion. Cook for 3 minutes, stir in ginger, cumin and paprika and cook for a further 30 seconds. Add the pumpkin, parsley, coriander, lemon juice, the preserved lemon and 125 ml (4½ fl oz/½ cup) water. Season to taste, cover and simmer on low heat for 20 minutes until tender, tossing occasionally with a spatula, adding a little more water if necessary. Serve warm as an appetiser or hot as a vegetable accompaniment.

WARM PUMPKIN SALAD WITH PRESERVED LEMON

FROM ITALY

CHARGRILLED RADICCHIO

2 heads radicchio
60 ml (2 fl oz/¼ cup) olive oil
1 teaspoon balsamic vinegar

SERVES 4

TRIM the radicchio, discarding the outer leaves. Slice into quarters lengthways and rinse well. Drain, then pat dry with paper towels.

PREHEAT a chargrill pan (griddle) to hot. Lightly sprinkle the radicchio with some of the olive oil and season. Cook for 2–3 minutes, until the under leaves soften and darken, then turn to cook the other side. Transfer to a dish and sprinkle with the remaining oil and vinegar. Serve with grilled (broiled) meats, or cold as part of an antipasto platter.

There are several types of radicchio available in Italy, all from the North. This round variety, *rossa di Verona*, is from Chioggia. The longer-leaved type is from Treviso.

CARDOONS WITH PARMESAN

CARDOONS, LIKE ARTICHOKES, ARE A TYPE OF THISTLE, GROWN FOR THEIR STALKS. THEY BROWN WHEN CUT, SO USE A STAINLESS STEEL KNIFE AND KEEP THEM IN ACIDULATED WATER. THE SICILIANS ALSO CALL THE YOUNG STALKS OF ARTICHOKES CARDOONS AND COOK THEM IN THE SAME WAY.

juice of 1 lemon
750 g (1 lb 10 oz) cardoons
1 tablespoon plain (all-purpose) flour
60 g (2 oz) butter
1 small onion, thinly sliced
4 tablespoons grated parmesan cheese

SERVES 4

PUT half the lemon juice in a large bowl of cold water. Discard the green leaves, outer stalks and tough parts of the cardoons, leaving the tender white stalks. Cut into 8 cm (3 inch) lengths and toss into the bowl of water.

BRING a large saucepan of water to the boil. Add the remaining lemon juice, the flour and a large pinch of salt. Add the cardoons. Simmer for about 50 minutes, or until tender. Drain and plunge into a bowl of cold water. Remove the strings with a knife, as you would with celery.

PREHEAT oven to 180°C (350°F/Gas 4). Grease a shallow 25 x 15 cm (10 x 6 inch) casserole or baking tray. Melt butter in a small frying pan and add the onion. Cook over low heat for 10 minutes, or until soft and golden.

LAYER half the cardoons over the base of the casserole and season with freshly ground black pepper. Spoon half the onion over the top and sprinkle with half the parmesan. Repeat these layers and bake in the oven for 30 minutes.

CARDOONS WITH PARMESAN

CHARGRILLED RADICCHIO

FROM MOROCCO

ARTICHOKES WITH BROAD BEANS

GLOBE ARTICHOKES AND BROAD BEANS APPEAR IN THE SOUKS AT THE SAME TIME, BUT THE BEANS ARE AT THEIR BEST EARLY IN THE SEASON. MATURE BROAD BEANS SHOULD BE SKINNED BEFORE COOKING – BLANCH, COOL, PEEL. WATERCRESS SUBSTITUTES FOR A WILD HERB CALLED BAKOOLA.

1 lemon
4 globe artichokes
3 tablespoons olive oil
1 white onion, finely chopped
2 garlic cloves, finely chopped
2 tablespoons chopped flat-leaf (Italian) parsley
2 tablespoons chopped fresh fennel leaves
1 kg (2 lb 4 oz) fresh broad (fava) beans, shelled
3 large handfuls cleaned watercress
1 preserved lemon (see recipe on page 485)
fennel sprigs, or chopped fennel, to serve

SERVES 4

HALVE the lemon and add juice of one half to a bowl of cold water. Cut remainder of the lemon in half and use to rub cut surfaces as artichokes are prepared.

CUT stem off artichoke close to base and cut a 12 cm (4½ inch) piece from the top of the stem, discarding remainder. Pull off and discard about 4 layers of the outer leaves, until the base of the remaining leaves is a light yellow–green. Trim carefully around base where leaves were removed. Each time you make a new cut or trim, rub the exposed surface with cut lemon. Cut and discard top quarter of artichoke, cut in half, remove hairy choke with a teaspoon, and cut again to make quarters. Drop into the lemon water. Peel the fibrous layer from the stem, cut across in half and add to bowl. Repeat until all are prepared.

WARM the oil over medium heat in a large stainless steel or enamelled saucepan. Add the onion and cook gently until soft, about 5 minutes. Add garlic, cook a few seconds, then stir in the herbs and drained artichokes and stems. Cook for 2 minutes, then add fresh broad beans and about 750 ml (26 fl oz/3 cups) water. Season and bring to the boil over high heat. Reduce to low–medium and simmer, partly covered, for 15 minutes.

MEANWHILE, chop watercress coarsely. Remove flesh from preserved lemon and discard. Rinse the rind well, cut into strips and set aside a quarter of them for garnish. Stir watercress and remaining preserved lemon strips into artichokes. Continue to cook, uncovered, for a further 12 minutes, or until artichokes and beans are tender. Boil rapidly towards the end of cooking so that only half the liquid remains. Transfer to a shallow serving dish and sprinkle with reserved lemon strips and fennel leaves. Serve with bread.

Cut tops off artichokes, halve and remove the hairy choke and prickly inner leaves with a spoon.

FROM ITALY

CHARGRILLED ASPARAGUS

24 asparagus spears
1 tablespoon extra virgin olive oil
2 tablespoons balsamic vinegar
parmesan cheese shavings

SERVES 4

WASH the asparagus and remove the woody ends (hold each spear at both ends and bend it gently; it will snap at its natural breaking point).

PUT the asparagus in a bowl, add the olive oil and toss well. Heat a chargrill pan (griddle) or barbecue and cook the asparagus for about 10 minutes, or until just tender. Drizzle with balsamic vinegar and sprinkle with parmesan, to serve.

OR, steam trimmed asparagus or boil it in salted water for about 6 minutes, or until just tender. Drain. Mix with olive oil, balsamic and parmesan.

STUFFED MUSHROOMS

8 large flat mushrooms
$1\frac{1}{2}$ tablespoons lemon juice
12 button mushrooms
1 tablespoon butter
1 French shallot, finely chopped
1 garlic clove, crushed
2 tablespoons white wine
100 g (3 oz/1 cup) grated parmesan cheese, plus 1 tablespoon to serve
60 g (2 oz/$\frac{2}{3}$ cup) fresh breadcrumbs
1 egg, lightly beaten
3 tablespoons thick (double/heavy) cream
1 tablespoon chopped tarragon
1 tablespoon chopped parsley

SERVES 4

PREHEAT the oven to 150°C (300°F/Gas 2). Wipe the large mushrooms with a damp cloth, remove and discard the stalks. Rub the caps with a little lemon juice to keep them white. Wipe the button mushrooms, chop them finely, then mix with the remaining lemon juice.

HEAT the butter in a small frying pan, add the shallot and garlic and cook, stirring, for 4 minutes. Add the chopped mushroom and the wine and cook, stirring, for another 4 minutes. Remove from the heat and stir in the parmesan, breadcrumbs, egg, cream and tarragon. Season.

PLACE mushroom caps on a lightly oiled baking tray and stuff with the filling. Bake for 12 minutes. Sprinkle with the parmesan and parsley and serve either warm or cold.

STUFFED MUSHROOMS

CHARGRILLED ASPARAGUS

BASICS

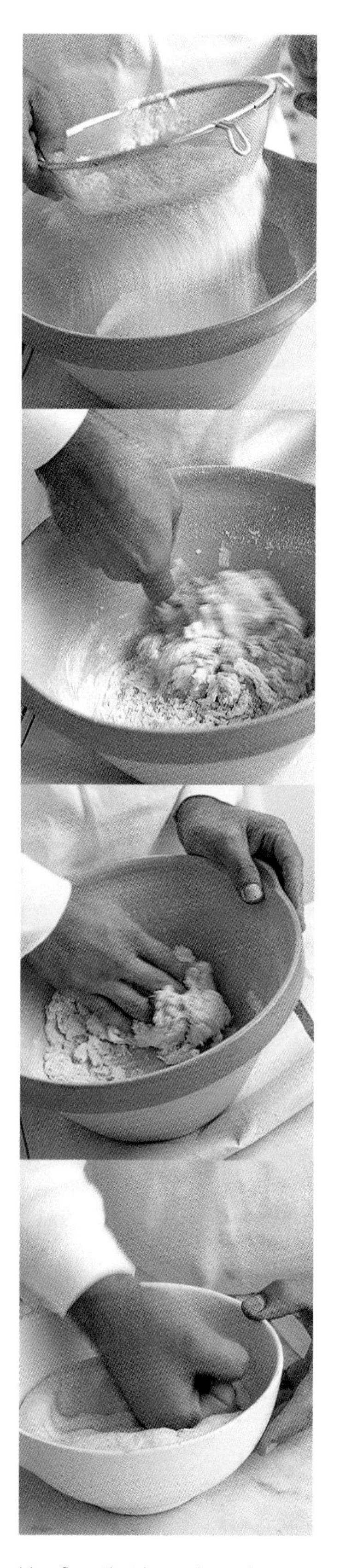

Use flour that is packaged as 'strong' or 'bread' flour. You can use plain flour or a mixture of plain and wholemeal, but the results won't be quite as good.

FROM FRANCE

BREAD DOUGH

LUNCH ON THICK SLICES OF THIS RUSTIC BREAD WITH UNSALTED BUTTER AND A GOOD CHEESE. THIS IS A BASIC BREAD DOUGH AND IS EASILY FLAVOURED. YOU COULD ADD CHOPPED WALNUTS, FRESH HERBS, OLIVES OR CHEESE.

2 teaspoons dried yeast or 15 g (½ oz) fresh yeast
250 g (9 oz) strong plain (all-purpose) flour
½ teaspoon salt
3 tablespoons olive oil

MAKES 1 LOAF

MIX the yeast with 125 ml (4fl oz/½ cup) warm water. Leave for 10 minutes in a warm place until the yeast becomes frothy. If the yeast does not bubble and foam in this time, throw it away and start again.

SIFT the flour into a large bowl and add the salt, olive oil and the yeast mixture. Mix until dough clumps together and forms a ball.

TURN out onto a lightly floured work surface. Knead the dough, adding a little more flour or a few drops of warm water if necessary, until you have a soft dough that is not sticky but is dry to the touch. Knead for 10 minutes, or until smooth, and the impression made by a finger springs back immediately.

RUB the inside of a large bowl with olive oil. Roll the ball of dough around in the bowl to coat it with oil, then cut a shallow cross on the top of the ball with a sharp knife. Leave dough in the bowl, cover with a tea towel (dish towel) or put in a plastic bag and leave in a draught-free spot for 1–1½ hours or until the dough has doubled in size (or leave in the fridge for 8 hours to rise slowly).

KNOCK back dough by punching it with your fist several times to expel the air and then knead again for a couple of minutes. (At this stage, the dough can be stored in the fridge for 4 hours, or frozen. Return to room temperature before continuing.) Leave in a warm place to rise until doubled in size. Place in a tin, on a baking tray or use as directed in the recipe, then bake at 230°C (450°F/Gas 8) for 30 minutes. When cooked, the base of the bread will sound hollow when tapped.

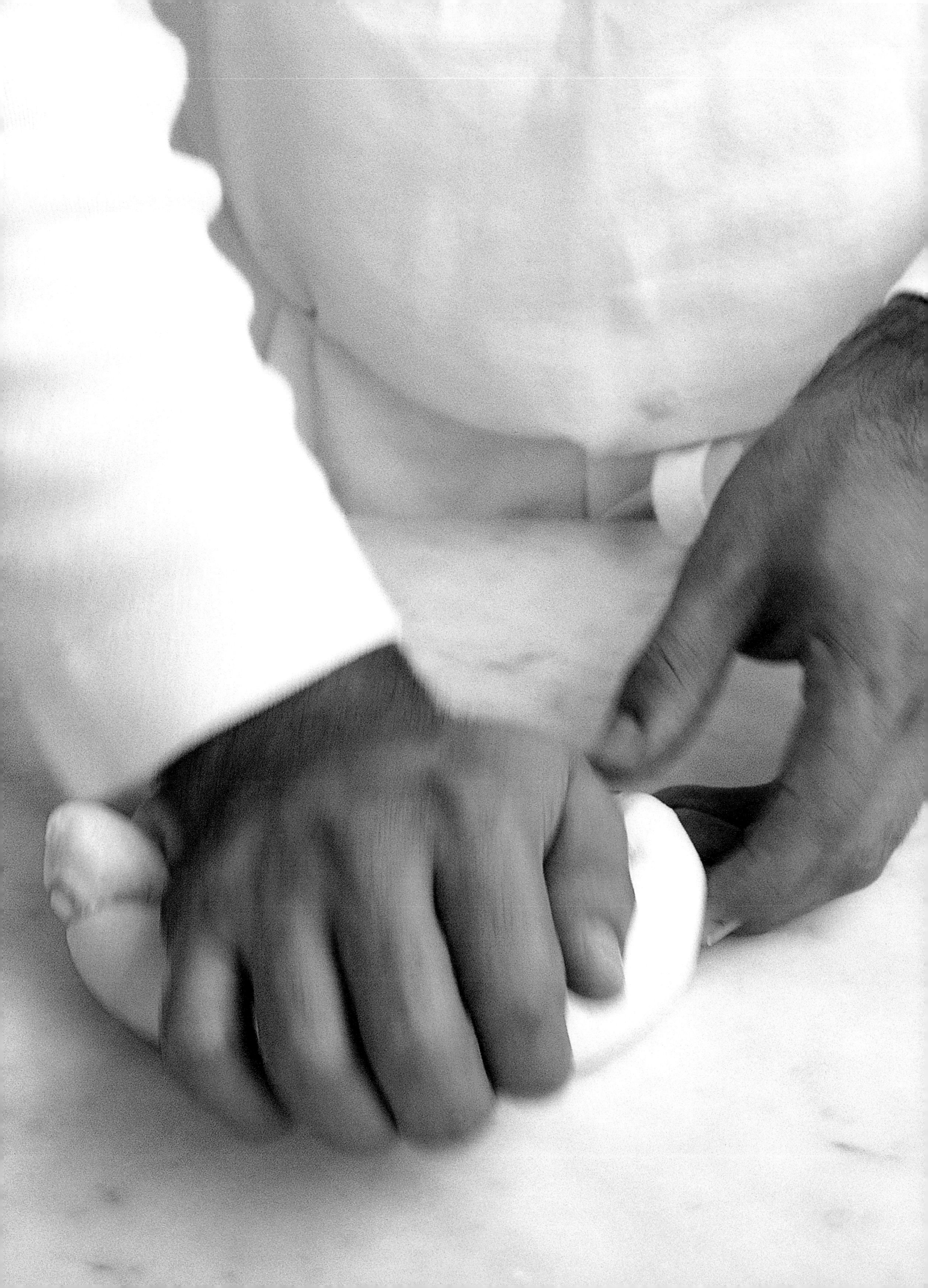

FROM MOROCCO

MOROCCAN BREAD

THE FIRST TASK IN A MOROCCAN HOUSEHOLD, ESPECIALLY IN RURAL AREAS, IS MAKING THE DAILY BREAD. AS IT ONLY HAS TO RISE ONCE, IT IS QUICK TO MAKE. COUNTRY BREAD USUALLY IS MADE WITH WHOLEMEAL (WHOLE-WHEAT) FLOUR, BUT THE FOLLOWING VERSION GIVES LIGHTER LOAVES.

- 3 teaspoons active dried yeast
- 500 g (1 lb 2 oz/3⅓ cups) strong flour or plain (all-purpose) flour, preferably unbleached
- 200 g (7 oz/1⅓ cups) wholemeal (whole-wheat) flour
- 125 ml (4 fl oz/½ cup) lukewarm milk
- 2 tablespoons yellow cornmeal
- 1 tablespoon whole aniseed, toasted sesame seeds, black sesame seeds or coarse salt, for topping

MAKES 3 LOAVES

DISSOLVE the yeast in 125 ml (4 fl oz/½ cup) lukewarm water. Sift the flours and 1½ teaspoons salt into a mixing bowl and make a well in the centre. Pour the yeast mixture into the well, then add 250 ml (9 fl oz/1 cup) lukewarm water and the milk. Stir sufficient flour into the liquid to form a thin batter, cover the bowl with a cloth and set aside for 15 minutes until bubbles form.

GRADUALLY stir in the remaining flour, then mix with your hands to form a soft dough, adding a little extra water if necessary. Turn out onto a lightly floured work surface and knead for 10 minutes, or until smooth and elastic and the dough springs back when an impression is made with a finger. Knead in extra plain flour if dough remains sticky after a few minutes of kneading.

AS the dough requires only one rising, divide into 3 even-sized pieces. Shape each piece into a ball and roll out on a lightly floured work surface to rounds 23 cm (9 inches) in diameter or 26 cm (10½ inches) for flatter breads.

SPRINKLE cornmeal onto baking trays. Lift the rounds onto the trays, reshaping, if necessary. Brush the tops lightly with water and, if desired, sprinkle with any one of the toppings, pressing it in lightly. Cover loaves with clean cloths and leave in a warm, draught-free place for 1 hour to rise. The bread has risen sufficiently when a depression remains in the dough after it is pressed lightly with a fingertip.

WHILE the loaves are rising, preheat the oven to 220°C (425°F/Gas 7). Just before baking, prick them with a fork. Put the breads in the hot oven and bake for 12–15 minutes, or until the bread is golden and sounds hollow when the base is tapped. Cool on a wire rack. Cut in wedges to serve. Use on the day of baking.

Roll out balls of dough, cover and leave to rise on baking trays. Prick with a fork just before baking.

FROM ITALY

COUNTRY-STYLE BREAD

THIS IS ONE OF THE BASIC LOAVES OF ITALY (ALTHOUGH NOT TUSCANY, WHERE THE REGIONAL *PANE TOSCANO* IS MADE WITHOUT SALT). IF YOU'RE SERVING IT FRESH WITH BUTTER, IT'S BEST EATEN ON BAKING DAY, BUT THE DAY-OLD BREAD IS EXCELLENT FOR MAKING BRUSCHETTA AND CROSTINI.

STARTER
185 ml (6 fl oz/¾ cup) milk, warmed
2 teaspoons honey
1 teaspoon dried yeast or 7 g (¼ oz) fresh yeast
125 g (4 oz/1 cup) plain (all-purpose) flour

DOUGH
1 teaspoon dried yeast or 7 g (¼ oz) fresh yeast
2½ teaspoons salt
500 g (1 lb 2oz/4 cups) plain (all-purpose) flour

MAKES 2 LOAVES

TO MAKE the starter, mix the milk and honey in a large bowl with 3 tablespoons warm water. Sprinkle yeast over the top and stir to dissolve. Leave in a draught-free place to activate. If the yeast does not bubble and foam in 5 minutes, throw it out and start again. Add flour and whisk to form a thick paste. Cover loosely with plastic wrap. Leave at room temperature overnight.

TO MAKE the dough, sprinkle yeast over the starter. Using your fingertips, break up the starter by squeezing it between your fingers. Gradually add 250 ml (9 fl oz/1 cup) water, combining it with the starter. Mix in salt and flour with your fingers until mixture comes together to form a soft dough.

PLACE dough on a lightly floured work surface and knead for 10 minutes, or until smooth and elastic. Place dough in a lightly oiled bowl and cover with a damp tea towel (dish towel). Leave to rise in a draught-free place for 1–1½ hours, or until doubled in size. Knock back, place on a lightly floured surface and knead for 1–2 minutes until smooth.

DIVIDE the dough into half and shape into round loaves, then flatten them slightly. Lightly grease a large baking tray with oil and dust with flour. Put loaves on the tray and score a crisscross pattern about 5 mm (¼ inch) deep on top of each loaf. Dust lightly with more flour.

COVER with a damp tea towel and leave to rise in a draught-free place for about 40 minutes, or until doubled in size. Preheat the oven to 200°C (400°F/Gas 6). Bake for about 35 minutes, or until bread sounds hollow when tapped underneath. Cool on a wire rack.

FROM ITALY

PIZZA DOUGH

PIZZA BEGAN LIFE AS A FAST FOOD, EATEN HOT ON THE BACKSTREETS OF NAPLES. TODAY IT IS FOUND ALL OVER THE WORLD, BUT IT IS STILL IN NAPLES THAT SKILLED *PIZZAIOLI* (PIZZA-MAKERS) USE WONDERFUL LOCAL TOMATOES, MOZZARELLA AND BASIL TO PRODUCE THE FINEST OF PIZZAS.

- 1 tablespoon caster (superfine) sugar
- 2 teaspoons dried yeast or 15 g (½ oz) fresh yeast
- 215 ml (7 fl oz) lukewarm water
- 450 g (1 lb/3⅔ cups) plain (all-purpose) flour
- ½ teaspoon salt
- 3 tablespoons olive oil
- cornmeal

MAKES TWO 30 CM (12 INCH) PIZZA BASES

PUT the sugar and yeast in a small bowl and stir in 90 ml (3 fl oz) of the water. Leave in a draught-free spot to activate. If the yeast does not bubble and foam in 5 minutes, discard it and start again.

MIX the flour and salt in a bowl or in a food processor fitted with a plastic blade. Add the olive oil, remaining water and the yeast mixture. Mix until the dough loosely clumps together. Transfer to a lightly floured surface and knead for 8 minutes, adding a little flour or a few drops of warm water, if necessary, until you have a soft dough that is not sticky but is dry to the touch.

RUB the inside of a large bowl with olive oil. Roll the dough in the bowl to coat it with oil, then cut a shallow cross on the top of the ball with a sharp knife. Leave dough in the bowl, cover with a tea towel (dish towel) or put in a plastic bag and leave in a draught-free spot for 1–1½ hours until it has doubled in size (or leave in the refrigerator for 8 hours to rise slowly).

PUNCH DOWn the dough to its original size, then divide in half. (At this stage, dough can be stored in the fridge for up to 4 hours, or frozen. Bring it back to room temperature before continuing.)

WORKING with one portion at a time, push the dough out to make a thick circle. Use the heels of your hands and work from the centre of the circle outwards, to flatten dough into a 30 cm (12 inch) circle with a slightly raised rim. (If you find it difficult to push the dough out by hand, use a rolling pin.) The pizza dough is ready to use, as instructed in the recipe. Cook on a lightly oiled tray, dusted with cornmeal. (Be sure to put it in the oven as quickly as possible.)

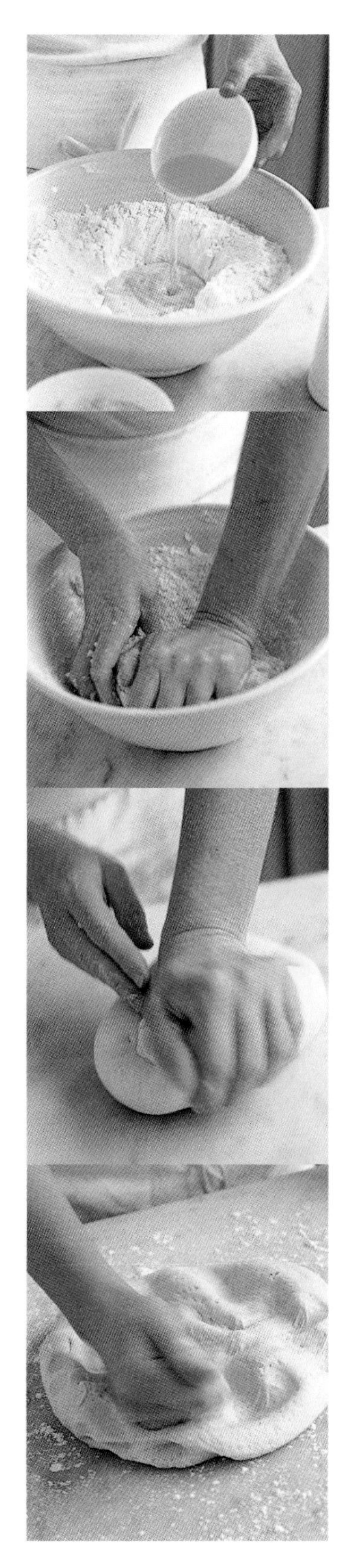

Knead dough by stretching it away from you and then folding it back on itself. Use your fist to squash it into a flat circle. You will need to push quite hard.

FROM ITALY

PASTA

PASTA WAS ORIGINALLY A SOUTHERN ITALIAN, PARTICULARLY SICILIAN, DISH, WITH THE FIRST PASTA INDUSTRY LOCATED IN NAPLES TO TAKE ADVANTAGE OF ITS PURE WATER, LOCAL GRAIN AND ABUNDANT SUNSHINE.

Pasta is traditionally made on a work surface and not in a bowl. Roll it by hand or with a pasta machine. Whichever method you choose, it must be thin enough to read a newspaper through.

500 g (1 lb 2 oz/4 cups) 00 (*doppio zero*) or plain (all-purpose) flour
4 eggs
chilled water

MAKES 700 G (1 LB 9 OZ)

MOUND the flour on a work surface or in a large bowl. Make a well in the centre. Break eggs into the well and whisk with a fork, incorporating the flour as you whisk. You may need to add a little chilled water (1/4 teaspoon at a time) to make a loosely massed dough. Turn the dough onto a lightly floured surface. It should be soft, pliable and dry to the touch. Knead for about 8 minutes, or until smooth and elastic with a slightly glossy appearance. Cover with a tea towel (dish towel) and leave for 30 minutes. The dough is then ready to roll out.

TO MAKE dough in a processor, mix flour for about 3 seconds, then, with the motor running, add the eggs. Mix again for 5 seconds, or until the mixture resembles coarse meal. Mix until a loose ball forms, then continue for 5 seconds until the machine slows and stops. If the dough seems too sticky to form a smooth ball, add 2 teaspoons flour and mix briefly. Add more small amounts of flour until the ball forms. If the mixture is too dry, add chilled water, a teaspoon at a time. Transfer to a lightly floured surface and knead for about 3 minutes until smooth and elastic. Cover with a tea towel and leave for 30 minutes.

TO ROLL OUT the dough, divide into two or three manageable portions. Work with one portion at a time, keeping the rest covered. Flatten the dough on a lightly floured surface and roll out from the centre to the outer edge, rotating the dough often. When you have a 5 mm (1/4 inch) thick circle of dough, fold it in half and roll it out again. Do this eight times to give a smooth circle of pasta, then roll to a thickness of 2.5 mm (1/8 inch). (Mend any tears with pasta from the outside of the circle and a little water.) Transfer to a lightly floured tea towel. If pasta is to be filled, keep it covered and don't allow it to dry out. If the sheets are to be cut into lengths or shapes, leave them uncovered while you roll out the other portions, so the surface moisture will dry slightly before cutting.

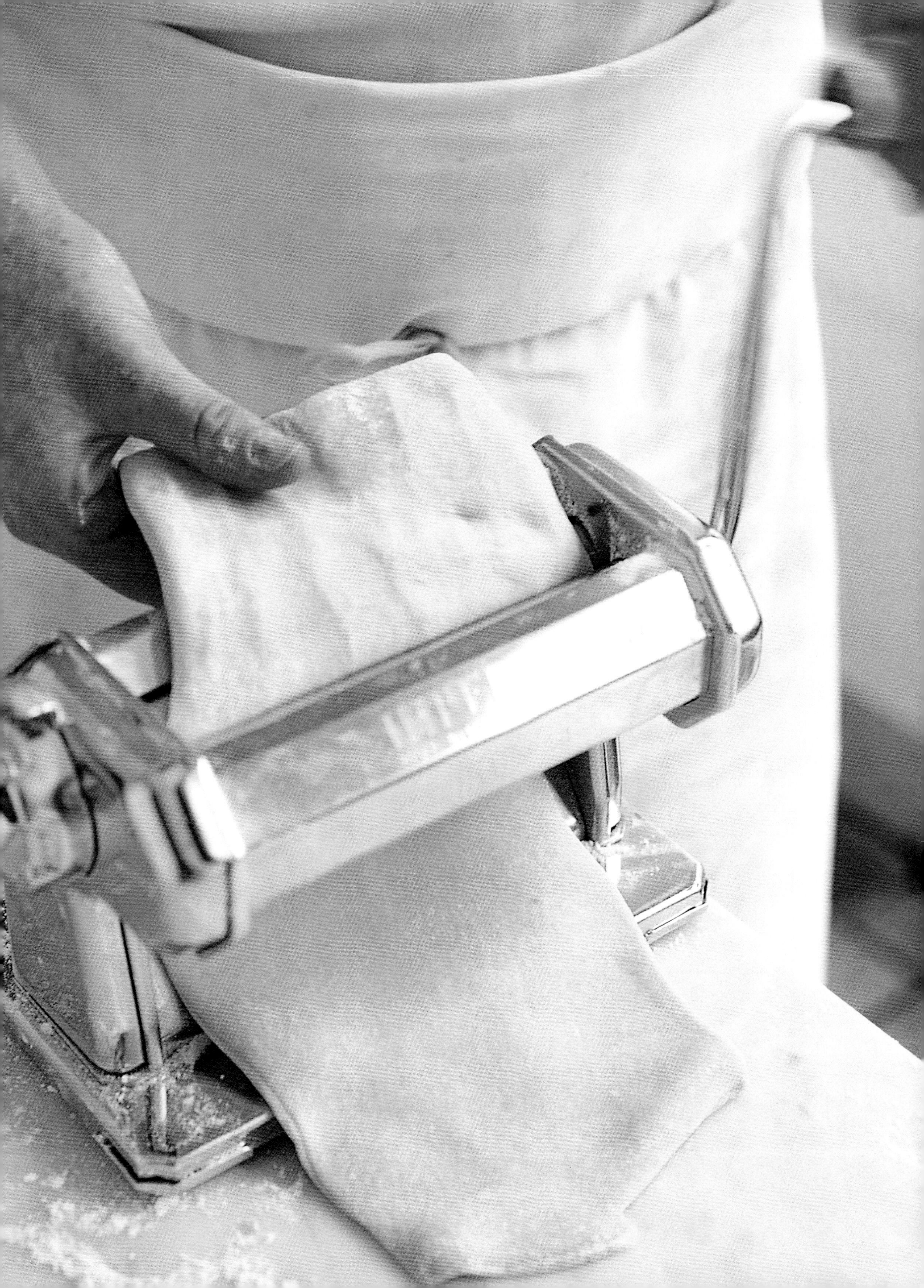

FROM MOROCCO

COUSCOUS (STEAMING METHOD)

BOTH REGULAR COUSCOUS AND INSTANT COUSCOUS SHOULD BE PREPARED IN THE SAME WAY, BY STEAMING THE GRAINS TO MAKE THEM LIGHT AND FLUFFY. THE TRADITIONAL METHOD OF RUBBING GRAINS TO REMOVE LUMPS AND 'AIR' THE GRAINS HAS BEEN REPLACED WITH A MODERN METHOD.

500 g (1 lb 2 oz/2¾ cups) regular couscous
90 g (3½ oz) clarified butter, smen or herbed smen (see recipe on page 486) or butter, diced

SERVES 6

PUT couscous in a large, shallow bowl, cover with cold water, stir with a balloon whisk and pour water off immediately through a strainer to catch any grains. Return the grains to the bowl and set aside for 10 minutes to allow couscous to swell, stirring occasionally with the whisk to keep the grains separate.

USE the steamer section of a *couscoussier* (a steamer that fits snugly over a large saucepan), or a metal colander. If steamer does not fit snugly, put a long, folded strip of foil around the rim of the pan, place steamer in position and press firmly.

IF THE steamer has large holes, line with a double layer of muslin (cheesecloth). Spread couscous grains in steamer and place over the pan of food being cooked, or over a saucepan of boiling water. The base of the steamer must not touch the top of the stew or water. Cook until steam rises through the grains, cover and steam for 20 minutes. Fork through couscous occasionally to steam it evenly.

TIP couscous into the bowl, add clarified butter and ½ teaspoon salt and sprinkle with 125 ml (4 fl oz/½ cup) cold water. Stir again with the whisk to separate the grains. At this stage, couscous may be covered with a damp cloth and left several hours, if necessary. About 20 minutes before stew is cooked, return couscous to the steamer and replace over stew or boiling water. Do not cover while steaming. Fluff up occasionally with a fork. Turn into the bowl, stir well with the balloon whisk and serve according to recipe.

INSTANT COUSCOUS: Follow above directions but only steam for 10 minutes each time.

Pour water onto regular couscous in a bowl, stir, drain off and leave 15 minutes; stir occasionally. Between steamings, traditionally the couscous grains are rubbed with the hands to break up any lumps. Fork through couscous while steaming.

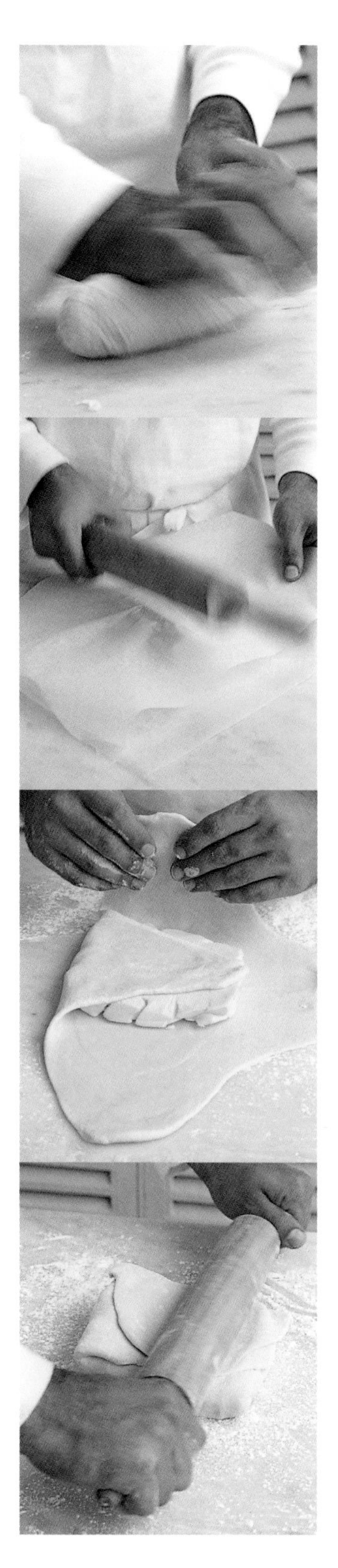

Although time-consuming to make, home-made puff pastry that uses butter tastes better than commercial pastry, which is often made with vegetable fat.

FROM FRANCE

PUFF PASTRY

LIGHTNESS IS THE HALLMARK OF GOOD PUFF PASTRY AND THE MANY LAYERS SHOULD RISE WITHOUT STICKING. THE KEY IS TO HAVE THE BUTTER AND PASTRY AT THE SAME CONSISTENCY WHEN YOU ROLL THEM OUT, AND TO KEEP THE ROLLING AND FOLDING AS NEAT AS YOU CAN.

250 g (9 oz/2 cups) plain (all purpose) flour
1 teaspoon lemon juice
1 teaspoon salt
30 g (1 oz) butter, melted
200 g (7 oz) butter, chilled

MAKES 650 G (1 LB 8 OZ)

SIFT the flour into a bowl and make a well in the centre. Pour in 125 ml (4 fl oz/½ cup) water, the lemon juice, salt and melted butter. Draw in flour with your fingertips, little by little, until you have a rough dough. Turn out onto a work surface and knead with the heel of your hand until the dough is smooth. Shape into a ball and cut a cross on the top. Wrap with plastic wrap and refrigerate for 1–2 hours.

PLACE the chilled butter between two pieces of baking paper and beat with a rolling pin to make a square 1.25 cm (½ inch thick). Keep the butter cool so that it doesn't harden again or melt any further. It needs to be about the same softness as the pastry or it will break up when you roll it.

ON A lightly floured surface, roll out the dough in four different directions to form a cross large enough to hold the square of butter in its centre. Put the butter in the centre and fold the four arms of dough over it, one by one, to enclose the butter completely. Position the dough so that it looks like a book with the spine to the left and the open piece of dough to the right. Roll the pastry away from you into a rectangle, keeping the corners as square as you can, then fold the top third down and the bottom third up to make a parcel of three even layers. Turn pastry 90 degrees to the right and repeat the rolling, folding and turning, trying to keep the corners neat and square. This will help make the pastry layers even. Wrap in plastic wrap and chill for 30 minutes. (You can mark the pastry with finger indents each time you refrigerate so you remember how many turns you have made.)

REPOSITION the pastry as before, with the hinge to your left, then roll out, fold, turn and chill twice more. Rest for 30 minutes, then make two more turns as before. The pastry is now ready to use.

FROM FRANCE

TART PASTRY

220 g (7¾ oz) plain (all-purpose) flour
pinch of salt
150 g (5½ oz) unsalted butter, chilled and diced
1 egg yolk

MAKES 450 G (1 LB)

SIFT flour and salt into a large bowl, add the butter and rub in with your fingertips until the mixture resembles breadcrumbs. Add the egg yolk and a little cold water (about 2 teaspoons) and mix with the blade of a palette knife until dough just starts to come together. Bring the dough together with your hands and shape into a ball. Wrap in plastic wrap and put in the refrigerator to rest for at least 30 minutes. You can also make the dough in a food processor, using the pulse button.

ROLL OUT pastry into a circle on a lightly floured surface. Use to line a tart tin, as directed in the recipe. Trim the edge. Pinch up the pastry edge to make an even border raised slightly above the rim of the tin. Slide onto a baking tray and rest in the fridge for 10 minutes.

When making the sweet pastry, it is easiest to work directly on the work surface.

SWEET PASTRY

350 g (12 oz) plain (all-purpose) flour
small pinch of salt
150 g (5½ oz) unsalted butter
100 g (3½ oz) icing (confectioners') sugar
2 eggs, beaten

MAKES 700 G (1LB 9 OZ)

SIFT the flour and salt onto a work surface and make a well in the centre. Put the butter into the well and work, using a pecking action with your fingertips and thumb, until it is very soft. Add the sugar to the butter and combine. Add eggs to the butter and combine.

GRADUALLY incorporate the flour, flicking it onto the mixture and then chopping through it until you have a rough dough. Bring mixture together with your hands and then knead a few times to make a smooth dough. Roll into a ball, wrap in clingfilm and put in the fridge for at least 1 hour.

ROLL OUT pastry into a circle on a lightly floured surface and use to line a tart tin, as directed in the recipe. Trim the edge. Pinch up the pastry edge to make an even border raised slightly above the rim of the tin. Slide onto a baking tray and rest in the fridge for 10 minutes.

SWEET PASTRY

Sift in the flour and stir until the choux dough comes away from the side of the pan.

FROM FRANCE

CRÊPES

250 g (9 oz/2 cups) plain (all-purpose) flour
pinch of salt
1 teaspoon sugar
2 eggs, lightly beaten
400 ml (14 fl oz) milk
1 tablespoon melted butter
butter or oil, for frying

MAKES 12 SMALL OR 6 LARGE CRÊPES

SIFT flour, salt and sugar into a bowl and make a well in the centre. Combine the eggs and milk with 100 ml (3½ fl oz) water and pour slowly into the well, whisking all the time to incorporate the flour until you have a smooth batter. Stir in the melted butter. Cover and refrigerate for 30 minutes.

HEAT a crêpe pan or a deep non-stick frying pan. Grease with a little butter or oil. Pour in enough batter to coat the base of the pan in a thin, even layer and tip out any excess. Cook over moderate heat for about a minute, or until the crêpe starts to come away from the side of the pan. Turn the crêpe and cook on the other side for 1 minute, or until lightly golden. Stack crêpes on a plate with pieces of baking paper between them and cover with foil while you cook the rest of the batter.

CHOUX PASTRY

CHOUX PASTRY

150 g (5½ oz) unsalted butter
225 g (8 oz) plain (all purpose) flour, sifted twice
7 eggs
1 tablespoon caster (superfine) sugar

MAKES 500 G (1LB 2 OZ)

MELT the butter with 375 ml (13fl oz/1½ cups) water in a saucepan, then bring it to a rolling boil. Remove from the heat and add all the flour at once and a pinch of salt. Return to the heat and beat continuously with a wooden spoon to make a smooth shiny paste that comes away from the side of the pan. Cool for a few minutes.

BEAT IN the eggs one at a time, until shiny and smooth – the mixture should drop off the spoon but not be too runny. Beat in the sugar. Store in a pastry bag in the fridge for up to 2 days.

FROM FRANCE

CRÈME ANGLAISE

300 ml (10½ fl oz) milk
1 vanilla pod
2 egg yolks
2 tablespoons caster (superfine) sugar

MAKES 300 ML (10 FL OZ)

PUT the milk in a saucepan. Split the vanilla pod in two, scrape out the seeds and add pod and seeds to the milk. (The custard will have small black spots in it, but if you don't want that, leave vanilla pod whole.) Bring just to the boil. Whisk the egg yolks and sugar until light and fluffy. Strain the milk over the egg mixture, whisking continuously.

POUR the custard back into the saucepan and cook, stirring, until it is thick enough to coat the back of a wooden spoon. Do not let it boil or the custard will split. Strain into a clean bowl, then lay plastic wrap on the surface to prevent a skin forming. Refrigerate for up to 2 days.

CRÈME PÂTISSIÈRE

CRÈME PÂTISSIÈRE

6 egg yolks
125 g (4 oz/½ cup) caster (superfine) sugar
30 g (1 oz) cornflour (cornstarch)
10 g (¼ oz) plain (all-purpose) flour
550 ml (19 fl oz) milk
1 vanilla pod
15 g (½ oz) butter

MAKES 500 G (1 LB 2 OZ)

WHISK together the egg yolks and half the sugar until pale and creamy. Sift in the cornflour and flour and mix together well.

PUT the milk, remaining sugar and vanilla pod in a saucepan. Bring just to the boil and then strain over the egg yolk mixture, stirring continuously. Pour back into a clean saucepan and bring to the boil, stirring constantly. It will be lumpy at first but will become smooth as you stir. Boil for 2 minutes, then stir in the butter and leave to cool. Transfer to a clean bowl, lay plastic wrap on the surface to prevent a skin forming and refrigerate for up to 2 days.

FRANGIPANE

FRANGIPANE

250 g (9 oz) unsalted butter, softened
250 g (9 oz/2 cups)) icing (confectioners') sugar
250 g (9 oz) ground almonds
40 g (1½ oz) plain (all-purpose) flour
5 eggs, lightly beaten

MAKES 800 G (1 LB 12 OZ)

BEAT butter until very soft. Add the icing sugar, ground almonds and flour and beat well. Add the egg gradually, beating until fully incorporated. Transfer to a clean bowl, cover with plastic wrap and refrigerate for up to 24 hours.

CRÈME ANGLAISE

FROM MOROCCO

HARISSA

Chop the dried chillies before soaking. The food processor makes short work of preparing harissa. This is a very hot paste.

HARISSA IS EXTREMELY HOT, SO YOU SHOULD USE WITH CAUTION. FOR A MILDER VERSION OF THIS FIERY PASTE, SLIT THE CHILLIES (INSTEAD OF CHOPPING THEM) BEFORE SOAKING IN THE BOILING WATER. THEN SCRAPE OUT THE SEEDS BEFORE PROCESSING AS PER THE RECIPE.

125 g (4 oz) dried red chillies, stems removed
1 tablespoon dried mint
1 tablespoon ground coriander
1 tablespoon ground cumin
1 teaspoon ground caraway seeds
10 garlic cloves, chopped
125 ml (4 fl oz/½ cup) olive oil

FILLS A 600 ML
(21 FL OZ/2½ CUP) JAR

TO PREPARE a storage jar, preheat the oven to 120°C (235°F/Gas ½). Wash the jar and lid in hot soapy water. Rinse with hot water. Put the jar in the oven for 20 minutes, or until fully dry. Do not dry with a tea towel (dish towel).

ROUGHLY chop the chillies, cover with boiling water and soak for 1 hour. Drain, put them in a food processor and add the mint, spices, garlic, 1 tablespoon of the olive oil and ½ teaspoon salt. Process for 20 seconds, scrape down the side of the bowl, then process for another 30 seconds. With motor running, gradually add remaining oil. Scrape down the side of the bowl, when needed.

SPOON paste into the clean jar, cover with a thin layer of olive oil and seal. Label and date. Harissa will keep in the refrigerator for up to 6 months.

SAFFRON RICE

SAFFRON RICE

500 g (1 lb 2 oz/2½ cups) short-grain rice
2 tablespoons olive oil
¼ teaspoon ground saffron threads
20 g (¾ oz) butter

SERVES 6

WASH the rice in a sieve until water runs clear, then drain well.

HEAT the oil in a heavy-based saucepan over medium heat. Add the rice, stirring so that it is coated evenly with oil. Add 900 ml (31 fl oz/3⅔ cups) water, the saffron and ¼ teaspoon salt and stir well. Bring to the boil over high heat and boil for 1 minute.

REDUCE the heat to low, cover and cook for about 10 minutes, or until all the water has been absorbed. Steam tunnels will form holes on the surface of the rice. Turn off heat, then leave the pan, covered, for 10 minutes. Add the butter and fluff lightly with a fork. Transfer to a serving bowl. Saffron rice is used to accompany fish dishes, but can also be used as a substitute for couscous.

FROM MOROCCO

PRESERVED LEMONS

MAKE PRESERVED LEMONS WITH RIPE, NEW-SEASON FRUIT THAT HAVE NOT BEEN WAXED. STORE-BOUGHT LEMONS ARE USUALLY COATED WITH A WAX, WHICH HAS TO BE REMOVED BY SCRUBBING IN WARM WATER WITH A SOFT-BRISTLE BRUSH; EVEN THEN IT IS VERY DIFFICULT TO REMOVE.

8–12 thin-skinned new-season lemons
rock salt
1–2 extra lemons
black peppercorns, optional
bay leaves, optional

FILLS 1 x 2 LITRE (70 FL OZ/8 CUP) JAR OR 2 x 1 LITRE (35 FL OZ/4 CUP) JARS

TO PREPARE a storage jar, preheat the oven to 120°C (235°F/Gas ½). Wash the jar and lid in hot soapy water and rinse with hot water. Put the jar in the oven for 20 minutes, or until fully dry. Do not dry with a tea towel (dish towel).

IF LEMONS are very firm, soak in water to cover for 3 days, changing water daily. Wash lemons if soaking is not required. Cut from stem end into quarters almost to the base. Insert 1 tablespoon rock salt in each lemon, close it up and place in a jar. Repeat until jar is filled, sprinkling 1 tablespoon salt between layers. Pack lemons into the jar as tightly as possible and add a bay leaf and a few black peppercorns to each jar, if desired.

WASH extra lemons and add the juice of 1 lemon to each jar. Fill with slightly cooled, boiled water. Put the washed skin from a squeezed-out lemon half on top so that if any white film forms on top (which is harmless), the skin can be discarded when the jar is opened. Seal and store in a cool, dark place for 4 weeks, gently shaking jars daily for the first week to dissolve the salt. The cloudy liquid clears in this time. Lemons will keep for 6 months or more. Once jar is opened, store in the refrigerator.

TO PREPARE for cooking, remove a lemon with a clean fork. Separate it into quarters and rinse under running water. Remove pulp and discard. Rinse the rind, pat dry with paper towel and use as directed in recipes.

To prepare for recipes, rinse preserved lemon and remove pulp with a spoon. Rinse rind and pat dry with paper towel, then cut as directed.

As the butter bubbles, the froth sinks. When the milk solids begin to colour, strain into a bowl.

FROM MOROCCO

CLARIFIED BUTTER (SMEN)

BUTTER IS MELTED AND HEATED FOR A LENGTHY TIME UNTIL THE MILK SOLIDS SINK AND BEGIN TO BROWN, GIVING A NUTTY FLAVOUR. FOR TRADITIONAL CLARIFIED BUTTER, SKIM THE FROTH AND POUR THE CLEAR FAT INTO A CONTAINER BEFORE THE MILK SOLIDS BROWN. GHEE IS A SUBSTITUTE.

250 g (9 oz) salted or unsalted butter, diced

MAKES 175 G (6 OZ)

PUT the butter in a heavy-based saucepan over low heat. If using gas, place over the smallest burner with a heat diffuser, as butter has a tendency to spit if the heat is not low enough.

SIMMER very gently for 25 minutes. Pour through a sieve lined with muslin (cheesecloth), set over a bowl. The clear oil is the smen and has a slightly nutty taste. Store in a sealed jar in the refrigerator. It can also be stored safely at room temperature, as is done in Morocco. Clarified butter keeps for many months.

FOR sweet pastries that use filo, smen is recommended, even with its slightly nutty flavour, because if melted unclarified butter is used any milk solids brushed onto the filo become dark when cooked, spoiling the appearance of the baked pastry.

HERBED CLARIFIED BUTTER

HERBED CLARIFIED BUTTER

TRADITIONALLY, THIS IS STORED IN A STONE JAR AND BURIED FOR A YEAR OR MORE, GIVING IT A STRONG CHEESY FLAVOUR. IT IS MUCH LOVED STIRRED THROUGH COUSCOUS. A SHORT CUT IS TO COMBINE EQUAL QUANTITIES OF HERBED SMEN AND BLUE CHEESE.

2 tablespoons dried za'atar, or dried Greek thyme
2 teaspoons coarse salt
250 g (9 oz) salted or unsalted butter

MAKES 175 G (6 OZ)

PUT the za'atar and salt in a sieve lined with muslin (cheesecloth). Following the directions above, heat the butter and slowly pour it through the herb and salt mixture. Store in a sealed jar in the refrigerator. In Morocco, herbed smen is aged for months, even years, and has a strong, cheesy flavour. This is a milder version.

FROM FRANCE AND ITALY

PESTO

2 garlic cloves
60 g (2 oz/⅓ cup) pine nuts
80 g (2½ oz/1⅔ cups) basil leaves
4 tablespoons grated Parmesan
150 ml (5 fl oz) extra virgin olive oil

MAKES 185 ML (6 FL OZ/¾ CUP)

PUT the garlic, pine nuts, basil and Parmesan in a mortar and pestle or a food processor and pound or mix to a paste. Add the oil in a steady stream, mixing continuously. Add salt if necessary. Refrigerate in a sterilised jar, covered with a layer

BECHAMEL SAUCE

BÉCHAMEL SAUCE

65 g (2¼ oz) butter
40 g (1⅓ oz/⅓ cup) plain (all-purpose) flour
pinch of grated nutmeg
610 ml (20 fl oz/2½ cups) milk
1 bay leaf

MAKES 810 ML (27 FL OZ/3¼ CUPS)

HEAT the butter in a saucepan over low heat. Add the flour and nutmeg and cook, stirring, for 1 minute. Remove from the heat and gradually stir in the milk. Add bay leaf, return to the heat and simmer, stirring often, until the sauce thickens. Season, cover with plastic wrap to prevent a skin

TOMATO SAUCE

TOMATO SAUCE

120 g (4 oz) roma (plum) tomatoes
3 basil leaves
2 garlic cloves, crushed
1 tablespoon tomato passata
2 teaspoons extra virgin olive oil

MAKES 185 ML (6 FL OZ/¾ CUP)

CORE the tomatoes and purée in a food processor with the basil leaves (or chop the tomatoes and basil very finely and stir together). Stir in the garlic, passata and olive oil and season well. Leave for at least 30 minutes before serving to allow the flavours to blend. Use on pizzas, toss

SALSA VERDE

1½ tablespoons fresh white breadcrumbs
1 tablespoon milk
1 hard-boiled egg yolk
2 anchovy fillets
1 tablespoon capers
5 tablespoons finely chopped parsley, mint and basil
1 garlic clove, crushed
80 ml (2½ fl oz/⅓ cup) extra virgin olive oil

MAKES 185 ML (6 FL OZ/¾ CUP)

SOAK breadcrumbs in the milk for 10 minutes. Finely chop together the egg yolk, anchovy and capers. Add herbs, garlic and the breadcrumbs and mix with a fork. Slowly blend in the olive oil until the sauce is smooth and thick. Season with pepper. Set aside for at least 1 hour before using.

SALSA VERDE

PEELED TOMATOES

FROM SPAIN

ALLIOLI

THE ORIGINAL OF THIS CATALAN CLASSIC WAS SIMPLY MADE WITH GARLIC AND OLIVE OIL. TODAY, EGG YOLKS ARE ADDED, BUT IT SHOULD STILL BE STRONGLY GARLIC IN FLAVOUR AND SMOOTH AND WHITE IN TEXTURE. IT'S PERFECT WITH SEAFOOD AND POTATOES.

2 egg yolks
4 garlic cloves, crushed
60 ml (2 fl oz/¼ cup) white wine vinegar or lemon juice
250 ml (8 fl oz/1 cup) mild olive oil

MAKES ABOUT 250 ML (9 FL OZ/1 CUP)

PUT egg yolks, garlic and half of the vinegar or lemon juice in a bowl. Using a balloon whisk, or electric beaters, whisk until well combined. While you continuously whisk, gradually add the oil in a slow stream until you have a thick mayonnaise. If at some point the mayonnaise becomes too thick, add the remaining vinegar and continue adding the rest of the oil. Season well. This keeps

ROASTED RED CAPSICUMS

PEELED TOMATOES

ripe tomatoes

SCORE a cross in the base of each tomato with a knife. Put tomatoes in a bowl of boiling water for 10 seconds, then plunge into a bowl of cold water. Remove from the water and peel the skin away from the cross. It should slip off easily. If desired, remove seeds with a teaspoon, and chop flesh.

ROASTED RED CAPSICUMS

capsicums (peppers)

CUT each capsicum (pepper) into four flattish pieces and carefully remove the seeds and membrane. Arrange pieces in a single layer on a baking tray and cook under a hot grill (broiler) until the skins are blackened and blistered.

PUT the capsicums in a large bowl and cover with plastic wrap (or put them in a plastic bag) and leave to cool for 10 minutes.

GLOSSARY OF MEDITERRANEAN FOOD AND COOKING

al dente Italian meaning 'to the tooth'. Pasta and risotto rice are cooked until they are al dente – the outside is tender but the centre still has a little resistance or 'bite'. Pasta cooked beyond this point becomes soggy.

almonds Whole, slivered and ground almonds are often used in sweet and savoury dishes. If ground almonds (almond meal) are not available, use whole or slivered almonds and grind in a food processor. Use very fresh, dry almonds for this, and process them as briefly as possible to prevent them from becoming oily; for this reason, slivered almonds are the better option. Pack well when using cup measures, as freshly ground almonds are lighter in texture than the packaged variety.

almonds, blanched Almonds keep better if purchased with skin on and have a better flavour when freshly blanched. To blanch, place in a bowl, cover with boiling water and leave for 5 minutes, drain and slip off skins when cool. Spread onto a paper towel–lined baking tray and leave until dry and crisp, or put in a slow oven for 5 minutes to dry thoroughly. Store in a sealed container in the refrigerator.

almonds, green These appear in Moroccan souks in mid-summer, when the drupe is green and the almond shell is still soft within – test with a pin. They are left to soak in salted water for a day or two, then eaten whole as a snack.

andouillette A French sausage made from pork or veal chitterlings or tripe. Andouillettes are usually grilled and often served with mustard, potatoes or cabbage. Some have an outer layer of lard that melts as they cook.

aniseed These greenish brown, licorice-flavoured seeds are used in both sweet and savoury cooking and also to make anís, an alcoholic beverage similar to schnapps. Buy the seeds whole as once ground, they lose flavour.

artichoke The edible flower of a member of the thistle family. Some have thorns and the types vary greatly in size. The largest are usually boiled, but the smallest and most tender can be eaten raw as antipasto.

asparagus Has been used from very early times as a vegetable and medicine, owing to its delicate flavour and diuretic properties. There is a recipe for cooking asparagus in the oldest surviving book of recipes, Apicius's third century AD De re coquinaria, Book III. It was cultivated by the ancient Egyptians, Greeks and Romans, who ate it fresh when in season and dried the vegetable for use in winter. Asparagus is low in calories, contains no fat or cholesterol.

bacalao The Spanish term for cod which has been salted and dried. It must be soaked for about 20 hours before use to rehydrate the fish and to remove the excess salt. Once prepared, the bacalao flakes easily and is popular in fritters, but is also cut into larger pieces for poaching, simmering or baking in various sauces.

bain-marie A French term, literally a 'water bath' for gentle oven-cooking of delicate terrines and desserts. Usually the dish is placed in a roasting tin, which is half-filled with water.

balsamic vinegar The home of balsamic vinegar is Modena, Italy, where authentic vinegars aged for at least 12 years (usually much more) are labelled *aceto balsamico tradizionale di Modena*. Originally made only by wealthy families who could afford to wait for their vinegar to mature, a version is now produced commercially and sold without the 'tradizionale' label. *See page 282.*

basil Was introduced to Europe in the sixteenth century from India. It is generally added to dishes at the last moment, as cooking quickly destroys the flavour. The fresh herb can be kept for a short time in plastic bags in the refrigerator, or for a longer period in the freezer, after being blanched quickly in boiling water. The dried herb also loses most of its flavour, and what little flavour remains tastes very different, with a weak coumarin flavour, like hay. It can be bought in pots or as bunches, or you can grow your own.

bay leaves Glossy green leaves sold fresh or dried and used to add a strong, slightly peppery flavour to wet savoury dishes and occasionally to puddings and custards. The fresh leaves are a little stronger than the dried.

besan (chickpea flour) A high-protein flour made by finely grinding chickpeas. Chickpea flour has a nutty flavour and is ideal for making batter for deep-fried foods and for thickening sauces.

beurre manié A French term for a paste made by combining butter and flour. Stirred into sauces at the end of cooking to thicken them.

beurre noisette A French term for a simple sauce made by cooking butter until it is brown and 'nutty'.

bocconcini Means literally 'small mouthful' and is used to describe various foods, but generally refers to small balls of mozzarella, about the size of walnuts.

bouquet garni A bundle of herbs used to flavour dishes. Made by tying sprigs of parsley, thyme, celery leaves and a bay leaf in either a piece of muslin or portion of leek.

bresaola Lean beef that is cured and air-dried for 2–3 months – a speciality of the Valtellina Valley in Lombardia. Has a dark red colour and a stronger flavour than prosciutto. Serve thinly sliced.

broad (fava) beans A Moroccan staple. Fava beans may be shelled and then dried or bought dried. Dried beans need to be first soaked for 48 hours in a cool place such as the refrigerator, changing water 3–4 times, and the leathery skins removed before use.

brown stock Stock made from browned beef or veal bones. As beef and veal stock are usually interchangeable, the term 'brown stock' is used. The best commercial stocks come freshly made in tubs, though stock sold in cartons and catering-quality powdered stock can also be good.

bruschetta Is a traditional Italian antipasto. Use slightly stale bread (this is an excellent dish for using up leftovers) that is dense enough to stop the olive oil seeping through. Technically speaking, bruschetta is just plain grilled (broiled) bread, rubbed with garlic while it is hot and then drizzled with good-quality olive oil. *See page 24.*

butter Butter is flavoured both by the lactic fermentation of cream and the diet of the cows from whose milk it is made. Use either salted or unsalted for savoury dishes, but unsalted in sweet recipes.

Calasparra rice A medium-grained, high-quality absorbent white rice grown in the Calasparra region of Spain that is traditionally used to make paella. *Bomba* is one variety of Calasparra rice and can sometimes be found labelled as such.

calzones Are an Italian delicacy that means 'baggy pants'. They are turn-overs filled with cheese and other ingredients. Calzones are made with floppy soft doughs. *See page 31.*

cannellini beans There are white, kidney-shaped beans, also known as Italian haricot beans or white kidney beans. Available fresh, dried or tinned.

cantucci Tuscan almond biscuits, also known as *biscotti di Prato*. These hard, double-baked biscuits often contain whole almonds. They are usually eaten dipped into a dessert wine such as *vin santo*.

caperberries The fruit of the caper bush, which appear after the flowers. They are usually preserved in brine and served as an accompaniment or garnish (much like olives).

capers The small flowers of the caper bush, which are preserved in brine and sometimes just salt. They should be rinsed well before use. They have a piquant flavour and are used in small amounts in dressings, salads and as a garnish. The smaller the caper, the more aromatic and, therefore, expensive.

capsicum This is also given as 'pepper' in recipes. In Morocco they use a sweet pepper that is thinner-fleshed, not as broad as a capsicum, and tapering to a point. The Capsicum genus also includes chillies. *See also chillies.*

cardoons Similar to the artichoke plant, cardoons have large leaves and long stems. Unlike artichokes, it is the stems that are eaten rather than the flowers. The stalks are usually blanched like celery.

casalinga Italian meaning 'home-made' or 'homely'. When attributed to sausages or salami, it generally means having a coarse texture and earthy flavour.

cava A quality Spanish sparkling white wine made by the same bottle fermentation method as Champagne. Cava is refreshing to drink, and can also be used to make sweet and savoury sauces.

cavolo nero A cabbage with long leaves that are so dark green they appear to be almost black. Used mainly in Tuscan cooking. If unavailable, Savoy cabbage can be used.

cayenne Also known as *cayenne pepper*. A powder made from ground red chilli peppers native to South America. It is very pungent and spicy and should be used sparingly. It is often added to wet dishes for heat and is sometimes sprinkled over cheese-topped dishes before baking or grilling (broiling) as the flavours are complementary.

cervelas A long, fat French pork sausage, often flavoured with garlic, pistachios or truffles. It is a boiling sausage *(saucisse à cuire)* and should be poached before browning under the grill. Ordinary pork sausages flavoured with pistachios can be used instead if cervelas are unavailable.

cetriolini Small gherkins. If unavailable, use cornichons or small cocktail gherkins.

chard Also known as silverbeet and Swiss chard, it is a member of the beet family. The leaves are bright green and crinkly in texture, with a white rib running through the leaf widening into a stem. It is much loved by North African and Middle Eastern people, probably as it grows prolifically in their gardens.

chickpea flour *See besan.*

chickpeas Small legumes commonly used in rustic, home-style cooking. Pale brown or yellow, they are commonly available dried and need to be soaked and cooked before being consumed; however, you can now find them already prepared and tinned for convenience. Once soaked, or after the initial boiling, chickpeas should be rubbed between your hands and rinsed to help remove their skins.

chillies Available fresh, dried or roasted, chillies belong to the capsicum (pepper) family and are native to South and Central America, from where they were taken by the Spanish and Portuguese into the Mediterranean. There are many different varieties of chilli and they vary dramatically in size, heat and flavour. The seeds and inner membranes of the chillies should be removed if less heat is desired.

chipolata In Britain, chipolata means any small sausage. In France, however, a chipolata can be as long as an ordinary sausage but is always much thinner. Usually made from pork and pork fat, chipolatas are used as a garnish in French cooking.

chorizo The best known of all Spanish sausages, chorizo is made from minced (ground) or chopped pork and pork fat, flavoured with sweet and hot paprika, garlic and black pepper. Sometimes sold soft for cooking in wet dishes (such as soups or stews), it is more commonly found as a hard, cured sausage that can be eaten as is, but is often sliced and fried, then eaten as a snack or added to wet dishes. *See page 80.*

ciabatta Slipper-shaped Italian bread with a rough, open texture. They are made from a very wet dough, which allows large bubbles to form and gives a thin crust. Ciabatta quickly goes stale and is best eaten on the day it is bought or made.

cilantro *See coriander.*

cinnamon Finely shaved bark from the cinnamon tree (*Cinnamomum zeylanicum*), which is interleaved and rolled to form sticks or quills. Both sticks and ground cinnamon are widely used. Ground cinnamon often includes cassia, which is actually from another species of cinnamon tree. Cassia is more reddish-brown than cinnamon and can be used in place of cinnamon sticks; in fact, it is often sold as such. Cinnamon is used in savoury and sweet dishes.

cipolline Small white Italian onions, usually flattened in appearance rather than round.

clarified butter (smen) Made by melting butter so that the fat separates out from the impurities and water. The fat is then either spooned off or the water tipped away and the butter reset. Clarified butter keeps for longer than ordinary butter because all the water has been removed and can be used for cooking at higher temperatures because it has a higher burning point. *See page 486.*

confit From the French word for 'preserve', confit is usually made from goose or duck meat, cooked in its own fat and then preserved in a jar or pot. It is eaten on its own or added to dishes such as cassoulet for extra flavour.

coppa An Italian type of cured pork made from half pork fat and half pig's neck and shoulder. It is rolled and cured in a casing and, when sliced, resembles a fatty sausage.

coriander (cilantro) Fresh coriander has feathery green leaves with a somewhat pungent flavour. Coriander seeds are ground and used as a spice.

cornichon The French term for a small gherkin. It you can't find cornichons, use cocktail gherkins instead.

cornmeal Dried yellow corn kernels ground to a meal, available in fine, medium and coarse grades; choose the medium grade. Do not confuse with polenta, which is a granular form. Cornmeal is used to add to bread, for sprinkling on baking trays, or on top of loaves to add crunch and flavour.

cotechino An Italian sausage made from pork and pork rind, giving it a gelatinous texture. Cotechino is flavoured with cloves and cinnamon and needs to be cooked before eating.

country-style bread Any bread that is bought as a whole loaf and has a rough texture. Pugliese, ciabatta and pane Toscano are all examples. Other white bread is not a suitable substitute. *To make your own see page 466.*

court bouillon A flavoured poaching liquid, usually for cooking fish.

couscous Made from very tiny balls of dough, couscous is usually steamed and served like rice with a main meal. Couscous was traditionally made by hand from freshly milled flour and came in different sizes of grain. Now that it is commercially produced, the grains tend to be uniformly quite tiny.

couscoussier The French name for the utensil in which couscous is steamed; in Moroccan the base is *qadra* and the top steamer is *keskes*, but the French name is in popular use even in Morocco. The base is tall and slightly bulbous, with the steamer section fitted on top for cooking couscous. The traditional couscoussier of tin-lined copper does not have a lid, but aluminium versions usually do. The original couscoussier of the Berbers was earthenware.

crème de cassis Originating near Dijon in Burgundy, France, crème de cassis is a blackcurrant liqueur used in desserts.

crème fraîche Often used in place of cream in the French kitchen. Lightly fermented, it has a slightly tart taste. Crème fraîche from Isigny has AOC status.

croccante Caramelised nuts, usually almonds but sometimes hazelnuts (these are also know as pralines).

cumin The elongated ridged seeds of a plant of the parsley family, these have a peppery, slightly bitter flavour and are used whole or ground to flavour savoury dishes and breads. The pungent, slightly nutty flavour is enhanced by dry-roasting before use. Available whole or ground.

curd cheese A smooth soft cheese made from curds that have not undergone lactic fermentation. Curd cheese is lower in fat than cream cheese but higher in fat than cottage cheese. The flavour is mild with about the same firmness as cheese, but has a springy or rubbery texture. Fresh curds squeak against the teeth when bitten into, which some would say is their defining characteristic.

dates Have played an important part in Moroccan cuisine for thousands of years. Archaeological evidence suggests the cultivation of dates all the way back in 6,000 BC in Arabia. The date palm was a major source of life for thousands of people throughout the Middle East and Northern Africa and is said to have provided people with thousands of different uses including thread, mattresses, lumber, rope, and many other household and dietary uses.

Dijon mustard A pale yellow mustard, made from verjuice or white wine and mustard seeds that have been ground to a flour. Originating in Dijon, this style of mustard is now made all over France.

doppio zero (00) flour In Italy, flour is classified either as 1, 0, or 00, and refers to how finely ground the flour is and how much of the bran and germ have been removed. Doppio zero is the most highly refined and is talcum-powder soft, made from soft wheat (grano tenero) and mainly used for making cakes and fresh egg pasta.

farro A type of spelt grain, farro is used in soups and stews in a similar way to barley. If farro is unavailable, spelt or barley can be used. Farro is most commonly used in the cuisines of the areas where it is grown – Tuscany, Umbria and Lazio.

figs This remarkable fruit has been important to the Mediterranean region from early days. The fresh fruit, both the purple (black) variety and the green, begins to appear early in summer. The majority of figs, however, are consumed dried. The fresh fruit is enjoyed as an ending to a meal, the dried for snacks, cooking and combined with dates for sweet pastry fillings.

filo pastry Paper-thin sheets of raw, unleavened flour dough used for making pastries. It is important how it is handled. Thaw as directed on package if frozen; whether frozen or chilled, it must be left in its package at room temperature for 2 hours before opening and unfolding the sheets. Place the sheets flat on your work surface, and while working with them, keep the sheets covered with dry, folded cloths or plastic sheeting; never put damp cloths in contact with the pastry. Keep the kitchen cool and draught-free if possible.

finocchiona A type of salami from Tuscany, flavoured with wild fennel seeds. The salami is very often large and is aged for up to a year before use. It also comes in a more crumbly version called sbriciolona.

flat-leaf parsley Also known as Italian or continental parsley. Used as an ingredient rather than a garnish, unlike curly parsley.

foie gras The enlarged livers of fattened geese or ducks. Regarded as a delicacy, with foie gras from Strasbourg and southwest France both highly regarded.

fontina A traditional Italian mountain cheese from the Valle d'Aosta in Piemonte. Full-fat and semi-soft with a sweetish flavour, fontina melts evenly and well and so is particularly good for cooking.

French olives Grown all over the South, the main varieties of French olives include the green pointed Picholines, purple-black Nyons and the small black olives of Nice, used in traditional Niçoise cooking. Fresh green olives are available from the summer and are picked before they start to turn black, while fresh black olives are available from the autumn through to winter. Though green and black olives have a different flavour, they can be used interchangeably in recipes unless the final colour is a factor.

fromage frais A fresh white cheese with a smooth creamy consistency. There are a number of varieties, many artisan-produced. The fat content of fromage frais varies, which may affect its cooking qualities, but generally it makes a good low-fat alternative to cream.

garlic Is a close relative of the onion, shallot, leek, and chive. Garlic has been used throughout recorded history for both culinary and medicinal purposes. It has a characteristic pungent, spicy flavour that mellows and sweetens considerably with cooking. A bulb of garlic, the most commonly used part of the plant, is divided into numerous fleshy sections called cloves.

ginger Available fresh or dried. Do not use more than is given in recipes as too much ginger can impart a bitter taste.

goose fat A soft fat that melts at a low temperature and is used a lot in the cooking of southwest France to give a rich texture to dishes. Available in tins from butchers. Duck fat can be substituted, although it needs to be heated to a higher temperature.

Gorgonzola A blue cheese, originally made in Gorgonzola in Lombardia but now produced in other regions as well. It melts well and is often used in sauces. If not available, use another full-fat blue cheese.

grape leaves *See vine leaves.*

Gruyère A pressed hard cheese with a nutty flavour. French Gruyère is available as *Gruyère de Comté*, which can have large holes, and *Gruyère de Beaufort*, which has virtually no holes. Although French Gruyére does have a different flavour to Swiss, the two are interchangeable in recipes.

gsaa From Morocco, a large, shallow wooden or earthenware bowl in which bread is kneaded or couscous grains made. An earthenware gsaa is also used for soaking couscous before cooking, and for rubbing and separating the grains during and after cooking.

hamed markad *See preserved lemons.*

haricot beans The general French name for beans, though the term is also used to mean just a kind of small, dried bean. Dried haricot beans come in many different varieties, including cannellini (kidney-shaped beans), flageolet (white or pale green beans) and navy beans (used to make baked beans). When slow-cooked in stews such as cassoulet they become tender. They also break down very well when mashed to give a smooth purée.

harissa A Tunisian condiment popular in Morocco, harissa is available from gourmet food stores and Middle Eastern markets, or make your own *(see page 482)*. Use with caution as it is extremely hot.

Italian olives Eating olives generally come from southern Italy. They can be picked when green and unripe or be allowed to ripen to dark purple or black. Though green and black olives have a different flavour, they can be used interchangeably in recipes unless the final colour is a factor.

jamón Spanish ham, resembling good-quality prosciutto, is available in different grades and varies in flavour and texture, depending on its region of origin. *Jamón Ibérico* is ham from the black Iberian pigs, which are fed mainly on acorns, figs and sometimes olives, giving the meat great flavour and aroma. The ham is salted, air-dried and then matured for about 2 years. *Jamón serrano*, or *mountain ham*, is from the fattened white pigs of the Sierra Nevada region, which are salted, and then air-cured for at least a year. Jamón is extremely flavoursome and tender and is often added to cooked dishes or simply eaten on its own. *See page 67.*

juniper berries Blackish-purple berries with a resinous flavour. Used in stews and robust game dishes. Use the back of a knife to crush the berries lightly before use to release their flavour.

Madeira A type of fortified wine from the Portuguese island of Madeira. There are a number of different varieties of Madeiras, from sweet (Malmsey or Malvasia and Bual), to medium (Verdelho) and dry (Sercial).

Manchego cheese One of Spain's most famous cheeses, originally made from the milk of Manchego sheep from the La Mancha region. A semi-firm cheese with a rich but mellow flavour which alters with age. Sold as fresh, semi-cured and cured – the texture firming and flavour deepening at each of these stages. It is perfect for everyday eating and has wonderful melting properties.

Maroilles A square soft cheese with an orange washed-rind and a strong smell but sweet flavour. As an alternative, you could use other washed-rind varieties, such as Livarot, or a cheese with a white moulded rind, such as Camembert.

Marsala A fortified wine from Marsala in Sicily that comes in varying degrees of dryness and sweetness. Dry Marsalas are used in savoury dishes, and sweet ones in desserts. Do not try to use sweet Marsala in savoury dishes. *See page 281.*

mascarpone A cream cheese originally from Lombardia. Made with cream rather than milk, it is very high in fat. Mascarpone is generally used in desserts such as tiramisu or instead of cream in sauces.

mastic Tears of resin from a small evergreen tree that grows in regions of the Mediterranean, especial the Greek island of Chios. Used to flavour sweet pastries, especially in Marrakesh, where it is added to almond paste for filling pastries. Do not confuse with gum arabic – this is an incense and a glue.

merguez A lamb sausage of Tunisian origin, popular in Morocco. It is spiced with harissa, paprika, allspice, fennel, black pepper, cumin and coriander seeds and flavoured with garlic. It is usually very hot, but the degree of heat depends on the manufacturer.

mesclun A salad mix containing young lettuce leaves and herbs such as rocket, lamb's lettuce, dandelion leaves, basil, chervil and endive. Traditionally found all over the south of France.

misticanza A Roman salad that was once made of wild greens. Today, it is generally a mixture of rocket, purslane, sorrel, mint, dandelion, wild fennel and endive with some lettuce. In Umbria, it also refers to a mixture of dried beans used for soups.

Moroccan rice Short- or medium-grained rice is preferred. Moroccans steam rice three times in a couscoussier, or in a colander lined with muslin over boiling water. Traditional rice-cooking methods have been used in the recipes.

morcilla A northern Spanish sausage made from pig's blood, similar to black pudding. It is very rich and often spiced with cinnamon, cloves and nutmeg. Some variations include rice, potato, garlic, white beans, onion or fennel. They are boiled before being hung up to dry and are then sometimes smoked. Often added to stews or casseroles or sautéed and crumbled into stuffings and dishes such as scrambled eggs.

mortadella A large, finely textured pork sausage, with lengths of lard running through it. Some versions contain pistachio nuts and all should be eaten very thinly sliced and as fresh as possible. Traditionally made in Bologna, the sausage is also known as bologna or boloney.

mozzarella Originally, all mozzarella in Italy was made from the prized milk of water buffaloes, which gives a creamy, fragrant fresh cheese. Most mozzarella is now made with cow's milk, with the resulting texture and taste being slightly different. Buffalo milk mozzarella is available in some places.

navy beans Also known as *haricot beans* or *pea beans*. One of the many members of the haricot bean family, navy beans are small white legumes sold dried, and are perfect for soups and stews as they require long, slow cooking. If not available, other members of the haricot bean family can be substituted (for example, *cannellini, pinto* or *borlotti [cranberry] beans*).

nigella seeds These little black seeds are usually sprinkled on bread before baking, and on steamed chicken. They have little aroma, but have a nutty flavour and are a little peppery. Black cumin seeds and black sesame seeds are often mistakenly called nigella.

noodles *See sheriya.*

olives *See French olives and Italian olives*

olive oil Extra-virgin and virgin olive oils are pressed without any heat or chemicals and are best used in simple uncooked dishes and for salads. Pure olive oil can be used for cooking or deep-frying. Different varieties of olives are grown all over the Mediterranean and the oil of each region has a distinctive taste.

orange flower water Also called *orange blossom water*, this is made from a distillation of the flowers of the bitter bigarade (seville) orange. A delicate flavouring used in beverages, and sweet and savoury food. *See also 'rosewater'.*

pancetta Cured Italian belly of pork, somewhat like streaky bacon. Available in flat pieces or rolled up (arrotolata), and both smoked and unsmoked. Generally used, either sliced or cut into cubes, as an ingredient in dishes like spaghetti carbonara.

paprika Small red capsicums (peppers) varying in heat from mild to hot are dried, sometimes smoked, then ground for use in savoury dishes both for flavour and colour. The rusty red powder is most commonly sold as sweet or mild *(dulce)*, medium hot *(agridulce)* and hot *(picante)*. Smoked paprika is also popular in certain regions and a small amount adds a distinctive smoky flavour to savoury foods.

parmesan (Parmigiano-Reggiano) Is a hard, fat granular cheese, cooked but not pressed, named after the producing areas of Parma, Reggio Emilia, Modena, Bologna, in Emilia-Romagna, and Mantova, in Lombardy, Italy.

Parma ham This prosciutto comes from traditionally reared pigs fed on the whey from making Parmigiano Reggiano. It has a sweet taste and is only flavoured with salt. Parma hams can be identified by the stamp on the skin showing the five-pointed star of the Dukes of Parma. Other prosciutto can be used if Parma ham is unavailable.

parsley Flat-leaf (Italian) parsley is used. Alternatively, use curly parsley and include some stalks when chopping to increase its flavour in cooking.

passata Italian meaning 'puréed', this most commonly refers to a smooth uncooked tomato pulp bought in tins or jars. Best without added herbs and flavourings.

pâté Is a mixture of minced meat and fat in the form of spreadable paste, generally made from a finely ground or chunky mixture of meats and liver, and often with additional fat, vegetables, herbs, spices or wine. In French cuisine, pâté may be baked in a crust as pie or loaf, in which case it is called *pâté en croûte* or baked in a terrine (or other mold), in which case it is known as *pâté en terrine*.

pecorino One of Italy's most popular cheeses, virtually every region produces a version. Made from sheep's milk and always by the same method, although the result varies according to the milk and ageing process used. *Pecorino Romano* is a well-known hard variety from Lazio and Sardinia.

peperoncino The Italian name for chillies, these are popular in the cooking of the South, and are also served there as a condiment. The smallest are called *diavolilli*.

pimiento/pimientos del piquillo Pimientos del piquillo are small, hot, red capsicum (pepper), which are preserved in oil in a tin or jar after being roasted and charred, then carefully peeled. Ready for use, the whole pimiento del piquillo can be stuffed and then deep-fried or baked in sauce, or chopped and added to salads or other dishes. Pimiento can also be puréed to form the basis of a sauce or soup. Small amounts of the red pimiento are often used to stuff green olives.

polenta The name of the dish and also the ingredient itself, which is ground corn. The cornmeal comes in different grades of coarseness. Finer varieties are better in cakes and coarse ones to accompany stews. A white cornmeal is also available.

porcini The Italian name for a cep or boletus mushroom. Usually bought dried and reconstituted in boiling water, but available fresh in the spring and autumn. *See page 193.*

poussin A baby chicken weighing about 450–500 g (1 lb-1 lb 2 oz). Poussin are often spatchcocked and grilled or stuffed. Usually one poussin is served per person, though slightly bigger ones are adequate for two people.

preserved lemons (hamed markad) Used in many Moroccan dishes to give a distinctive flavour. Make your own *(see page 485)* or buy those that are preserved in the

Moroccan manner (no oil) from gourmet food stores or good delicatessens.

prosciutto Italian name for ham. Prosciutto crudo is cured ham and includes *Parma ham* and *San Daniele*. *Prosciutto cotto* is cooked ham.

provolone Curd cheese made from cows' milk. The curds are spun and worked into large pear-shaped cheeses, then immersed in brine and bound with string. Available fresh or matured and eaten as a table cheese or used in cooking.

prunes The prune is the dried version of various species of the *damascene (damson) plum*. It is often a substitute for dates in meat and fruit dishes – an intensely flavoured sweet–sour fruit that marries well with spices. Today's prunes do not need soaking – they are moist and succulent and add a wonderful flavour. While it is an easy (though somewhat sticky) task to remove the pits, pitted prunes are readily available.

Puy lentils Tiny green lentils from Puy in central France that are AOC graded. They do not need to be presoaked and do not break down when cooked. They have a firm texture and go very well with both meat and fish. Traditionally, they are cooked and served with a mustard vinaigrette.

quince This interesting fruit can also be eaten cooked or raw. They are an excellent source of vitamin C. When quinces are not in season use quince paste instead.

radicchio An Italian salad leaf of the chicory family with slightly bitter red leaves. There are several varieties: *radicchio di Castelfranco*, *di Chioggia* and *rosso di Verona* are similar to a red cabbage with round leaves; *radicchio di Treviso* has longer, pointed leaves.

ras el hanout A Moroccan blend of many spices, which vary according to the maker. Some blends are kept a closely guarded secret. You can make your own version *(see page 482)* or buy a ready-made ground spice mix from gourmet food stores or herb and spice stores.

rashasha From Morocco – an ornate flask of coloured glass with a rounded body and a tall and slender neck, ornately decorated with silver metalwork. It is filled with orange flower water or rosewater, and after the Moroccan ritual handwashing before and after a banquet or formal meal, the hands are lightly sprinkled with the flower water.

rice *See Calasparra rice, Semifino rice, Moroccan rice*

ricotta Is a fresh cheese (as opposed to ripened or aged), grainy and creamy white in appearance, slightly sweet in taste, and contains around 5% fat. In this form, it is somewhat similar in texture to some cottage cheese variants, though considerably lighter. Like many fresh cheeses, it is highly perishable. Ricotta may also be used in sweet and savoury dishes. It also makes a delicious substitute for mayonnaise in traditional egg or tuna salad and as a sauce thickener.

risotto rice Round-grained, very absorbent rice, cultivated in northern Italy. The longer cooking and more absorbent the variety, the better it is for risotto. Semifino rice includes varieties like vialone nano and is quick to cook (about 15 minutes). This is good for soups and salads. Fino takes longer to cook (about 16 minutes) and has more bite – this is good for risotto. Superfino is the most sought after variety and includes arborio and carnaroli. It takes about 20 minutes to cook and is the best for risotto.

rosewater A distillation of fragrant rose petals, originating in Persia and introduced to North Africa by the Arabs. Many locals distil their own using an *alembic*, a superseded distiller that remains in use in Morocco and the Middle East. Where obtainable, orange blossoms *(see 'orange flower water')* are also distilled. It is bottled and kept for 4–5 months before use and claimed to be superior to that made by distilleries. Rosewater is used to flavour beverages and sweet and savoury foods.

roux Is a cooked mixture of wheat flour and fat, traditionally clarified butter. It is the thickening agent of three of the mother sauces of classical French cooking: *sauce béchamel, sauce velouté,* and *sauce espagnole*. Butter, vegetable oils, or lard are common fats used. It is used as a thickener for gravy, other sauces, soups and stews. It is typically made equal parts of flour and fat by weight.

saffron The orange–red stigma of one species of the crocus plant is the most expensive spice in the world due to the fact that one flower contains only three stigmas, which are laboriously hand picked and then dried. Fortunately, only a little is needed when cooking. Sold in both thread and powdered form, beware of cheap imitations. Saffron is best toasted, then soaked in warm liquid for a few minutes before use – this process helps to bring out the flavour and colour.

saucisse à cuire A French cooking, or specifically boiling, sausage that is usually larger than an ordinary sausage. Saucisses à cuire are poached in liquid, either as part of a dish like choucroute garnie or just with red wine.

semolina The milled inner endosperm of hard or durum wheat, pale beige or yellow in colour and granular in appearance. It can be very fine (almost like a flour), fine or coarse, the latter used in the manufacture of couscous. Fine and coarse semolina are sold as breakfast cereals. Do not confuse semolina with semolina flour, which is used in pasta making, and is durum wheat flour.

sesame seeds Their use dating back some 4,000 years, sesame seeds have been part of the North African diet for millennia. It was the first seed from which oil was extracted for use in food, and while it isn't used in Morocco, the seeds certainly are. They are used to top breads, toasted and sprinkled on savoury foods, and sprinkled on many sweet pastries. To toast the seeds, use a dry frying pan, add seeds and place over medium heat. Stir often until lightly toasted and tip immediately into a shallow dish to prevent them burning. When cool, store in a sealed jar in the refrigerator and use as required. They can also be spread into a roasting dish and stirred occasionally until golden. Again transfer immediately to another container.

sheriya A Moroccan pasta. Sheriya are little pellets of dough rolled into thin strips a little thicker than vermicelli. They are usually steamed three times, and gently rubbed in cold water between steamings, then used in stuffings, or simply tossed with butter and served with sugar and cinnamon. However, most cooks these days prefer to crumble vermicelli to add to soups or to use in stuffings.

sherry vinegar (vinagre de Jerez) A gourmet wine vinegar made from Sherry. It is produced in the Spanish province of Cádiz and inside the triangular area between the city of Jerez de la Frontera and towns of Sanlúcar de Barrameda and El Puerto de Santa María, known as the 'sherry triangle'. *See page 148.*

smen A clarified (drawn) butter with milk solids that have been allowed to brown slightly, giving it a nutty flavour. Ghee can be used as a substitute; in many recipes, butter can also be used. An aged smen is made by the Berbers by storing it in a sealed earthenware jar, which is then placed in the cellar or buried for a year or longer until it ages; it has a flavour resembling strong blue cheese.

soffritto The flavour base for many soups, stews and risottos. Soffritto is a mixture of fried ingredients like onion, celery, carrot, garlic, pancetta and herbs. It means literally to 'under-fry' and the mixture should be sweated rather than coloured.

soufflé Is a light, fluffy, baked dish made with egg yolks and beaten egg whites combined with various other ingredients and served as a savoury main dish or sweetened as a dessert.

Spanish olive oil Olive oil is an integral part of Spanish cooking and has been since the Phoenicians and Greeks introduced the olive tree to the Iberian Peninsula in ancient times. The Spanish word for oil is *aceite* which originates from the Arabic word *al-zait*, meaning 'olive juice'. *See page 92.*

Spanish sweet paprika Is also known as *pimentón*. It is a popular ingredient in many Mediterranean recipes. Anyone from Spain swears by this paprika, and its flavour is essential for authentic Spanish cooking. The peppers are dried, slowly over an oak burning fire for several weeks. The result is a sweet, cool, smokey flavour. *See page 19.*

squid/cuttlefish ink Used to colour and flavour pasta and risotto. It has a subtle savoury flavour that is not at all fishy, as one might expect.The ink is stored in a sac that can be removed from whole squid and cuttlefish or bought in sachets from fishmongers or delicatessens.

sweetbreads The pancreas and thymus glands of calves or lambs, sweetbreads are white in colour, soft in texture and have an irregular shape. Sweetbreads should be soaked in cold water to remove any blood before they are cooked.

tagine A Moroccan earthenware dish with a conical lid, and also the food cooked in this dish. Such food is really a stew or braise.

Taleggio An Italian mountain cheese originally from the Italian Alps near Bergamo, but now also made in other regions. Taleggio is a very good table cheese and benefits from being eaten young – its flavour becomes more acidic with age. It is made in squares and has a pink-yellow crust and creamy centre.

tangia A Moroccan pottery vessel shaped like a small amphora. The food cooked in it is also called tangia, known as the bachelor's dish; young men or soldiers away from home put chunks of meat (beef, lamb or goat) in it, add tomato, preserved lemon, sprigs of coriander (cilantro) and flat-leaf parsley, season and tie on parchment to cover it, making a handle with the string. This is taken to the hammam (bathhouse) furnace to be cooked on the embers for several hours.

tapenade *See page 16.*

tobsil From Morocco, a round shallow pan of tin-lined copper or aluminium, with two handles. The warkha pastry is made on the base of the pan, set upside-down over a brazier or a pan of boiling water. Turned right side up, the bestilla (pigeon or chicken pie encased in warkha) is placed in it and deftly fried on each side.

tocino Spanish fat bacon which is salted and air-cured but not smoked. Often sold covered with a layer of crystalline salt. It is used in stews and soups and, when made from Iberian pigs, is much sought after.

Toulouse sausage A general French term for meaty pork grilling sausages, usually sold in a coil.

truffles Considered an expensive delicacy, truffles are a type of fungus and have an earthy smell. The black truffles found in France, specifically around Périgord, are often considered the best black truffles in the world. In Italy the black ones come from Umbria (especially around Norcia), Piemonte and Emilia-Romagna. The white ones come from Alba (considered the best), Emilia-Romagna, Le Marche, Tuscany and Umbria. Truffles are best eaten fresh, but can also be bought preserved in jars. They are used in small amounts to flavour dishes.

vanilla extract Made by using alcohol to extract the vanilla flavour from pods and not to be confused with artificial vanilla essence made with synthetic vanillin. Vanilla extract is very strong and should be used sparingly.

vinagre de Jerez *See sherry vinegar.*

vin santo A golden dessert wine, tasting rather like sherry and eaten with cantucci biscuits. Now made in many regions of Italy, but the best known is made in Tuscany.

vine leaves (grape leaves) Large green leaves of the grape vine are used in Mediterranean and Middle Eastern cookery, mainly to wrap foods before grilling (broiling), roasting or simmering. Commonly available in brine in jars, tins or packets, they are also sometimes sold fresh (these should be blanched in hot water until pliable before use). Vine leaves in brine should be rinsed or briefly soaked in cold water to remove the salty brine.

yeast Active dried yeast is available in bulk or in sealed 8 g (¼ oz) sachets that each measure 2 teaspoons. Always store yeast in a sealed container in the refrigerator.
For yeast past its use-by date, dissolve a teaspoon in 125 ml (4 fl oz/½ cup) warm water with 1 teaspoon sugar and leave in a warm place for 15 minutes. If it is frothy in this time, the yeast can be used, otherwise discard it and purchase a fresh packet.

za'atar Arabic word for thyme. The Mediterranean climate gives certain wild herbs a pungency and flavour difficult to duplicate with cultivated herbs. If you cannot find dried za'atar from Morocco in food markets, use the dried thyme available at Greek markets or fresh lemon thyme; recipes indicate which substitutes are suitable. Do not confuse this with the Lebanese herb and spice mix of za'atar, used to sprinkle on bread.

zucchini The Italian name for courgettes. *See page 43.*

INDEX

Published in 2010 by Bay Books, an imprint of Murdoch Books Pty Limited.

Murdoch Books Australia
Pier 8/9
23 Hickson Road
Millers Point NSW 2000
Phone: +61 (0) 2 8220 2000
Fax: +61 (0) 2 8220 2558
www.murdochbooks.com.au

Murdoch Books UK Limited
Erico House, 6th Floor
93–99 Upper Richmond Road
Putney, London SW15 2TG
Phone: +44 (0) 20 8785 5995
Fax: +44 (0) 20 8785 5985
www.murdochbooks.co.uk

Chief Executive: Juliet Rogers
Publishing Director: Kay Scarlett
Commissioning Editor: Lynn Lewis
Design Concept: Vivien Valk
Senior Designer: Heather Menzies
Designer/cover design: Wendy Inkster
Photographers: Jason Lowe, Alan Benson, Gorazd Vilhar, Ian Hofstetter
Production: Alexandra Gonzalez
Index: Jo Rudd

ISBN 978-1-74266-113-1

Printed by C & C Offset Printing Co. Ltd in 2010. PRINTED IN CHINA.

IMPORTANT: Those who might be at risk from the effects of salmonella poisoning (the elderly, pregnant women, young children and those suffering from immune deficiency diseases) should consult their doctor with any concerns about eating raw eggs.

OVEN GUIDE: You may find cooking times vary depending on the oven you are using. For fan-forced ovens, as a general rule, set the oven temperature to 20°C (32°F) lower than indicated in the recipe.